Efficiency,
Equity, and
Legitimacy

Efficiency, Equity, and Legitimacy

The Multilateral Trading System at the Millennium

Roger B. Porter
Pierre Sauvé
Arvind Subramanian
Americo Beviglia Zampetti
Editors

CENTER FOR BUSINESS AND GOVERNMENT
HARVARD UNIVERSITY

BROOKINGS INSTITUTION PRESS
Washington, D.C.

Copyright © 2001
CENTER FOR BUSINESS AND GOVERNMENT

Library of Congress Cataloging-in-Publication data

Efficiency, equity, and legitimacy : the multilateral trading system at the millennium / Roger B. Porter, Pierre Sauve, Arvind Subramanian, and Americo Beviglia Zampetti, editors.
    p.   cm.
Includes bibliographical references and index.
ISBN 0-8157-7162-2 (cloth : alk. paper)
ISBN 0-8157-7163-0 (pbk. : alk. paper)
1. Commercial policy. 2. International trade. 3. Foreign trade regulation.
I. Porter, Roger B.

HF1411 .E37 2001
382—dc21   2001003373

9 8 7 6 5 4 3 2 1

The paper used in this publication meets minimum requirements of the American National Standard for Information Sciences—Permanence of Paper for Printed Library Materials: ANSI Z39.48-1992.

Typeset in Adobe Garamond

Composition by Northeastern Graphic Services
Hackensack, New Jersey

Printed by R. R. Donnelly and Sons
Harrisonburg, Virginia

Contents

Preface

As the collapse of the World Trade Organization (WTO) Seattle Ministerial meeting vividly demonstrates, the multilateral trading system finds itself under increasing strain, lacking both in leadership and strategic, longer-term direction. In the United States, traditionally the driving force behind multilateralism, there seems limited enthusiasm for further liberalization.

The WTO finds itself at a critical juncture. After the successful conclusion of the Uruguay Round in 1994, the world's leading trade powers—the United States, Japan, and the European Union—and the multilateral trading community more broadly, confront the challenges of globalization, challenges that the very successes of the system have helped produce.

Multilateral trade confers large efficiency benefits by fostering the international division of labor and by disseminating the gains from technological progress. Yet achieving efficiency gains involves adjustments. Support for measures that will yield greater economic efficiency requires a sense that the benefits and burdens of the necessary adjustments are shared equitably across and within countries, both to maximize the gains from trade and to sustain support for the system. In addition, the system requires political legitimacy if it is to deliver sustained benefits. Finally, the governance of the WTO, the modalities of trade negotiations, and the broader international political context remain critical to the success and functioning of the trading system.

Raymond Vernon was an astute observer of the forces that have transformed the economic landscape in recent decades. He also was among the world's preeminent scholars on international political economy. To honor his memory and the lasting contributions he made to our understanding of the multilateral trading system—a system whose architecture he helped shape in the aftermath of the Second World War—Harvard University's Center for Business and Government organized a conference on a topic dear to his heart and central to his scholarship: the challenges faced by the multilateral trading system in the new millennium.

This volume brings together contributions from many of the world's leading specialists on the four themes—efficiency, equity, legitimacy, and governance—that run through the current debates about the WTO. The individual chapters were originally presented at the conference held at Harvard University in June 2000. Also included are comments delivered at the conference as well as four summaries of the discussions that ensued and a summary of the concluding session. The contributions have since been revised for publication under the editorial guidance of Roger B. Porter (Harvard University), Pierre Sauvé (Organization for Economic Cooperation and Development), Arvind Subramanian (International Monetary Fund), and Americo Beviglia Zampetti (European Commission). The latter three editors were fellows of the Center for Business and Government at the time of the conference. The conference was sponsored by the Kansai Keizai Doyukai of Japan and the Center for Business and Government.

Financial support for this project was provided by a research fund established at the Center for Business and Government by the Kansai Keizai Doyukai; we appreciate the support of the Kansai Keizai Doyukai Partnership companies, Daikin Industries, Ltd., Kansai Electric Power Co., Inc., Kawasaki Heavy Industries, Kobe Steel Ltd., Matsushiita Electric Industrial Co., Ltd., Nippon Life Insurance Company, Obayashi Corporation, Osaka Gas Co., Ltd., Sumitomo Electric Industries, Ltd., Sumitomo Metal Industries, Ltd., Suntory Limited, Takenka Corporation, and West Japan Railway Company. Raymond Vernon's influence was felt far and wide, and it is appropriate that individuals and organizations from across the globe would support this effort in his honor.

Our thanks to Janet Walker, managing editor at Brookings Institution Press, and Chris Kelaher, acquisitions editor, for their encouragement and assistance. We also thank Barbara de Boinville for her patience and skill in editing the manuscript. In addition, Carlotta Ribar proofread the pages and Robert Elwood prepared the index.

We thank Dow Davis for his support on administrative and financial matters and Maureen Caulfield, Darcie Dennigan, and especially Amy

Christofer for their help organizing the conference. Carolyn Lips and Daniel Braga were helpful in producing the manuscript.

The views expressed in this book are exclusively those of the authors and should not be ascribed to the institutions with which they are affiliated, to the people whose assistance is acknowledged, or to the organizations that supported the project.

ROGER B. PORTER

Raymond Vernon

Raymond Vernon's life spanned nearly the whole of the twentieth century, and his public service and academic career were at the center of many of its most important economic developments. Born in the South Bronx in 1913, he spent most of his eighty-six years in the arena where economic policy issues are shaped and implemented. He devoted his life to thinking and writing about these issues and to teaching others. After graduating from high school at the age of fifteen (the same high school that produced Colin Powell), Ray attended the City College of New York, where he concentrated in economics and statistics. He took every course offered in those subjects and hit the job market in 1933 asking a simple question: Do you want a statistician?

At the National Bureau of Economic Research (the home of Arthur Burns and Simon Kuznets), he found employment from nine to five at $40 a week, and in the evenings he worked at an advertising agency. In the course of solving a series of problems there, he tactfully taught his supervisor multiple regression analysis. Two years later he was restless and eager for new challenges. Washington beckoned and would hold him and his talents for two decades.

In 1935 he took a job at the newly created Securities and Exchange Commission, where he wrote the early SEC reports from his perch in the research department before moving into and overseeing stock market operations. He assisted in writing guides for the military regarding Japan and

Germany (the structure of their economies and governments and the nature of their business-government relations). Ultimately, in 1946, he was
invited to go to Japan with a group advising General Douglas MacArthur
on restructuring the Japanese economy, with special emphasis on antitrust
provisions.

While working at the SEC during the day, Ray managed to get a
Ph.D. in economics at Columbia University. He attended classes during
his summer vacations and also received credits from George Washington
University, American University, and the U.S. Department of Agriculture
(which had some superb statisticians). By 1941 he had earned his doctor-
ate, but at that time he was not thinking of an academic career. A love of
learning and the challenge of completing the degree motivated his studies.

Having come to the attention of officials at the State Department, he
left the SEC in 1946 for a position at State. After working on patents and
trademarks, he soon gravitated toward trade policy. Working with Paul
Nitze, Dean Acheson, John Leddy, and Clarence Randall, he helped shape
economic relations in the postwar world (including the Marshall Plan and
GATT). He was, to borrow Dean Acheson's phrase, present at the creation
during one of the most remarkable periods in our history.

In 1954 a new challenge beckoned, and he left government to work
for Mars Candy Company, a privately held firm. Forest Mars administered
an examination (which Ray passed with a score of 100 percent), and he
became comptroller and planner for the company. During the evenings he
wrote articles and was active in the Council on Foreign Relations. Among
his many accomplishments at Mars Candy Company was the peanut
M&M, an achievement much appreciated by many of us. Because of his
quick mind and tremendous abilities, he found himself confronted with a
decision: did he want to consider the position of president of the company? His beloved Josie encouraged him: "Let's get out of here before we
can't afford to leave."

In his mid-forties Ray transitioned to the world of academia. Within
two years the Harvard Business School offered him a full professorship to
teach international business. He accepted and organized the Harvard Multinational Enterprise study—a multiyear effort that produced 30 books, 200
articles, 30 doctorates in business administration, and about half the international business professors in the country.

While at the Harvard Business School, Ray Vernon reached across the
river and became a full member of the Harvard community by serving as
director of the Center for International Affairs. He also helped to establish

the Development Advisory Service—what was later the Harvard Institute for International Development (HIID). Ray was always a bridge builder. Nearing the mandatory retirement age at the business school, he was enticed by Harvard University's Department of Government in the Faculty of Arts and Sciences to accept the Clarence Dillon Professorship of International Affairs.

In 1980 he joined the faculty of the Kennedy School of Government and became the founding editor of the *Journal of Policy Analysis and Management* (JAPAM), a position he filled for five years. Nearly two decades were spent at the Kennedy School—a remarkably productive period. He wrote many books and articles on trade policy and the role of multinational enterprises. Not least, he was someone who exhibited little regard for his own recognition and devoted much time, effort, and attention to helping others.

Raymond Vernon was not only a great man but also a good man. The outpouring of interest in the Center for Business and Government's conference in June 2000 reflects more than the timeliness of the topic: it demonstrates the affection and admiration that was felt around the world for Raymond Vernon. In this life we have the opportunity to swing in close with only a relatively small number of people. For those who swung in close to Ray Vernon, it was an experience they will never forget and will always treasure.

He thought deeply and puzzled over problems long and hard. Rarely have I met anyone with a stronger work ethic. Literally, to the end of his life, he never flagged or failed—teaching students, writing books and articles, consulting with colleagues and friends. For a decade our offices were located next to one another, and I saw each day his stamina and benefited from the countless ways in which he enriched the lives of those around him.

Ray was encouraged by four women in his life—his mother, his wife, Josie, and his two daughters, Heidi and Susan. He liked to talk to me about his early years growing up in the Bronx and came to our home to share some of those experiences with our children. His mother held high expectations for her son and demonstrated through her actions the deep belief she had in him.

Josie was the great joy of his life. For Ray, there was never anyone quite like her. She performed that invaluable service for him that we all need in our lives: she helped him keep his life in perspective. Above all, she inspired him to do his best and to be his best. And he reciprocated, building with her a marvelous relationship that involved genuine commitment and unconditional love. He spoke often about his daughters, Heidi and Susan, and about the pride he felt in them and their work. Not surprisingly, they both pursued academic careers and have passed on to their students many of the qualities Ray helped inculcate in them.

Ray Vernon was drawn to the practical rather than the abstract. He liked to work on concrete problems rather than elaborate theories. A careful and systematic thinker, he engaged the world as he found it and tried to make it better. He had much optimism, but given his long experience in government, business, and academia, he was, not surprisingly, a realist. John F. Kennedy once described himself as an idealist without illusions. Ray Vernon shared that outlook.

His idealism tempered by realism is an important reminder to us today. This is a time when two dangers loom large. For those who are experiencing great prosperity, there is the danger of complacency. For those who are experiencing poverty, the challenges of adjusting to a global trading system seem almost overwhelming. This is precisely the kind of challenge that would excite Ray. He would bring to that challenge an attitude developed over a lifetime of experience.

Ray Vernon held a positive view of the world and of its governments. He believed that most public officials sought the welfare of their citizens most of the time. Having experienced the Great Depression, the Second World War, and the events in the war's immediate aftermath, he saw the powerful force for good that governments can be and the important role played by sound policies and institutional arrangements. At the same time he understood the virtues of markets and the need to rely on them in allocating resources. He recognized the power of utilizing incentives. One often felt in his presence a sense of urgency, but he was a patient man in many ways. He knew that progress comes incrementally and that there are powerful rewards for the persistent.

The virtues he embodied are worthy of emulation. They will serve well those whose task it is to write the next chapter in the evolution of the global trading system, a system about which Ray Vernon cared deeply and to which he contributed so much.

PART ONE

Introduction and Overview

ROGER B. PORTER

1 | Efficiency, Equity, and Legitimacy: The Global Trading System in the Twenty-First Century

Scholars will undoubtedly judge the twentieth century as one of the most remarkable in history. It was
a century filled with troubled times and with astonishing accomplishments. Among its most notable developments were the twin triumphs of
democratic political institutions and market-oriented economic arrangements. The ascendancy of democracy and free enterprise were anything
but assured as the century began. As the century closed, much of the globe
enjoyed a time of both peace and prosperity.

The first fifty years of the twentieth century witnessed two world wars
and a deep, prolonged depression. Unemployment in the United States
never fell below 14.5 percent in any month for a full decade. Many factors contributed to this economic distress, including well-intentioned but
misguided policies such as a dramatic increase in tariffs among the world's
trading nations. This led to a sharp decline in global trade, which fell to
approximately one-third its previous level.

The second half of the twentieth century represented a marked contrast. While there was a prolonged cold war, in military terms it was a time
of relative peace. There were regional conflicts to be sure, but, as Richard
Cooper has reminded us, Europe has experienced its longest period of
peace since the Roman Empire.

Moreover, the second half of the century has witnessed unprecedented
global prosperity. During the period from 1950 to 1990, world per capita

3

income increased by 2.2 percent per year, a more rapid rate of growth than in any previous period. Per capita income was more than two and a half times larger at the end of the century than it was in 1950. This remarkable material improvement is especially evident in many of today's economically prosperous countries such as Japan, South Korea, Italy, and Spain, to name just four, nations that were much poorer only fifty years ago.

Not only has the production of goods and services greatly increased, but advances in health care reflected in the decline of infant mortality and progress in treating communicable diseases have led to substantial increases in longevity. Life expectancy for someone born in the United States in 1900 was forty-six years of age. One hundred years later, life expectancy had increased more than three decades. Partially as a result, the global population, which was approximately 1.9 billion in 1900, exceeded 6.0 billion as the century drew to a close.

Many factors influenced this remarkable rise in prosperity. Not least among them is the growth of trade in goods and services, which is widely acknowledged to have made a significant contribution. During the last fifty years, international trade outpaced the growth in economic output, growing more than 6 percent annually. This was partly a result of the decline in import protection during this period following eight rounds of multilateral tariff reductions.[1]

Developments in transportation and communications helped to fuel trade in goods and services. Between 1920 and 1990, average ocean freight and port charges for U.S. import and export cargo fell almost 70 percent. Between 1930 and 1990, average air-transport fares per passenger mile fell by 84 percent, and the cost of a three-minute telephone call between New York and London plummeted 98.6 percent.[2] By 1995 tariffs on manufactured goods into developed economies were only about 10 percent of the levels they were in 1947, the year of the first multilateral round.

Yet at the beginning of a new century the prospects for the global trading system are anything but settled. The disappointing ministerial in Seattle in December 1999 underscored the uncertainty and divisions that exist about what direction the multilateral trading system should take, what next steps are both feasible and desirable, and what processes should govern negotiations and the implementation of agreements in the future.

The enthusiasm for a bold new round of trade negotiations is surprisingly muted. A sense of urgency regarding the next steps in trade liberalization is strangely absent. Why, when increased trade appears to have benefited so many to such an extent, does there appear to be so little agreement on where to go from here?

In some respects the trading system is a victim of its own success. As societies become more affluent, the attraction of and interest in pursuing noneconomic objectives become stronger and the capacity to provide greater and greater amounts of security for citizens increases. Likewise, as societies prosper, distributional issues tend to loom larger. Most advanced industrial economies in the twentieth century adopted governmental programs designed to provide a floor, a safety net, for those with the fewest economic resources. At the same time the spread of democracy in the developing world, and the growth of organized groups, which understandably seek a greater voice in shaping public policies, have made reaching decisions and agreements more challenging.

Thus the discussion of the global trading system is not the province of a select number of officials and experts seeking to find mutually beneficial reductions in border barriers. In many respects trade has become the major game in town. The number of players eager to get on the field has grown. The range of considerations that various participants press has expanded. The process of fashioning agreements and getting them approved and implemented is increasingly complicated and difficult. In short, the discussions and debates about global trade today revolve around efficiency, equity, and legitimacy.

Efficiency

Having raised tariffs sharply in the early 1930s, policymakers concluded that such actions were counterproductive. In the United States, Cordell Hull championed passage of the Reciprocal Trade Agreements Act of 1934, but most of the significant tariff reductions came after 1947. Today tariff rates on manufactured goods are approximately one-tenth what they were in 1947. The average rate of duty on manufactured goods was over 40 percent in 1947 but less than 4 percent at the conclusion of the Uruguay Round in 1994.[3]

The success in reducing tariffs on manufactured goods has led many to question the size of the potential remaining gains. It is commonplace to assume that with average tariff levels one-tenth what they were a little more than fifty years ago, the remaining efficiency gains from further reductions are relatively modest. Moreover, many question whether more gains in efficiency can be achieved without forestalling a movement toward greater equity and without impeding progress on valued noneconomic objectives such as the environment and workplace standards.

Critics of globalization advance a host of subtexts, but their essential arguments fall generally into a three-pronged attack: the economic benefits from globalization are essentially complete; the complexity of deeper integration will entail a substantial transfer of nation-state sovereignty; and desirable noneconomic goals will suffer from a continued emphasis on the pursuit of economic efficiency. The low-hanging fruit has already been harvested. Retrieving the remaining crop is not worth the costs associated with capturing it.

Jeffrey Frankel's thoughtful assessment of what potential efficiency gains remain, however, posits a far different reality. Whether one measures against the standard of what trade flows would look like in a fully integrated global economy (assuming the absence of transportation costs or cultural differences) or one examines the real impediments that exist in many economic sectors, Frankel appropriately concludes that the global economy is still far from complete integration and that large gains are still available.[4]

One source of these gains comes from achieving greater allocative efficiency utilizing the conventional rationale for trade that has been advanced since Adam Smith and David Ricardo. Some have underestimated these allocative efficiencies because focusing on average tariff rates is deceptive: actual tariffs include many peaks as well as valleys. The peaks (with tariffs as high as 20 and 30 percent) still significantly restrain trade flows. More important, many of the constraints on trade now consist of nontariff barriers—quotas, orderly marketing agreements, regulatory standards, procurement requirements, and the like—which often exist to advantage domestic firms.

Many economists, including Robert Willig, have noted an increase in international cartel-type behavior during the past five years and that the increasing frequency with which antidumping provisions are sought and applied has also had the effect of reducing the rate of growth of trade in goods and services. Significant barriers remain in agriculture and textiles, in government procurement and transportation, particularly ocean transport. As Jeffrey Frankel reports, several computable general equilibrium (CGE) models have estimated that further gains from a new round of multilateral liberalization to achieve allocative efficiencies would improve world income by $350 billion, or roughly 1 percent of global GDP. In addition, as the new trade theory posits, pure gains in efficiency also result from the powerful effects that flow from constraining rents, from achieving greater economies of scale, from stimulating technological innovation, and from accelerating the diffusion of ideas and processes. A rough estimate of Frankel's suggests that, when these dynamic effects are included, the effect of a new round could be to raise world GDP by 2 percent over the subsequent twenty-five years.

It is a mark of modern market-based economies that they usually are highly efficiency conscious, implicitly recognizing the enormous economic gains that can come from appropriate investments and allocating those resources to their most efficient uses. With respect to international trade, the answer to the question of what remaining efficiency gains are possible is clearly that substantial potential gains still exist. Barriers remain and, if reduced or eliminated, can contribute to major gains.

How best to achieve them remains an open question. Alan Sykes adopts a realistic approach, accepting that nations for the foreseeable period will, for a variety of reasons, act to restrain trade in some ways. Accordingly, he calls for making those constraints as nondistorting as possible, all the while seeking to remove them as quickly as is politically feasible.

Advancing the efficiency agenda is also likely to be aided by encouraging greater transparency. Tariffication helps individuals and societies understand the price they are paying for trade barriers, and therefore it illuminates the choices they make. In doing so, societies come to understand the economic costs associated with restraints on trade. This makes those barriers seem less attractive. Another tool in dealing with many barriers that are regulatory in nature is to pursue performance-based regulation, a more efficient approach than traditional command and control regulatory schemes.

The evidence that a half-century of policy-driven increases in trade flows has yielded substantial aggregate economic benefits is overwhelming. The argument that restraints on trade remain and that further potential gains exist is equally powerful. Yet the debate over next steps engages competing values beyond the quest for efficiency.

Equity

A second powerful idea helped shape policy during the twentieth century, a concern about equity both within and across nations. During the past seventy years, and increasingly in the past fifty years, governments in Europe, the United States, Canada, Japan, and elsewhere have adopted programs designed to redistribute income as a means of providing citizens with greater security—job security, health security, retirement security.

In 1930 U.S. federal government spending was approximately 3 percent of gross domestic product. Today it is roughly seven times that level, with more than 60 percent of spending devoted to so-called entitlement programs. The figures are equally striking in other developed economies. The rise of mandated or entitlement spending is driven partly by the pursuit of greater security and stability but also by an interest in an equitable distribution.

Likewise, the past fifty years raised several questions: How should the unprecedented gains that efficiency has helped produce be allocated among and within nations? What share of the expanding pie should be devoted to public purposes and to the achievement of public goods such as a clean and inviting environment and a safe and healthful workplace? Policymakers debate not merely how best to increase the size of the pie, but how the pie should be divided up. The debates over equity tend to take three forms: equity between nations, equity within nations, and an equity concern that involves the tension between economic and noneconomic objectives.

Equity between Nations

There is a feeling on the part of many developing nations that they are being left behind, that they are receiving a disproportionately small share of the benefits of a more liberal global trading system. Jeffrey Sachs reminds us that trade is only a part of the process of economic development. Equally important, investment, technology, and the capacity to use that technology are essential. Addressing the gap between developed and developing economies will require not only much effort, but also receptivity and a willingness to engage on the part of developing countries—a readiness to accept foreign investment and to make what changes are needed to facilitate the transmission of new technologies throughout their economies.

Equity within Nations

A second equity concern involves the distribution of benefits within countries. The recognition that increased trade in goods and services occasions adjustments by individual workers and firms has prompted much deliberation over whether and how best to ease those adjustments. Affected groups, including organized labor, have resisted efforts to reduce trade barriers in an attempt to avoid such adjustments altogether.

Provisions that ease or cushion these adjustments have played a prominent role in securing approval to negotiate a reduction in trade barriers.

For more than four decades, provisions on trade adjustment assistance for workers, firms, and communities have been among the most fiercely fought provisions in U.S. trade legislation. Proponents of such measures have argued that while all citizens receive the benefits from trade in the form of favorable effects on price, quality, and selection, displaced workers bear a heavy burden and therefore merit special assistance.[5]

The negotiations over these provisions involve how much assistance, for how long, in what form, and with what conditions. The arguments revolve around what level of "compensation" is equitable and over whether the form the assistance takes will facilitate or prolong the period of adjustment. The persistence and growth of such provisions underscore the reality that equity considerations within national economies remain a prominent feature of the landscape for trade policymakers.

One striking aspect of this debate is the comparison between adjustments occasioned by technological innovations and adjustments driven by increased trade. The rapid diffusion of technological innovations has contributed to the increased dynamism that characterizes modern economies. Indeed, the amount of adjustment that is driven by technological change and innovations is much larger than the adjustments occasioned by changes in trade policies.

Those seeking to reduce barriers to trade must address how they propose to ease the adjustments that increased trade will produce in ways that those urging governmental spending on programs designed to expand research and development and increase the pace of technological innovation do not. Arguably, the connection with job losses is more distant and more difficult to establish in the case of technological innovations. Moreover, the changes driven by technological innovations are less easily attributable to specific governmental actions. Not least, foreigners do not vote. The difference between the treatment of workers displaced by trade and those displaced by technology reflects in part the strength of equity concerns in trade policy.[6]

Economic and Noneconomic Objectives

A third equity concern involves the tension between economic and noneconomic objectives. The growth of per capita incomes and increased affluence in many societies have produced an intensified debate about not simply the allocation of income between individuals, but also the allocation of national income between economic and noneconomic objectives.

This debate has increasingly revolved around the environment and around the conditions under which employees work. Attention to environmental quality and workplace standards has risen dramatically since the 1970s and now plays a significant role in trade policy discussions as well as in debates over appropriate social regulation.

Environmental policy is an interesting case in point. Environmental considerations played virtually no role in the deliberations leading to the Trade Expansion Act of 1962, and an extremely limited role in passage of the Trade Act of 1974 and the Omnibus Trade and Competitiveness Act of 1988. Likewise, when the phalanx of advisory committees was established to assist the Office of the U.S. Trade Representative, little, if any, thought was devoted to whether to establish a committee dealing with the environment.

The past decade, however, witnessed a marked change. The environmental effects of trade agreements, and whether trade agreements should be used to seek improvements in environmental quality, played a pivotal part in the debates over fast-track authority for a North American Free Trade Agreement (NAFTA), the negotiation and approval of NAFTA, and the intense debates over fast-track authority in 1995 and 1997.

Proponents of greater trade liberalization have sought to draw attention to the long-term effects of trade liberalization and to shift the focus from an emphasis on short-term considerations. While acknowledging that the increased economic activity resulting from trade liberalization may contribute in some instances to modest short-term increases in pollution, they point to a remarkably consistent pattern in economies that achieve higher levels of prosperity. Greater economic prosperity is almost uniformly associated with an increased interest in the environment and more willingness by nations to devote greater resources to improving it.

By the end of the twentieth century, the U.S. economy was producing more than twice as many manufactured goods as in 1970, and it was doing so with less absolute pollution. Indeed, the attention and resources devoted to environmental protection in developed economies during the last three decades of the century were remarkable.

Rather than a feared "race to the bottom" with respect to environmental standards, whether measured by resources devoted or results achieved, a healthier environment has accompanied the prosperity in developed economies associated with liberalized trade. Yet despite this pattern, trade and the environment are likely to remain linked in the future.

Likewise, workplace standards have received much attention in recent trade rounds with the oft-asserted fear that the demands associated with an integrated and competitive global economy will produce a race to the bottom. Many have claimed that the result of greater trade is a reduction in workplace standards for health and safety. Yet the evidence of a race to the bottom is difficult to find. More frequently, workplace standards in developing economies rise than workplace standards in developed countries fall. Indeed, in the United States there has been a steady, decade-by-decade rise in workplace standards in the last half century, a time when the share of the U.S. economy engaged in trade roughly trebled. One of the driving forces behind this phenomenon is the rise of multinational enterprises. They have tended to encourage the diffusion of best practices in manufacturing processes with safer equipment and fewer workplace injuries. Whether between nations, within countries, or with respect to such non-economic objectives as labor standards and the environment, equity considerations now claim a much larger place in trade discussions than in past decades.

Legitimacy and Governance

The modern age accords much attention not only to the substantive outcomes of policy but also to the process by which decisions are reached. Internationally, policymakers vigorously debate the procedures by which disputes should be settled and what institutional arrangements should govern global economic activity.

Any discussion of legitimacy and governance should acknowledge the patterns of the past as well as the challenges for the future. The successful multilateral trade rounds during the second half of the twentieth century produced trade agreements that were highly technical in nature filled with specialized jargon and classifications. As in many other arenas, a cadre of officials expert in the substance and nuances of trade policy negotiated the agreements.

These agreements were built around the nation-state and were fueled by the opportunity to reach, in the aggregate for a country, Pareto optimal outcomes. Political leaders who provided direction to their trade negotiators justified the final agreements to their citizens by saying that the net benefit to the nation would exceed the costs or adjustments. Once agreements were adopted, the decisions reached by international bodies in resolving disputes have largely been self-enforcing. The entire system has relied heavily on trust between participating countries.

New Elements

Several developments have challenged the old regime in trade policy. First, the number of countries with membership in the World Trade Organization (WTO) has sharply increased, complicating the task of reaching consensus in future negotiations.[7] As was abundantly clear at the Seattle Ministerial, a broad consensus is necessary to make even modest progress, and the ability of the WTO to reach a consensus is complicated by the range of views and interests represented by member countries. Overlaid on the increased number of participants is the reality that participating countries vary widely in population, economic output, and trading interests.

Second, the task of reaching agreements has become more complex, and concluding multilateral agreements has taken longer. Negotiations that revolved around reducing tariff barriers, largely on manufactured goods, have been replaced by more contentious issues—agriculture, services, intellectual property, investment, competition policy, and restraints associated with regulatory regimes.

Third, perhaps the most striking new element wrought by the Uruguay Round was adoption of the single undertaking. It greatly expanded the reach of the new World Trade Organization by establishing binding disciplines on all members in those areas covered by WTO agreements. Given that all members are now bound by changes in the rules, one effect of the single undertaking is to entrench the principle of consensus.

Fourth, the other major structural change adopted during the Uruguay Round was the Disputes Settlement Understanding (DSU), which has the effect of establishing a more juridical system for resolving disputes. To the extent that rulings by panels and the appellate body are seen as balanced and unbiased, and to the extent that parties abide by the decisions, a body of WTO law will gradually be established. In the end, final sovereignty still rests with member nations who are able to determine, subject to WTO rules, whether they will modify their practices consistent with the ruling or suffer the trade consequences. But clearly, the new DSU represents a departure from the past.

Fifth, recent decades have seen a dramatic rise in the proliferation and sophistication of organized interests at all levels of government and across national boundaries. Many of these have sought to infuse the agenda with new issues, complicating the task of negotiation. Their insistent and persistent efforts have raised the question of what roles these organizations and their concerns should play in future negotiations.

Sixth, as reaching large multinational agreements has become more difficult, the number of regional agreements has grown, more than doubling during the past decade. Indeed, in the United States the trade policy advanced during the 1990s was specifically multipronged: a series of unilateral and plurilateral initiatives accompanied the commitment to seek a multilateral agreement.

In one sense the negotiation of regional agreements demonstrates an interest by countries in reaping the benefits of freer trade and helps maintain momentum toward reducing barriers to the movement of goods and services. A real question is whether regional agreements will complement, or serve as a substitute for, a more comprehensive multilateral agreement. The events in Seattle as the millennium drew to a close are a sobering reminder of the challenge posed by this series of recent developments. The lack of agreement, even on next steps, illuminates how difficult fashioning the next multilateral round will undoubtedly prove.

What Is Needed?

As discussion about the longer term occurs, four immediate tasks deserve attention. First, there is value in pursuing a realistic, if limited, short-term agenda. This agenda should include at a minimum the Uruguay Round mandated negotiations on agriculture, the commitment in the General Agreement on Trade in Services (GATS) for negotiations on liberalizing trade in services, and the negotiations mandated by the Agreement on Trade-Related Aspects of Intellectual Property Rights (TRIPs).

Second, there is a need to develop credibility for the new disputes-settlement procedures. The WTO is a fledgling organization with a modest staff and greater responsibilities than resources; greater expectations than capacity. Strengthening the WTO machinery can assist in helping to produce fair, balanced, expert, and credible decisions.

Third, governments must attend to establishing improved relationships with the increasingly active phalanx of nongovernmental organizations (NGOs). The advisory committee structure in the United States is one avenue for constructive exchanges. Less formal but sustained interactions between government officials and NGO representatives is another. There is evidence, in fact, that officials are engaging NGOs more actively. In the United States the formal advisory committee structure within the executive branch has been expanded. As more and more congressional committees have successfully laid claim to elements of the trade policy agenda, a wider range of voices has been heard in legislative branch deliberations.

Officials, however, should carefully pursue more actively engaging NGOs given two sobering realities. The first concerns the issue of formal standing. The second concerns the scope of trade negotiations. Granting standing in legal or quasi-legal proceedings or a place at the negotiating table to insistent parties is a slippery slope. Democratically elected governments have a responsibility to consider the concerns and interests of all citizens. There is some evidence this is occurring. Many of the debates over trade policy have acquired greater visibility and received more press attention. In that sense more aggressive and pervasive media have helped illuminate and convey views and positions. Second, elected and appointed officials have engaged in greater outreach to organized groups through formal advisory bodies and greatly augmented informal consultations.

At issue is the extent to which certain groups are entitled to a more definitive role in the process of negotiating agreements and resolving disputes. What groups? Under what conditions? In what ways? With what rights? These are questions worth measuring carefully. Precedents once created are difficult to reverse. Sensitizing government officials to the need to genuinely engage organized interests has many advantages over granting nongovernmental entities a more formal role.

It is understandable why a wide variety of groups wants to use trade negotiations (and sanctions) to address issues these groups consider urgent, but such a path is fraught with risk. Trade negotiations have themselves become more complicated as the number of parties involved has grown and the range of trade issues under consideration has expanded. Expanding the agenda even further undermines the prospects for achieving the kind of consensus that is needed to reach agreements. Moreover, many developing countries view NGOs, which are largely based in and driven by individuals and groups in developed countries, as often hostile to their trade interests. Given adoption of the single undertaking, creating binding disciplines that apply to all WTO members, future trade negotiations will engage those from developing countries to an even greater degree than in the past.

Fourth, the Seattle Ministerial reminded us that careful preparation is essential. Some of that preparation is formal; much of it is informal. A central task of political leadership is to build support for an undertaking before beginning a journey. The muted reaction to the Seattle Ministerial in many quarters in the United States and elsewhere illuminated how disengaged those in the business community were and how little they felt was genuinely at stake. By contrast, the vote on a permanent normal trading relationship with China illustrated the willingness of business interests to become active when they saw real benefits and tangible markets.

The new world of trade policymaking now involves in a more intense way not merely the quest for efficiency but also the search for equity. More nations are more actively engaged. More organized interests are pressing their claims for a voice. The challenge for political leaders is not only to articulate the benefits of further trade liberalization but also to fashion a broader set of policies that will help ease the inevitable adjustments, policies that can generate the broad base of support that will be needed to make that agenda a reality.

Notes

1. Richard E. Caves, Jeffrey A. Frankel, and Ronald W. Jones, *World Trade and Payments: An Introduction,* 8th ed. (Addison-Wesley, 1999), p. 5.
2. Council of Economic Advisers, *Economic Report of the President, 1997,* p. 243.
3. Caves, Frankel, and Jones, *World Trade and Payments,* p. 165.
4. See Jeffrey Frankel's chapter in this volume.
5. See Roger B. Porter, "The President, Congress, and Trade Policy," *Congress and the Presidency,* vol. 15 (Autumn 1988), pp. 165–84.
6. André Sapir has written perceptively about many of the differences between how U.S. and European policymakers have struggled with the type of domestic adjustment assistance that is preferable. See his chapter in this volume.
7. The General Agreement on Tariffs and Trade numbered twenty-three members when it was formed in 1948. By the time the Uruguay Round concluded and the WTO replaced it, GATT had 110 members. As of March 2001, the WTO has 140 members and more than 30 applicants eager to join.

PIERRE SAUVÉ
ARVIND SUBRAMANIAN

2

Dark Clouds over Geneva? The Troubled Prospects of the Multilateral Trading System

There can be little doubt that the December 1999 Seattle Ministerial of the World Trade Organization (WTO) was an unmitigated fiasco. All it seemingly achieved was to embolden the crusade of those who want to slow down the pace of market liberalization or indeed reverse the liberal framework of policies that underpinned five decades of postwar trade and investment growth and the worldwide improvement in living standards associated with such growth. Much of the débâcle in Seattle bore a "made in the USA" label. The paradox is of a host country lurching between unprecedented economic prosperity and technological dominance on the one hand and growing public angst directed at policies that engage the world economy on the other.[1]

To be fair to those directly involved, Seattle certainly was not the first *rendez-vous manqué* of the sort. Nor will it probably be the last. Several survivors of the Seattle gathering were quick to recall past instances of failed ministerial gatherings or missed negotiating deadlines. Such is life in the trenches of trade policy.

The proximate causes for the failure of the Seattle meeting were many, and we will cite just a few: the host government's sagging commitment to multilateral trade diplomacy and its overriding preoccupation with

The authors are grateful to Aaditya Mattoo for very helpful discussions on and contributions to this chapter.

short-term domestic politics; the incompetent handling of the consensus-building process leading up to Seattle, which would have made success elusive even had the political environment been more propitious; and the divisive atmosphere created by the bitter wrangling over the choice of the new director-general of the WTO.

The End of the End of History? A Seductive but Incomplete Tale

The jury is still out on the fundamental lessons to draw from Seattle. Should one essentially discount the whole affair and view it as a *hiccup*—a mere bump along the road to closer worldwide economic and political integration? Or should it rather be regarded as a *warning signal,* alerting governments that unless and until they more resolutely address some of globalization's fault lines—on the environment, the North-South divide, social safety nets, or the perceived exclusion of civil society from decision-making—a sustained commitment to market openness may prove politically untenable? Or, more ominously still, should one view Seattle as a possible *turning point* in the benign climate afforded by nation states to multinational enterprises during the past few years of Washingtonian consensus? Stated differently, might Seattle have in any way signaled what French economist Pierre Jacquet has usefully coined the "end of the end of history"?[2]

Much as the "end of the end of history" story has great intuitive appeal and certainly makes for better headlines, the failure of Seattle is more readily explained in traditional trade policy terms. We offer three core explanations in support of this view.

First, the bargaining dynamic that lies at the heart of the multilateral trading system has broken down for a number of hitherto unexplored reasons. To put it succinctly in Yeatsian terms, it was not so much the passionate intensity of "civil society"—or at least those within it who view themselves as mantle bearers of the antiglobalization and pro-democracy crusade that derailed Seattle—as the lack of conviction of private sector interest groups that traditionally have driven the trade policy machine.

Seattle failed less because civil society, deeply distrustful of globalization and the creeping power of greedy, stateless, and unregulated multinational corporations, had found its voice. Rather, in the battle over trade policy the proverbial good guys—and traditional drivers of the liberalization process—were simply nowhere to be found or, worse still, were in retreat.

Second, much as it is not the root cause of the problem, there is little denying that civil society activism contributes to the breakdown of the trading system's bargaining dynamic. The vocal demands of civil society for higher labor and environmental standards increasingly constrain the ability of the North to satisfy the growing assertiveness of the South's market access demands.

And third, the perceived erosion of the system's legitimacy once again has conventional trade policy origins. While claims that the WTO system is deficient in its democratic and participatory foundations have some validity, other factors, including increasing judicialization and the fractured nature of the relationship between the United States and the European Union, arguably play an even more important part.[3]

If our hypothesis has validity, the prognosis for the future of the multilateral trading system might well be bleaker than a version that attributes failure primarily to a resurgent civil society. We say "bleaker" because if the system is to keep delivering the considerable benefits that remain to be reaped from further global integration, not only must globalization's fault lines be addressed, but the multilateral community must find ways of kick-starting the trade policy machine. The famous metaphor for trade negotiations used to be the bicycle, which had to be in constant, forward movement to avert a system breakdown. Post-Seattle, the trading system above all needs a cyclist—and preferably a long-distance specialist rather than a sprinter. Only then can the notions of forward movement, or merely standing still, acquire renewed meaning.

A comparison between Seattle and the congressional vote on China's permanent normal trading relationship (PNTR) status illustrates well our main contention. Opponents of globalization, ranging from organized labor to those who care about human rights, labor standards, the environment, and other important causes, targeted the China vote with as much vehemence as they did Seattle. Few countries are perceived as so wholly at odds with the core values—human rights, environmental protection, participatory democracy, labor standards—espoused by civil society as China. And yet the outcome of the PNTR vote shows that civil society's voice was successfully muzzled.

This was so because powerful corporate interests, which had a lot at stake in terms of increased access to the Chinese market, threw their considerable weight behind the trade opening deal. To be sure, the vote in

Congress was not about increased penetration of U.S. markets, and hence insecure import-competing interests were conveniently taken out of the political equation. Despite strong opposition from organized labor, environment-related nongovernmental organizations (NGOs), and human rights groups, the lure of access to large untapped markets ultimately prevailed. In Seattle, by contrast, no corporate *demandeurs* could be found. What explains this puzzle?

The North as Demandeur

The WTO is quintessentially a bargaining framework—a peace treaty among mercantilists—where "concessions" (the progressive opening of markets) are exchanged. The system is ultimately powered and driven by private sector interests that seek market opening abroad. Consider, in turn, two major sets of demandeurs for market opening—private sector interests in industrial countries ("the North") and developing countries ("the South"). Table 2-1 outlines schematically our arguments relating to each of these.

Why is the private sector in industrial countries seemingly disenchanted with the multilateral trading system or not willing to invest in it as much as it once did? Could it be that the scope for global integration has been exhausted? The answer must be an emphatic no. Several studies demonstrate that the process of global integration is, to put a crude quantitative number on it, less than one-sixth complete.[4] Disenchantment simply cannot be attributed to the accomplishment of the WTO's job. Rather, the source of the problem must be located in a combination of success and failure, to which we now turn.

The North's Demands for Market Access in the South

As developing countries have improved their economic situation, they have offered increasingly important markets for suppliers in industrial countries. Accordingly, enhanced entry to these markets should be of great interest to industrial country exporters. They should be active *demandeurs* in the WTO, working hard with their governments to lower trade and investment barriers in developing countries—in goods, intellectual property, and services. But why is this less the case than common sense should dictate?

Table 2-1. *The North as Demandeur of Market Opening*

Region and subject	Level of North's interest in opening	Comment
In the South		
Manufacturing	Low	Credible unilateral reform and regional agreements have made multilateral reform less important
Intellectual property	Low	Successful Uruguay Round and strengthened dispute settlement disciplines have reduced importance of IP as a rulemaking challenge
Services—Access	Low to medium	Developing country resistance to multilateral reform
		Perverse effect of monopoly/ dominant foreign incumbents
		Slowness of negotiated regulatory convergence
In North and South		
Regulatory barriers (goods and services)	Low	Regulations impinge upon domestic policy objectives and countries are reluctant to cede sovereignty
		Increasing gap between accelerating product cycle and lengthening negotiating cycle breeds private sector indifference
Investment	Low and declining	Unilateral investment regime liberalization continues unabated in the absence of multilateral rules
		Bilateralism yields superior outcomes for home country investors in matters of investment protection
		Increased judicial activism à la NAFTA lessens negotiating interest of OECD governments (fearing loss of regulatory sovereignty)

TRADE IN GOODS.   Consider first the traditional area of trade in goods. Developing countries have long maintained, and continue to maintain, high barriers to goods trade, largely in the form of tariffs. The average tariff in developing countries is over 20 percent, compared with less than 5 percent in industrial countries. In the WTO developing countries have undertaken a commitment not to raise their tariffs above certain levels, called the bound level. This represents their international legal commitment, the breach of which would trigger action by trading partners. A common feature of WTO bindings in the tariff field is for bound tariffs to be well above the actual tariff level maintained by developing countries.

Consider a few examples. Chile, typically touted as a paragon of openness, applies a uniform tariff of 9 percent to all imports. It has nonetheless bound its tariff at 35 percent. The gap between Mexico's and India's applied and bound tariff rates is well above 15 percent. And the list goes on. The wedge between the actual and bound tariff is important because it is the margin that countries retain for themselves to reverse policies without breaching their WTO obligations. Even if this represents an undesirable state of affairs from the viewpoint of the country seeking flexibility and negotiating coinage (the case for small countries less likely to offer attractive locations to foreign investors), the more puzzling question is why partner countries—and especially the industrial countries—willingly accept this state of affairs. Why have they not pushed developing countries harder to reduce their bound tariffs at least closer to actual levels? Are they merely grateful for the fact that developing countries have some, minimal, commitments, no matter how commercially meaningful? Or do they no longer care much—or care much less—about such barriers?

Two arguments favor the latter view. For one, many developing countries, imbued in recent years with the policy precepts of the so-called Washington consensus, have been unilaterally dismantling their trade barriers, typically at the urging of the World Bank and the International Monetary Fund. Between the early 1980s and today, quantitative restrictions have been eliminated, and tariff barriers have been lowered considerably, from an average of over 35 percent in the early 1980s to about 20 percent in the late 1990s. With all this happening outside the WTO framework, suppliers in industrial countries do not have to expend negotiating coinage within the WTO to secure outcomes that can be obtained costlessly.

Nonetheless, industrial countries should be interested in ensuring that the far-reaching reforms enacted by developing countries in recent years, the bulk of which were unilaterally decreed and hence subject to reversal, are "locked in," in trade policy parlance. The WTO offers a mechanism for doing precisely that.[5] Countries commit to tariff "bindings"—that is, to not raising tariff levels above bound levels. Yet evidence from the Uruguay Round and more recently from the run-up to Seattle suggests that exporters in industrial countries are not overly concerned by the specter of policy reversal. They have been willing to allow developing countries to bind their tariff levels well below actual tariff rates. The only convincing explanation for this apparent permissiveness must be that partner countries no longer see the prospect of policy reversal as very likely. Ironically, by achieving credibility of policy, developing countries have less to offer—or rather their partners have less to seek of them—in the WTO context. This is yet another manifestation of the WTO becoming a victim of its very success.[6]

Second, just as countries continue to lower trade and investment barriers unilaterally, they increasingly do so in the context of regional trade agreements (RTAs). The WTO received notification of no less than forty-five RTAs in its first two years of operation. Of the WTO's 140 members, 82 are party to an RTA.[7] The RTA contagion includes a large number of agreements reached between the members of the European Union (EU) and countries in eastern Europe and other regions of the world (for example, Turkey, the Mediterranean countries, most recently Mexico), along with an expanding web of agreements closer to home in the Americas. Interestingly, an important feature of such agreements has been their North-South character. Weakly constrained by multilateral disciplines, regional integration may be lessening private sector interest in pursuing bargains at the multilateral level. What is more, the systemic effects of regional agreements for multilateral bargaining may well be perverse: countries in a regional arrangement may actually want less broad-based liberalization in the WTO since their preferential access to each other's main export markets will likely be eroded. The revealed preference of WTO members for weak provisions under Article 24 of the General Agreement on Tariffs and Trade (GATT) and Article V of the General Agreement on Trade in Services (GATS) is more easily understood in this light.

INTELLECTUAL PROPERTY.   One of the major driving forces in the Uruguay Round was the intellectual property (IP) lobby. However bitter the pill may have been for developing countries to swallow, a successful conclusion to the round would have likely proved elusive without a strong result on intellectual property.[8] Of all the Uruguay Round breakthroughs, the Trade-Related Aspects of Intellectual Property Rights (TRIPs) Agreement was one of the few that had a real impact in the sense of compelling what in some cases were far-reaching changes to domestic IP regimes and institutions.[9] This interest group is no longer a major *demandeur* in a multilateral context because many of the commercially important issues of concern to firms in the pharmaceutical, chemical, and entertainment goods (but not services) industries were settled in the Uruguay Round. The IP lobby was seldom seen and barely heard in Seattle. Here, too, the WTO may be characterized as a victim of its own success.[10]

TRADE IN SERVICES. If private sector disinterest springs from success, it also owes to failure. Globalization and the unfurling advances in information technology have shifted policy attention from goods to services, the tradability of which has increased significantly in recent years and is widely expected to expand further as the e-commerce revolution, both business to business and business to consumer, takes firmer root around the world. Services remain an area where opportunities for enhancing national and global welfare have only begun to be tapped.

Developing countries have long resisted calls for the multilateral liberalization of service regimes. It is undoubtedly an exaggeration, but only a mild one, to suggest that developing countries as a group largely gave a pass to the inaugural set of multilateral negotiations on trade in services. Evidence of the "success" of developing-country resistance—and of commensurate precaution by indsutrial country regulatory authorities—is the generally weak and unfinished framework of rules that emerged from the Uruguay Round in the services area, as well as the minimal level of liberalization commitments undertaken by countries. And here again, as with tariffs, the wedge between the reality of present-day regulatory regimes and the level of bound commitments often remains quite large.[11]

To date, the only true success under GATS has come in the core infrastructure sector of basic telecommunications, where a sense of shared urgency led to significant regulatory convergence and a willingness to commit to WTO-anchored trade and investment liberalization in the mid-1990s. Still, the architectural weaknesses of GATS, its "user-unfriendliness," and the difficulty of achieving much by way of negotiated regulatory convergence in most sectors, have fueled the growing private sector realization that the multilateral system may not be overly effective—and may be decidedly slow—in delivering the real opening of services markets around the globe.

TECHNOLOGY VERSUS NEGOTIATING CYCLES. This perception is strengthened by the increasing disjunction between the accelerating product cycle

firms must contend with and the lengthening negotiating cycle governments must contend with as the trading system moves inland. The accelerating pace of technological progress has had profound implications for
the operation of a number of key sectors, such as telecommunications
goods and services and finance. Even national regulation of these sectors
tends to be one step behind technological changes. But if multilateral regulation proves slow and ponderous as recent experience has shown, private
sector enthusiasm will wane. Nongovernmental routes to securing market
access and standard setting will prove more attractive for the private sector than the WTO route. So, too, will the call of *regional* intergovernmental sirens.

THE SPECIAL CHALLENGE OF FOREIGN INCUMBENCY.   Compounding these
developments in the services sector has been another phenomenon with
perverse consequences for the liberalizing dynamic on the multilateral
front. Where service sector liberalization has taken place in developing
countries, most notably in areas such as telecommunications, finance,
transportation, or energy, emphasis has often been on privatization-
induced liberalization rather than on rendering domestic markets more
contestable. To a considerable degree, such policies were pursued out of
the belief that private ownership was inherently preferable to state control.
As a result, monopoly profits that were dissipated by inefficient domestic
firms in the public sector were transferred to foreign firms as rents.[12] These
domestic policy choices have entrenched dominant foreign interests,
which may now have a stake in resisting further liberalization and the
adoption of procompetitive regulatory regimes (including the adoption or
more activist enforcement of competition policy regimes) for fear that
such enlightened actions might threaten their privileged position. The end
result is a threefold problem: the disappearance—or benign indifference—
of more private sector interests as *demandeurs* in the multilateral arena,
lessened pressures for liberalization, and heightened civil society antago-
nism (in the North and South) toward multinational enterprises.

The Plot Thickens: The North's Other Demands for Market Access

Owing to increasing success in dismantling border barriers such as tariffs, quantitative restrictions, and export subsidies, the focus of multilateral rulemaking in the area of trade in goods, especially between industrial
countries, is shifting to behind-the-border regulatory measures. This shift

becomes even more pronounced as liberalization focuses on services, where regulatory measures are pervasive, and in most instances the sole barrier to competition through trade and foreign direct investment.

THE REGULATORY DILEMMA. Regulations typically exist to further a legitimate public policy objective, be it environmental protection, consumer safety, competition, or social protection. But regulations can and regularly do become trade barriers if they inflict an undue burden—a burden over and above what is necessary to achieve the stated domestic policy objective—on trading partners. Finding a workable trade-off between the two is fiendishly difficult. Moreover, regulations get embedded because of political capture, as vested interests perceive economic advantage in their maintenance. Even where capture is not a serious problem, governments are loath to abandon or change domestic regulation to accommodate the commercial interests of trading partners. Recent disputes in the WTO—for example the case of hormone-treated beef and the controversy surrounding genetically modified organisms—demonstrate how difficult these are to resolve even among countries at similar stages of development.

INVESTMENT. A topic with both northern and southern dimensions to it, investment rulemaking, stands out as one that has proven ominously problematic of late. Here again, owing to a combination of success and failure, and the subtle (but crucial) differences in the political economy of trade versus investment regime liberalization, the scope for useful multilateral bargaining appears to be dwindling. The failed attempt anchored by the Organization for Economic Cooperation and Development (OECD) to conclude a Multilateral Agreement on Investment illustrates our argument well.

There has been major *unilateral* reform of foreign direct investment (FDI) regimes all over the world. As recent surveys by the United Nations Conference on Trade and Development show, policy change on the FDI front has been, and remains, a one-way street and a strongly liberalizing one at that, with close to 95 percent of changes in FDI regimes worldwide during 1991-98 being of a liberalizing nature.[13] This benign policy climate has spurred a remarkable growth in cross-border FDI activity, which in recent years has increased by close to 60 percent, far outstripping growth in cross-border trade and domestic production over the past fifteen years.

FDI reform is unique in having a powerful (and self-reinforcing) market mechanism against policy reversal embedded in it. The reason is sim-

ple: in a world of considerably heightened capital mobility, foreign investors increasingly vote with their feet. This sets investment policy apart
from its trade cousin, whose political economy of cyclical protectionist
capture is more likely to generate de-liberalizing changes in policy.

Faced with unabated, unilateral benevolence on the part of host-
country governments, corporate indifference to multilateral rulemaking is
hardly surprising. Because global firms get much of what they want
unilaterally, OECD governments are all too happy to stay away from international investment agreements. The considerable intrusiveness of comprehensive investment rulemaking, which works well in the one-way street
of North-South investment treaty making, is decidedly trickier when pursued among countries with high regulatory density and a legal industry
willing and able to guard against the alleged confiscatory tendency of governments. As the increasing number of investor-state disputes under the
North American Free Trade Agreement (NAFTA) is showing, investment
agreements can significantly empower private investors to challenge host-
country regulatory authority.

Diminishing Negotiating Coinage: The South as Demandeur

Industrial countries are increasingly withdrawing from their traditional role of *demandeurs* in seeking the multilateral dismantling of trade
barriers in foreign markets. But with the emergence of large developing nations as important traders on the global scene, the WTO system must increasingly accommodate the market access demands of these new players.
They, too, have become *demandeurs* (see table 2-2). This newfound assertiveness was much in evidence in Seattle, as developing countries emitted
a collective *no mas* in the wake of then-president Bill Clinton's plea to enforcing multilaterally agreed labor standards with trade sanctions.

But their comparative advantage lies in precisely those labor-intensive
sectors that are the most difficult for the United States, the European
Union, and Japan to contend with. In both the EU and Japan, agriculture
is a sacred, multifunctional cow, and in the United States, liberalizing textiles and clothing is a red rag, since this sector represents one of the last bas-
tions of deeply entrenched protectionism.[14] There is also growing concern
among the trade policy cognoscenti that the dismantling of quotas on textiles and clothing, agreed under the Uruguay Round and scheduled to take
effect in early 2003, may not proceed smoothly. The signal that would send

Table 2-2. *The South as Demandeur of Market Opening in the North*

Subject	Level of North's ability to deliver opening	Comment
Agriculture	Low	Sacred cow in the EU, Japan, Korea
Textiles and clothing	Low	Red rag to a bull in the United States
Labor-based services	Low	High domestic sensitivities over immigration-related matters
All areas: existing access	Potentially threatened	Northern civil society activism in areas such as labor and environmental standards increasingly seen by developing countries as threat to existing market access

to developing countries could scarcely be good news for the trading system as a whole. And the precedent it would set would hardly embolden the EU and Japan to soften their resistance to agricultural trade liberalization when the peace clause embedded in the Uruguay Round's Agreement on Agriculture expires in 2003. Both deadlines are literally just around the corner.

Another area where developing countries are *demandeurs* is labor-based services. In software, accountancy, and legal, medical, and other professional services, developing countries have real comparative advantage and significant opportunities to enhance their exports of high-skilled labor and services. For the great majority of OECD countries, however, especially in Europe and Japan, undertaking multilateral commitments with regard to the inward movement of labor, even on a temporary entry basis, is anathema and has axiomatically been considered out-of-bounds in multilateral bargaining. Despite the pressure of some developing countries, most notably India and the Philippines, WTO provisions dealing with such issues (in the GATS) are remarkable for their weakness and the caution labor market regulators and immigration officials continue to display.

Civil society's criticisms of the World Trade Organization can be broken down into procedural and substantive matters. On procedure, the main claim is directed at the nonparticipatory and insufficiently democratic nature of the WTO. On substance, the disaffection concerns the trumping by liberal trade of allegedly more important values—environment, labor and human rights, respect for animals.

The putative legitimacy that emerges when the question is so posed—that is, trade versus other values—obscures the divisive nature of the policy diagnosis and the prescriptive cure on offer. Invariably, the latter takes the form of unilateral (or multilaterally mandated) demands for higher standards in the South on the environment and labor, standards that have the potential of jeopardizing even the existing market access that developing countries have been able to derive from the multilateral trading system.

To many developing countries, heightened civil society activism in the North, steeped as it may be in the rhetoric of compassion for the weak and downtrodden and rejection of the animal spirits of market-based competition, has the ring of a new form of policy imperialism. Most important, civil society activism is constraining the ability of the North to deliver on the demands of the South—not just to provide new market access opportunities but to maintain existing markets. As a result, the WTO's bargaining quagmire worsens.

The inferences that flow from the preceding analysis are somewhat gloomy. We are left with a bargaining arena where the North is not interested enough to make demands of the South. In turn, the South, which has serious demands to make, runs up against the North's inability to satisfy them. Worse still, the North's ability to maintain the South's existing access is threatened by civil society "imperialism." And both North and South seem unable to accede to demands to change deeply cherished and/or captured regulatory systems. What kinds of bargains are possible in such an environment? And what added layers of difficulty (and gloom) must one face when globalization and its discontents are added to the mix?

Enter Judicialization and the Crisis of Legitimacy

As if the aforementioned ailments were not enough, the multilateral trading system is further buffeted by the WTO's crisis of legitimacy. The popular impression, and one that the mass demonstrations at Seattle and Washington lent credence to, is that this crisis emanates from some fundamental disaffection with globalization. This stems from the perception that newly emerging (or resurging) voices—civil society, organized labor, environmentalists, human rights activists—have been, and remain, excluded from the trading system's decisionmaking processes.

While there is substance to some of these claims, the crisis of legitimacy is once again partly attributable, in our view, to more traditional failings in the trading system. These failings have not been given adequate attention in the now-proliferating exegeses of Seattle.

A major outcome of the Uruguay Round was to strengthen the old GATT institutionally, and one key element of the strengthening was the judicialization of dispute settlement. Legal verdicts, in the manner in which they were derived and implemented, now have a distinctly judicial ring to them. In the old GATT, there was always the restraining (sometimes overly so) hand of politics and the diplomatic order even when it came to the adoption as law of panel rulings.

Judicialization was a conscious choice made by countries as a response to the diminishing effectiveness of the old GATT system. Judicialization per se may not be bad. It may, indeed, be the only way to contend with the WTO's considerably expanded agenda of domestic rulemaking. And the sight of many developing countries making use of the Disputes Settlement Understanding (DSU) to defend their hard-fought rights is without a doubt a welcome sign. Yet in conjunction with two parallel developments—the desultory state of the United States' relationship with the European Union and the creeping insularity of the U.S. Congress—judicialization may have fueled the current crisis of legitimacy.

Trade Relations between the United States and the European Union

It is a truism that the state of the trade relationship between the United States and the European Union determines the overall health of the trading system. Before the 1990s, the GATT, with only a little exaggeration, *was* the U.S.-EU relationship. Today, with the emergence of large trading nations in the developing world, that synonymity obviously no longer holds, but it is fair to say that healthy U.S.-EU relations are a necessary, although not sufficient, condition for the vibrancy of the multilateral trading system. That relationship is today fractured, tense, and riddled with reciprocal suspicion. A series of high-profile disputes, from bananas to beef hormones, aircraft subsidies, and tax policy, has created the impression of a relationship that is largely adversarial rather than bound by a shared purpose that is mutually beneficial. The disputes over bananas and beef hormones have bred brinkmanship. There has been a familiar and distressing pattern of provocation, escalation of conflict, flirting with the precipice, toying with the consequences of nonimplementation, and grudging retreat from the brink without real resolution.

The disputes themselves are the most immediate and obvious manifestation of the lack of trust between the two transatlantic partners. Yet the drift in U.S.-EU trade relations creates a deeper crisis of legitimacy for the trading system as a whole. The long history of divide between the two sides (particularly over agriculture), coupled with the push of WTO rulemaking behind the border, has led to the negotiation of rules in the Uruguay Round that are ambiguous and deliberately nebulous. The constructive ambiguity of rules that delivered the short-term gain of diplomatic success and conclusion of agreements in the Uruguay Round has carried with it the significant risk of their nonjusticiability, sowing the seeds of future conflict. This is most evident in the areas of standards and food safety, as well as in services (as the bananas case so vividly showed).

Failure to agree on clear rules in the legislative or negotiating process has been compounded by irresponsibility and escalating judicial activism by the two sides. By carelessly allowing some of the weakest links in the WTO chain to be tested before WTO dispute settlement panels, the two sides have in effect sought to impose judicial solutions on political failures. It is in the nature of such solutions to bring political surprises, not all of which will be pleasant or properly anticipated.[15]

But more important, such tactical judicial activism has exposed the WTO's fledgling legal order to damaging allegations of intrusiveness, and it has eroded political and regulatory sovereignty. These criticisms carry sting because the WTO's legal order does not have the legitimacy of national judicial systems. After a famous environmental dispute, ads placed in major American newspapers accusing "faceless Geneva bureaucrats" of altering sovereign policy choices have had a telling impact. In this troubled environment it is hardly surprising that civil society has had a field day challenging the trading order.

Creeping Isolationism

Judicialism can be successful if the underlying system commands legitimacy, as the Supreme Court in the United States or the European Court of Justice in Europe so obviously do. Judicialism also can succeed if the dominant players in the system accept that they will lose some disputes. Both transatlantic partners, however, have been prone to playing with fire. Examples include the European Union's recurring tendency to skirt compliance with WTO panel decisions and the recent decision by the United States to resort to so-called carousel retaliation (which it now sadly targets at poor countries in Africa and the Caribbean).

Equally troubling are the recurring attempts by the U.S. Congress to claw back from the executive branch powers that it voluntarily ceded in the aftermath of the disastrous Smoot-Hawley tariff. This owes in no small measure to the fact that WTO rulemaking is today chiefly concerned with regulatory barriers—the traditional domain of Congress (and of NGOs). The more insular perspective of Congress, typified in recent years by its reluctance to renew fast-track negotiating authority and its call for a vote on continued U.S. membership in the WTO, has created a mind-set where the prospect of losing WTO disputes somehow seems less politically palatable than it once did.

Conclusion

The ills of the trading system are increasingly laid at the door of glob-alization's discontents, ably articulated by and represented in resurgent civil society. While there is some truth in this, it is an essentially incomplete depiction of the formidable challenges confronting the multilateral trading system at the dawn of the new millennium. The failure of Seattle and the current vacuum in the trading system can be explained in more traditional policy terms. This chapter has offered three reasons for coming to this conclusion.

First, the traditional bargaining dynamic in the WTO has broken down because corporate interests in the North—the traditional drivers of the trade policy machine—are increasingly in retreat and because the North is increasingly unable to meet newly assertive demands by the South for market access.

Second, civil society discontent over matters of substance is not the root cause of the trading system's current malaise. Yet there is little denying that the rising chorus of public opposition to a liberal world order contributes to the breakdown of the WTO's bargaining dynamic. It does so, in part, by constraining the ability of northern governments to fulfill the market access demands of the South.

Third, while the procedural sources of civil society discontent—the claim that WTO processes are undemocratic and insufficiently participatory—have some validity, the organization's current crisis of legitimacy is attributable in large measure to more traditional failings. Chief among them are the judicialization of the WTO and a U.S.-EU relationship that is fraught with tension and suspicion.

If this analysis has some merit, the prognosis for the multilateral trading order is bleak. Of course, the procedural and substantive sources of civil society disquiet must now be addressed. The traditional bargaining dynamic that underlies the WTO must be rescued from the apathy of northern corporate interests, the profound distrust of the South, and the angst of civil society.

Notes

1. See André Sapir's chapter in this volume for a cogent discussion of why globaphobia has been predominantly a North American phenomenon.

2. Pierre Jacquet, "WTO's Future Is a Beginning, not History's End," *The WorldPaper* (May 2000).

3. See Robert Keohane and Joseph Nye's chapter in this volume for a fuller discussion of such claims.

4. See Jeffrey Frankel's chapter in this volume.

5. It also allows countries to negotiate what Alan Sykes in this volume has dubbed "efficient protection."

6. Part of the reason for this paradox must lie with the very process of globalization and the attendant dispersion in production it brings in its wake. Domestic policymakers in developing countries realize that if any one policy environment becomes overtly inimical to foreign commercial interests, many alternative sources of supply can be found along global or regionally integrated production chains. The rising share of intrafirm trade brought about by globalization has similarly altered the political economy calculus of trade and investment rulemaking.

7. See Robert E. Hudec and James D. Southwick, "Regionalism and WTO Rules: Problems in the Fine Art of Discriminating Fairly," in Miguel Rodriguez Mendoza, Patrick Low, and Barbara Kotschwar, eds., *Trade Rules in the Making: Challenges in Regional and Multilateral Negotiations* (Brookings, 1999), p. 47.

8. See Sylvia Ostry's chapter in this volume.

9. See Arvind Subramanian, "TRIPs and the Seattle Round," paper presented at the Conference on Developing Counries and the Seattle Round, Harvard University, 1999.

10. The meaning of "success," however, has become a highly contested matter. A rising chorus of voices questions the purported benefits of the TRIPs agreement on equity and developmental grounds. Many also question what its precedent portends for the treatment of the slew of other "trade and" issues knocking at the WTO's door.

11. The level of bound liberalization embodied in GATS is widely seen as inimical to the pursuit of economically efficient policymaking. See Aaditya Mattoo, "Developing Countries in the Next Round of GATS," *World Economy,* vol. 23, no. 4, pp. 471–90; Pierre Sauvé and Christopher Wilkie, "Investment Liberalization in GATS," in Pierre Sauvé and Robert M. Stern, eds., *GATS 2000: New Directions in Services Trade Liberalization* (Brookings, 2000), pp. 331–63; Bernard Hoekman and Patrick Messerlin, "Liberalizing Trade in

Services: Reciprocal Negotiations and Regulatory Reform," in Sauvé and Stern, *GATS 2000*, pp. 487–508.

12. The most egregious example is the extended monopoly granted to the telecommunications operator Cable and Wireless by a number of Caribbean countries. But other examples abound throughout the developing world, as well as in central and eastern Europe.

13. United Nations Conference on Trade and Development (UNCTAD), *World Investment Report 2000—Cross-Border Mergers and Acquisitions Development* (Geneva: United Nations, 2000).

14. The tortuous legislative journey of the Africa Growth and Opportunity Act, enacted in 2000, speaks legion in this regard. The initiative long floundered on the rocks of the textiles lobby. U.S. textiles producers argued that the possible extra imports of half of 1 percent of current imports would pose a significant threat to them.

15. A recent WTO panel found the U.S. government guilty of granting WTO-prohibited export subsidies to foreign sales corporations. It is well known that this case was in no small measure the result of a vengeful move by the European Union in response to perceptions of U.S. aggression in previous disputes—especially over bananas and hormone-treated beef, which put the EU on the defensive. The beef hormones verdict exposed the WTO to allegations of intrusiveness on the part of environmental NGOs, while the verdict on export subsidies is undermining private sector support for the WTO in the United States. Meanwhile, the protracted dispute over the bananas case has not only damaged trade. It has also opened the door to criticisms that the WTO is insufficiently sensitive to the interests of the poorest countries while it allows its powerful members to skirt panel rulings.

AMERICO BEVIGLIA ZAMPETTI

3

A Rough Map of Challenges to the Multilateral Trading System at the Millennium

For more than half a century, the multilateral trading system has known failure and success, bad as well as good times, as Raymond Vernon could attest, having worked in the group of enlightened planners that designed the postwar economic institutions.[1] Today, as the collapse of the World Trade Organization's Seattle Ministerial meeting undoubtedly shows, the multilateral trading system finds itself under renewed and increasing pressure. This is due to a confluence of factors, which may point to somewhat more structural difficulties than the unfavorable political economy conjuncture existing at Seattle.[2] A nonexhaustive account of them follows.

First, interest groups in civil society—including labor, environment, and consumer groups in the developed world and increasingly in developing countries as well—have mounted a vocal backlash against globalization; international trade liberalization, with its emphasis on economic efficiency, is considered one of the main driving forces.

Second, a sense of discontent has grown in many developing countries that the trading system is tilted against them, a conviction stemming from their belief that the Uruguay Round imposed substantial obligations on them without delivering commensurate benefits.

The author is grateful to Pierre Sauvé and Arvind Subramanian for many stimulating discussions on the issues covered in this chapter.

Third, growing tensions between major trading partners on matters of domestic regulation—straddling societal, cultural, and scientific issues—have proven intractable as they impinge upon deeply held notions of sovereignty in the pursuit of public policy objectives. By far the largest share of these tensions to date has involved advanced industrial economies, principally the United States, Japan, and the European Union.

Fourth, progress in the preparation for new negotiations in areas such as trade in services, foreign direct investment, competition policy, and government procurement has proven difficult. Questions are being asked regarding achievable progress on some inherently complex issues and the developing countries' interest in, and ability to deal with, those issues. Furthermore, debates on what are seen by some as spurious issues, such as the environment and core labor standards, have become quite divisive.

Finally, the legitimacy of WTO processes and outcomes, including the organization's ability to credibly arbitrate and resolve commercial disputes, is subject to serious scrutiny in some capitals and by several elements of civil society. This has prompted calls to reflect on the existing governance structure of the WTO and on ways to improve its effectiveness.

All of these important challenges to the WTO and the multilateral trading system largely derive from the increasing integration and complexity of the world economy and the difficulty of providing the requisite supply of international governance. After the successful conclusion of the Uruguay Round, the multilateral trading community confronts what might loosely be termed the challenges of globalization, challenges that the very successes of the system have helped produce. Whether signs of a deep, structural crisis or a fleeting *crise de croissance*, these challenges revolve around four main issue areas: efficiency, equity, legitimacy, and governance.

One of the few certainties that the "dismal science" provides and that economic reality has confirmed is that international trade confers large efficiency benefits by fostering the international division of labor and by disseminating the gains from technological progress. This validates the policy prescription of trade and investment liberalization, both domestically and through international cooperative efforts. Yet efficiency gains sometimes involve painful adjustments. Support for measures that will yield greater economic efficiency requires a sense that the benefits and burdens of the necessary adjustments are shared equitably across and within countries.

Facing up to the equity challenge and to the calls to broaden the system's policy objectives to encompass environmental, development, and social considerations is crucial to maintaining the political legitimacy of the international trading order. At the same time, the trading system's legitimacy is strongly affected by the way the WTO discharges its two main governance functions: rulemaking through trade negotiations and conflict resolution through its dispute settlement mechanism. The emerging "global" civil society of nonstate actors, including interest groups, professional associations, and corporations, is posing renewed risks and opportunities for the development of the hitherto state-centered multilateral trading system.[3]

Finally, the broader international political context and the capacity of trading nations to tackle these challenges remain critical to the success and functioning of the WTO and to the effective and coherent governance of the international system, of which the WTO is a key element.

Efficiency

Multilateral trade negotiations traditionally have covered trade in goods but, increasingly, they are encompassing new areas such as services, investment, intellectual property, government procurement, and domestic regulation. Despite the recurrent overselling or underselling, depending on political opportunity and ideological preferences, the economic case for further trade and investment liberalization remains compelling.[4] Trade liberalization has been successful over the years, but there is still a long way to go in virtually all areas. Although many efficiency gains are there to be reaped through further negotiations, attaching a precise monetary value to specific liberalization efforts remains difficult and somewhat risky in the tense political debates surrounding trade policy in many countries because it could be seen as a sort of pass-fail test for liberalization.[5] Furthermore, the exercise becomes exceedingly complicated when the assessment is extended from border to nonborder regulatory measures, which are key to furthering the liberalization process, for instance in the area of services. It remains even more complicated if the set of indicators is broadened in order to assess effects in areas such as employment or income distribution. Hence, trying to select, prioritize, and agree on a negotiating agenda on this basis would prove elusive. The only econometric estimations that count in political terms, if any, are the very country-specific ones, inevitably bound to produce rather differentiated wish lists.

If we move from the general policy prescription in favor of trade and investment liberalization, which flows from economic theory, to the messier world of political economy and trade negotiations, the challenge is to find the most "efficient" outcomes by reducing trade distortions and restrictions as much as possible, in a context still dominated by the political imperative to ensure broad reciprocity of benefits. The multilateral trading system remains a world where producer interests are more powerful than consumer interests and where mercantilist and protectionist impulses must constantly be tamed by those in government who, with a true sense of leadership, look at trade negotiations as a way to promote national (and sometimes even global) welfare through enhanced economic efficiency. The ability of countries to fend off protectionist pressures in order to proceed along the path of economic efficiency through liberalization remains a key challenge for all countries and for the future of the trading system.

While it is true that politicians and officials often succumb to mercantilist and protectionist pressures, the track records of GATT and WTO negotiations and outcomes are remarkably positive. GATT and WTO disciplines have ensured that the degree of politically unavoidable protection at any particular time has been achieved in ways that are generally the least harmful to economic welfare. Pursuing economic efficiency through GATT and WTO trade liberalization has worked, and the policy prescription of continuing on this path remains robust. As Alan Sykes put it in his chapter in this book, WTO rulemaking can steer countries toward "efficient protection." It has done so to a considerable extent in goods markets, where the learning curve is being climbed, and more tentatively in services markets, where more experience and analysis are needed and the issues, mainly pertaining to domestic regulation, are inherently more complicated.

Indeed, following the remarkable success in tariff liberalization, the WTO system has shifted its focus much more to domestic regulation. In order to encourage efficiency, its rules aim at removing market distortions caused by "unjustified" regulation of a naked protectionist kind or, more often nowadays, facially neutral but *de facto* discriminatory.[6] Through this efficiency gate, and mainly as a result of the Uruguay Round negotiations, a good deal of new subject matter has been brought, at least partially, within the WTO remit. The cluster of environmental and food safety issues falls into this category. Moreover new issues, ranging from competition policy to social issues, are actively being debated.[7] It will be a key challenge for future negotiations to ensure that rulemaking in these areas leads to the most efficient outcome possible. This is increasingly important, since, when dealing with domestic regulation, beyond "economic" efficiency proper, other—at least as important—public policy objectives need to be taken into account.[8] In the end, as Frankel notes, "efficiency means maximizing one's objective, whatever it may be, subject to the constraints of nature and man. The objective is not limited to GDP but includes such noneconomic goals as the equality of income distribution and the quality of the environment. The principle remains that countries can better achieve their goals through free international exchange—subject to rules mutually agreed in international forums such as the World Trade Organization, the International Monetary Fund, the International Labour Organization, and the UN Framework Convention on Climate Change—than they could if they hid behind barriers to trade and investment."[9]

Equity

Since the beginnings of GATT, the multilateral trade system has included the promotion of economic development as one of its goals.[10] The experience of the past few decades has shown that, with very few exceptions, the contribution of the trading system and of trade liberalization to the process of development has been useful, necessary some would argue, but certainly neither sufficient nor decisive enough to set it on a sustainable path. As a result, trade and trade liberalization, through their contribution to economic growth, play an important supporting role in development and in the fight against poverty.[11] The GATT and WTO approach to economic development has been mainly based over the years on the granting of tariff preferences and on the "Special and Differential Treatment" instrument, as adapted by the requirements, sometimes very protectionist, of the political economy of the day.[12] More recently, the importance of removing market distortions, also through trade and investment liberalization, has become rather ubiquitously recognized, but many restrictions remain to both North-South and South-South exchanges.[13]

Moreover, there is a growing awareness that a successful approach to development must take account of the whole range of institutional, social, and structural needs of a well-functioning society, such as good governance, an appropriate institutional and regulatory framework, social inclusion policies, public services, physical infrastructure, and environmental protection policies.[14] Again, the pursuit of efficiency, or at least of economic efficiency strictly construed, is only one, albeit essential, element of development policy. The multilateral trading system can contribute to the realization of a wider set of objectives, which go beyond opening markets by "strengthening" them in a broader sense.[15]

As a framework of rules, the WTO system already makes a major contribution to good governance. In particular, the body of WTO rules ensures predictability, stability, and enhanced transparency. It also offers protection to developing countries, which, in the absence of the multilateral shelter, may be exposed to the unilateral trade policies of more powerful partners. Beyond this, the development of new rules and market access commitments in the WTO provides many countries, both developing and developed, with the additional external pressure they sometimes need for important domestic reforms.

Although trade policy reform, and fuller integration in the trading system, contribute to higher economic growth and good governance, they also entail significant costs. Today the increasing complexity and globalization of world markets, as reflected in the Uruguay Round agreements, demand a high degree of institutional sophistication and impose a broad range of obligations and implementation costs. Such requirements are inescapable, but if the growth payoff flowing from integration in the world economy is to be reaped, developing countries, in particular the least developed, must engage in complex institutional and regulatory reforms and accept considerable adjustment costs.[16] Even the multilateral shelter represented by the WTO's dispute settlement mechanism is far from free of charge.[17]

This is fueling discontent in many developing countries and in large sections of civil society and public opinion in the North and South. The trading system, many say, is not affording an "equitable" distribution of benefits and market opportunities between countries. Whereas globalization is bringing, on balance, a lot of benefits to emerging economies, the least developed countries, including almost the entire sub-Saharan region, has not yet benefited likewise.[18] There is, in fact, a worrisome split between a group of middle-income developing countries that are successful participants in global trade and nearly eighty developing and transition economies (comprising 35 percent of the world's population) that are virtually excluded from it.[19]

The blame for this cannot be laid at the door of the multilateral trading system. It is true that the "balance of power" in the system has meant that trade negotiations have generally privileged issues and sectors of direct interest to the developed countries, and protectionism has been dismantled much more vigorously there, while significant barriers and distortions still remain in sectors such as agriculture and textiles. But in most cases the enduring predicament of developing countries is chiefly the result of the structural weaknesses of their economies much more difficult to correct than any imbalance in trade negotiation outcomes. These weaknesses are compounded by nonexistent or inadequate institutions and policies in the fields of law and order, sustainable macroeconomic management, and public services.[20]

Hence, the integration of these economies in the world economy cannot be seen as an end in itself but must be placed in the context of a comprehensive development strategy. This strategy needs to be backed by enhanced international support. The international donor community and the Bretton Woods institutions must increase their attention and adapt their policies to tackle the key public health and technological challenges facing developing countries (in particular, the more marginalized among them).[21] Moreover, coherence in global economic policymaking means involving all international organizations in the pursuit of the development agenda.

In the specific area of trade, it is essential that the multilateral trading system take full account of developing countries' interests, needs, and constraints, thus allowing these countries to make use of existing trade-related opportunities for development and to enjoy the benefits open trade promises to all.[22] Translating such promise into reality would go a long way toward realizing the "equitable" multilateral trading system to which all countries appear to be committed.[23] For future negotiations there is no dearth of areas to make up a development-friendly agenda: agricultural export subsidies and the needs of net food importing countries, accelerated removal of restrictions in textile and clothing trade, liberalization of the movement of natural persons as service providers and of the cartelized ocean shipping lines, reform of the antidumping regime and of the Trade-Related Aspects of Intellectual Property Rights (TRIPs) Agreement, in particular with regard to access to essential medicines and the protection of indigenous knowledge. In addition, a new approach toward incentives to attract foreign direct investment (FDI), a reappraisal of special and differential treatment provisions, and an enhanced commitment to technical cooperation and trade-related capacity building would also be crucial elements. Such an agenda could contribute substantially to economic growth and the development of the poorer members of the WTO.

Further opening of trade and investment policies in developing countries needs to be complemented by sound domestic policies aimed at ensuring an equitable distribution of the benefits of economic growth and support for the necessary adjustments. In particular, the establishment of a sound regulatory framework and improvement in human and institutional capacities will be essential for fostering "good governance" domestically, which are key to achieving a more equitable distribution of gains within societies.

Indeed, the equity debate cannot remain confined to the economic relations between nations. In democratic societies foreign economic policy is ultimately meant to improve the welfare of the people.[24] While international trade unequivocally does so overall, it also produces some losers. This happens in developing and developed economies. In some cases the success of developing countries in certain industries (such as textiles, apparel, and steel) dislocates workers in developed countries, which heightens the demand for protection.[25] In many other cases the forces of global markets produce, together with many benefits, significant adjustment costs. But in general, as Richard Cooper has noted, "foreign trade is small potatoes when it comes to disturbing modern economies, compared to technological change." However, a good deal of technology (as embodied in goods, investment, and intellectual property rights) moves easily across borders thanks to the rules of the WTO.[26] Hence the wholesale backlash against trade, the trading system, and more broadly "globalization." Confused as this reaction may be, it needs to be addressed. As experience has consistently shown, restricting and distorting markets through protection, although perhaps politically appealing, generally worsens instead of alleviating the problem. It remains incumbent upon governments, while repelling protectionist calls, to provide the necessary adjustment mechanisms to help those who are hurt. Labor market flexibility, retraining schemes, trade-adjustment assistance, social inclusion, and redistributive policies are possible approaches.[27] In addition, policymakers need to pay increasing attention to sustainability or the intergenerational equity aspects of the policies they promote. Failing to meet the equity challenge in all its facets, both within the trading system and domestically, abdicates an important leadership responsibility and leads to a loss of legitimacy for the multilateral system.

Legitimacy

Both the efficiency and the equity debates vividly demonstrate the depth of the trading system's impact on national economies and societies.

In keeping with the requirement of a more integrated world economy and as a result of the Uruguay Round, the multilateral trading system has gone well beyond the liberalization of border measures into policy areas that were formerly within "domestic jurisdiction."

Hence the trading system appears to be moving in the direction of integrating even more its policymaking and rulemaking objectives and issue areas other than economic efficiency through trade liberalization, which was the main original function of GATT. These new issues include competition, investment, environmental protection, health and safety, and sustainable development. Examples of this trend were already abundant in the Uruguay Round and were at the core of the discussions leading up to the Seattle Ministerial. As Frankel has noted, "the most important lesson from the Seattle demonstrations of November 1999 is that these issues will increasingly dominate public debate regarding globalization and multilateral institutions. They cannot simply be shunted off to the side, with pure trade issues occupying alone the center stage of international negotiations."[28]

Even accepting a strictly functionalist (trade only) perspective, the trading regime, through its normal operation, seems bound to extend its coverage, as the trade implications of other policy areas become apparent. If the European Community's experience is instructive for the multilateral trading system, this broadening suggests a gradual shift toward a more demanding (intrusive, some would say) "positive integration" paradigm, even if only to keep fulfilling the system's trade liberalization mandate. As a result, the linkage across international regimes and vis-à-vis domestic policy areas is here to stay.

This poses the fundamental constitutional challenge of how to reconcile the tension between various economic and noneconomic objectives that are relevant for the trading system and of great interest to WTO members, and their citizens.[29] Trade-offs of this kind are controversial in domestic settings, but they are even more so in an international context where state and nonstate actors exhibit different social preferences, attach unequal importance to economic and "noneconomic" values, and jealously guard their regulatory prerogatives. As Joel Trachtman notes, "The WTO cannot avoid these issues: it can only decide them."[30] Even failing to decide is to decide by favoring the status quo and the interests it represents.

How the "balancing" challenge is resolved has broad implications for the international legal order. It bears on whether international trade rules are considered "higher law" vis-à-vis environmental, human rights, and similar rules or vice versa, and whether a coherent approach is followed across different international regimes and institutions. It affects the relationship between international trade law, as part of the international legal order, and municipal legal orders of Members, and in particular, whether domestic regulatory choices should be trumped—the so-called deference issue. Moreover, the sensitivity that surrounds the balancing of economic and noneconomic objectives affects the equilibrium between powers within the organization, specifically, the extent to which the WTO "judiciary" should engage in the balancing exercise, if at all, in order to cover for the lack of rulemaking or rule interpretation by "legislators," the WTO Members.[31] Ultimately, how the balancing challenge is resolved has a key impact on the political legitimacy of the WTO.[32]

The legitimacy of international regimes has many facets.[33] A fundamental one is the "effectiveness of governance" and the ability to realize constituents' preferences and goals. The WTO is part of the international system of governance. To the extent that it does not reflect the preferences of the system's members, it is perceived as illegitimate. Even if a narrow state-centered approach to the trade system is adopted, full legitimacy is difficult to achieve. There will often be states that feel the system is tilted against them and they are somehow losing out. The problem becomes acute when the sentiment is widely shared. Many developing countries' perception of the trading system's "inequity," in terms of negotiated outcomes and procedures, has severely dented the legitimacy of the WTO, at least as far as they are concerned. If the approach is broadened to encompass people, producers and consumers, and civil society, perceptions will be differentiated even more widely and full legitimacy will be more elusive.

With globalization, the "relevant constituency" of the global governance system is broadening.[34] In the trading system the rule-making (legislative) function is still exercised through the mediation of the nation state, but the legal and policy relevance of the individuals and groups (often straddling national borders) is growing, fully in line with developments in other areas of international law and policy.[35] Furthermore, since the governance decisions taken within the system are sometimes considered unsatisfactory and it is increasingly easier to forge transnational coalitions, there is a growing tendency to try and influence decisionmaking at the national, but also "directly" at the international, level.[36] A reversal of this trend seems rather unlikely and is perhaps undesirable if the democratic legitimacy of the system is to be bolstered.

Within the multilateral trading system, policies and rules in new areas are being set that elicit significant attention from the public. Governments are then exposed to the allegation that sovereignty has been compromised, leading to a loss of decisionmaking transparency and democratic accountability. There is a tendency in certain quarters to think that difficult policy trade-offs should be sorted out in the domestic arena, since that is the legitimate locus to mediate and reconcile different values and policy objectives.[37] International cooperation in these situations is seen as undesirable if not dangerous.[38]

The system is thus confronted with a double challenge. Many individuals, groups, and countries feel excluded and want effective access to the international decisionmaking space; others think that space has grown too large and want to reduce it. There are those who want more or different international governance and those who want less. This structural opposition is compounded by many substantive differences on specific policy trade-offs. Failure to respond to these challenges could undermine support for the system and its further development as well as its perceived legitimacy and salience in the global economy.

Governance

Faced with the many complex issues that global economic integration has created, the multilateral trading system needs to adapt. Since widespread "outcome legitimacy" will prove elusive across all member countries and their peoples, at least the process through which outcomes are reached must be seen as effective, transparent, fair, and thus legitimate. This may require institutional reform of the WTO.[39]

Especially in the wake of the Seattle Ministerial meeting, many developing countries have complained about their *de facto* exclusion from the decisionmaking process. They point to their more modest negotiating capabilities, and the scarce attention paid to their demands. This structural bias would also be responsible for the limited economic benefits they have been deriving from the system. On the other hand, some developed countries have criticized the increasing difficulty of reaching consensus in a near-universal organization such as the WTO, with individual countries able to paralyze its entire decisionmaking machinery.

However, the formal, sovereignty-based equality on which the international system rests appears unchangeable in the foreseeable future, even if it has not delivered the degree of equity that developing countries desire or the standard of efficiency developed countries are seeking.[40] This means that there is no viable possibility of altering in any substantive way the existing intergovernmental, consensus-based setup of the WTO. The obvious innovation compatible with the equality principle—some form of simple or weighted majority voting—would be unacceptable alternatively to developed or developing countries. Leaving aside the daily administration of existing rules where some attempt could be envisaged, majority voting appears more adapted to situations when rulemaking is exercised on a continuous basis and not through intermittent and uncertain rounds of negotiations. However, the challenge to improve the inclusiveness, efficiency, and effectiveness of the WTO governance structure remains. An increased role (and resources) for the director-general and the independent WTO secretariat as consensus facilitators could be explored.

Numerous developing countries encounter serious problems in day-to-day participation in the WTO and in negotiating situations. The conduct of the Seattle Ministerial meeting was a painful reminder of the urgent need to improve developing countries' involvement through capacity building and innovative forms of issue-based and regional representation.[41] Doing so not only would help these countries participate in the organization more fully, but it also could facilitate consensus building in negotiations and WTO decisionmaking effectiveness more generally.

Furthermore the WTO, and in particular, each of the more than 140 countries cooperating in that institution, must face the parallel challenge of interfacing with the various national civil societies as well as the incipient "global civil society," where nongovernmental organizations, corporations, and business and professional associations have forged broad transnational links. The notion that civil society should be dealt with only in the domestic political space is somewhat misleading, since what every WTO member does in Geneva is part of its policy- and rule-making activity. Allowing effective transparency in order to hold government representatives accountable and providing an opportunity to express views and concerns in the institutional contexts where decisions are taken seem difficult to deny in democratic polities, and in any event, hard to accomplish in light of the advances in communication technologies. Whether this kind of participation is to be achieved piecemeal or through institutional engineering is an important challenge for the future of the WTO.

The introduction of an advisory body, with which civil society groups could have consultative status, may allow the institutionalization of their participation, in a sense providing them with a microphone to replace the megaphone.[42] An institutional venue of this kind, where national parliamentarians could also be asked to participate, would allow for a more structured discussion of issues and concerns of relevance to the trading system, from development to the environment, from consumer safety to technological developments. More specifically, the body could carry out studies, hold hearings, issue recommendations, and prepare opinions as requested by other WTO bodies. These activities would contribute to the important goal of fostering the WTO's "supportive politics," as Pierre Jacquet put it.[43] Such politics could help win the broad public support necessary for the further development of the multilateral trading system. Moreover, a heightened competition of ideas could, in turn, improve the quality of the decisionmaking process and outcomes.

Conclusion

At the dawn of the new millennium the system is confronted with some daunting and interconnected challenges. To fulfill its original mission to foster efficiency through trade liberalization, it needs to promote a more equitable distribution of benefits across its membership. Indeed, globalization must be harnessed for the benefit of all countries and peoples in a sustainable fashion. Since the Uruguay Round at least, trade rules and policies have influenced many other areas and activities, while different rules and policies at virtually all levels of governance have affected trade and trade rules and policies. The challenge is to retain sufficient legitimacy for the process and outcomes of international cooperation in the trade area, writ large. In the years to come, many difficult and interlinked issues will have to be analyzed and probably negotiated. The contribution of Raymond Vernon to these endeavours will be sorely missed.

Notes

1. For his own analysis of the beginnings of GATT, see Raymond Vernon, "America's Foreign Trade Policy and the GATT," Essays in International Finance 21 (Princeton University, October 1954).

2. For a rather gloomy account of the trading system's immediate prospects, see the chapter by Pierre Sauvé and Arvind Subramanian in this volume.

3. The idea of a "global" civil society is explored in Jessica T. Matthews, "Power Shift," *Foreign Affairs* (January–February 1997), pp. 50–66.

4. See Jagdish Bhagwati's chapter and also that of Jeffrey Frankel and the accompanying comment by Alan Winters in this volume.

5. See Winters's comment.

6. See David Leebron's comment in this volume.

7. See Frankel's chapter.

8. This challenge may not be entirely novel, as Robert Hudec recalls in his comment in this volume. Even in the "good old days" of straightforward trade liberalization under GATT, important "noneconomic" dimensions, such as "the suffering of workers being thrown out of work, and the decimation of communities dependent on these noncompetitive firms," were actively debated.

9. See Frankel's chapter.

10. See, for instance, Article XVIII (Governmental Assistance to Economic Development) of GATT 1947.

11. Outward-oriented strategies were applied in Southeast Asia, with export promotion followed by import liberalization; Latin-American countries in the decades following World War II followed inward-oriented strategies, or import substitution. These choices contributed to the difference in growth performance in the 1960s and 1970s between the Asian tigers and Latin American countries, which were initially at the same level of GDP per capita. The Asian experience helped form a consensus in favor of outward orientation as the optimal foreign trade strategy for development. However, the Asian tigers accomplished their integration in the world economy in an environment that differs from the global economy that developing countries are trying to catch up with. On the relationship between trade, growth, and poverty, see Dan Ben-David and L. Alan Winters, "Trade, Income Disparity and Poverty," WTO Special Study 5 (Geneva, 1999); Jeffrey Frankel and David Romer, "Does Trade Cause Growth?" *American Economic Review*, vol. 89, no. 3 (June 1999), pp. 379–99; David Dollar and Aart Kray, "Growth Is Good for the Poor," mimeo, World Bank, March 2000; Dani Rodrik, "Can Integration into the World Economy Substitute for a Development Strategy?" note prepared for the World Bank's ABCDE-Europe Conference, Paris, June 26–28, 2000; and David Dollar's chapter in this volume.

12. Giving exemptions to developing countries that allowed them to maintain high levels of protection in the GATT and the WTO was "the worst 'favor' we ever did them." See Dollar's chapter. See also John Whalley, "Special and Differential Treatment in the Millennium Round," paper prepared for the Workshop on Developing Countries and the New Round of Trade Negotiations, Harvard University, November 5–6, 1999.

13. See Alan Deardorff's chapter in this volume.

14. See Dollar's chapter.

15. See Jonathan Fried's summary in this volume.

16. For an average developing country to implement the WTO obligations in the areas of sanitary and phytosanitary measures, intellectual property rights, and customs reforms would require investments on the order of $150 million, equal to a full year's development budget for many of the least developed counties. Moreover, implementation alone would not ensure immediate and sizable benefits. Although it would contribute to create a business-friendly environment, common supply problems and bottlenecks would remain to be addressed. See J. Michael Finger and Philip Schuler, "Implementing the Uruguay Round

Commitments: The Development Challenge," Policy Research Working Paper (Washington: World Bank, October 1999).

17. See Bernard Hoekman and Petros Mavroidis, "Enforcing WTO Commitments: Dispute Settlement and Developing Countries: Something Happened on the Way to Heaven," mimeo, June 2000.

18. Consider some illustrative economic data. The share of least developed countries in world trade declined steadily from 0.8 percent in 1980 to 0.4 percent in 1997. The same is true for sub-Saharan Africa, which has gone down from 1.2 percent to 0.8 percent of world trade. Foreign direct investment is also very limited. For instance in 1997, FDI into the whole of Africa remained a mere 3 percent of total FDI flows into developing countries. This was comparable to foreign direct investment in Malaysia in that year. In terms of world GDP, sub-Saharan Africa's share declined from 2.5 percent in 1980 to 1.2 percent in 1998.

19. See International Bank for Reconstruction and Development and the International Monetary Fund, "Trade, Development and Poverty Reduction," paper prepared for the Development Committee, April 17, 2000, p. 3.

20. See Dollar's chapter.

21. See Jeffrey Sachs's chapter in this volume.

22. See Rubens Ricupero, "A Development Round: Converting Rhetoric into Substance," mimeo, June 2000; UNCTAD, *A Positive Agenda for Developing Countries: Issues for Future Negotiations* (New York: United Nations, 2000).

23. See United Nations, "Millennium Declaration," A/RES/55/2 (September 8, 2000):

> 12. We resolve therefore to create an environment—at the national and global levels alike—which is conducive to development and to the elimination of poverty.
>
> 13. Success in meeting these objectives depends, inter alia, on good governance within each country. It also depends on good governance at the international level and on transparency in the financial, monetary and trading systems. We are committed to an open, equitable, rule-based, predictable and non-discriminatory multilateral trading and financial system.

24. This is quite well expressed already in the preamble to GATT 1947: "Recognizing that their [the signatories'] relations in the field of trade and economic endeavour should be conducted with a view to raising standards of living, ensuring full employment and a large and steadily growing volume of real income."

25. See Deardorff's chapter.

26. See Richard Cooper's comment in this volume.

27. See André Sapir's chapter in this volume.

28. See also Bhagwati's chapter.

29. See the contributions by Robert Howse and Kalypso Nicolaïdis and by Steve Charnowitz in this volume; and Thomas Cottier, "Limits to International Trade: The Constitutional Challenge," paper presented at the meeting of the American Society of International Law, Washington, D.C., 2000.

30. See Joel Trachtman's summary in this volume.

31. See Frieder Roessler's chapter and the accompanying comment by William Davey in this volume.

32. See the comments by Gary Horlick and Hudec in this volume. In particular, Hudec notes that "without trying to predict the answers to those yet-to-be-answered substantive

policy questions, suffice it say that these answers will be a large part—perhaps the largest part—of the answer to today's legitimacy problem."

33. See Thomas M. Franck, *The Power of Legitimacy among Nations* (Oxford University Press, 1990).

34. See David Held, "Democracy and the New International Order," in Daniele Archibugi and David Held, eds., *Cosmopolitan Democracy: An Agenda for a New World Order* (Cambridge, Mass.: Polity Press, 1995).

35. See Steve Charnowitz's comment in this volume.

36. See the chapters by Robert Keohane and Joseph Nye Jr. and by Sylvia Ostry and the comment by Daniel Esty in this volume.

37. See Hudec's comment.

38. The "anti-globalizers" share this call for restraint with the "GATT-nostalgics." In their view, the WTO should not meddle with these difficult and controversial issues and just forge ahead with its traditional trade liberalization agenda.

39. See the chapters by Keohane and Nye, by Ostry, and by Robert Hormats in this volume.

40. Efficiency in this context can be understood as the amount of time, effort, and resources needed to forge consensus. See Oran R. Young, *Governance in World Affairs* (Cornell University Press, 1999). See also Benedict Kingsbury, "Sovereignty and Inequality," *European Journal of International Law*, vol. 9 (1998), pp. 599–625.

41. See Zutshi's comment in this volume.

42. The experience of the United Nations is relevant. See UN Economic and Social Council, Res. 1996/31 (July 25, 1996). An advisory body could bring together all members of the World Trade Organization or could have a restricted but geographically representative and rotating membership.

43. See Jacquet's comment in this volume.

JAGDISH BHAGWATI

4 | *After Seattle: Free Trade and the WTO*

R ay Vernon, the inspiration for this chapter, was both prolific and profound. He also wrote with an uncanny sense of what was important. Indeed, one might say that Ray's most enviable anatomical asset was his nose: like a bloodhound, he zeroed in on the leading public policy issues, not just of the day but of the next. I need only recall his celebrated book *Sovereignty at Bay: The Multinational Spread of U.S. Enterprise.*

We should also remember his integrity. In the intellectual milieu in which many of us live, it is not difficult to find men and women of brilliance. But we see integrity far less often. Ray had it in abundance. Few of you may know that Ray resigned from the U.S. government because he refused, on principle, to take a lie detector test. In fact, that was why Ray joined Mars Co. before winding up in academe. He was the one who suggested putting peanuts into M&Ms, a great commercial idea but probably the only act of inspiration where I part company with Ray: I like my M&Ms plain.

The topic of the conference from which this book stems, the multilateral trading system at the millennium, is timely; it is also important. We have recently been through a roller coaster, with bad and good news coming at us in tandem and in spades.

Bad News on Trade

The bad news has come mainly from Washington, the city and the state. Then-president Bill Clinton failed to secure fast-track authority. Seattle wound up in chaos. Paris, never happy about letting Washington get ahead, has joined in: the Multilateral Agreement on Investment (MAI) at the Organization for Economic Cooperation and Development (OECD) ran aground over French withdrawal of its consent before Seattle. This gave nongovernmental organizations (NGOs) a victory that only added fuel to their anti-trade agitations. There is a sense of despair among some pro-trade groups in the United States: if trade is such a difficult case to sell at a time of unprecedented prosperity and employment, what could happen when the economy turns down, as it almost certainly will some day?

The good news is that the antiglobalist NGOs, politicians, and labor unions can no longer talk of an unending streak of victories against the freeing of trade. The vote on China's entry into the World Trade Organization (WTO) was critical, since it was won against an intensive campaign by most unions and by some influential NGOs like Ralph Nader's Public Citizen. And it was also won even though China is about the worst country that you can point to if you wish to argue against freer trade on moral grounds.

Yet this victory was important to the pro-trade groups only in the sense that a defeat would have made the victorious anti-trade groups ever more fierce and effective in the public domain. In an important sense its value is limited because the deal was astonishingly one-sided in terms of concessions: China made virtually all of them, the United States practically none.[1] No trade deal of that kind can be repeated—all normal trade negotiations involve give, not just take.

Moreover, I would not call the passage in 2000 of the Africa Growth and Opportunity Act, which is in many respects a trade bill, a major indicator of a changed sentiment in Congress or in the country in favor of trade. This act is a Trojan horse masquerading as a gift horse.[2] Cast in the mold of preferential access, it extracts more than it gives. U.S. lobbies, both protectionists and unions, have imposed restrictions and made successful demands for reverse preferences for the United States that make this act an example of how not to liberalize trade for poor countries.[3]

Good News on Trade

The really good news about trade lies elsewhere. The following developments provide reason for a measure of optimism. First, trade in the past decade has continued to grow at a faster rate than incomes, despite the financial crises in Asia and Russia.

Second, trade barriers did not escalate sharply during the financial crisis; indeed, little protectionism emerged, except for antidumping actions and voluntary export restraints (on steel, in particular), plus some rise in tariffs toward their higher bound levels (as with 504 items by Mexico after the November 1994 peso crisis). Why? Partly because the architects of the General Agreement on Tariffs and Trade (GATT), who were seeking institutional mechanisms such as bindings to prevent a ready outbreak of competitive raising of trade barriers as had happened after the Great Crash in 1929, turned out to be right: GATT and its successor, the WTO, did work.

Other factors also helped. Economic doctrine has changed: many now believe that macroeconomic adjustment is best undertaken through macroeconomic policies and that trade policies should focus on the gains-from-trade target. This view was the basis of conditionality in the extraordinary assistance from the World Bank and the International Monetary Fund (IMF) during the financial crisis.

Even without new negotiations, trade will grow in the next few years. The fruits of the Uruguay Round are still kicking in. The services and agriculture negotiations, part of the agenda unfinished from the Uruguay Round, will surely register some progress, even if slowly. Concessions on the Multi-Fiber Agreement, which are end-loaded, are still to materialize. The vastly more effective disputes settlement mechanism continues to open markets. For example, India lost its Article xviii(b) case to the United States and is now beginning to remove its balance-of-payments quantitative restrictions on consumer goods imports.

Finally, in the past two decades countries worldwide have unilaterally reduced trade barriers outside the framework of trade negotiations characterized by reciprocity. This process of unilateral trade liberalization continues apace for a variety of reasons.[4]

Yet there are major reasons to worry. In doing so, it is useful to distinguish issues relating to free trade itself and those concerning the WTO.

Free Trade

In the late 1980s and early 1990s, the challenges to the prescription for freeing trade came from several younger theorists, including Paul Krugman and Gene Grossman. When imperfect competition exists in product markets, as the Nobel laureate John Hicks saw clearly over forty years ago, the case for free trade is compromised. The benefits of free trade depend in part on whether market prices reflect social costs. With imperfect competition, this is no longer so, generally speaking. Krugman, in his youthful surrender to irrational exuberance, went so far as to advance the view that it was no longer possible to defend free trade on theoretical grounds.

The new theorists have finally come around to propagating free trade again. Some buy into the argument that there is "no beef": imperfections are not significant enough to justify protectionism; others argue that intervention will make things worse. Moreover, the economic sentiment has grown that, for a variety of possible reasons—including the x-efficiency effects of competition and the benefits from exploiting scale economies—free trade can bring big gains and protection can produce big losses.

Less than a decade after the burst of sentiment in favor of protectionism, the case for free trade stands on solid ground. But a new set of opponents of free trade has emerged. Their complaints range over a wide arena.

Trade is a threat to culture. In France, Monsieur Bové has fused culture with agriculture—marrying conventional protectionism with the protection of culture—into a populist and powerful objection to further trade liberalization. The Canadian minister of culture has taken nearly two dozen of her counterparts in other nations down the road of alarm over the cultural threats posed by trade and globalization.

Trade harms the environment. The 1991 *Tuna-Dolphin* case and the recent *Shrimp-Turtle* decisions illuminate the conflict that can arise between market access and "values"-related desires to restrict it. Potential conflicts between the trade restrictions contemplated in the multilateral environmental agreements (against "free riders" and defectors) and those implied by the WTO need clarification and reconciliation. These conflicts, while often generated by institutional questions relating to the WTO, have spilled over into the case against free trade.

Trade overrides human rights and labor rights. It is amusing that human and worker rights are listed additively by activists, as if "human" does not embrace "workers." Human rights activists and the unions argue that free trade overrides "values" and undermines attaining better standards. Both groups aim at putting restraints on free trade.

Trade increases poverty. Some free trade opponents believe that trade (and direct foreign investment, that is to say, multinational corporations) accentuates poverty instead of reducing it.

Two Common Fallacies

Two common fallacies produce much of the heat against free trade. The first relates to the common tendency to assume that if the (imprudently hasty) freeing of financial flows played a major role in precipitating the Asian financial and economic crisis, then free trade is equally to be condemned. That is a non sequitur, of course, but its appeal to the antiglobalists is so strong that even a remarkably accomplished economist, my good friend Dani Rodrik, has succumbed to it. In his recent essay, "The Global Fix," in the *New Republic,* he started with the financial crisis and proceeded illogically to fix the trade system instead.[5]

The second problem arises because of the widespread concern with poverty. For those of us who come from India, the notion that such concerns automatically imply sensible diagnoses and effective policies is not compelling. Indian planners, politicians, and economists talked of little else. Contrary to James Wolfensohn's belief that he and his advisers at the World Bank discovered poverty, reducing poverty was at the center of development economists' and indeed Indian planners' attention from the outset of the postwar developmental efforts. Yet poverty failed to decline significantly in India until abysmally low growth rates, produced by illiberal, antimarket, and antiglobalization policies, compounded by an inefficient public sector, were reversed.

The fallacy that dominates much public discussion today, especially among the antiglobalists and the politicians who pander to them, is that talking about poverty is tantamount to reducing it. Talk comes cheap; getting policies right is the hard part. Many denounce pro-market, pro–free trade policies as the cause of persistent poverty when, in fact, such policies are part of the solution, not just on an a priori basis but also on the basis of convincing evidence. In considering these concerns, I focus on two "fair trade" arguments and two "distortions"-related principles.

Fair Trade

Some free trade opponents make two fair trade arguments with particular political salience. First, if a country's trade partners have lower environmental and labor standards, they are indulging in "social dumping" that needs to be countervailed by a tariff. Second, a "race to the bottom" will ensue, leaving countries with lower standards than they want.

Neither argument is compelling, however. Differences in standards typically reflect differences in fundamentals: in initial conditions, endowments, and preferences. Thus, even when countries have an identical desire to prevent domestic pollution per se, and they accept the "polluter pay principle," the pollution tax rates for identical carcinogens dumped into the local waters or the air will differ across countries.[6] Diversity of tax burdens is fully legitimate; to call it "unfair" competition is to betray an ignorance of elementary economics: a charge that can be laid at the door of Messrs. Bonior, Boren, Gephardt, and Gore, who have all written erroneously on the subject and most of whom have also sought to legislate on their misguided convictions.

By contrast, the race to the bottom argument is theoretically valid; where it fails is in its empirical relevance. An uncoordinated Nash equilibrium could well produce, under second-best conditions, outcomes where each country, or a subset of countries, will underachieve with respect to economic welfare or environmental goals or both, compared to what a coordinated equilibrium would achieve. That is not to say that this coordinated equilibrium will be characterized by lower-standard countries in the Nash equilibrium moving upscale. Indeed, the economist John Wilson has shown that the world may be characterized by a race to the top.

The real problem is not theoretical. It is simply that we have little evidence that governments choose to attract investments by offering to cut standards, or that multinational corporations actually are attracted by such concessions. A great deal of empirical evidence suggests that multinationals do not choose environmentally unfriendly technologies, for example, or even locations, because the environmental regulations are less stringent.[7] The race to the bottom occurs far more in tax concessions offered by governments (including local and state governments in federal countries) to attract multinationals. Few governments are likely to say to multinationals, "Come and make profits by polluting our water and air!"

My own view is that since there is little evidence of multinationals (which account for the bulk of the direct investments, as distinct from small firms) choosing to exploit lower environmental standards, countries should simply extend their standards (as distinct from wages, of course) to their firms abroad on a mandatory basis: do in Rome as New Yorkers do, not as Romans do. This would assuage the fears of environmentalists, and of those seeking dignity and safety for workers abroad, without imposing serious constraints that these firms do not already impose on themselves. Alongside this mandatory action, I would encourage the development of voluntary codes, such as the social accountability label, SA8000, which is now in business with more than fifty factories certified in twelve countries.

The mandatory codes will differ across the countries that adopt them, since they merely reflect an extension of national codes and laws; the voluntary codes will differ among themselves but are identical across countries for everyone who adopts them. Between them, they provide a more efficient and equitable alternative to the demands for countervailing social dumping and for legislation aimed at preventing a hypothetical race to the bottom.

Principles of Commercial Policy

If some politicians succumb to demands for a "social tariff" on the basis of dubious economics, their lack of comprehension of the central prescriptions in the theory of commercial policy accounts for further policy confusions that imperil the cause of free trade. One such confusion is the notion that free trade, relative to protection, harms causes such as the environment. Another is that the use of trade sanctions is necessary to advance social agendas, such as good labor standards, abroad.[8]

We know from the theory of intervention under distortions (that is, market failures) the value of two principles:

—In the presence of market failure, free trade may be worse than (a given level of) protection; but it is also possible that such protection may be worse than free trade.

—If governments fix market failures through suitable policy interventions, then free trade regains its claim as the necessarily appropriate welfare-improving policy.

These principles sound straightforward to most economists today, but they were revolutionary when developed in the 1960s. For nearly two centuries after Adam Smith's *The Wealth of Nations* and the simultaneous discovery of the "invisible hand" and the case for free trade, economists had conceded that for varying types of market failure the case for free trade collapsed, and therefore protectionism could not be ruled out.

At the onset of the 1990s environmentalists agitated against free trade, assuming that absent a good environmental policy (say, the polluter pay principle was inoperative), free trade was no longer appropriate. Yet the first principle above shows that any given level of protection may be worse, not better, than free trade. The 1991 GATT report on trade and the environment demonstrated in two empirical cases that freeing trade while leaving environmental policies at their presumably inefficient level improved both economic welfare and the environment.

At the same time it follows that if, for example, the polluter pay principle is pursued, thereby addressing the market failure of an absence of markets where pollution can be priced and paid for, free trade will enhance economic welfare and environmental protection. If policymakers have two targets, they will generally require two instruments to achieve them optimally. In plain words, you cannot kill two birds with one stone.

This principle applies to other issues as well. For example, should one pursue a reduction in child labor through an institution such as the International Labor Organization (ILO) or at the WTO through trade treaties and trade sanctions? Pursuing social agendas through trade treaties and institutions implies using one stone to kill two birds. It will miss both birds, slowing trade liberalization and impairing the advancement of social agendas.

The failure to renew fast-track authority and the Seattle debacle slowed down the freeing of trade, the former at home and the latter in relation to the developing countries. At the same time, the morality of the agenda has been devalued. Most developing countries, their intellectuals, and NGOs now see the deliberate resort to trade sanctions as a thinly disguised attempt to moderate competition from the developing countries in labor-intensive products.

It makes more sense to develop another stone, perhaps even several pellets. That endeavor underlies the proposals to pursue these agendas through appropriate and appropriately strengthened agencies such as the ILO, and with policy instruments other than trade sanctions. The heavy lifting needed to accelerate the reduction of child labor requires collaboration with governments, NGOs, and aid agencies, all working at the ground level.

This is also the way to answer Pascal Lamy's demands to look at the "multifunctionality" of agriculture. We should be able to find suitable policies that promote the other functions of agriculture while freeing trade. Greenery could be subsidized directly rather than indirectly—and inefficiently—through trade barriers protecting agricultural production.

The "trade and culture" conflict is amenable to similar solutions based on the doctrine of matching the number of instruments with policies. Rather than protect French cinema by restricting the screening of Hollywood movies, why not subsidize it?

The WTO at Risk

Let me now turn to problems that have arisen regarding the World Trade Organization itself. To understand these, it is essential to recognize three major changes that took place with the founding of the WTO. First, whereas GATT was relatively free from extraneous issues, the WTO is increasingly under pressure to introduce a variety of "trade-unrelated" preconditions for market access (as it did with intellectual property protection). Second, in contrast to GATT, which was a weak organization institutionally, with optional codes and a nonbinding disputes settlement mechanism, the WTO is now a single undertaking and has a binding disputes settlement mechanism. Third, demands to change not only the WTO but also other international agencies to accommodate greater transparency and participation by nongovernmental actors have multiplied.

Trade-Unrelated Issues: Daggers Aimed at the Developing Countries

The Uruguay Round saw the WTO turn into a tripod, with its three legs being the old GATT, the new General Agreement on Trade in Services (GATS), and intellectual property protection. The last leg really did not belong at all. If the only criterion for getting an issue into the WTO is that your issue affects trade, then virtually everything gets in. The underlying principle of what issues are addressed in a trade institution such as GATT or the WTO must be the principle of mutual gain.

In essence, noncoercive trade is a mutual-gain phenomenon. It is true that, if two parties liberalize trade, a third party can get hurt. Thus two operating principles are needed to ensure that a multicountry trade institution, such as the WTO, functions in greater conformity with the principle of mutual gain, at least as far as the developing countries are concerned:

—First, if a major trade negotiation (such as the Uruguay Round) affects adversely a specific group of developing countries (as did the Uruguay Round for Africa, according to several calculations), then the Bretton Woods institutions, such as the World Bank and the IMF, should provide supplementary short-term finance for adjustment and long-term concessionary loans to cushion the blow.

—Second, if a disputes settlement panel or appellate court finding implies a major adverse side impact on developing countries, as in the *Bananas* case, then the Bretton Woods institutions should cushion that impact.

But the principle of mutual gain does not obtain in any significant degree for intellectual property protection, which was worked into the WTO because of intense lobbying pressures in the United States from the pharmaceutical and software industries. Instead of mutual gain, intellectual property protection represents a transfer of royalties from the using countries to the producing countries.

Having introduced something contrary to the essence of a trade institution into the WTO, the third leg of the tripod has naturally attracted the attention of others. Labor unions say, "You did it for capital; you must do it for labor." Environmentalists add, "You must do it for nature." The door has swung open to those who can muster enough voices. The tripod is in danger of turning into a centipede. And the centipede will slow down the progress to trade liberalization. Why?

These trade-unrelated issues are defined and advanced by rich-country NGOs and other lobbies. Just as intellectual property protection is a dagger aimed at developing countries, so are these other demands. The social clause views the developing countries as defendants. I have yet to see any developed country seriously worried about being taken to the WTO: the contents of that clause and the matters selected for fast-track implementation (such as child labor) are always those on which the developing countries are expected to be found wanting.

Developing countries, which had viewed GATT as an institution that would defend the weak against the strong in trade matters, now view the WTO as turning, under rich-country pressure, into an assault on weak countries on trade-unrelated matters. In Seattle overnourished workers demonstrated against undernourished workers in poor countries, pretending that it was in the latter's interest; turtles were preferred over poor fishermen by young environmentalists who knew little better; uncomprehending children were cynically made to march against child labor in poor countries that have no magic wand that could relieve millions of children in poverty from working to support themselves and their families. This made the developing-country delegations ever more aware that the game at the WTO had changed against them—and that it was a deadly contest, because the unions and the NGOs were crowned with halos, whereas the traditional protectionist lobbies were at least seen for what they were when they sought measures against the exports of the developing countries.

No wonder, the developing countries walked away rather than broker a deal such as the innocent-sounding but potentially deadly attempt to establish a "study group" under WTO auspices, with or without the participation of other institutions. They would not hear of it as long as the WTO was involved in any way. The WTO will not successfully initiate a new round until these trade-unrelated issues are shifted to other arenas; indeed, that is exactly what the basic principles of international trade theory suggest.

Introducing Flexibility into the WTO

The WTO also needs to lighten up. The single undertaking approach is now irreversible, in my view. But the disputes settlement mechanism can be separated from the notion that nations must always comply by vacating legislation. That invites an unnecessary anti-WTO political response. Consider the approach of the 301 panel, which essentially came out against the 301 legislation but said that 301 legislation was kosher until used. As a result, the United States was able to declare that it had won; the legislation was not found in violation of the WTO agreement; and the European Union saw that, in fact, it had won and did not seek an appeal. The political fallout in the United States was avoided.

Remedies must also move away from massive trade retaliation, as in the banana and hormone-fed beef disputes. Such actions disrupt huge quantities of trade and encourage hostility to the WTO, which is seen as authorizing trade disruption. In this context, the carousel proposal to rotate the targets of retaliation is absurdly counterproductive. Remedies should include the use of a labeling scheme where acceptable and, if not acceptable, cash compensation, a small fraction of the trade affected if estimated as the gains from trade lost rather than the total value of trade lost. Compensation could be directed to the industry whose market access has been lost: the hormone-fed-beef firms, for instance.

I have some sympathy for Frieder Roessler's view that the dispute settlement panels and the appellate court must defer somewhat more to the political process instead of making law in controversial matters. I was astounded that the appellate court, in effect, reversed long-standing jurisprudence on process and production methods in the *Shrimp-Turtle* case. I have little doubt that the jurists were reflecting the political pressures brought by the rich-country environmental NGOs and essentially made law that affected the developing countries adversely. Unless the WTO legal process understands that NGOs do not necessarily speak for developing countries, the WTO will stand in danger of accentuating the problems of the North-South divide already exacerbated by Seattle.

Transparency and Participation

Finally, there is the question of transparency and participation by civil society, that is, by NGOs and union lobbies. It is useful to distinguish among three components of the WTO: the working of the secretariat, trade negotiations, and the dispute settlement mechanism. Each deserves a separate discussion.

The dispute settlement process is now legal rather than political. Clearly, it should be open. But matters such as *amicus* briefs raise difficulties. To permit them only after standing is allowed restricts entry. Moreover, it gives better access to well-heeled rich-country groups like the Sierra Club. So there should be free entry: a website, perhaps, where anyone can send in briefs. As for inviting such briefs by the panel or the court, they must always be balanced between the developing and the developed countries, or the interests of the developing countries will be compromised.

I would consider remedies that remove the inequities of the adversarial system, in which rich countries spend huge sums on their side but poor countries are resource constrained. Why not get a rich country to give the poor countries against which it is bringing a case a sum that matches its own estimated legal expenses, so that the contest is equal? The liberal establishment in U.S. law schools should find this and other remedies (perhaps a limit on what might be spent relative to what the poor defendant can afford) to the unbalanced battles between rich and poor a matter of some interest.

As for trade negotiations, it is up to the governments that negotiate to give their preferred NGOs, business, and union lobbies a place on their negotiating teams. To give the nongovernmental organizations a second shot independent of their governments that they have elected has no rationale. To do so would give rich-country negotiators added weight because it is rich-country NGOs that are effectively going to receive a greater voice through their resources, clout, and lobbying experience.

As for the secretariat, there are now several opportunities in seminars and conferences for regular contact with civil society groups. This development would benefit from greater institutionalization, balanced representation from the developing and the developed countries, and adequate regular funding.

Notes

1. I recognize, as do all good economists, that a trade concession is generally good for oneself, too. But in a political context one's own trade barrier reductions are considered a concession against which every trade negotiator looks for corresponding concessions by the other side.

2. See Jagdish Bhagwati and Arvind Panagariya, "A Trojan Horse for Africa," *Financial Times,* June 30, 2000.

3. By contrast, genuine and outright most favored nation (MFN) liberalization of products of the greatest interest to the poor African countries, along with aid and technical assistance to enable these countries to take advantage of the trading opportunities created, would have made more sense.

4. See Jagdish Bhagwati, ed., *Going Alone: The Case for Relaxed Reciprocity in Freeing Trade* (MIT Press, 2001).

5. Dani Rodrik, "The Global Fix," *New Republic,* November 2, 1998.

6. This applies, of course, to domestic pollution and not to cross-border pollution. I am also abstracting from the notion of "values"-related objections to granting market access, which raises other issues.

7. This was the burden of Arik Levinson's well-known research, reviewed in his contribution to Jagdish Bhagwati and Robert E. Hudec, eds., *Fair Trade and Harmonization: Prerequisites for Free Trade?* vol. 1 (MIT Press, 1996). In chapter 4 of that book, T. N. Srinivasan and I offer a number of reasons why multinationals may be indifferent to playing down to lower standards.

8. The fair trade arguments relate to "egoistical" reasons to suspend trade access (that is, reasons related to one's own interest), whereas the argument that such suspension of trade access is for advancing social agendas abroad is based on "altruism." This distinction is absolutely critical and leads to very different arguments as to why the advocacy of trade sanctions (that is, trade access) is to be deplored. I have dealt with these distinctions at length in a paper on linkages, reprinted in Jagdish Bhagwati, *The Wind of the Hundred Days: How Washington Mismanaged Globalization* (MIT Press, 2000).

JEFFREY D. SACHS

5 | *A New Framework for Globalization*

The cold-war world was divided into a capitalist first world, a socialist second world, and a developing-country third world that tried to mix markets with socialism. Although these ideological divisions collapsed in the past generation, as virtually all nations proclaimed allegiance to global markets, a more intractable three-way division is taking hold, this time based on technology rather than ideology. A small part of the world, maybe 15 percent of the world's population, provides most of the world's technological innovations. A second part of the world, involving as much as half of the world's population, is able to incorporate these new technologies into national production and consumption structures. A third part of the world, covering around a third of the world's population, is technologically disconnected, neither innovating at home nor successfully adopting (on a large scale) the technologies produced abroad.

The boundaries, of course, are imprecise and depend on the indicators one chooses, but the general pattern is clear. My colleagues Andrew Warner, Michael Porter, and John McArthur and I are developing new measures of the technological divisions. In one schema that I have found useful, the technological first-world of innovators includes the United States and Canada, Western Europe (with the possible exception of some southern European countries), Japan, the Asian tigers (Korea, Taiwan,

Hong Kong, and Singapore), Israel, Australia, and New Zealand. These are the countries, specifically, which produced at least ten U.S. utility patents per million citizens in 1997.

The boundaries between the technological adopters and those that are disconnected are less certain, since all regions of the world succeed in at least a small amount of technological adoption. Evidence for broad-based technological adoption includes success in attracting large-scale foreign direct investment (FDI) in high-tech sectors (such as electronics, pharmaceuticals, information technology, biotechnology, automotive and aeronautical components, financial services), and at least some exports to first-world markets in high-tech sectors. In most cases these exports represent standardized production processes (for example, labor-intensive assembly) in the value chain of high-tech multinational firms. Taking a generous view of the matter, technology adopters include Mexico outside of the tropical South, much of the Caribbean and Central America, southern Brazil, Argentina, and Chile; Central European states that border the European Union, the Baltic states, the Balkan states of Bulgaria and Romania (at least prospectively), part of the Mediterranean basin of North Africa (Morocco, Tunisia, and Egypt), Turkey and the Levant; the southern states of India, parts of southern Africa, Mauritius and Sri Lanka in the Indian Ocean; and the Asian Pacific Rim regions of coastal China and Southeast Asia.

The technologically stagnant regions are the rest: southern Mexico and pockets of tropical Central America, the Andean countries, most of tropical Brazil, tropical sub-Saharan Africa, most of the former Soviet Union aside from the areas nearest to European and Asian markets, and landlocked parts of Asia such as the Ganges valley states of India, landlocked Laos and Cambodia, and the far-interior states of China. Many of these regions, especially in the tropics, are caught in a poverty trap. Key problems—such as tropical infectious disease, low agricultural productivity, environmental degradation—require technological solutions not available within these countries. Technological stagnation contributes to high childhood mortality, rapid population growth that results from (more than offsetting) high fertility rates, and ecological stress on regions of great importance to the world, such as tropical rainforests and other areas of exceptional biodiversity.

Occasionally, the needed technologies are available from the outside world, but the countries are too poor to purchase or license them at needed scale. Too often the technologies do not yet exist in appropriate form, and the impoverished markets of the poor countries offer scant market incentives for the needed research and development. Even the scientists and engineers at work in the poorest countries are frequently induced by market forces to work on rich-country problems, if not to migrate to the rich countries. Solutions will be easier for poor regions in richer countries (Mexico, Brazil, India, China), and hardest when entire countries within a region are technologically stagnant.

It is time for the rich countries to recognize, and then respond to, the structural features that are leaving 2 billion people or more behind in the current practice of globalization. Broader based globalization will not only help to stabilize the world politically and environmentally, but it will also provide economic benefits to the rich countries through expanded world markets at the same time that it rescues the poor countries from their current misery. Success in this effort will require three things. The first is a better framework for understanding globalization, one that properly incorporates geography, public health, and ecology into the analysis of technological change and economic growth. The second is the willingness to re-invigorate international assistance by spending more money and spending it more wisely. The third is the readiness to create a new structure of international assistance. On the one hand, we need new participants in global assistance, including a much larger assistance role of multinational firms, first-world universities, and first-world scientific establishments. On the other hand, we need a redesign of the official multilateral institutions charged with global development, including the International Monetary Fund, World Bank, and relevant agencies of the United Nations. The world has changed, but the multilateral institutions have not kept up.

Toward an Improved Theory of Globalization

The simplest theory of globalization holds that countries are rich or poor depending on their levels of capital per worker. Development is seen, essentially, as a process of accumulation of physical and human capital. Poor countries, when they are well governed, are assumed to have an advantage in capital accumulation, on the grounds that the scarcity of capital in those countries will tend to be associated with high returns to new investments, thereby encouraging high rates of domestic saving, high returns to incremental investments, and inflows of capital from abroad. Rapid capital accumulation in the poor countries is expected to produce a narrowing of income gaps between rich and poor, a process known as "convergence."

The picture is optimistic for globalization. It is also too simplistic. We have known since at least 1957, when Robert Solow published his seminal analysis of the sources of U.S. growth, that technological change, as much or more than capital accumulation, lies at the base of long-term improvements in living standards.[1] It was the ability of the now-rich countries to produce and harness key technologies in the past two centuries that produced the historically unprecedented era of sustained economic growth. And it was the relative failure of the rest of the world to adopt these technologies, or to invent their own when local conditions required it, that accounts for the vast gulf in income levels now seen in the world.

Technological levels are less likely to converge than the levels of capital. One key reason is that innovation seems to have properties of increasing returns to scale, meaning that regions that already have advanced technologies are probably best placed to achieve further innovation. New ideas are typically produced from a recombination of existing ideas (to use the phrase of my colleague Martin Weitzman), so that idea-rich environments produce chain reactions of innovation. But as in a nuclear chain reaction, a critical mass of existing ideas and technology is needed before the spontaneous process can unfold. Another reason for lack of convergence is that the market incentive to innovate depends on the size of the market. Innovation has a strong fixed-cost element—a new blueprint or design needs to be produced just once—and a larger market supports a larger amount of such fixed-cost activities. Inventors producing for large integrated markets have higher incentives to undertake the requisite fixed costs of research and development than inventors producing for smaller markets.

The public goods aspect of ideas (the fact that they can be used over and over again without being "used up") leads to further complexities in the industrial organization of innovation. Free markets, even free markets supplemented by patent protection, are not sufficient to create a dynamically innovative economy. Successful innovation requires a complex system of supporting institutions. A commercial innovation today is generally a product of two things: basic scientific insight, where ideas are not generally privately owned, and applied engineering backed by patent protection. Much of the basic science is likely to originate in universities and government research laboratories, backed by public sector and philanthropic support, while applied engineering is more likely to be undertaken by private firms motivated by profit considerations. Thus successful innovation requires a complex interplay of academia, government, and industry, a combination that very few countries have mastered.

Consider one of today's leading technological breakthroughs, the Internet. Computer networking originated as a U.S. Defense Department project in the 1970s. It was then nurtured in the 1980s within U.S. universities, with financial support from the public sector, specifically the U.S. National Science Foundation. The requisite software for the World Wide Web was written by university researchers in the early 1990s. And then public use exploded in the second half of the 1990s as a largely private sector phenomenon.

Taken together, the main characteristics of innovation are excellent news for the United States, which enjoys the world's largest national market, secure property rights for innovation, a large existing pool of high technology and science, a remarkably fruitful system of university-industry relations, and large-scale government support for science, now around $85 billion a year. The main characteristics of innovation are not good news for a poor country in the tropics, where markets are small, property rights are insecure, the existing pool of technologies and scientists is small, and support from governments for R&D is generally lacking. Seventy countries with populations of at least 1 million in 1995 had half or more of their populations in the geographical tropics. All told, these countries produced just 255 of the roughly 50,300 U.S. utility patents issued to foreign inventors in 1997, despite having a combined population of more than 2.4 billion people.

Of course, the technological capacity of an economy depends not just on its own innovations, but on its capacity to adopt the technologies produced elsewhere in the world. There are three major channels for adopting technologies from abroad. Technologies may be imported through their embodiment in capital and consumer goods (cell phones, fax machines, personal computers, immunizations). Technologies may be licensed from patent holders for domestic production. And technologies may be imported via FDI, wherein a multinational enterprise with proprietary technology sets up production operations in another country. In all cases countries must be successful as exporters in order to be able to pay for the imports of technology (or to pay dividends on foreign investment).

Many economists assume that all developing countries are equally well placed to absorb technologies from abroad, but this is wishful thinking. Whether the technologies are brought in by export, licensing, or FDI, two geographical conditions are extremely important for success. First, the major technology importers tend to be close to major markets, or on favorable sea routes, or both. Mexico's success in raising export earnings from

$80 billion in 1995 to $136 billion in 1999 is a tribute to wise policies of the United States, Canada, and Mexico in creating the North American Free Trade Agreement, and to the 2,000 mile border of Mexico with the United States, which allows Mexican-based plants to serve the U.S. market with little delay and low shipping costs.

More generally, foreign direct investments from the United States, Europe, or Japan to developing countries—other than for primary commodities like oil—flow mainly to nearby countries (such as Mexico and Costa Rica in the case of the United States; Poland and Hungary in the case of the European Union; and Thailand and Malaysia in the case of Japan); or to regions that share a common ecology (such as temperate-zone southern Brazil and Argentina, rather than the tropical Andean countries); or to countries or parts of countries with low-cost access to sea-based trade (such as coastal China, Hong Kong, Singapore, port cities of Southeast Asia, and coastal states of southern India). Foreign direct investment does not flow (except, again, in the case of natural resources) to distant mountainous regions (the Andean countries), landlocked developing countries (Central Asia), or regions within countries far from seaports (inland China or northern India).

Countries that fail to keep up with global technology often collapse, unable to maintain a given standard of living, much less to increase it. These countries are typically stuck in a narrow range of export sectors that gradually lose their relevance and profitability in the world economy. Copper producers are displaced by fiber optics. Natural rubber and jute producers are displaced by new synthetic materials. The long-term decline in the terms of trade of many primary commodities is the side effect of innovation, which produces a continuing flow of substitutes for traditional products and production processes.

The risks of collapse are magnified by demographic pressures. Poor countries typically experience rapid population growth until urbanization, the education of girls, and declines in childhood mortality rates combine to induce couples to reduce their formerly high rates of fertility. In technologically stagnant countries, however, these fertility-limiting processes are all blocked or weakened. The growing labor force in rural areas finds few outlets in urban jobs because the technologically stagnant economy is unable to achieve export competitiveness in urban-based manufactures and services. Children continue to die at shockingly high rates, so households are loath to reduce fertility. And since families continue to have so many children, investments in the health and education of each child is reduced.

Environmentalists should recognize that the demographic pressures of marginalized regions, as least as much as the rapid growth of the rich countries, pose serious threats to global ecosystems. Population pressures, much more than economic growth in the rich countries, are currently responsible for deforestation and degradation of the world's biodiverse "hot spots" (the regions of extraordinary biodiversity) throughout the world. Population pressures rather than the export of tropical hardwoods are leading to the decimation of the world's tropical rainforests. Developing countries able to produce or absorb high technologies are more likely to protect biodiversity by creating viable urban economies. (Of course, this is not to absolve the richer countries of their predominant contribution to global climate change through fossil fuel emissions, a process that also poses grave long-term threats to the global ecosystems.)

Rethinking the Strategy of Globalization

Without a complete change in international strategy, much of the world, perhaps 2 billion people or more, will fail to share in the benefits of global growth. There are three priorities. First, the rich countries need to do much more to help the poor countries to break the vicious circle of impoverishment, health crisis, and rapid population growth. It is time for a vastly enhanced global commitment to public health, directed at the killer infectious diseases of the tropical world, combined with enhanced family planning. Second, new approaches are needed to connect remote regions with the main world markets—to increase noncommodity exports from the marginal areas and to induce multinational firms to locate in these shunned regions. Third, a major, multifaceted international effort should be launched to establish long-term scientific and engineering capacity in the poorer regions of the world. This can happen only with a redesigned strategy of global assistance, one with a much larger role for the multinational enterprises and first-world universities, a thoroughly revamped role of the World Bank, IMF, and specialized UN agencies.

Meeting the Public Health and Population Challenge

The disease burden of poor countries, especially in sub-Saharan Africa, is simultaneously a humanitarian catastrophe, a steep barrier to economic development, and a first-order threat to the global environment

through the effects on population growth. Foreign investors shun economies with high disease prevalence because they seek to avoid huge medical costs, disruptions to their labor force, and risks to their expatriate
workers. The burdens of ill health block economic development in other
ways as well. Sick children can face a lifetime of diminished productivity,
as repeated bouts of illness contribute to school absences and premature
school leaving, and long-term cognitive and physical impairment. Parents
in high-disease environments adjust by having more rather than fewer
children and then invest less in the health and education of each individual child.

Efforts by the donor community to control killer infectious diseases
in the poor countries are shockingly small. Total worldwide efforts for malaria control in Africa are little more than $50 to $75 million a year,
though malaria claims perhaps 2 million lives a year (1 million or more directly from malaria and another million or so from diseases in which malaria is a contributing factor). In the past decade, donor efforts for AIDS
control in Africa have amounted to no more than a few tens of millions
of dollars a year, even as the disease was reaching historic proportions.
AIDS now claims more than 2 million lives a year in Africa, and new in-
fections number around 4 million a year. There are about 23 million in-
fected persons overall on the continent. The World Bank estimates that its
worldwide concessional lending for AIDS totaled no more than $341 mil-
lion during the twelve years from 1986 to 1998, as the epidemic became
a pandemic.[2] Donor contributions for immunizations have been so small
that many poor countries have not even begun to introduce important
vaccines that have been in routine use in the rich countries for years—vaccines that could substantially reduce death and disease in Africa at very low
cost. A remarkable donation of up to $1 billion by the Gates Foundation
will at last address this urgent problem.

A serious effort to extend the benefits of globalization would start with
a proper battle against these killer infectious diseases, a point that is at least
starting to be acknowledged. The Clinton administration, rightly if belat-
edly, recognized AIDS in the developing world as a national security problem for the United States because of the potential of the disease to
destabilize vast regions. Africa's own leaders have pleaded for $1 billion a
year in donor support to help them partially reverse the devastation of malaria. The United Nations has pleaded for another $4 billion a year to ad-
dress the HIV/AIDS epidemic before it destroys Africa's population the
same way the bubonic plague destroyed Europe six and a half centuries

ago.[3] A few billion dollars more are needed to address the growing tuberculosis (TB) epidemic, and the millions of deaths still attributable to measles, diarrheal diseases, and other communicable diseases. Direct outlays would be combined with new incentives for research and development on more effective long-term approaches to these diseases, especially new vaccines for malaria, TB, AIDS, and killer respiratory and diarrheal diseases. Note that a program like this would cost perhaps $10 billion a year from the first-world countries, which is no more than $10 per person a year for the billion people in the rich countries, a rather paltry sum to save millions of lives, especially when compared with the vast sums expended in Kosovo, East Timor, and Gaza, where the beneficiaries are vastly smaller in number.

Connecting the Marginalized Regions

The rich regions have taken some care in recent years to integrate their poor next-door neighbors into regional production structures. The United States has backstopped Mexico's modernization with NAFTA and financial bailouts when necessary. These policy measures have been followed by massive foreign investments that are succeeding in a dramatic upgrading of Mexico's technological capacities. The European Union has created similar, though so far less bold, trading arrangements with North Africa and Central Europe. Such preferential approaches, though clearly beneficial for the immediate neighbors, have unintended adverse consequences for the more distant regions because they divert FDI and trade from them. Policy bias thereby compounds geographical disadvantage. The cartelization of global shipping generally adds another barrier to the remote regions, since the trade routes linking the marginal traders with the major markets tend to be much less competitive than the high-volume trade routes. The lack of rich-country interest in dismantling these shipping cartels is scandalous.

These considerations suggest that a new multilateral trade round could do much to offset the effects of regional preferences and thereby reduce the marginalization of more distant regions. A development agenda for trade should include improved market access for the poorest countries, liberalization of global shipping, and more balanced arrangements on intellectual property rights, as discussed later.

Life in the marginalized regions is hard enough without the simplistic advice they receive from the World Bank and IMF, where advice should be read as policy commands from Washington. The Bretton Woods institutions have a remarkably weak record in helping marginalized regions to "hook up" to the world economy in effective ways. Both institutions improperly reject the use of special incentives to attract FDI, such as export processing zones, tax holidays, and joint ventures between host governments and potential foreign investors, even though these incentives have proven to be important in a wide range of successful economies. When Costa Rica wanted to attract Intel, it rightly gave special tax incentives. The Israeli government similarly cofinanced some ventures with Intel. Ireland's rapid growth was supported by a special low corporate tax rate applied to foreign investments. The rich and poor countries could actually design cooperative tax incentive schemes to bring new technologies to the marginalized regions in ways that would share the fiscal costs between the source and host countries.

In addition to improved policies in trade, shipping, and taxation, information technology (IT) offers another huge opportunity for the currently marginalized regions of the world. Information technology can overcome many of the disadvantages of geographic distance. A landlocked region, say Mongolia, surely would have a comparative advantage in IT-based service exports (software, data transcription, telemarketing) compared with export-oriented manufactures. The problem, of course, lies in closing the "digital divide," so that the poor countries develop the bandwidth and the human resources needed for an effective IT sector. Just as the United States has a sophisticated industrial policy for the uptake of IT (including tax holidays on e-commerce, subsidies for getting schools and local governments on line, and policies to spread coverage to remote areas), the developing countries should create national policies to promote information technology. Even more important, the political leadership of the developing countries should work together with leaders of the IT industry to develop policies for a rapid increase in bandwidth in the poor countries.

Fostering Long-Term Technological Advance

At the core of the global divide is the vast inequality in the innovation and diffusion of technology. Globalization policy has barely addressed this central problem. The World Bank, for example, has had no coherent science and technology policies for at least a generation. Its own contributions to the support of science are minimal. The combined World Bank lending and grants for science and technology in a year are probably less than one-tenth of the R&D budget of a single large U.S. pharmaceutical company. The World Bank puts in around $50 million a year toward tropical agricultural research and around $10 million or so for tropical health research. Merck's R&D budget in 1999 was $2.1 billion.

International policies could help to foster new technologies for development, as well as long-term innovative capacity in the poor countries. Surely the single most important example of this approach in the twentieth century was the Rockefeller Foundation, which showed the world what grant aid targeted on knowledge could really accomplish. Rockefeller funds supported the successful eradication of hookworm in the U.S. South, the discovery of the yellow fever vaccine, the accelerated development of penicillin, the establishment of public health schools worldwide (the ones that are the undisputed leaders in the field today), the establishment of medical faculties in all parts of the world, the establishment of great research centers (such as the University of Chicago, the Brookings Institution, Rockefeller University, and the National Bureau of Economic Research), the control of malaria in Brazil, and the support of scientific research centers that accomplished the Green Revolution in Asia and, in turn, became the Consultative Group for International Agricultural Research. Not one of these earth-shaking accomplishments was a high-conditionality country loan. All required access to large-scale grants ready to back the pursuit of knowledge. And the donor, incidentally, wanted to build strong and independent institutions, so the Rockefeller Foundation consciously and explicitly eschewed conditionality.

Probably the big difference between the Rockefeller Foundation strategy and the one needed now is the requirement of a greatly increased role for the private sector. The Rockefeller Foundation worked mainly with universities and governments (often helping to create new faculty departments or even whole universities, as well as government agencies, when they were needed). Now, with high technology increasingly developed and controlled by private business, an updated strategy of technological promotion must be based on a three-sided interplay of academia, government, and industry. In fact, there are at least six parties at the table, since a coherent strategy will need to include academia, government, and industry from the advanced countries and from developing countries.

A first step should be the commitment of major international high-technology firms to increase their technological cooperation with developing countries, combined with a much greater commitment of the poor countries to the promotion of science and technology through their own national policies. Already the leading pharmaceutical companies give away hundreds of millions of dollars of medicines to low-income countries, and under international pressure they have recently agreed to supply anti-AIDS medicines at low cost. But much more should be done. The leading companies in the United States have an extensive involvement in corporate philanthropy and joint-venture arrangements with U.S. universities. Companies like IBM, Microsoft, Monsanto, and Merck should avidly pursue similar long-term arrangements with universities and private firms in the poor countries—establishing departments and research centers, donating funds for student and research support, and helping to foster the critical linkages between universities and domestic industry. Governments should augment those efforts with a much-heightened role for scientific advice in the formulation of national priorities.

First-world universities and scientific associations could also do much more. One of the ironic effects of the World Bank's traditional insistence on the primacy of primary education was the neglect of tertiary education in many developing countries. This has had seriously adverse consequences that should now be put right, in part through the active support of first-world universities. Of course, many U.S. and European universities have established overseas campuses or long-term exchange relationships, but these relationships are typically oriented toward undergraduate education rather than long-term collaborative research. The research links are underfunded. American universities are the recipients of billions of dollars each year of philanthropic and foundation giving, and they could and should devote much more of these funds to deepening their research and teaching relationships with partner institutions in developing countries. As a result, universities that foster deeper international connections in developing countries will establish long-term competitive advantages over more inward-looking universities. Similarly, scientific associations, such as the U.S. National Academy of Sciences, could play an increased role in cooperative research undertakings.

Philanthropy, of course, is only a part of the story. Considerable public funding must underwrite the effort at long-term technological advance as well (just as in the rich economies). In 2000 my colleague Michael Kremer and I proposed to use public sector pledges to purchase new vaccines as a mechanism to induce more global research attention to malaria, TB, and AIDS. Then-president Clinton adopted that approach in new proposals for tax breaks for successful vaccine developers. Public funding should combine "push" strategies (R&D efforts directed at poor-country problems are explicitly subsidized) and "pull" strategies (the market incentive for supplying the new technologies is enhanced by rich-country commitments to purchase the resulting technologies on behalf of the poor countries).

At the government-to-government level, the international community should make a firm commitment to the promotion of scientific and technological capacity in the poor countries. Such a call for increased technology transfer is already part of the World Trade Organization agreements, but so far it is a dead letter. National science foundations should be pressed into active service, with supporting budgets for such an undertaking. Additionally, the rich countries need to exercise much greater self-control in the definition and use of property rights surrounding high technology. In the nineteenth century, the "liberals" repeatedly dispossessed powerless indigenous populations by demanding "modern" property rights in land and rejecting the long-standing "pre-modern" communal ownership of land by the indigenous groups. In the early twenty-first century, the rich countries are unilaterally asserting the rights of private ownership over human and plant genetic sequences, or basic computer codes, or chemical compounds long in use in herbal medicines in traditional rainforest communities. These approaches are of questionable legitimacy and threaten to exacerbate serious global inequities. Similar demands by rich countries (mainly the United States) for enhanced patent protection directly threaten the access of impoverished peoples to essential medicines. We still need to find international arrangements that protect property rights and innovation while promoting the interests of the poorest of the poor.

Redefining the International Institutions

For the past twenty years, the Bretton Woods institutions have been at the forefront of global development practice. Their delivery mode is high-conditionality lending to member governments. This approach was fashioned in the cold war era, when the United States sought to engage governments of the developing world to win their hearts and minds, or at least to use the power of the pocketbook to keep them in the fold. In a world dominated by concerns over technology, disease, and environment, the country-based model is passé. The multilateral institutions need to change and address issues beyond those that can be negotiated one-at-a-time in agreements with member governments. If these institutions do not change, they will become irrelevant.

Part of the resistance to needed change relates to money: more of it would be needed in donor support within a properly structured system of institutions. And here the United States may be the greatest obstacle. The technological leader and beacon of hope for much of the world, the United States has been the stingiest aid giver of all. It now musters all of $5 per American each year in budget assistance for the 600 million people of the least developed countries. Successive U.S. administrations have sought to define development assistance in the cheapest possible way. And what could be cheaper than lecturing poor countries about their weak governance while providing precious little in monetary support for technological advancement, public health, and other needs?

With more funding the international aid agencies could engage in very different missions. In reflecting on the future of the World Bank, the donor governments should finally recognize that there is much more to development assistance than high-concessional country lending programs. We have plenty of banks that can make country loans. We really need a global foundation that provides grants for urgent human needs and for long-term technological development of the poorer regions, essentially a modernized Rockefeller Foundation for the twenty-first century. The World Bank now has $30 billion of paid-in capital. This endowment could usefully be increased to $50 billion or even $100 billion by the rich countries, in tandem with a fundamental change of mission toward knowledge creation and dissemination for development rather than country lending.

The specialized U.N. agencies are perhaps the most in need of new funds and new organizational design. No agency has a more important mandate for development in the poorest of the poor countries than the World Health Organization, but no critical agency has been more starved for funds (with the United States at the lead in insisting on a freeze of the core budget). The WHO and similar institutions, however, need organizational change to allow them to play a much more dynamic role in fostering linkages among academia, industry, and government. They have not played that role effectively in the past decade.

The IMF, for its part, should get out of the development business altogether and go back to its mandate to monitor global financial markets. Every serious independent review of the IMF in recent years—by the Council on Foreign Relations, the Overseas Development Council, the Meltzer Commission, and the Center for Economic Policy Research—has reached a similar conclusion. The concessional aid now given by the IMF would be delivered much better by the World Bank, or World Health Organization, or UNICEF, or other agencies.

In conclusion, the time is ripe for a rethinking of globalization. There are no fundamental disagreements on basic economic ideology. The prosperity and self-assurance of the richest countries is at an all-time high, and the ability of the rich countries to look beyond their immediate needs is strong. At the same time, the crisis of the poorest of the poor countries is acute, and the shortcomings of the current strategy of globalization are painfully evident. The world's leaders are convening a Millennium Assembly at the United Nations.[4] What better opportunity to set high goals and practical means to achieve the kind of globalization that can serve all of the world?

Notes

1. Robert M. Solow, "Technical Change and the Aggregate Production Function," *Review of Economics and Statistics,* vol. 39 (August 1957), pp. 312–20.

2. See (www.worldbank.org/html/extdr/pb/pbaidsactivites.htm [June 2000]).

3. In April 2001, just before the publication of this book, UN Secretary General Kofi Annan called for a Global AIDS and Health Fund of between $7 billion and $10 billion to combat the crisis caused by the disease in the world's smallest countries.

4. The UN Millennium Assembly took place in September 2000 and reached agreement on broad goals for equitable globalization, setting a number of specific targets in health, education, and economic development. The goals have been set; the realistic plans for action are yet to come.

PART TWO

Efficiency

JEFFREY A. FRANKEL

6

Assessing the Efficiency Gains from Further Liberalization

In engineering, efficiency means getting the most output out of a given input—for example, getting the most energy out of a given quantity of fuel—subject to the laws of physics. In economics, efficiency means getting the most of an objective such as GDP out of given inputs, subject to the laws of human behavior.

The idea that it is more efficient for countries to engage in international trade than to produce everything they want domestically is as old as the field of economics itself. The current vantage point in history, the year 2001, is a time when the gains from trade should be abundantly tangible. During the first half of the twentieth century, governments turned back the hands on the historical clock of international integration. The resulting decline in trade was implicated in world depression, political upheaval, and war. During the second half of the twentieth century, the leadership of the western alliance, in general, and the United States, in particular, turned forward the hands of international integration. The resulting increase in trade has been accompanied by overall world prosperity and the spread of western economic and political values to virtually all parts of the globe.

Nonetheless, the turn of the millennium is a time when critics are questioning the gains from further efforts to liberalize trade. Many are not con-

I thank Ha Yan Lee for research assistance and Ash Carter, Philippa Dee, Thomas Hertel, Gary Hufbauer, Dani Rodrik, Pierre Sauvé, Ira Shapiro, Rob Stavins, Arvind Subramanian, and Dan Tarullo for helpful suggestions.

vinced that historical correlation implies causation. Others might agree that the increase in trade has contributed to economic growth, but they argue that concerns other than GDP—such as equality or the environment —point to a different judgment regarding the desirability of trade. Still others might agree with the characterization of the last half-century but contend that little more remains to be done. After all, most tariffs are now close to zero, and globalization seems to be complete and irreversible.

How Far Has Globalization Gone?

It is easy to get the impression that globalization is almost complete, that most trade barriers have already been dismantled, borders are irrelevant, nation states are inconsequential. It is easy to imagine that American citizens already trade with buyers or sellers on the other side of the globe as easily as the other side of town. But this is not the reality.

How Much Farther Do We Have to Go?

Globalization of trade still has a lot farther to go. Although trade as a share of the U.S. economy, for example, has tripled over the past half-century, the increase is less impressive when viewed by the hypothetical standard of complete global integration. The trade share is now about 12 percent (exports or imports of goods and services as a fraction of GDP). But this is less than one-sixth of the way toward complete global integration, defined as the hypothetical condition that would hold if Americans were no more likely to buy from, and sell to, each other than to trade with residents of other economies.[1]

Similar statistics hold for other countries, even those that are smaller and naturally more open. Figure 6-1 illustrates for twenty-three countries the importance of purchases from and sales to foreign residents (that is, imports and exports) relative to purchases from and sales to domestic residents. The countries are arrayed horizontally according to size in the figure; greater openness is the downward direction, closedness is the upward direction. The United States is far above the 45° line; openness would have to increase more than sixfold before U.S. transactions with the rest of the world were in proportion to size. Other, smaller, countries have a higher ratio of trade to GDP because they are less self-sufficient. But even for them, openness is still far less than it would be in a borderless world.

Figure 6-1. *Openness and Size of Twenty-Three Countries*[a]

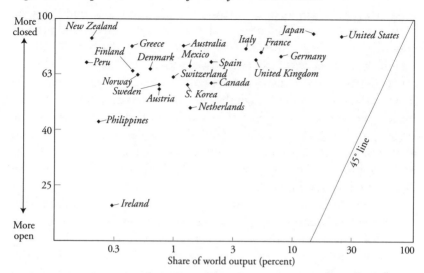

Source: Author's calculations based on national accounts data from International Monetary Fund, *International Financial Statistics.*
a. Closedness = {1 − [(X+M)/(GDP*2)]}*100.

We are still far from the day when we buy from across the globe as easily as from across the country. At any point in history there are many powerful forces working to drive countries apart, at the same time as there are other powerful forces working to shrink the world. The shrinking forces have dominated over the past fifty years, but there is nothing inevitable about that. From 1914 to 1944 the fragmenting forces dominated, and it could happen again.

What Are the Barriers?

It is not difficult to identify some of the impediments to international economic integration that remain. Geographical, social, and policy factors all play a role. Their effect can be quantified in many ways. The following discussion of effects on bilateral trade draws on statistical estimates from the so-called gravity model.[2] Other approaches, such as tests of the ability of cross-border arbitrage to narrow differentials in prices, give similar results.

Statistically, when two firms are located on opposite sides of a national border, operating for example under different legal systems, trade between them falls by an estimated two-thirds—that is, to one-third of what it would be if they were located in the same country. This estimate even allows that the two countries in question officially have free trade between them, speak the same language, and use the same currency. If the two countries use different currencies, trade again falls by a further two-thirds, even if they fix the exchange rate between them. That is, the two border effects together reduce trade to one-ninth of what it would be within the same country. In addition, when the exchange rate is as variable as it is for the average pair of currencies, currency risk and transactions costs reduce trade by another 13 percent. Such factors together explain why Canadians are ten times more likely to trade with other Canadians than with Americans, despite the physical and cultural proximity of the two countries.[3] National borders still matter.

For most pairs of countries, the impediments to trade are much higher still. If the two countries do not belong to a free trade area but have typical tariffs and other trade barriers between them, trade again falls by roughly two-thirds. (It falls by even more if the trade barriers are at levels typically found in poor countries.) If the two share no common historical or cultural links, the impediments are greater still. If they speak different languages, for example, trade falls by half.

Finally, notwithstanding the long-term historical decline in physical shipping costs, geography still matters. If two countries are not adjacent to each other, trade falls by half. In addition, for every 1 percent increase in the distance between them, trade falls by another 1 percent. Small wonder, then, that U.S. purchases from and sales to the European Union, for example, are less than 3 percent of the level of U.S. purchases from and sales to the United States, even though the EU economy is as large as the U.S. economy.

The threefold increase that the United States has experienced in trade as a share of the economy over the past fifty years can be attributed in large part to declining trade barriers and declining transport costs. But neither of these sources of friction is yet close to zero. Differences in currencies and languages and the other factors mentioned earlier have diminished little. Globalization, though not in its infancy, has not yet reached full maturity. Unless we do something to screw it up, trade barriers and transport costs are likely to continue to fall during the twenty-first century. It follows that there are still large gains to be reaped from further reductions in trade barriers. That is, it follows provided integration is viewed as beneficial—the question to which we now turn.

The Economic Benefits from Globalization

Why do economists consider free trade so important? What exactly are the benefits?

The Theoretical Case for Trade

Classical economic theory tells us that there are national gains from trade, associated with the concept of comparative advantage. Over the past two decades, scholars have developed an alternative New Trade Theory. Though often misinterpreted, it suggests the existence of possible additional benefits from trade, which are termed dynamic. Let us consider each theory in turn.

The classical theory goes back to Adam Smith and David Ricardo. Adam Smith argued that specialization—the division of labor—enhances productivity. David Ricardo extended this concept to trade between countries. The notion is that trade allows each country to specialize in what it does best, thus maximizing the value of its output. If a government restricts trade, resources are wasted in the production of goods that could be imported more cheaply than they can be produced domestically.

What if one country is better than others at producing *every* good? The argument in favor of free trade still works. All that is required is for a country to be *relatively* less skilled than another in the production of some good in order for it to benefit from trade. This is the doctrine of comparative advantage—the fundamental (if perhaps counterintuitive) principle that underlies the theory of international trade. It makes sense for Tiger Woods to pay someone else to mow his lawn, even if Woods could do it better himself, because he has a comparative advantage at golf over lawn mowing. Similarly, it makes sense for the United States to pay to import certain goods that can be produced with relatively greater efficiency abroad (apparel, shoes, tropical agriculture, and consumer electronics) because it has a comparative advantage in other goods (aircraft, financial services, wheat, and computer software).

This is the classical view of the benefits of free trade in a nutshell. Two key attributes of the classical theory are worth highlighting. First, it assumes perfect competition, constant returns to scale, and fixed technology—assumptions that are not very realistic. Second, the gains from trade are primarily static in nature—that is, they affect the *level* of real income. The elimination of trade barriers raises income, but this is essentially a one-time increase rather than a permanent rise in the rate of growth.

The New Trade Theory is more realistic than the classical theory because it takes into account imperfect competition, increasing returns to scale, and changing technology. It ultimately provides equally strong, or stronger, support for the sort of free-trade policies that the United States has followed throughout the postwar period (that is, multilateral and bilateral negotiations to reduce trade barriers) than did the classical theory.

Much has been made of the result from these theories that, under certain very special conditions, one country can get ahead by interventions (for example, public subsidies to strategic sectors), provided the government gets it exactly right and provided other countries do not retaliate or emulate. But these theories also suggest that a world in which everyone is subsidizing at once is a world in which everyone is worse off—a classic "prisoner's dilemma"—and that we are all better off if we can agree to limit subsidies or other interventions. An example would be the agreement between the United States and Europe to limit subsidies to our respective aircraft manufacturers. Assume for the sake of argument that the U.S. government is knowledgeable enough to use aircraft subsidies in such a way as to reap extra profits for the American producer (Boeing) at the expense of the EU producer (Airbus) if the Europeans do not retaliate. But how does that help? The Europeans would, in fact, retaliate.

Bilateral or multilateral agreements in which other sides grant concessions in favor of U.S. products, in return for whatever concessions we make, are almost the only sorts of trade agreements we have made. Indeed, most recent trade agreements—like the North American Free Trade Agreement (NAFTA) or the agreement to give China permanent Normalized Trade Relations have featured much larger reductions in import barriers on the part of our trading partners than we are required to make ourselves. The explanation for this is that their barriers were higher than ours to start with. But the implication is that such agreements raise foreign demand for our products by more than they raise our demand for imports. Hence the United States is likely to benefit from a positive "terms of trade effect." This just adds a bonus on top of the usual benefits of increased efficiency of production and gains to consumers from international trade.

Even when a government does not fear retaliation from abroad for trade barriers, intervention is usually based on inadequate knowledge and is corrupted by interest groups. Special interests waste money lobbying to get the government to raise the price of whatever they are selling or lower the price of whatever they are buying. Ruling out all sector-specific intervention is the most effective way of discouraging such "rent-seeking" behavior. Globalization also increases the number of competitors operating in the economy. Not only does this work to reduce distortionary monopoly power in the marketplace (which corporations exercise by raising prices); it can also reduce distortionary corporate power in the political arena (which they exercise by lobbying).

Most important, new trade theory offers a possible reason to believe that trade can have a permanent effect on a country's rate of growth, not just on the level of real GDP. Openness allows firms to keep in touch with global markets. A high rate of economic interaction with the rest of the world speeds the absorption of frontier technologies and global management best practices, spurs innovation and cost cutting, and competes away monopoly.

The Empirical Case for Trade

Citing theory is not a complete answer to the question "How do we know that trade is good?" We need empirical evidence.

There are a number of studies of the static microeconomic costs of protection by tariffs, quotas, and other trade barriers. It has been estimated, for example that the European Union's distortions impose costs on it as high as 7 percent of European GDP. These studies do not attempt to include possible dynamic effects on growth rates.[4]

Economists have undertaken macroeconomic statistical tests of the determinants of countries' growth rates. Investment in physical capital and education are the two factors that emerge the most strongly in these studies. But other determinants matter as well. There is a correlation of growth with openness (measured, for example, as the sum of exports and imports as a share of GDP). David Romer and I looked at a cross-section of 100 countries during the period since 1960.[5] We sought to address a major concern regarding simultaneous causality between growth and trade: Does openness lead to growth, or does growth lead to openness? We removed the complication of simultaneous causality by isolating variation in trade patterns that could be clearly attributed to geographical influences such as distance, borders, language, and so forth. We found that the effect of openness on growth is even stronger when we correct for the simultaneity, as compared with standard estimates.

The estimate of the effect of openness on income per capita varies, depending on the particular data set and equation, but it is on the order of 0.3 over the span of twenty-five years, and perhaps four times that in the truly long run. That estimate means that when trade increases by one percentage point of GDP, income increases by about one-third of a percent over twenty-five years. By way of illustration, the increase in U.S. openness since the 1950s has been 12 percentage points. The numbers imply that increased integration has had an effect of about 4 percent on U.S. income over this period, or about 15 percent in the very long run. More dramatically, compare a stylized Burma, with a trade ratio close to zero, and a stylized Singapore, with a ratio close to 200 percent. Our ballpark estimate, the coefficient of 0.3, implies that as a result of its openness Singapore's income is about 60 percent higher than Burma's over a thirty-year period, or about 250 percent higher in the very long run.

One possible response to these claims is that this approach demonstrates only the growth benefits from geographically induced trade and need not extend to the effects of policy-induced trade. But it is not obvious why the benefits of one impetus to trade should be so different from those of another. In any case, popular critics of globalization seem to think that increased international trade is the problem, regardless of whether it comes from technological progress or market-opening negotiations. If the question is the broad-brush phenomenon of globalization, the answer seems to be that the effect on incomes is clearly positive.

The case for free trade has more widespread support in most countries now than it did thirty years ago. Trade has been a major component of the growth that has visibly lifted East Asia out of poverty during the past forty years. The rest of the world now wants the same. Poor countries do not want to be protected from "exploitation"—the exploitation of having the opportunity to sell their products abroad to willing buyers and thereby to raise their incomes.

The Noneconomic Benefits or Costs of Trade

Many critics of globalization today do not dispute the claim that international trade has positive effects on gross domestic product. Rather, they have in mind other concerns: noneconomic goals such as the promotion of labor rights and protection of the environment. The most important lesson from the Seattle demonstrations of November 1999 is that these issues will increasingly dominate public debate regarding globalization and multilateral institutions. They cannot be shunted off to the side, with pure trade issues occupying alone the center stage of international negotiations.[6]

International trade and investment have implications, in such areas as income distribution or environmental quality, that are sometimes favorable and are in some cases unfavorable. Facile generalizations are likely to be wrong. In particular, it is misleading to talk as if the partners in U.S. trade or investment are generally countries that have lower wages, labor standards, and environmental standards than does the United States and that these partners will inevitably pull down American standards. In more than half of U.S. trade and direct investment, the partners are high-wage countries that are likely to have "higher standards" than the United States has.

From the viewpoint of Europe, the *United States* is the low-wage country with less-regulated labor markets. Environmental standards are sometimes lower in Europe than in the United States, but just as often they are higher. A case in point is European resistance to genetically modified organisms (GMOs) crossing the Atlantic. In fact, there is as yet no scientific evidence that GMOs are harmful. But if European consumers, guided by the precautionary principle "better safe than sorry," want to avoid buying foods that have had the benefit of such technology, that should be their right, so long as their governments avoid discriminatory trade policies.[7]

Even when the partner country is at income levels below the U.S. level, the feared undercutting of U.S. standards is less in evidence than one might think. When American multinationals locate in developing countries, for example, they tend to raise labor and environmental standards relative to local employers. Once a technology or a management practice has become well established in the United States, the world's biggest market, trade and investment spread the same techniques to partner countries. The major effect, in practice, is often upward pressure on the poor-country standards, rather than downward pressure on rich-country standards.

The Case of the Environment

There is no question that the early stages of industrialization bring environmental damage. But a clean environment is a "superior good"—something that societies wish to purchase more of, even though at some cost to aggregate income, as they grow rich enough to be able to afford to do so. If this effect is strong enough, then trade might be expected eventually to improve the environment, once the country gets past a certain level of per capita income. There is some empirical support for this pattern. Gene Grossman and Alan Krueger popularized what is called the environmental Kuznets curve: growth is bad for air and water pollution at the initial stages of industrialization, but later on reduces some forms of pollution, as countries become rich enough to pay to clean up their environments.[8] A substantial literature has followed.

The idea that trade can be good for the environment is surprising to many. The pollution-haven hypothesis instead holds that trade and investment encourage firms to locate production of highly polluting sectors in low-regulation countries, in order to stay competitive. But research suggests that environmental regulation is not a major determinant of firms' ability to compete internationally.[9] In a model that combines various effects of trade, including via the scale and composition of output, Werner Antweiler, Brian Copeland, and M. Scott Taylor estimate that if openness raises GDP by 1 percent, then it reduces sulphur dioxide concentrations by 1 percent.[10] The implication is that, because trade is good for growth, it is also generally good for the environment.

It is important to note that government intervention is the primary channel whereby people enact their desire for a cleaner environment as they grow richer. There is no reason to think that the market can take care of it by itself.

Most of the econometric studies of effects of trade and growth on the environment are limited, in that they examine only a few specific measures of pollution. There is a need to look at other environmental criteria as well. It is difficult to imagine, for example, that trade is anything but bad for the survival of tropical hardwood forests, absent substantial international efforts by governments to protect them.

The argument that richer countries will take steps to clean up their environments is likely to hold only for issues where the primary effects are felt domestically—where the primary "bads," such as smog or water pollution, are external to the firm or household but internal to the country. Two important environmental externalities are global, however: greenhouse gas emissions and depletion of stratospheric ozone. A ton of carbon dioxide has the same global warming effect regardless of where in the world it is emitted. In these cases, individual nations can do little to improve the environment on their own, no matter how concerned their populations or how effective their governments. International cooperation is required, which inherently means a trade-off at the margin against national sovereignty. The same is true about those environmental concerns over so-called nonuse values that are increasingly cross-border, such as the value placed on endangered species. Governments have negotiated international treaties in an attempt to deal with each of the three problems mentioned—ozone depletion, greenhouse gases, and biodiversity. Of the three, however, only the attempt to save the ozone layer, the Montreal Protocol, can be said as yet to have met with much success. The Kyoto Protocol on Global Climate Change faces political hurdles that approach the insurmountable. Desire by countries to protect their national sovereignty is one of the most important hurdles.

Is the popular impression then correct, that international trade exacerbates global environmental externalities? Yes, but only in the sense that trade promotes economic growth. Clearly if mankind were still a population of a few million people living in pre-industrial poverty, greenhouse gas emissions would not be a big issue. Industrialization initially leads to environmental degradation, and trade is part of industrialization. But virtually everyone wants industrialization, at least for themselves. Deliberate self-impoverishment is not a promising option.[11] Once this point is recognized, there is nothing special about trade, as compared to the other sources of economic growth, such as capital accumulation, rural-urban migration, and technological progress.

The popular impression is that trade is somehow different. U.S. congressional opponents of the Kyoto Protocol fear that if the industrialized countries agreed to limit emissions of carbon dioxide and other greenhouse gases, there would be an adverse effect on American trade competitiveness vis-à-vis the developing countries, who are not yet covered by the treaty. This is partially true: those U.S. sectors that are highly carbon-intensive, such as aluminum smelting, would indeed suffer adversely. But other U.S. sectors would be *favorably* affected by trade with nonparticipating countries.

The real issue—the true reason why we need the developing countries to participate in a global climate change agreement—has little to do with competitiveness. It is that the industrialized countries would otherwise make little progress on aggregate global emissions over the coming decades, even if they were willing to cooperate to achieve the emission targets of the Kyoto Protocol and to bear the moderate costs involved in gradually restructuring their domestic energy economies. The big increases in emissions will come from developing countries. This point has little to do with trade. It would be the same in a world where industrialization took place without globalization. International trade, whether in goods or in emission permits, actually offers a way of bringing down the economic cost of attaining any given reduction in global emissions, or a way of obtaining deeper cuts in emissions for any given economic cost. Elimination of such distortions as subsidies to agriculture, logging, and coal can be pro-environment and pro-free-trade at the same time.

Efficiency as the Achievement of Objectives

As noted at the outset, efficiency means maximizing one's objective, whatever it may be, subject to the constraints of nature and man. The objective is not limited to GDP but includes such noneconomic goals as the equality of income distribution and the quality of the environment. The principle remains that countries can better achieve their goals through free international exchange—subject to rules mutually agreed in international forums such as the World Trade Organization (WTO), International Monetary Fund (IMF), International Labor Organization (ILO), and UN Framework Convention on Climate Change (UNFCCC)—than they could if they hid behind barriers to trade and investment.

What Areas Should Be Priorities for Negotiation?

Now that most tariffs have been reduced substantially, the remaining nontariff barriers are more important, and merit more attention, even though they are inherently more complicated to negotiate over. This has been said during the past forty years, at each round of the General Agreement on Tariffs and Trade (GATT). But it has been true each time.

The challenge in proposing multilateral negotiations is not to identify sectors that remain to be liberalized. There are lots of those. Rather it is to identify a set of liberalizations that is perceived by each major participant as a package that, on net, offers it major benefits. Furthermore, under a well-known principle of political economy, which might be called reciprocal mercantilism, the benefits had better accrue to important producer interests in each country. The economist's argument that liberalization is beneficial to *consumers* in the importing country does not carry much weight in the political sphere.

There have been exceptions to this rule of political economy in recent years. One type of exception is unilateral liberalizations in some countries that had become disenchanted with old import-substitution policies. Another is recent post–Uruguay Round multilateral liberalizations in single sectors such as information technology, financial services, or telecommunications. These single-sector negotiations succeeded despite the absence of scope for trading concessions across producers because they involve sectors that firms in many countries see as *inputs* important to industrial development.[12] But it is unlikely that those single-sector negotiations can be repeated for many other industries.

The Form of Negotiations: Where and Who?

Should attempts at further liberalization be negotiated regionally or multilaterally? Who are the key players who must agree to the agenda?

Regional or Multilateral Negotiations?

Given the difficulty of reaching agreements at the multilateral level, the question arises whether more progress might be made at the regional level, where fewer players are involved, political goals might help, and the countries might in any case be natural trading partners.[13] From 1982 to 1994, regionalism had a lot of momentum, in part because progress at the multilateral level was so slow (blocked largely by failure of the EU to agree to U.S. demands to liberalize agriculture). But regional arrangements no longer look like such a promising alternative, outside of Europe. On the one hand, the Uruguay Round was successfully concluded; on the other hand, regional clubs in the Western Hemisphere have made no further progress and in Asia have come to little. The major 1982 shift in U.S. policy, the decision to accept regional free trade areas (FTAs) as an alternative to multilateral negotiations, has become less relevant recently, during a period when Congress has refused to give the president fast-track authority for trade negotiations of any sort, in part because of a perceived popular backlash against NAFTA. This is not to say that the new president, George W. Bush, might not do better using a modest objective like Chilean accession to NAFTA for selling fast-track to Congress than a big WTO objective. Nevertheless, the current obstacles to liberalization exist as fully at the regional level as at the multilateral level. We might as well have the debate at the global level where it really counts.

The general rule stands: packages must offer perceived benefits to producer interests in each major country. This means a package of market-opening measures in a variety of well-chosen areas. It probably should come in the form of another WTO round, even if it does not turn out to be called the Millennium Round and even if it is decided to lock in a first set of concessions after a few years of negotiations (a "roundup"), rather than waiting until the end.

The Developing Countries

Even though decisions in GATT and the WTO are technically made by consensus (each country has an equal vote), some players, in practice, count far more than others. The pattern in past GATT rounds has been that the negotiations were dominated by fencing between the United States and Europe, and when those two powers agreed, the rest of the world generally fell into line. Other countries had little influence over the agenda.[14] Little vote was given to the developing countries, largely because they had little in the way of lucrative concessions to offer the rich countries.

Increasingly, however, the developing countries are important players, at least collectively. Asia and Latin America now constitute major markets. Under the new rules agreed in the Uruguay Round, they, like other WTO members, are generally no longer able to opt out of aspects of an agreement.[15] Nor can they block decisions by panels under the dispute settlement mechanism. Furthermore, in the Uruguay Round developing countries were asked to put energy into enforcement of a set of rules on intellectual property rights that, whatever their economic justification, benefit rich-country corporations and not them. This time their interests will have to be taken into account. This means liberalization of textiles trade, for one thing. It also means protection against arbitrary antidumping measures, if the United States would agree, and liberalization in agriculture, if Europe would agree. If a new round has nothing to offer the developing countries, they might this time try to block it.

Environment, Food Safety, and Labor Standards

Other players who have gained a new seat at the table de facto if not de jure are the nongovernmental organizations (NGOs) in areas such as environmental and social policy. They are often confused and inconsistent about what they want. It was surprising at the time of the Seattle Ministerial to see demonstrators from the environmentalist and labor movements claim to share some beliefs about the proper role for multilateral institutions. (Environmentalists see the WTO as an obstacle to enforcing regulations like the Kyoto Protocol on global climate change. Those in the labor movement are the strongest opponents to the Kyoto Protocol.) It was even more surprising to see them claim to share some interests with the populations of poor countries. (The labor and environmental groups want western countries to import less from poor countries; the poor countries want them to import more.)

Nevertheless, the day has passed when those working to advance free trade can respond to the environmental and labor concerns of the NGOs by simply explaining that the WTO deals only with trade. Discussion of these issues may have to take place under the auspices of the WTO, and the organization may have to go beyond the step taken at the Singapore Ministerial of 1997, when the words "labor and environment" were mentioned in the agreement.[16] Even if the discussion remains outside the WTO, some acceleration of effort toward international agreements on environmental and labor standards is necessary. It is necessary if only to convince an important bloc of public opinion that the world's governments are not just paying lip service to these concerns. Otherwise, again, trade negotiations are likely to be blocked.

The ultimate goal should be international agreements voluntarily entered into. There is no alternative in a world of sovereign countries. An agreement on genetically modified food concluded in Montreal in January 2000, under the 1992 UN Convention on Biological Diversity, might be a model. (U.S. grain exporters, for example, will have to identify shipments that "may contain living modified organisms," in effect allowing those farmers eschewing GMOs to appeal to consumers who prefer "natural" foods and are prepared to pay the cost premium.) This global Biosafety Protocol, if it works out, will show that it is possible to marry international progress on health and environment issues with trade rules that protect producers from arbitrary or discriminatory actions by importing countries. Furthermore, in a move to transparency, environmental NGOs were included in the negotiations and supported the outcome.

The logical locus for most international agreements is designated multilateral institutions, such as the International Labor Organization in the case of labor standards and the UN Framework Convention on Climate Change in the case of greenhouse gases. In the meantime, one must recognize, as the NGOs point out, that the World Trade Organization is a more credible institution than the ILO or the UNFCCC—in part because withholding trade is one of the few powerful weapons that countries have, short of military action. The ILO and UNFCCC have no teeth. The United Nations Environment Program (UNEP) is so weak an institution that it should be replaced from scratch.

The reason these institutions lack teeth, however, is because the member countries, so far, want it that way. The failure to agree on binding international standards enforced by sanctions is attributable to the desire to retain national sovereignty, to disagreements among countries, and to internal disagreements within each country on what priority to assign labor rights and the environment. It is the fault neither of globalization nor the international institutions themselves. Agreements should include sanctions if and only if members, acting through their chosen national governments, can agree that they want them to.

Multilateral institutions can play a major constructive role in the areas of

—*certification,* that is, monitoring multinational corporations that commit to particular codes of conduct, along the lines of the UN Global Compact;

—*labeling,* so that consumers can exercise their right not to consume products they view as environmentally or socially harmful or objectionable —for example, dolphin-unfriendly tuna or turtle-unfriendly shrimp; and

—*scientific fact finding and risk assessment,* to offer an unbiased expert judgment on, for example, the state of scientific knowledge regarding the effects of hormone-treated beef and GMOs, thus refereeing where countries hold vastly different perceptions.

The aim is to help individuals use their purchasing power as a signal to express their values and beliefs and as a weapon to pressure corporations and countries to behave in particular ways. Such signals and weapons can help pressure the system to move in the direction of international agreements of the sort noted earlier. They successfully persuaded Mexican tuna fishermen to protect the dolphins, a process that was not impeded by the GATT panel ruling.

Countries must not make up their own rules for international trade, imposing trade penalties on other democratic countries to bully them into changing their environmental or social policies, in violation of WTO rules. Without this assurance, developing countries will refuse to discuss the whole subject of environmental and labor standards in the context of the WTO.

Priority Sectors for Negotiation

In what sectors are the prospects of efficiency gains from liberalization promising?

Textiles and Other Manufactures

The World Trade Organization has not finished lowering tariffs and quotas on manufactured products. This is especially true of manufactured imports into developing countries.

I have already mentioned textiles and apparel, the first rung of manufacturing exports for poor countries seeking to climb the ladder of development. Rich countries agreed in 1995, under the Uruguay Round, to phase out over the next ten years the quotas that under the Multi-Fibre Agreement (MFA) have long kept the textile sector highly protected. An acceleration of the schedule is the simplest concession to offer the poor countries in exchange for the many demands being placed on them. But little liberalization has occurred to date. The difficult time the Clinton administration had convincing the U.S. Congress to support the elimination of barriers to apparel exports even from Africa and the Caribbean is revealing. China's accession to the WTO alarms some with the prospect of a huge increase in the global supply of inexpensive textiles and apparel. There are grounds for skepticism, given domestic politics in the United States and other rich countries, regarding whether the MFA phase-out that was promised in 1995 will actually happen. If rich countries fail to deliver on this promise, it is hard to see what incentive developing countries have to go along with a new round, or even to carry out their Uruguay Round commitments in the area of intellectual property rights.[17]

Built-In Agenda: Agriculture and Services

Agriculture and services were both exempted from the original GATT rules. Both were formally brought under the WTO in the Uruguay Round that was completed in 1994. But in both cases, serious liberalization was postponed. Agriculture and services constitute the "built-in agenda" of negotiations that was supposedly scheduled to resume by the year 2000, and are the most likely core of a new round. Distortions in agriculture—import barriers, export subsidies, and producer subsidies—remain as high as ever, especially in industrialized countries.[18] The Uruguay Round only got as far as expressing these distortions in terms of tariffs, with an eye toward facilitating future negotiated reductions. Of the total worldwide gain from rich countries' elimination of distortions in their goods markets, Kym Anderson, Bernard Hoekman, and Anna Strutt estimate that one-third is to be had in agriculture.[19]

Services constitute a diverse category of sectors. Historically, most of these have been less affected by trade than have goods sectors, but many (for example, business services) increasingly engage in trade, in part because of the Internet and other advances in telecommunications and computer technology.

Within the large and diverse category of services, perhaps the greatest efficiency gains are to be had by liberalizing transportation services. Protection levels tend to be higher for transport services than for construction and business services.[20] The airline industry is heavily regulated internationally—passengers, air cargo, and express—with an overabundance of national champions and a lack of competition. The shipping industry is even more highly regulated and cartelized, and unevenly so around the globe. "Liner conferences" operate as cartels. Thus the airline, shipping, and trucking sectors are prime candidates for liberalization. Their role as inputs into international trade makes them doubly important candidates: liberalization would reduce costs in the transport sector, and the enhanced ease of international trade would confer additional gains throughout the global economy. The United States has been a leader in negotiating bilateral open skies agreements, but the maritime industry firmly blocks multilateral efforts at liberalization in shipping.

Other Issues for Negotiation

An increasing number of issues cut across sectors of the economy. Although trade distortions have been reduced in many areas and are roughly unchanged in others, there is one kind of distortion that is on the upswing: antidumping (AD) measures.

Antidumping Measures

In 1999, 328 antidumping cases were launched, up 41 percent from 1998, and more than double the rate in 1995.[21] The term "antidumping" sounds like it has something to do with antitrust enforcement against predatory pricing; thus it gives the press and public the impression that these measures are a tool to combat trade distortions and increase competition. But they have nothing to do with predatory pricing, they suppress competition rather than defend it, and they are among the costliest of trade barriers.[22]

The use of AD measures increased rapidly in the United States in the 1980s and 1990s because firms hit by increased imports found it much easier to gain protection under the antidumping laws than under the safeguard laws. Subsequently, their use increased rapidly in other countries as they emulated and retaliated against the United States. An attempt to rein in the indiscriminate use of antidumping would rank near the top of the economist's wish list of priorities for the next round of multilateral negotiations. It could be coupled with some steps toward a multilateral competition policy, to reassure those who are under the illusion that the AD laws have some pro-competition value. Unfortunately, the United States is unlikely to agree to the inclusion of the AD issue.

Competition Policy and Investment

The Uruguay Round already included an agreement on Trade-Related Investment Measures, but its effects were minimal. Some hoped to generalize provisions in NAFTA to the multilateral level. But opposition from suspicious developing countries led to an attempt to begin by using the OECD, rather than the WTO, as a venue for negotiating a Multilateral Agreement on Investment (MAI) among industrial countries alone. Notwithstanding the inadequacy of the MAI, nongovernmental organizations rallied opposition in a surprising first display of successful electronic populism that presaged Seattle. Some combination of that opposition and French intransigence killed the MAI in 1998. Investment may not now be the most promising issue with which to make progress in multilateral negotiations. If it is to be pursued, which would require more thought regarding environmental and labor standards, it should probably be moved back to the WTO.[23]

The world is probably even less ready for a comprehensive multilateral agreement in the related area of competition policy.[24] Countries vary widely in their conception of what sort of competition policy is desirable, even at the domestic level. History suggests that formation of a consensus worldview on an issue, even before horse-trading begins, is a prerequisite for international cooperation.[25]

Government Procurement

Potential gains to an agreement for enhanced market access in public procurement would be substantial, particularly covering construction, maintenance, and repair services.[26] But this is another area where developing countries are being asked, in effect, to make larger concessions than industrialized countries.

Enforcement of DSM Rulings

The Uruguay Round created in the World Trade Organization a dispute settlement mechanism (DSM) purged of the crippling limitation that the losing country could block a panel ruling. On the whole, it has worked well. But a mechanism to compel enforcement is still lacking. Nothing has forced the European Union to comply with adverse panel rulings in the cases of bananas and hormone-treated beef.[27] The EU has retaliated with a complaint, now upheld by a WTO panel, that U.S. foreign sales corporations constitute a subsidy to exports in violation of WTO rules. One hopes that the EU and United States can work out their differences before they undermine the legitimacy of the dispute settlement mechanism.

An immediate need for the dispute settlement panels is an expansion of personnel, as in the WTO more generally. A more ambitious need for the longer term is agreement among the members over enforcement.

Estimates of Efficiency Gains from Multilateral Liberalization

How can we estimate the magnitude of gains from multilateral trade liberalization? Statistical estimates of the association between trade and growth cannot be used by themselves to put a number on the benefits of specific negotiations to liberalize trade. Too many factors in addition to past liberalization have contributed to the observed increase in trade. For example, there have been technological reductions in the costs of transportation and communication. To assess the gains from multilateral negotiations aimed at further liberalization, we must turn to microeconomic models. Of the various econometric approaches to modeling trade, the computable general equilibrium (CGE) models are the most popular for evaluating multilateral negotiations because they attempt to take into account interactions across sectors. An evaluation of the effects of lifting steel quotas, for example, would include not just the savings to firms that buy steel, but also the impact on the prices and sales of products made from steel, the impact on industries that produce other materials that might compete with steel, the diversion of resources out of the steel industry in steel-importing countries and into other industries, the reverse movement within steel-exporting countries, and so forth.

A number of researchers have recently used versions of a global CGE model called the Global Trade Analysis Project to evaluate the possible effects from a new WTO round. Thomas Hertel estimates that the global welfare gains from reducing trade barriers in manufacturing, services, and agriculture, to take effect in 2005, would amount to nearly $350 billion.[28] Agricultural liberalization contributes the most, followed by manufacturing and services. The services experiment is knowingly limited, excluding, for example, transportation services. Nigel Nagarajan includes in his experiment a modest reduction in trade costs from a WTO agreement on trade facilitation, coupled together with a 50 percent across-the-board cut in worldwide protection in all agricultural, industrial, and services sectors. He estimates resulting annual welfare gains of around $400 billion for the world economy, or about 1.4 percent of global income.[29] In addition, a WTO agreement on competition is said to generate an annual welfare gain of approximately $85 billion. Philippa Dee and Kevin Hanslow use a version of the model that has been modified to include the effects of foreign direct investment, so as to be better able to get at liberalization in services.[30] They project an increase in world real income of more than $260 billion in current dollars as a result of eliminating all post-Uruguay trade barriers.[31] About $50 billion of this would come from agricultural liberalization, $80 billion from liberalization of manufactures, and $130 billion from liberalizing services trade. Overall, then, the static gains are estimated on the order of 1 percent of world income.[32]

The estimates of the CGE models are not designed to take into account the possible long-term effects on the growth rate, as opposed to a one-shot effect on the level of real income—the dynamic benefits mentioned earlier in this chapter as opposed to static effects. As already noted, these potential dynamic gains include the benefits of technological improvements through increased contact with foreigners and their alternative production styles. Such interactions can come from direct investment by foreign firms with proprietary knowledge or from the exposure to imported goods that embody technologies developed abroad. For a back-of-the-envelope calculation that includes all growth effects, we must return to something like the Frankel-Romer estimate of the coefficient on openness. The results in Hertel estimate that a new round entails a 20 percent increase in global trade volumes (three-fourths of it coming from cuts in manufacturing tariffs and most of the rest from agricultural liberalization).[33] This would raise the global levels of merchandise exports plus imports as a share of income from a ratio of about 37 percent to 45 percent.[34] Thus the 0.3 Frankel-Romer coefficient implies that the round might raise global income per capita by 2 percent over a twenty-five-year period, and four times that in the truly long run. Needless to say, such a calculation merits many qualifications. Nevertheless, if trade can have long-term effects of this nature, further liberalization negotiations have an even more compelling case.

Notes

1. The U.S. trade-output ratio would have to rise from 12 percent to 75 percent before it fully reflected the share of non-U.S. producers and consumers in the world economy. Even this statistic of a sixfold gap is an understatement because exports and imports are gross transactions, not net value added; Singapore and Hong Kong, for example, export and import well over 100 percent of their GDPs.

2. These estimates of the gravity model of bilateral trade are from Jeffrey Frankel, *Regional Trading Blocs* (Washington: Institute for International Economics, 1997); Andrew Rose, "One Money, One Market? The Effect of Common Currencies on International Trade," *Economic Policy*, vol. 15, no. 30 (2000), pp. 7–46; and Jeffrey Frankel and Andrew Rose, "An Estimate of the Effect of Currency Unions on Trade and Output," Working Paper 7857 (Cambridge, Mass.: National Bureau of Economic Research, August 2000).

3. John Helliwell, *How Much Do National Borders Matter?* (Brookings, 2000), especially chapter 2.

4. Patrick Messerlin, *Measuring the Costs of Protection in Europe* (Washington: Institute for International Economics, 1999). Gary Hufbauer and Kim Elliott perform the analogous exercise for the United States in *Measuring the Costs of Protection in the United States* (Washington: Institute for International Economics, 1994).

5. Jeffrey Frankel and David Romer, "Does Trade Cause Growth?" *American Economic Review*, vol. 89, no. 3 (1999), pp. 379–99. Frankel and Rose, "An Estimate of the Effect of Currency Unions," contains updated estimates.

6. Two key references in this rapidly growing field are Jagdish Bhagwati and Robert Hudec, eds., *Fair Trade and Harmonization,* vol. 1, *Economic Analysis* (MIT Press, 1996), and Dani Rodrik, *Has Globalization Gone Too Far?* (Washington: Institute for International Economics, 1997).

7. The precautionary principle cannot always answer the question, even for the risk averse. In the case of GMOs designed for agriculture in poor countries, doing without them may be the riskier strategy.

8. Gene Grossman and Alan Krueger, "Economic Growth and the Environment," *Quarterly Journal of Economics,* vol. 110, no. 2 (1995), pp. 353–77. An earlier reference is International Bank for Reconstruction and Development, *World Development Report 1992: Development and the Environment* (Oxford University Press, 1992).

9. Adam Jaffe and others, "Environmental Regulation and the Competitiveness of U.S. Manufacturing: What Does the Evidence Tell Us?" *Journal of Economic Literature,* vol. 33 (1995), pp. 132–63.

10. Werner Antweiler, Brian Copeland, and M. Scott Taylor, "Is Free Trade Good for the Environment?" Working Paper 6707 (Cambridge, Mass.: National Bureau of Economic Research, August 1998).

11. In any case, indoor air pollution (particulate matter from cooking and heating fires) and lack of clean drinking water are larger environmental threats in poor countries; each claims millions of premature deaths a year. Economic development is the best way to address these threats.

12. Council of Economic Advisers, *Economic Report of the President, 1999,* pp. 224–26; Gary Hufbauer and Erika Wada, *Unfinished Business: Telecommunications after the Uruguay Round* (Washington: Institute for International Economics, 1997).

13. See Jeffrey Frankel, *Regional Trading Blocs* (Washington: Institute for International Economics, 1997). I evaluate whether regional trading arrangements are natural—more likely to be trade-creating than trade-diverting—and provide an extensive review of the literature, including the political economy of regional arrangements.

14. In the case of Japan, anything that maintained the momentum of a rule-based multilateral trading system was beneficial, since it constitutes insurance against unilateral demands against Japan.

15. Jagdish Bhagwati, "Fifty Years: Looking Back, Looking Forward," paper prepared for the Symposium on the World Trading System, organized by the WTO and the Graduate Institute of International Studies, Geneva, April 30, 1998. The requirement that WTO members must adhere to all negotiated obligations as a "single undertaking" still has exceptions for the poorest developing countries. Two areas, government procurement and civil aviation, remain under "plurilateral accords" of the WTO. Jeffrey Schott, "The World Trade Organization: Progress to Date and the Road Ahead," in J. Schott, ed., *Launching New Global Trade Talks: An Action Agenda* (Washington: Institute for International Economics, 1998), p. 3.

16. In addition to the fundamental political obstacles, there has been a legal obstacle to including most environmental and labor issues: the key distinction between internationally traded goods, which are the proper subject of internationally agreed rules, and the processes by which the goods are produced within each country, which have not been considered an appropriate subject for the WTO. It might be argued that the inclusion of intellectual property rights in the Uruguay Round has shattered the distinction regarding

processes. Keith Maskus argues that labor issues lack the international externalities of competition policy or cross-border environmental problems. Keith Maskus, "Regulatory Standards in the WTO," Working Paper 00-1 (Washington: Institute for International Economics, January 2000).

17. Zhen Kun Wang and L Alan Winters, "Putting 'Humpty' Together Again: Including Developing Countries in a Consensus for the WTO," Policy Paper 4 (London: Centre for Economic Policy Research [CEPR], 2000); Arvind Subramanian, "Intellectual Property Rights," paper presented at the Conference on Developing Countries and the New Round of Multilateral Trade Negotiations, Harvard University, Cambridge, Mass., November 5–6, 1999.

18. Developing countries tend to tax agriculture rather than subsidize it. In OECD countries agricultural protection, measured as the rate of assistance, rose from about 30 percent in 1968 to about 60 percent in 1998, a period during which tariffs on industrial goods fell sharply. Thomas Hertel, "Potential Gains from Reducing Trade Barriers in Manufacturing, Services and Agriculture," paper presented at the 24th Annual Economic Policy Conference, Federal Reserve Bank of St. Louis, Oct. 21–22, 1999; and I. Roberts and others, "The Dynamics of Multilateral Agricultural Policy Reform," paper presented at the 1999 Global Conference on Agriculture and the New Trade Agenda from a Development Perspective, World Bank and WTO, Geneva, October 1–2, 1999.

19. Kym Anderson, Bernard Hoekman, and Anna Strutt, "Agriculture and the WTO: Next Steps," paper presented at the workshop on New Issues in the World Trading System, CEPR, London, February 19–20, 1999.

20. Bernard Hoekman, "Assessing the General Agreement on Trade in Services," in Will Martin and L. Alan Winters, eds., *The Uruguay Round and the Developing Economies,* Discussion Paper 307 (Washington: World Bank, 1995).

21. "Overprotective?" *Economist,* April 22, 2000, p. 5.

22. The enactment of antidumping duties means import quantities on average fall by almost 70 percent and import prices rise by more than 30 percent. Thomas Prusa, "On the Spread and Impact of Antidumping," Working Paper 7404 (Cambridge, Mass.: National Bureau of Economic Research, 2000).

23. Bhagwati, "Fifty Years"; Edward Graham, "Trade and Investment at the WTO: Just Do It," in Schott, *Launching New Global Trade Talks.* See also Edward Graham, *Antiglobalism and the Demise of the Multilateral Agreement on Investment* (Washington: Institute for International Economics, 1999).

24. J. David Richardson, "The Coming Competition Policy Agenda in the WTO," in Schott, *Launching New Global Trade Talks,* pp. 179–88.

25. Richard Cooper, "International Cooperation in Public Health as a Prologue to Macroeconomic Cooperation," Brookings Discussion Papers in International Economics 44 (March 1986).

26. Joseph Francois, Douglas Nelson, and N. David Palmeter, "Public Procurement: A Post-Uruguay Round Perspective," Discussion Paper 1412 (London: CEPR, June 1996).

27. John Jackson, "The Role and Effectiveness of the WTO Dispute Settlement Mechanism," in Susan Collins and Dani Rodrik, eds., *Brookings Trade Forum: Policy Challenges for the New Millennium* (Brookings, 2000), p. 13.

28. Hertel, "Potential Gains from Reducing Trade Barriers in Manufacturing, Services and Agriculture," pp. 17, 30.

29. Nagarajan, Nigel, "The Millennium Round: An Economic Appraisal," Economic Paper 139 (Brussels: European Commission, Directorate General for Economic and Financial Affairs, November 1999).

30. Philippa Dee and Kevin Hanslow, "Multilateral Liberalisation of Services Trade," Staff Research Paper (Ausinfo, Canberra: Productivity Commission, 2000), pp. 17–18.

31. The most obvious reason why these estimated effects are less than Hertel's is that they are in current dollars; his are in terms of 2005.

32. Welfare gains on this order are often described as disappointingly low. But an annual gain of $300 billion is in fact a huge number, especially when one takes the (present discounted) sum over time. Perhaps it would sound more impressive as the numerator of a benefit-cost ratio, where the denominator is the budget of the WTO (a mere $76 million a year) and of national trade negotiators.

33. Hertel, "Potential Gains from Reducing Trade Barriers in Manufacturing, Services and Agriculture," pp. 15–16.

34. For 1998, ($11 trillion)/($29 trillion) = 0.37.

COMMENT BY

L. Alan Winters

I find myself in almost total agreement with Jeff Frankel's essay and therefore will try to complement it rather than comment on it. My focus is the efficiency gains that may be available from negotiations in the so-called "new" and "new new" issues, including services, government procurement, and various regulatory areas. I also consider these issues primarily from the point of view of developing countries.

The "new issues" still offer huge returns to liberalization but not necessarily in obvious ways. In many respects these issues are the same as the old ones. The economist's long-held presumption in favor of competition as a route to both static efficiency (resource allocation) and dynamic efficiency (loosely, maximizing growth) continues to hold. So do firms' and labor's equally long-held tendencies to feel that, while competition is fine for everyone else, they are a special case. Moreover, given the large sizes of the sectors affected by new issues and the evidence of either their closedness to international trade or the big wedges between domestic and world prices in them, I instinctively believe that the potential gains from further liberalization are large.

In 1997 services accounted for 43 percent of GDP in low-income countries, 52 percent in middle-income countries, and 63 percent in high-income countries, making a world average of 61 percent.[1] Yet services account for perhaps a quarter of world trade, albeit by a long way the more dynamic part of it. Identifying wedges between world and domestic prices is not easy in services, but, for example, in the early 1990s the United Nations Conference on Trade and Development (UNCTAD) and the World Bank estimated that credit for imports into Uganda cost around 20 percent of the imports' c.i.f. value![2]

Similarly, government procurement of goods and services (excluding capital expenditure) accounted for 36 percent of central government expenditure (7 percent of GDP) in middle-income countries and 25 percent (8 percent) in high-income countries.[3] Moreover, these purchases are pretty home-biased. For thirteen manufacturing sectors in seven European countries, the ratio of import penetration in the public sector to that in the private sector was below two-thirds in the majority of cases.[4] Finally, the benefits in terms of availability and lower costs arising from the competition associated with the deregulation of the telecom sector are well known.

The case seems plain: the new issues are huge and promise huge gains. However, within that broad case some care is required; in fact, the situation varies from case to case in terms of positive economics and in terms of the political economy of realizing the gains.[5] One's view of government procurement, for example, depends critically on whether one thinks goods are differentiated or not. If not, biased procurement policies do not matter per se for a small country. If government demand is less than local supply, any "excess" units of local output that the government buys are replaced on the local market by private sector imports at the world price.[6] Even if government demand exceeds local supply at free trade prices, there is no misallocation, provided there is free entry to the industry and the domestic industry's minimum long-run average cost equals the world price. The same is true for nontraded goods, provided the government does not prevent foreign access.[7] In these latter cases, changes in pure market access yield nothing, and attention should switch from procurement policy to competition policy to ensure that the conditions noted actually apply.

Alternatively, if one believes in product differentiation and imperfect competition, the home bias induced by procurement biases affects international specialization and offsets some of the forces of industrial agglomeration. Federico Trionfetti reports some evidence for both effects. The former is costly, but the latter is possibly not so, at least for the country concerned.[8] Overall, therefore, we need to be quite careful in assessing the likely gains from liberalizing government procurement. As Simon Evenett and Bernard Hoekman note, efforts might be better directed at first to achieving transparency and due process than to market access agreements per se.[9]

In services, the key is competition.   Major gains in services seem likely in a number of cases. The efficient provision of business services is an important component of competitiveness in many sectors, both by keeping costs low directly and by enhancing competition. Thus unilateral liberalizations of these sectors have much to commend them. The issue is less one of ownership than of competition, however. There is more to it for developing countries than just granting access to their markets: a foreign-owned private monopoly must be spectacularly efficient in a technical sense if it is to be the best way of providing a service. Market access must be tailored and supported by complementary policies in a way that increases competition.[10] Multilateral trade negotiations may help countries to achieve this by providing templates (for example, the Reference Paper in telecoms), by offering means to bind commitments to access, by creating coalitions for liberalization, and perhaps by offering pressure that can be harnessed for the policy reform. They are not very often sufficient, however.

It is very difficult to find convincing ways of quantifying the efficiency gains from such liberalizations. One important step toward doing so, even if only on a case-by-case basis, is to compile decent inventories of existing barriers and, where possible, their distortion cost. At present the World Trade Organization schedules are far too imprecise to make it clear what issues there are to negotiate, let alone what they are worth.

Beware the "ideas of much." Economists' measurements and quantifications of the benefits of policy reforms have become absolutely central to contemporary processes of liberalization and negotiation. We are constantly asked for estimates of the effects of this or that reform and have rapidly learned that little concentrates the minds of policymakers or the public as fast as dollar signs followed by lots of zeros. But as a small act of heresy, I confess that at least part of me regrets this. It is not that I dislike measurement. Indeed, my career has been primarily devoted to measurement and testing. However, a narrow focus on the numbers in policy debate places too great a strain on economists' ability to make reasonable estimates and for that reason opens debate up to less rather than more scrupulous arguments.

The giant leaps in liberalization, such as the creation of the United States, the General Agreement on Tariffs and Trade (GATT), and the European Economic Community (EEC) were all inspired by a strong belief in their efficiency benefits (among other things) but were undertaken without detailed balance sheets. Still less were they accompanied by the quantitative identification of losers and gainers that characterizes most current debates. I should like to see more attention given to broad principles and orders of magnitude and less to the details of particular gains and losses. I urge all economists who quantify policy impacts to stick firmly to their footnotes in which they qualify their numbers and not to enter into bidding races in which only larger and less conditional predictions of benefits can command attention. Such bidding races are ultimately prisoners' dilemmas for our profession.

The "movement of natural persons" is a key sector for developing countries. One area that I believe offers huge benefits to developing countries in any future negotiation is the temporary movement of natural persons to supply services in a foreign market.[11] The Uruguay Round's General Agreement on Trade in Services (GATS) contained few commitments in this area, and most of them were heavily qualified. Almost inevitably, the least liberal sectors were those in which developing countries have a comparative advantage (labor-intensive activities requiring low or medium skills). Four types of constraint on movement require negotiation: immigration regulations concerning the entry and stay of service providers; recognition of qualifications, work experience, and training; the differential treatment of domestic and foreign personnel; and regulations covering other modes of supply, particularly commercial presence, which indirectly limit the scope for the movement of natural persons. The fundamental problem is that there is no separation between temporary and permanent labor movement, even though GATS is meant to cover only temporary labor flows in services.

With suitable provision for *short-term* mobility of workers (which, I stress, is not migration), developing countries could greatly expand the supply of services to developed-country consumers and businesses (for example, in construction, distribution, environment, and transport). Moreover, temporary movement would enhance delivery through other modes. The current success stories of developing countries exporting services, such as Indian software or Cuban health services, rely significantly on provider mobility.[12] Industrial countries already compete to attract software engineers from the developing world, and there is no reason why that should not also apply to many other relatively low-skilled jobs such as caregivers, painters, plumbers, cleaners, or waiters.

On the back of the mythical envelope, one could sketch out the following. Suppose that when a worker moves from a low-income to a high-income country, she could make up one-quarter of the wage gap between the two countries. (That is, assume that three-quarters of observed wage gaps are attributable to differences in individual characteristics and hence would persist even after people started to work in the rich countries). Suppose also that 50 million additional people from developing countries worked abroad in any year, equivalent to an increase of about 5 percent in industrial countries' populations. With a wage gap of, say, $24,000 a year, the gains would be $300 billion a year.[13]

The politics of achieving such a deal are formidable. Not only would there be practical issues to be solved such as health coverage, but one would need to overcome genuine concerns that these workers lacked rights in their host countries. Of course, the likely losers from such arrangements are unskilled workers in the industrial countries. They have been the traditional beneficiaries of protection and so can be expected to mount fierce campaigns against any liberalization. In the name of reciprocity and national treatment, the developing countries must be prepared to accept inflows of workers as well as outflows, so they, too, will have political problems—from skilled elites, from traditional antagonisms, and in some cases from their own unskilled workers. Nonetheless, the gains are such that the attempt would surely be worthwhile. Moreover, such mobility will start to look even more attractive as the baby boomers in the industrial world retire and seek personal services.

Harmonizing regulations is not necessary. The final bit of the WTO agenda that I wish to consider is regulation. Jeff Frankel's comments on this matter are exactly right. Efficiency encompasses more than just GDP, although I do not like the term "noneconomic objectives" because many of these other objectives are economic in nature and assuredly involve the sort of trade-offs that are the bread and butter of economics.[14] If different peoples have genuinely different tastes for different goods, economists respect that and, indeed, place it at the heart of their theorizing. I believe that we should accord other tastes the same respect. Frequently labeling will be sufficient to ensure this, but if there are externalities, we may need to invoke standards.

Recent concerns over hormones in beef imports and genetically modified organisms (GMOs) illustrate the point quite well. Resolving these issues represents one of the major challenges for the trading system in the next decade. Europeans' resistance to imports of these goods lies in fears about their safety. These fears have not been scientifically substantiated, but given the long time horizons over which problems could arise, there is clearly some positive probability of harm occurring. The United States has been prepared to bear these risks, but Europe has not. If the difference between the two behaviors resides in different estimates of the risk, it may ultimately be resolvable through scientific work, discussion, and arbitration. This is the interpretation of the problem implicit in the relevant WTO agreements (on sanitary and phytosanitary measures and, relatedly, on technical barriers to trade). These agreements call for scientific risk assessments (albeit with a very catholic definition of science).

The alternative view is that there might be perfect agreement about the risk but different attitudes toward bearing it, reflecting differences in utility functions. If the risk involved (presumably a social, not a purely private, one) were in the consumption and use of hormone-fed beef or GMOs, import restrictions would be justified so long as equivalent restrictions were applied to domestic production. If the risk were only in production (for example, local dangers to wildlife), international trade would be part of the solution, not part of the problem. If Americans were happy to risk the wildlife consequences of GMOs, Europe should be pleased to import those products in order to preserve its own wildlife from any possible dangers. Only European concerns about U.S. wildlife, such as that it was vital for global biodiversity, or fears about the transcontinental migration of modified organisms would justify intervention.

The correct degree of intrusiveness of international bodies into domestic regulation will become an ever more pressing question as disputes pile up, and there is a good chance that this issue will have to be reopened in the WTO at some stage.[15] The current European position based on extreme caution is not fundamentally untenable, but it is confounded and obscured by the protectionist baggage that it currently carries. At present one cannot completely suppress the suspicion that part of the objection to hormone-fed beef and GMOs is that both techniques would permit large increases in yields, immediately and directly in the case of hormone-fed beef. If EU farmers adopted yield-increasing procedures, their extra output would bankrupt the Common Agricultural Policy. Thus it would be easier to debate the real issue if the European Union first slashed its agricultural protection; ultimately the correct treatment of risk might turn out to be the larger issue.

Big gains to liberalization, but distinguish between border and nonborder measures. In conclusion, I re-emphasize the distinction made by Finger and Hoekman between border measures, the traditional concern of the world trading system, and nonborder measures, which, broadly speaking, have only recently entered the system's ambit.[16] With regard to border measures, I am sure that there are huge gains to be won by extending the trade-liberalizing magic into new areas such as services. I also understand the necessity to quantify these, although, given the inevitable uncertainty surrounding such efforts, I would like to see more emphasis on the broad principles and orders of magnitude of the case and less on detailed distributional outcomes. The latter have a role but cannot be the only yardstick.

On nonborder measures the situation is considerably more complex. For many services border liberalization will not be sufficient to reap material benefits; appropriate domestic deregulation will be necessary as well. Similarly, in many other cases domestic regulations dilute border liberalization, and international constraints on them would be beneficial all around. There are cases, however, in which international constraints, especially in the form of the harmonization of regulations, would be inefficient, reducing welfare because it undermines individuals' objectives instead of extending beyond the simple maximization of immediate consumption. Economists should respect individuals' objectives—as, indeed, the GATT did, for it never outlawed protection in the form of tariffs nor even asked countries to justify it—and recognize that meeting them may legitimately reduce the amount of international trade.

I do not believe that the exceptions to effective liberalization will be widespread. Nor do I believe that the world should abandon the requirement that they be met in nondiscriminatory ways that impose the least possible cost on trade partners. However, the exceptions are likely to be important and sensitive when they arise. If the genuineness of certain differences in taste between countries and the right of governments to respond to these differences are not recognized, the whole of the trading system could be undermined. By pursuing a false efficiency through harmonization in these sectors, we run the risk of destroying genuine efficiency in the very many others where the usual prescription applies.

Notes

1. World Bank, *World Development Indicators, 1999.*

2. United Nations Conference on Trade and Development (UNCTAD) and World Bank, "Strengthening the Service Infrastructure: Uganda," UNCTAD/ITE/IIT/Mics.5 (New York, 1997).

3. These numbers are very approximate indicators: the shares in government expenditures are median values, while the shares of expenditure in GDP used to express these as percent of GDP are weighted averages. World Bank, *World Development Indicators, 1999,* tables 4.9, 4.14.

4. Federico Trionfetti, "Discriminatory Public Procurement and International Trade," *The World Economy,* vol. 23 (2000), pp. 57–76.

5. Given that in analyzing goods we distinguish, say, agriculture, clothing, and airliners, it would be surprising if we did not need to make distinctions within the new issues.

6. Robert Baldwin and J. David Richardson, "Government Purchasing Policies, Other NTBs and the International Monetary Crisis," in H. Edward English and K. Hay, eds., *Obstacles to Trade in the Pacific Area* (Ottawa: Carleton School of International Affairs, 1972).

7. Simon J. Evenett and Bernard M. Hoekman, "Government Procurement Discrimination and International Trade," World Bank, Development Research Group, September 1999.

8. Trionfetti, "Discriminatory Public Procurement."

9. Evenett and Hoekman, "Government Procurement Discrimination."

10. Aaditya Mattoo, "Developing Countries in the New Round of GATS Negotiations: Towards a Pro-Active Role," *The World Economy,* vol. 23 (1999), pp. 471–90.

11. See Rupa Chanda, "Movement of Natural Persons and Trade in Services: Liberalising Temporary Movement of Labour under the GATS," paper presented at workshop session 32 of the Global Development Network Conference: Bridging Knowledge and Policy, Bonn, December 6–8, 1999 (www.gdnet.org/bonn99/workshops/sessions32.htm/). For a summary, see Zhen Kun Wang and L. A. Winters, "Putting 'Humpty' Together Again: Including Developing Countries in a Consensus for the WTO," Policy Paper 4 (London: Center for Economic Policy Research, 2000).

12. Mattoo, "Developing Countries in the New Round."

13. Labor costs per manufacturing worker, which I take as an indicator of productivity, were about $32,000 in the United States in 1990–94, compared with $1,192 in India, $1,442 in Lesotho, $5,822 in China, and $6,138 in Mexico; high-income countries' population was 927 million in 1997. World Bank, *World Development Indicators, 1999.*

14. A decade ago I coined the term "so-called noneconomic objectives" (SNOs), but unaccountably it never took root. L. Alan Winters, "The 'So-Called Non-Economic Objectives' of Agricultural Policy," *OECD Economic Studies,* no. 13 (Winter 1989–90), pp. 237–66.

15. James Rollo and L. Alan Winters, "Subsidiarity and Governance Challenges for the WTO: The Examples of Environmental and Labour Standards," *The World Economy,* vol. 23 (April 2000), pp. 561–76.

16. J. Michael Finger and Bernard Hoekman, "Developing Countries and a New Trade Round: Lessons from Recent Research," World Bank, Development Research Group, 1999.

ALAN O. SYKES

7 | *"Efficient Protection" through WTO Rulemaking*

Free trade maximizes global economic welfare as conventionally defined but plainly does not maximize the joint political welfare of the government officials who control trade policy. Protectionist policies persist in many goods markets despite more than half a century of reciprocal trade negotiations. The process of opening services markets to international competition under the General Agreement on Trade in Services (GATS) has only begun. Future negotiations will no doubt make further progress in reducing the remaining trade barriers, but the ultimate demise of protectionism is hardly in sight. Accordingly, rulemaking by the World Trade Organization (WTO) can productively work to ensure that persistent protective measures cause no greater loss of economic welfare than is necessary to achieve protectionist goals that remain politically essential. In this sense, WTO rulemaking can facilitate "efficient protection."

The task of designing rules that promote efficient protection is a daunting one given the multiplicity of potentially protectionist policy instruments that nations have at their disposal, and the multiplicity of considerations that bear on the question of how protection ought best to be structured. The most fundamental consideration relates to the danger that

My thanks to Motoshige Itoh, David Leebron, Pierre Sauvé, and to the conference organizers, commentators, and participants for their many useful thoughts and suggestions.

trade commitments made with respect to one policy instrument (such as tariffs) may be undermined by new protectionist measures grounded in unconstrained policy instruments. Trade agreements of necessity, therefore, must address a wide range of potentially protective measures.

A second and related consideration arises because the multiplicity of potentially protectionist policy instruments makes it difficult for nations to evaluate the benefits of a concession on a single one of them, even if the policies in place elsewhere do not change. It is hard to know how much exports will increase as the result of a tariff concession, for example, if exporters must also contend with a variety of protective regulatory measures once they begin to export. The transaction costs of trade negotiations can thus be reduced if protection can be channeled into one policy instrument, or at least into as few as possible. The transaction costs of negotiation can likewise be reduced if the allowable protectionist instruments affect trade in ways that are transparent and predictable.

Finally, protectionist policy instruments do not have equivalent effects on economic welfare, even holding constant the amount of protection that they afford. Some have added costs associated with trade diversion, for example. Others have added costs because their protective effect is attributable to a direct increase in the marginal costs of production for foreign firms. Therefore, trade agreements can enhance welfare by channeling protection into the policy instruments that do the least damage.

WTO rules already do quite a bit to encourage efficient protection in goods markets.[1] A comparison of policy instruments suggests that nondiscriminatory tariffs, and perhaps domestic subsidies, tend to afford the most efficient protection. These instruments are, indeed, the least constrained in the WTO system. More destructive forms of protection, such as regulatory measures that raise foreign rivals' costs and create large deadweight losses in the form of wasteful compliance expenditures, are disfavored. This analysis is developed in the first section of the chapter.

I then consider services markets. Here the task of structuring protection efficiently is more difficult. Some of the best options for protection in goods markets (such as a nondiscriminatory tariff) will not work in services markets. Subsidies can be used, of course, but they are often politically unacceptable because of the drain on the treasury. Service market protection is typically achieved instead through domestic regulatory measures such as licensing restrictions, investment restrictions, restrictions on foreign ownership and partnership, and so on. Where complete liberalization is politically infeasible, at least for a time, some mix of these devices must likely be retained. Which ones should the system prefer? I offer some tentative answers, with the proviso that difficult empirical issues stand in the way of a confident response in many instances. The discussion also addresses an issue of current prominence in WTO services negotiations— whether liberalization should proceed on a sectoral basis as in the past, or whether broader principles applicable to all sectors would be preferable. Another lurking issue is whether WTO rulemaking can be used to dismantle foolish regulations that not only impair international trade in services, but also stifle domestic competition inefficiently.

Efficient Protection in Goods Markets

The protectionist policy instruments available in goods markets include tariffs (discriminatory and nondiscriminatory), quantitative restrictions (quotas), regulatory measures that impose higher compliance costs on foreign firms, subsidies, state trading monopolies, discriminatory procurement policies, discriminatory tax policies, and no doubt others. To illustrate what I mean by efficient protection, and to make the argument that the WTO already encourages it to a significant degree in goods markets, I focus on tariffs, quotas, subsidies, and regulatory measures.

Why All Protection Is Not Created Equal

Holding constant the amount of protection afforded (the quantity of imports allowed into the importing country and the resulting equilibrium market price received by domestic firms), tariffs, quotas, and protective regulations differ in their transparency and in the predictability of their impact on trade. They also differ in the static deadweight losses that they will cause.

NONDISCRIMINATORY TARIFFS.   Consider first a tariff that is uniform for all imports of a particular good, whatever their origin (a most-favored-nation tariff). The effects of such a nondiscriminatory tariff on trade are fairly transparent and predictable. Under competitive conditions, the tariff will drive a wedge between the delivered price of a good at the border and the price paid by the domestic importer in an amount exactly equal to the tariff. This wedge will be the same (or at least the same percentage of price) for all exporters. A sense of the pertinent supply and demand elasticities is then all that is required to forecast the effects of a tariff cut, at least when other protective policies will not restrain trade after the tariff is lowered.

As for the deadweight costs of nondiscriminatory tariffs, five sources of loss can be identified. The first is the loss of consumer surplus to consumers who are priced out of the relevant market by the price increase induced by the tariff. The second is the waste of resources caused by the substitution of higher-cost domestic production for lower-cost foreign production (to the extent that domestic producers expand output in response to the tariff). These losses reflect the conventional "deadweight loss triangles" in standard, partial equilibrium analyses of the effects of tariffs.[2] A third deadweight loss arises because a tariff requires resources for the creation of a tariff classification system and the customs bureaucracy to administer it. A fourth loss can occur because the elevated price that results from the tariff confers some additional surplus on domestic producers, and this additional surplus may be partially dissipated by the initial rent seeking activity necessary to induce the government to impose the tariff or by the subsequent rent seeking necessary to keep it in place. Finally, the tariff generates revenue for the government, and groups seeking to induce the government to transfer that revenue to them may make additional rent-seeking expenditures. Despite all of these deadweight costs, however, a nondiscriminatory tariff may be a comparatively efficient instrument of protection for the reasons given below.

DISCRIMINATORY TARIFFS.   Imagine a tariff system that permits tariff discrimination and thus departs from a most-favored-nation requirement. In comparison with the nondiscriminatory tariff, and holding constant the volume of imports allowed into the country, the deadweight costs under a discriminatory tariff due to the loss of marginal consumer surplus and the inefficient substitution of domestic production will be the same. The amount of rent seeking by the domestic industry that benefits from the tariff should also be the same (in expected value). The costs of the tariff system will increase, however, because it now becomes necessary to establish the origin of imported goods: rules of origin must be developed and administered.

Moreover, the discriminatory tariff complicates reciprocal trade negotiations. Exporters seeking market access commitments must now be concerned with the possibility that differential and more favorable treatment will be afforded to other exporters, undermining the value of the concessions that they receive. Therefore, they must undertake to predict and guard against such problems.

In addition, to the degree that more favorable tariff rates are applied to the goods of higher-cost foreign suppliers, the problem of trade diversion arises: the imports permitted into the country are no longer produced by the lowest-cost foreign producers as they would be under a nondiscriminatory tariff.[3] Tariff revenue falls as a result (holding imports constant), and an additional deadweight loss arises from the substitution of inefficient foreign sources of supply.[4]

These considerations suggest that the discriminatory tariff is likely to be inferior to the nondiscriminatory tariff as an instrument of protection. The one caveat lies in the possibility that a nondiscriminatory tariff will complicate trade negotiations in a different way by introducing the possibility of free riders.[5] If nations are entitled to the benefits of lower tariff rates negotiated between other countries because of some legal principle that mandates most-favored-nation tariff treatment (such as Article I of GATT), all nations may attempt to free ride, and fewer trade concessions may result. In the abstract, a system allowing discriminatory tariffs could then dominate even though it has the additional costs noted earlier. To ameliorate the free rider problem, however, trade negotiators in practice resort to tariff cutting formulas that apply to everyone. Negotiators can delay making any final deals until all nations' offers are on the table and can be evaluated for their adequacy. Given the relative success of these negotiation strategies at lowering tariffs within the WTO/GATT system to date, it seems reasonable to conclude that the free rider problem with nondiscriminatory tariffs is not intolerable. The opportunity for nations to create customs unions and free trade areas may represent a sensible accommodation between the free rider problem on the one hand and the competing considerations that favor nondiscriminatory tariffs on the other.[6]

QUOTAS.   Now compare quotas to the nondiscriminatory tariff. Under competitive conditions, and again holding the volume of imports allowed into the country constant, the losses from the exit of marginal consumers, the inefficient substitution of domestic production, and rent seeking by the domestic industry in pursuit of protection should be the same. A system for the classification of goods into categories is necessary for the administration of quotas, so that cost is about the same as well.

Other costs depend on how the quota is administered. If rights to import are auctioned, the system looks very much like a nondiscriminatory tariff system in its welfare effects. Lowest-cost foreign suppliers will ordinarily pay the most for the right to import, so little trade diversion should occur. Much more commonly, however, quota rights are simply given away to importers or exporters. Plainly, unauctioned quota rights confer quota rents on some private party, and rent seeking to secure the property rights in the quota may then occur, although it is unclear that rent dissipation in pursuit of quota rights will exceed rent seeking in pursuit of the revenues raised by tariffs. But other sources of deadweight loss enter as well. If the quota rights are extended to all exporters on a global first-come, first-served basis until the quota is exhausted, deadweight losses can arise because of the resulting "quota race" where all foreign suppliers strive to be first in line. They may arrange their production schedule uneconomically to accelerate output, for example, or invest uneconomically in trying to locate and secure necessary import licenses before someone else does. Trade diversion can also occur because there is no reason to suppose that the lowest cost suppliers will always be first in line under the quota.

If the quota is allocated by giving fixed shares to individual exporting nations, the danger arises that less efficient suppliers will be given an allocation (trade diversion). Although the global quota race is averted, unproductive quota races may still occur within each exporting nation. Further, when shares are allocated by country, rules of origin are again required, and bring with them associated administrative costs.

Some of these problems can be ameliorated by giving the quota rights to importers, who can then search the world for the lowest cost sources of supply to maximize the wedge between what is paid for the imports at the border and the resale price. But if shares are allocated by country, trade diversion may still arise.

Quotas also complicate trade negotiations by making it harder to value concessions, again depending on how they are administered. A global first-come, first-served quota raises the problem of how to predict who will be at the head of the line before the quota is filled. If quota shares are allocated by country, the problem of predicting each nation's share of exports is eliminated, but the transaction costs of fighting over shares during the course of negotiations must be incurred.

From a welfare standpoint, therefore, a quota system is no better than a nondiscriminatory tariff, and it is likely to be comparable only if quota rights are auctioned. Where quota rights are given away free to exporters as is commonly the case (often to bribe them into tolerating the quota), a quota system seems inferior to the nondiscriminatory tariff because of the costs associated with quota races, trade diversion, and increased difficulty for trade negotiators in reaching an accord on concessions.

SUBSIDIES.   It is difficult to determine how the welfare consequences of domestic subsidies compare with nondiscriminatory tariffs. Holding constant the expansion of the domestic industry across the two instruments, the deadweight loss from the substitution of domestic for foreign production will be the same. The surplus gained by domestic producers, and their rent-seeking efforts in pursuit of it, also ought to be about the same. Subsidies have the apparent advantage that they do not reduce consumer surplus in the affected market and may increase it. This benefit may be offset in whole or in part, however, by distortions in the market(s) taxed to raise the money for the subsidy. These distortions will depend on the precise taxes at issue and may include rent seeking by parties who want to avoid or repeal the tax. Subsidies do not require a tariff classification system for their administration, of course, but in a country that has one anyway for other reasons, there may be little savings. Finally, subsidies have somewhat less transparent effects on trade than do tariffs, perhaps, but as long as their magnitude is known to trading partners, their impact may not be much harder to forecast than that of a tariff. About all that can be said, therefore, is that subsidies are neither obviously inferior to nor obviously superior to nondiscriminatory tariffs from a welfare standpoint. They may often be inferior from a political standpoint, of course, because they require an on-budget expenditure of resources by the government.

REGULATORY MEASURES.   Protective regulatory measures can take many forms. The easiest way to disadvantage foreign rivals through regulation is to enact a regulation that applies only to them (imported automobiles are subject to emissions control rules, for example, but not domestic automobiles). But facially nondiscriminatory regulations can also have a dramatic protective effect. Products can be required to be made of some input product, or to incorporate some technology, that is much more expensive abroad than it is domestically. Or imported products might be required to obtain some expensive quality or safety certification at a domestic facility that is redundant of quality or safety certification costs incurred abroad. Innumerable other examples might be offered.

Regulations may also confer benefits in the form of improved product quality or safety, improved consumer information, and the like. In analyzing the welfare consequences of protective regulatory measures, therefore, an additional set of considerations enters the mix that can make the analysis quite difficult. Suppose, however, that the regulatory measures at issue serve no regulatory objective aside from protection and exist solely to disadvantage foreign rivals. This is a strong assumption that may not describe many regulations in practice, but let us see where it leads us.

Continuing with the nondiscriminatory tariff as a benchmark and again holding constant the level of protection afforded to the domestic industry, the loss of consumer surplus to marginal consumers will be the same and the extent of inefficient substitution between domestic and foreign production will be the same. This is also true regarding the value of protection to domestic firms and thus the expected amount of rent seeking in pursuit of protection. As for administrative costs, regulatory protection substitutes costs of the regulatory system for the costs of the tariff system. It is by no means obvious which is greater.

But there is a critical difference between regulatory protection and a tariff that can make the former far more pernicious. The protective effect of the regulation arises because of the differential compliance costs for domestic and foreign firms. Let us suppose, as is commonly the case, that compliance measures consume resources and do not simply transfer them. That is, let us suppose that to comply with the regulations, firms expend real resources on changing product design and engineering, on testing and certification services, and the like. If those resources are priced at marginal social cost, and if their consumption yields no benefit to the regulating jurisdiction other than protection (my strong assumption above), then these regulatory compliance expenditures become a pure deadweight loss. In the limit, an amount of surplus equal to the revenue that could have been transferred to the government under a tariff system—only some of which would have been dissipated through rent seeking in pursuit of it—is entirely wasted on useless regulatory compliance measures that have no purpose other than to raise the costs of foreign firms and protect domestic rivals.

Regulatory protection also poses difficult problems for trade negotiators. It is often quite lacking in transparency, and the magnitude of its impact on trade can be quite hard to predict. Accordingly, the task of valuing trade concessions in the face of possible regulatory protection can be quite difficult. For these reasons, regulatory protection is likely inferior to nondiscriminatory tariffs from a welfare standpoint, potentially by a wide margin. The system will have more surplus to distribute, and trade agreements will be easier to negotiate, if protection is instead channeled into tariffs.

Of course, if we relax the assumption that the regulation yields no benefits to the importing nation aside from the protection, the analysis becomes more complicated. And the reader may suspect that few regulatory measures in practice are purely protective with no benefits relating to other regulatory goals. Yet many regulations require an unnecessary expenditure of resources that produces a protective effect when all regulatory objectives (other than protection itself) could be achieved more cheaply without the protective component of the regulation. In this sense, even regulations that promote some nonprotectionist regulatory goal can have a protective aspect to them with adverse welfare consequences that can be eliminated through the substitution of a tariff, as suggested earlier.

For example, consider a regulation that requires the producers of children's clothing to use a particular flame retardant that is far more expensive abroad than domestically. Assume further that alternative flame retardants, available more cheaply abroad, would work just as well. Then the benefits of reduced flammability could be obtained more cheaply through a regulation that simply specified a flammability standard, which manufacturers could meet through the cheapest technology available. The regulation that requires a particular flame retardant has a purely wasteful protective component, even though it does in some sense yield regulatory benefits by reducing the flammability of children's clothing. Welfare would increase if foreign manufacturers were allowed to use the least-cost flame retardant. And if the protection afforded to domestic manufacturers by the wasteful version of the flammability regulation were a political imperative, welfare could still be improved by adopting the more sensible flammability standard and then imposing a nondiscriminatory tariff on imports to achieve the needed protection. The welfare gain arises for exactly the reason given above: protection is achieved by a device that effects a transfer to the government rather than one that induces a wasteful increase in foreign production costs.

The Response of the WTO/GATT in Goods Markets

WTO rules applicable to goods markets seem broadly consistent with the logic of promoting efficient protection. The one instrument of protection that is completely unconstrained, save for the voluntary bindings entered by trading nations during the course of negotiations, is the nondiscriminatory tariff (GATT Article II). Discriminatory tariffs, on the other hand, are generally prohibited by the most-favored-nation obligation (GATT Article I). The principal exception is found in the authorization for free trade areas and customs unions (GATT Article XXIV), which must eliminate substantially all barriers to trade among their members. A possible explanation for this exception, as suggested above, is that it allows nations a way to reduce the free rider problem that arises under the most-favored-nation obligation in a way that does not seriously undermine the results of multilateral negotiations or create too great a danger of trade diversion.

Quotas are prohibited in the system (GATT Article XI) with a few exceptions. The most important exceptions relate to quotas in connection with balance-of-payments crises (GATT Article XII) and as part of safeguard actions (GATT Article XIX). Both uses of quotas are supposed to be temporary. The logic of these exceptions would take us afield; suffice it to say that the use of quotas is much more limited than the use of nondiscriminatory tariffs.

For many years domestic subsidies were unconstrained in the system, save for the introduction of a new subsidy that frustrated market access expectations under a tariff commitment.[7] The WTO Subsidies Code and Agriculture Agreement introduce a number of additional disciplines on subsidies, but the use of subsidies remains fairly widespread in the WTO, especially in the agricultural sector.

Regulatory protection is handled in a complicated fashion, initially through a national treatment obligation (GATT Article III) and now through the broader WTO Agreement on Technical Barriers to Trade and Agreement on the Application of Sanitary and Phytosanitary Measures. Roughly speaking, regulatory discrimination among or against foreign firms is prohibited, as are regulatory measures that have an unnecessary protective component as described earlier. My hypothetical regulation requiring a particular flame retardant would violate several provisions of the technical barriers code, for example.[8] Regulations that are genuinely necessary to nonprotectionist regulatory objectives are allowed under the system.[9]

This patchwork of obligations, in a concededly crude fashion, channels protection into the policy instruments that do the least harm. The recent "beef hormones" dispute between the United States and the European Union illustrates its operation. Europe affords a considerable amount of protection to its beef industry through tariffs and farm subsidies. Its beef industry is also eligible for "special safeguard" protection should imports of beef surge. All of these measures are in accordance with WTO law.[10] Yet when Europe affords additional protection to its beef producers through a regulation that prohibits the importation of hormone-fed beef from abroad, it violates WTO law unless it can show that the prohibition is a legitimate public health measure bearing a rational relationship to a scientific risk assessment.[11]

Whether or not one agrees with the application of the rules to the hormones dispute, its underlying logic is to insist that Europe protect its beef industry through policy instruments that do less harm than regulatory protection does. Under the European hormone regulation, exporters wishing to do business with Europe must expend resources to keep track of animals that are hormone free, and additional resources to certify them as such on exportation. The resulting cost increases are considerable and greatly hamper exports from nations like the United States where hormones are allowed. Such protection creates the potentially large deadweight losses noted earlier and can also frustrate market access expectations associated with tariff negotiations. Unless the regulation has some legitimate regulatory benefits that can justify its protectionist consequences—rightly or wrongly the WTO found it does not—the regulation is inefficient protection. Surplus in the system will be greater, and trade negotiations will result in more credible and thus more valuable commitments, if protection can be directed into more transparent and less costly policy instruments.

The political economy explanation for the creation of such a system need not detain us. It likely lies, in part, in the insight that political officials prefer to undertake redistribution (here protection of domestic firms) in a way that minimizes the overall loss of surplus. The smaller is the loss of surplus from redistribution, the more will remain for officials to bestow on their constituents to gain political support.[12] Recognizing this fact, savvy politicians can maximize their joint political welfare by designing trade agreements that preserve as much surplus as possible conditional on the level of market access that each nation promises to others. Related, it is in the interest of all officials that they have the capacity to make credible market access commitments, and thus that they disable themselves from using potentially protectionist policy instruments in a way that would amount to reneging on the bargain.

Efficient Protection in Services Markets

With perhaps a few rare exceptions, units of services do not pass through customs or otherwise cross the border in a fashion that allows them to be counted and taxed. This fact dramatically alters the options available to governments that wish to protect their service providers against foreign competition; it implies that border measures such as tariffs and quotas will rarely be available to protect service industries.

This feature of trade in services can make protection more difficult to impose. For example, it is exceedingly difficult to prevent a citizen in one country from dialing into a telecommunications network located abroad or from seeking a legal opinion via the mails or e-mail from a foreign solicitor. For a government to limit such cross-border supply of services—mode 1 of services trade under the General Agreement on Trade in Services—will often require such extraordinary efforts at interdiction that they will not be worth the effort.[13] It is also exceedingly difficult for one nation to prevent its citizens traveling abroad from consuming services offered for sale in a foreign market (mode 2 under GATS).

Substantial services trade usually cannot occur, however, unless the foreign service provider establishes a legal presence in the market of the services consumer (mode 3 under GATS). The banking customer wants a local bank for certain services that require person-to-person contact, such as large withdrawals, certified checks, or safe deposit services. The bank itself wants a local presence to enable it to evaluate better the soundness of loan applicants. The insurance customer wants a local agent for claims service, and the insurer wants a local presence to guard against insurance fraud and overinsurance that might create excessive moral hazard. The telecommunications customer wants local access and technical support. The customer for legal services wants someone who can appear in court or file papers before an agency. And so on.

Not only is legal presence necessary for trade to occur in many instances, but foreign service suppliers will often want to staff their local offices with their own nationals, at least at the higher levels of management, and at a minimum during the start-up phase of the business when initial organization and hiring decisions are made. Thus trade will often require the physical presence of foreign nationals (mode 4 under GATS), at least on a temporary basis.

One important aspect of trade in modes 3 and 4 can make it less vulnerable to protectionist pressures: the hiring by foreign service establishments of domestic nationals, sometimes quite a high percentage of the work force. The rhetoric of "job loss" frequently heard with respect to trade in goods will be dampened here.

Protectionist pressures, however, remain. And the importance of a commercial presence and the presence of foreign natural persons provides the importing nation with tools to restrict trade in services even if the border measures used in goods markets are unavailable. All of the regulatory tools that govern domestic service providers—licensing and prudential regulations, network access restrictions, restrictions on ownership form and structure—can potentially be invoked to disadvantage foreign service providers. When these tools are blended with immigration restrictions, barriers to foreign access can quickly become insurmountable.

In devising rules in this area, GATS negotiators face the same challenges as the GATT negotiators before them—to ensure that unexpected protective policy changes do not undermine market access expectations, to reduce the transaction costs of negotiations by encouraging nations to use fewer instruments of protection and to emphasize those that are transparent and predictable in their effects, and to channel the remaining protection in services markets into the relatively less wasteful policy instruments. In the remaining discussion I tentatively inquire how well GATS is performing that function so far and what more can be done. A comprehensive survey of all of the issues in every sector is impossible, so I proceed in two stages: I discuss the overall architecture of the General Agreement on Trade in Services without regard to sectoral issues, and then discuss issues of particular importance to trade in legal services.[14]

The Structure of Protection under GATS

In contrast to GATT, GATS makes no direct reference to tariffs or quantitative border measures, a reflection of the minimal role that traditional instruments of protection in goods markets play in services markets. But under GATS, like GATT, members are free to make, or not to make, market access commitments respecting particular types of services. In addition, certain disciplines apply whether or not market access commitments have been made in a given sector. Here I consider the major features of this system, in each case asking the question whether the rules encourage efficient protection.

MOST-FAVORED-NATION OBLIGATION AND EXCEPTIONS.   GATS contains a most-favored-nation obligation in Article II. This obligation applies to all services sectors, including those not covered by market access commitments. The most-favored-nation commitment in GATS is weaker than in GATT, however, because GATS permitted members to schedule exceptions to it on a one-shot basis, subject to a ten-year sunset provision. Aside from these scheduled exceptions, GATS Article V further allows members to negotiate preferential access agreements akin to customs unions and free trade areas as long as they have "substantial sectoral coverage." This condition would seem easier to satisfy than the GATT Article XXIV requirement that customs unions and free trade areas eliminate barriers on "substantially all the trade" in goods between the parties. Finally, Article VII of GATS permits an important form of derogation from the most-favored-nation obligation in the form of mutual recognition agreements.[15] For example, such an agreement might exempt the financial services exporters of each party to the agreement from the prudential regulation of the other on the grounds that home-country regulation is sufficient. Plainly, the parties to these agreements can confer significant cost advantages on their respective service providers relative to providers from nations that are not entitled to mutual recognition.[16]

The wisdom of this structure, with its comparatively weaker commitment to the most-favored-nation principle, is difficult to assess. As indicated earlier, most-favored-nation obligations help to protect the value of trade commitments by disabling the parties to an agreement from giving subsequent and more favorable treatment to third parties. They also eliminate the deadweight costs of trade diversion that will occur if less efficient sources of supply are given market access on more favorable terms. They do so at a price, however, by creating a free rider problem and associated strategic behavior during the negotiation process. For this reason they may not always be beneficial.

As for the ability of the GATS system to protect the value of concessions against unexpected discrimination in favor of third parties, the requirement that nations schedule MFN exceptions plainly makes such discrimination more predictable than it otherwise would be (as will the sunset provision, assuming it is enforced effectively). Likewise, perhaps the memberships of preferential arrangements that are negotiated under GATS will parallel those of the ones in place for goods markets (the European Union, the North American Free Trade Agreement, and so on), and thus be fairly predictable as well. The emergence of bilateral mutual recognition agreements may be harder to forecast, but some comfort may be taken from the fact that Article VII requires that other nations be given an opportunity to negotiate for recognition as well. It also stipulates that mutual recognition agreements must not create discrimination in the application of service market regulations or a "disguised restriction" on trade in services. Plausibly, then, GATS members enjoy reasonable assurance that preferences given to others will not undermine the commitments that they have received.

But the opportunities for discrimination in GATS do raise concerns about trade diversion. It is very difficult to know whether the right balance has been struck, and whether GATS is properly more agnostic about the most-favored-nation obligation than the GATT. Perhaps the growth in WTO membership to more than 130 nations makes the free rider issue more acute than it was in 1947 when the original GATT was drafted. Or perhaps the free rider problem is greater in GATS because certain measures that have helped to address it in GATT—such as across-the-board formulaic tariff cuts—are difficult to adapt to services markets where tariffs are unimportant.[17] But a convincing assessment of the efficiency of this aspect of the system must plainly wait until any patterns of discrimination in the system have emerged and can be studied empirically.

MARKET ACCESS COMMITMENTS.   When a member undertakes market access commitments in a particular service sector, it must schedule all of the market access restrictions that it wishes to retain. These are defined in GATS Article XVI to include limitations on the number of service providers (by the use of numerical quotas, monopolies, exclusive service providers, or the requirements of an economic needs test); limitations on the total value of services transactions; limitations on the total number of services operations or on the total quantity of service output; limitations on the number of natural persons that may be employed in a particular service sector or that a service provider may employ; measures that restrict or require specific types of legal entity or joint venture through which a service supplier may supply a service; and limitations on the participation of foreign capital.

Plainly, these measures can hamper the ability of foreign service providers to compete with domestic providers, and a requirement that they be scheduled serves to protect market access expectations in the sectors where concessions have been negotiated. But the deadweight costs of these various types of restrictions may differ considerably. For example, a limitation on the total quantity of service output—an output quota—applicable to foreign firms or perhaps to all firms (with the established domestic firms filling most of the quota as first movers), or a limitation on the total number of service providers, probably has deadweight costs quite analogous to those associated with quotas in goods markets. Marginal consumers are priced out of the market because of elevated prices, some inefficient substitution of domestic production for foreign production occurs, rent-seeking expenditures are made in pursuit of protection, quota races may occur, and some trade diversion may arise depending on how quota rights are allocated.

Other types of restrictions can have additional types of deadweight costs. Limitations on the employment of natural persons, for example, may lead not only to the costs noted earlier but also to an inefficient shift toward capital-intensive technology for service provision. Requirements that service providers enter joint ventures with domestic nationals may force firms to be structured in ways that raise the marginal costs of production for the foreign provider and lead directly to an additional deadweight loss.

These observations suggest that the various market access limitations are unlikely to be equivalent in their welfare consequences. Presently, however, GATS treats all market access limitations equally as long as they are scheduled. Just as GATT seems to encourage efficient protection in goods markets, GATS could do more to channel market access restrictions into particular instruments based on an assessment of those that tend to do the least damage.

NATIONAL TREATMENT OBLIGATIONS.   National treatment obligations are handled in GATS much like market access restrictions: members need not commit to national treatment at all, but if they do make market access commitments in a particular sector, they must schedule all of the limitations on national treatment that they wish to retain (GATS Article XVII). Likewise, there are no constraints on the manner in which national treatment may be withheld. Any form of discrimination in favor of domestic suppliers is permissible in principle as long as it is scheduled. These rules contrast markedly with those of the GATT, where pursuant to Article III any policy that denies national treatment on like products is prohibited.[18]

This fundamental difference between GATT and GATS is unavoidable: a denial of national treatment—as in the licensing process, or in taxation, or in the details of regulatory supervision—will commonly be the most easily administered protective instrument in services markets. Tariffs generally will not work as noted, and the sorts of quantitative limits and investment constraints that GATS deems "market access restrictions" may be inadequate or too difficult to implement.

In the face of these difficulties, the first task is to ensure that departures from national treatment do not undermine the market access expectations associated with negotiated concessions. The requirement that national treatment limitations be scheduled serves this end.

But as in the case of the market access restrictions, measures that deny national treatment can have radically different welfare consequences. A discriminatory tax on services transactions with foreign providers might be the rough equivalent, in its welfare effects, of a nondiscriminatory tariff in goods markets. By contrast, a measure that requires foreign service providers to expend extra resources to establish their safety, soundness, or quality, and that is not essential to the domestic regulatory goals in question, can readily convert the transfer payment that a tax system generates into a deadweight loss. As with the market access restrictions discussed earlier, GATS could do more to channel the denial of national treatment for protective purposes into less destructive avenues.

To be sure, this problem sometimes takes care of itself. Consider two measures, both of which achieve equivalent levels of protection for domestic suppliers. One does so through a tax that raises revenue for the government, and the other does so through a discriminatory regulation that raises the costs of foreign suppliers wastefully. Most governments will probably prefer the former method to the latter, even absent any legal inducement to select it. Similarly, governments might at times prefer to use quantitative market access limitations rather than wasteful regulations because they can confer quota rents on foreign suppliers, making market access more valuable to them and thereby enabling the importing nation to obtain larger concessions in return.

The difficulty with this self-correction mechanism is that it may not always work. Revenue-raising protective devices may be impractical, as may be quantitative limits on service providers or transactions. And left to their own devices, national regulators may be largely oblivious to the different welfare consequences of particular instruments, especially if foreigners bear the burden of wasteful measures. Consequently, there is something to be gained by codifying principles that discourage unnecessarily wasteful protection.

CONSTRAINTS ON FACIALLY NONDISCRIMINATORY DOMESTIC REGULATION. Facially nondiscriminatory regulations can have a disparate impact on foreign suppliers and thus have a protective effect. WTO rules for goods markets have responded with technical barriers codes that impose a number of important obligations. These rules require, for example, that regulators use performance standards rather than design standards where feasible; that they employ the least trade-restrictive means necessary to achieve their objectives; that they rely on international standards where possible; and that they comply with a variety of notice, transparency, and publication requirements.[19]

The limited GATS counterpart to these technical barriers agreements is Article VI. Although it contains some due process requirements, most of its obligations are quite soft. Article VI simply provides that the Council on Trade in Services should establish bodies to develop greater discipline on matters such as transparency and least-restrictive-means requirements. Much remains to be done if the regulatory disciplines in service sectors pursuant to Article VI are to approach the rigor of the goods market commitments under the technical barriers agreements.[20]

Although GATS Article VI is far weaker than the corresponding obligations in goods markets, it is not clear whether GATS should be tightened to the point that its generic obligations are comparable. One feature of the technical barriers agreements—a tight national treatment obligation on all matters of tax and regulatory policy—is unlikely to be appropriate in services markets as long as some protection must survive for political reasons. Is it possible that facially nondiscriminatory regulations might also constitute efficient protection at times?

I suspect that the answer is no. In general, the protection achieved by facially nondiscriminatory regulations results from their disparate impact on the marginal costs of foreign suppliers. Typically, these increases in private marginal cost will be increases in social marginal cost as well (though obviously not to the extent that the resources used in regulatory compliance are earning economic rents). Such protective measures are precisely the ones that tend to be the most wasteful. They are usually dominated by other measures that achieve protection through transfers or otherwise preserve the rents attributable to protection. Further, the protection created by facially nondiscriminatory measures may tend to be less predictable and transparent than the protection associated with transparently discriminatory (and scheduled) limitations on national treatment.

Thus I tentatively conclude that most of the generic disciplines found in the WTO technical barriers agreements for goods might productively be brought into GATS as well. The important caveat relates to national treatment: certain measures that deny national treatment, and that are disclosed and scheduled appropriately under GATS, may represent the most efficient protection available.

SUBSIDIES.   For the reasons given earlier, domestic subsidies may be a comparatively efficient form of protection. They may not appeal politically because they are on-budget expenditures, but if nations are inclined to use them, they may do about as little harm as any other option.

Interestingly, GATS places little constraint on the use of domestic subsidies. Article XVI provides that members who believe themselves to be adversely affected by subsidies may request consultations, and it encourages members to negotiate over subsidy rules, but it does not create any rules. If a member negotiates a market access commitment in a service sector, however, and then the importing nation introduces a new and unexpected subsidy program that frustrates market access expectations, the exporting member has recourse to dispute settlement with a "nonviolation nullification or impairment" claim (GATS Article XXIII).

This structure appears consistent with the idea that subsidies may often be efficient protection. The nonviolation claim protects expectations under negotiated concessions against erosion by unexpected changes in subsidy policy, and members are otherwise free to use domestic subsidies more or less at will.

A Closer Look: Trade in Legal Services

Although generic principles can assist in structuring protection in all services markets, sector-specific clarification is helpful. Some clarification is provided in the sector-specific annexes to GATS, and some has been developed in later negotiations, but much remains to be done.

To illustrate how further guidance might be useful, I consider some of the issues that arise with trade in legal services. The WTO has recently released a survey of the major trading obstacles in this area, dividing them into market access restrictions, national treatment restrictions, and barriers attributable to domestic (nondiscriminatory) regulation.[21]

MARKET ACCESS RESTRICTIONS.   According to the WTO secretariat, the most common market access restrictions in legal markets are nationality requirements (prohibitions on the practice of certain types of law by noncitizens), restrictions on the movement of natural persons (generally immigration related), and restrictions on the legal form of entities permitted to do legal work. Important differences can exist among them from a welfare standpoint.

Nationality requirements are typically justified on the premise that the lawyer is in some way performing a "governmental function." Such claims are largely frivolous. There is no reason why a foreign national cannot certify a signature as a notary, for example, or appear in court and argue a case on behalf of a client. These restrictions should be understood for the most part as rather bald protection. Yet as protection goes, it may be reasonably efficient. If few lawyers will go to the trouble of changing their citizenship in order to practice abroad, expenditures to overcome this barrier may be minimal, and the only important deadweight costs will be the usual costs of protection.

Of course, depending on their reach, nationality restrictions can all but eliminate the importation of legal services. If a lesser degree of protection is desired, immigration restrictions may be a reasonable measure. A system of permanent entry visas for legal personnel, limited in quantity to some desired number, should function much like a quota in its welfare consequences. But one can also imagine immigration restrictions that create greater deadweight losses—if natural persons who supply legal services are limited to short stays in the importing country, for example, much may be wasted on the transaction costs of revolving personnel. And the ability of a single lawyer to build human capital in the form of a lasting client relationship, including close familiarity with the client's problems, may be compromised, leading to a further increase in costs if the lawyer can remain competitive at all.

Restrictions on legal form, such as a prohibition on incorporation, can also be problematic. The rationale for such limitations is questionable. If limited liability raises concerns about judgment-proof practitioners who cannot be penalized for malpractice, for example, mandatory insurance or bonding rules would seem a more sensible response. Or if the concern is for the existence of nonlawyer equity investors that would somehow distort the integrity of legal advice or compromise confidentiality, the sophisticated consumers of international legal services should act as an effective market check on firms that perform badly in this manner, without the need for any mandatory regulation that raises the cost of capital (more on these issues below).

Further, the practical effect of restrictions on form may be to prohibit the entry of foreign firms governed by different rules about legal form at home. The potential for significant trade diversion then arises if the established firms in some important trading nations will be excluded. And to avoid complete exclusion, some firms may disintegrate their operations and establish separate entities that cannot take advantage of the economies of larger firm practice. Then the source of the protective effect is an uneconomical increase in the marginal costs of foreign service suppliers.

NATIONAL TREATMENT LIMITATIONS.   The WTO secretariat notes three
principal barriers to trade in legal services that can be characterized as a
denial of national treatment. The first concerns prohibitions on partnership between foreign and domestic lawyers and related restrictions on the
hiring of locally licensed lawyers by foreign firms; the second involves restrictions on the use of firm names by foreign entities; the third involves
various kinds of residency requirements.

Restrictions on partnership between domestic and foreign lawyers
often flow from a more general prohibition on partnerships between lawyers and nonlawyers. A foreign lawyer, who lacks the qualifications necessary to practice domestic law in the host country, may be a "nonlawyer"
for purposes of these rules. This policy is typically defended as necessary
to protect consumers against the unauthorized practice of law by unqual-
ified individuals, or to avoid a situation in which a partnership between
lawyers and nonlawyers might lead the lawyers to compromise their professional judgment. Neither defense seems terribly plausible. Powerful re-
putational concerns militate against entrusting clients to incompetents (as
may the possibility of malpractice actions), particularly in firms that serve
sophisticated clients seeking legal advice on international matters. And if
there is any tendency to give legal tasks to nonlawyers imprudently, certainly the widespread use of para-professionals by large law firms affords
ample opportunity for that to happen without the presence of foreign attorneys in the firm. Likewise, it is totally unclear why a partnership with
a foreign lawyer would produce an environment in which the lawyer was
encouraged to give bad legal advice or representation, to the detriment of
the firms' clients and reputation.

The more likely explanation for these rules is a desire on the part of
the local bar to protect its rents against erosion by making it more costly
for clients to seek out foreign law firms for advice on international matters. It is noteworthy that the rules do not seem to prohibit a domestic law
firm from hiring a foreign lawyer on a salaried, nonpartnership basis to
serve the firm's clients, leaving to the firm and its clients the task of ensuring that no "unauthorized practice of law" results. Domestic firms may
thus present themselves as full service organizations, with in-house expertise on foreign law and salaried foreign lawyers on staff if necessary, while
foreign firms are denied the same opportunity. Likewise, foreign firms
with little reputation in the local market are disabled from acquiring an
established domestic firm, which may be the most efficient form of foreign entry.

In short, these measures appear to be a classic "raising rivals' cost" strategy. The most efficient way to provide full-service legal representation for clients operating in global markets may well be an agglomeration between an existing foreign firm and an existing domestic firm. Rules that prevent this agglomeration raise the costs of legal services across the board, but do so more for foreign firms than for domestic firms and thus can increase the profits of the latter. Such measures, of course, can be quite unfortunate in their welfare effects.

Restrictions on the ability of foreign firms to use the names by which they do business in the home country also have obvious protective consequences. Prominent international firms familiar to potential clients may be forced to change their name when establishing a presence in a new market, raising the costs of search for potential clients that might otherwise retain their services on the basis of their international reputation, and perhaps necessitating costly advertising efforts to inform potential clients of the firm's true pedigree.

Residency requirements, though nominally neutral in their application to all attorneys, can plainly disadvantage foreign lawyers disproportionately. Prior residency requirements, which require a lawyer to reside in the host jurisdiction for some time before a license to practice can be granted, can burden foreign lawyers with the costs of working in a less productive capacity while fulfilling the residency requirement. This is not only a disincentive to the entry of the foreign lawyer, but a deadweight cost, to the degree that the foreign lawyer has a higher marginal product as a practicing lawyer than while waiting to become one.[22] Permanent residency requirements can also impose considerably greater burdens on foreign lawyers. To the degree that they necessitate the forfeiture of home country residency by the foreign lawyer, they may create considerable personal dislocation and may also affect the lawyer's ability to remain fully qualified under home-country law. And if the lawyer instead maintains dual permanent residency, the cost increment can be substantial as well.

In short, the measures identified by the WTO secretariat as important limitations on national treatment not only restrict entry by foreign lawyers, but also raise their costs of doing business. The magnitude of these cost increases is, of course, an empirical issue, but one cannot help but wonder whether other protective devices (such as quantitative market access restrictions, discriminatory taxes, or licensing fees) that deny national treatment, might afford better options for protection than the ones now prevalent.

DOMESTIC REGULATION.   Many of the most important obstacles to trade in legal services are posed by nondiscriminatory domestic regulations. The WTO secretariat emphasizes three types of regulations as potentially important: qualification requirements for the practice of host-country law, licensing requirements for foreign legal consultants, and the prohibition of "multidisciplinary practice" law firms.

Although it is unclear why the market alone is inadequate to police incompetence in the legal profession, regulatory qualification requirements seem to be ubiquitous (at least for the practice of host-country law), and it is unlikely that nations will move away from them any time soon. Consumer protection justifications are generally offered in support of them, but it is equally clear that they serve as entry barriers that tend to protect existing lawyers from competition.

Qualification requirements typically include rules about the length of time that must be spent studying law and the degree that must be obtained, the period of apprenticeship that must be spent thereafter before full admission to the bar, and the need to pass a professional examination. They do not disfavor foreign aspirants to host-country practice per se, since foreign nationals can always obtain qualification in the same way as a domestic national (if the immigration laws allow it). But these rules are nevertheless perceived as having a disproportionate impact on foreign lawyers who have already qualified for practice in their home country. The process of qualifying abroad renders some of the qualification requirements in the host country unnecessary, runs the argument.

The response to this argument, of course, is that legal systems differ. The fact that a lawyer is qualified in one country in no way ensures that the lawyer can do an adequate job of practicing the law of another country. Indeed, taking the United States as an example, a lawyer's qualification to practice in one state does not entitle the lawyer to practice in another state automatically. And the differences between national legal systems are often far greater than the differences between the legal systems in the various American states.

But this response is inadequate. It seems most unlikely, for example, that a lawyer qualified to practice law in Europe and whose English is competent needs a from-the-ground-up American legal education in order to provide competent services as an American lawyer. An attorney familiar with European competition policy, for example, can learn the differences in American antitrust law easily. If the U.S. jurisdiction requires an American law degree as a precondition to entry into practice, such a requirement indeed seems out of proportion to the pursuit of any genuine consumer protection objective.

Unnecessary requirements that force foreign lawyers to waste months or years in superfluous educational pursuits rather than employing their labor productively produce large deadweight costs. Protection of domestic attorneys could likely be accomplished more efficiently through quantitative limits on entry or discriminatory licensing fees that transfer rents rather than destroy them. Host countries might argue that some sort of qualification check on foreign lawyers is necessary to protect against incompetence. If so, the less burdensome alternative is probably an examination process that tests the foreign lawyer on whatever subjects are deemed necessary, without forcing the lawyer to invest months or years in a domestic curriculum or apprenticeship. Examinations could include oral components that test for spoken language and advocacy competence.

Mutual recognition agreements might facilitate the reduction of entry barriers for foreign lawyers. Indeed, GATS Article VII both authorizes and encourages them. The risk of such agreements, however, is trade diversion and its attendant deadweight costs. One might question whether they are really desirable for this reason: if a lawyer has qualified abroad and can pass rigorous written and oral examinations in host-country law that ensure competence, should that not be enough? Why should entry be limited to the nationals of countries entitled to "mutual recognition"? And if the rate of new entry would be politically intolerable if qualification exams were open to all comers, less costly instruments of protection, such as discriminatory licensing fees, might be used to restrict it to acceptable levels.

Compared with the qualification requirements for the practice of host-country law, the licensing requirements for foreign legal consultants (who simply advise clients on the law of their home country or perhaps a third country) are typically much less burdensome. Indeed, they are de minimis if the advice is provided across the border, since such advice is almost impossible to interdict. But nontrivial obstacles to licensing occasionally do arise when the foreign legal consultant wishes to establish a presence in the host country. Some nations require foreign legal consultants to pass a professional examination. Others require that they have a certain number of years of practice experience before they can obtain a license.

Although these requirements need not be terribly burdensome, they are difficult to defend. It seems sufficient to require that an attorney who offers advice on the law of a particular nation be qualified to do so under the laws of that nation; for another country to insist that additional qualifications are necessary seems highly suspect. These additional obligations will entail some compliance costs that will unnecessarily raise the costs of foreign legal consultants and advantage domestic attorneys who can generally provide advice on foreign law without qualifying as a "foreign legal consultant." Again, if some perceived need to restrict competition from foreign legal consultants is present, other protective devices may dominate.

A number of countries (including the United States) have rules providing that lawyers cannot combine and share profits with nonlawyers. Thus they cannot enter partnerships with other professionals (such as accountants) and cannot sell equity shares in their firms to the public. These rules are sometimes referred to as a prohibition on multidisciplinary practice or partnership. The prohibition becomes a trade issue because a number of jurisdictions do not have it. Firms based in a jurisdiction that permits multidisciplinary practice can find themselves foreclosed from entry into a foreign market that does not permit it.

Multidisciplinary practice restrictions are usually defended as necessary to ensure the independent professional judgment of lawyers and, perhaps, to ensure the protection of client confidences. Neither justification is convincing, however, and scholars increasingly condemn these rules as protectionist folly—doubly so because they may actually reduce lawyers' incomes in the end.[23] Just as clients may wish to deal with firms that provide "one-stop shopping" for advice on domestic and foreign law, firms may develop considerable efficiencies in providing clients with a mix of legal, accounting, actuarial, economic consulting, and other services at a single location. Where the market would create such entities but for legal prohibitions against them, one can infer that the transaction costs to clients of securing these services independently are considerable and that their integration into a single firm is efficient.[24] Likewise, if the legal judgment of such firms were inferior or if confidential information were inadequately protected by them, sophisticated clients would not retain them.

Perhaps the argument against multidisciplinary practice rests on the premise that unsophisticated clients need protection from it, but this too rings hollow. Agglomerations of accountants, lawyers, and the like are unlikely to be the law firm of choice in a slip-and-fall case—virtually all of the clients of these firms will be sophisticated. And to the degree that lawyers in these firms can get away with providing shoddy legal services to the few unsophisticated clients, there are innumerable other ways for them to do so without entering multidisciplinary practice. Given the availability of close substitutes for any particular form of shoddiness, it is odd to prohibit multidisciplinary practice when it has obvious potential benefits to an important class of clients and is permitted without apparent ill effect in a number of prominent jurisdictions.

Another argument that is occasionally advanced against multidisciplinary practice rests on the relatively higher degree of market concentration in accountancy services. If accountants can merge with lawyers, the argument runs, only a few huge law firms will exist, and the sector will behave noncompetitively. This argument also seems quite weak. There is simply no reason to believe that the large accounting firms will affiliate with the bulk of the lawyers in any jurisdiction. And should the legal fees charged by lawyers affiliated with large accounting firms rise above their costs, new entrants and established nonaffiliated firms would be there to undercut them.

Accordingly, a strong argument can be made for the elimination of restrictions on multidisciplinary practice quite apart from any effect that they may have on international trade in legal services. Improved market access for multidisciplinary foreign firms would be icing on the cake. Any politically necessary protection against foreign competition might be supplied more efficiently through policy instruments that do not force uneconomical increases in the marginal costs of multidisciplinary services.

Conclusion

Many of the observations in this chapter about the relative merits of alternative instruments of protection are somewhat conjectural, to be sure. Far more information is needed before definitive judgments can be made. Likewise, the policy instruments that are discussed in the chapter are only a subset of all of those available to policymakers, especially in services markets. The analysis here is intended to be illustrative rather than comprehensive.

Nevertheless, even with this tentative and incomplete beginning, one can confidently say that instruments of protection are not perfect substitutes from a welfare standpoint. The trading community can gain from channeling protection into its least harmful manifestations and has already done so to a considerable degree in goods markets. Much less has been accomplished so far in services markets, in part because negotiated liberalization is so recent. I hope that I have suggested some considerations pertinent to the task of improving things.

Notes

1. For a discussion of why regulatory protectionism should be so disfavored in goods markets under WTO law, see Alan O. Sykes, "Regulatory Protectionism and the Law of International Trade," *University of Chicago Law Review*, vol. 66 (1999), pp. 1–46.

2. See, for example, Peter B. Kenen, *The International Economy* (Prentice-Hall, 1985), pp. 175–77.

3. See, for example, Richard Lipsey, "The Theory of Customs Unions: A General Survey," *Economics Journal*, vol. 70 (1960), p. 496.

4. This conclusion assumes that not all tariff revenue is dissipated by rent seeking in pursuit of it. If it were, the additional revenue raised by a nondiscriminatory tariff would be wasted anyway.

5. See, for example, Andrew Caplin and Kala Krishna, "Tariffs and the Most-Favored-Nation Clause: A Game-Theoretic Approach," *Seoul Journal of Economics*, vol. 1 (1988), p. 267; Warren F. Schwartz and Alan O. Sykes, "Toward a Positive Theory of the Most-Favored-Nation Clause and Its Exceptions in the WTO/GATT System," *International Review of Law & Economics*, vol. 16 (1996), p. 27; Kyle Bagwell and Robert Staiger, "Multilateral Trade Negotiations, Bilateral Opportunism, and the Rules of GATT," mimeo, Columbia University and University of Wisconsin, March 2000.

6. See Schwartz and Sykes, "Toward a Positive Theory of the Most-Favored-Nation Clause."

7. See, for example, "EEC—Payments and Subsidies Paid to Processors and Producers of Oilseeds and Related Animal-Feed Proteins," 37th Supp. BISD 86 (1991), GATT Panel Report adopted January 25, 1990.

8. Article 2.2 of the agreement condemns measures that create unnecessary obstacles to trade. Article 2.8 specifically condemns measures that unjustifiably employ design standards (use a particular flame retardant) rather than performance standards (a flammability standard).

9. For a fuller discussion, see Sykes, "Regulatory Protectionism," and Alan O. Sykes, *Product Standards in Internationally Integrated Goods Markets* (Brookings, 1995).

10. See Sykes, "Regulatory Protectionism," pp. 2–3.

11. See WTO, "EC Measures Concerning Meat and Meat Products (Hormones)," Appellate Body Report 1997-4 (January, 16, 1998).

12. See Sam Peltzman, "Toward a More General Theory of Regulation," *Journal of Law and Economics*, vol. 19 (1976), p. 211; Gary Becker, "Comment on Peltzman," *Journal of Law and Economics*, vol. 19 (1976), p. 245.

13. See General Agreement on Trade in Services (GATS), Art. 1(2).

14. For a related discussion, see Aaditya Mattoo, "Shaping Future Rules for Trade in Services, Lessons from the GATS," mimeo, World Bank, July 2000.

15. Mutual recognition agreements are also possible in goods sectors pursuant to the technical barriers agreements. Because regulatory measures are so much more central to market access in service sectors, however, their potential impact here is likely greater. On the potential for discrimination to arise through recognition agreements under GATS, see Kalypso Nicolaïdis and Joel Trachtman, "From Policed Regulation to Managed Recognition in GATS," and Americo Beviglia Zampetti, "Market Access through Reciprocal Recognition:

The Promise and Limits of GATS Article VII," both in Pierre Sauvé and Robert Stern, eds., *GATS 2000: New Directions in Services Trade Liberalization* (Brookings, 2000), pp. 24–82 and 283–306, respectively.

16. A more in-depth discussion of these issues may be found in Aaditya Mattoo, "MFN and the GATS," mimeo, World Bank, January 1999.

17. To be sure, various "formulaic" devices might be used to reduce the transaction costs of negotiations in services sectors. For example, model schedules of commitments might be developed to which all nations would adhere unless they scheduled a specific deroga-tion. On the devices for organizing services negotiations and overcoming some of their transaction costs, see Patrick Low and Aaditya Mattoo, "Is There a Better Way? Alternative Approaches to Liberalization under GATS," and Rachel Thompson, "Formula Approaches to Improving GATS Commitments," both in Sauvé and Stern, *GATS 2000*, pp. 449–72 and 473–86, respectively.

18. In both GATS and GATT, of course, exceptions exist for things such as national se-curity concerns and measures necessary to protect public health.

19. See Alan O. Sykes, *Product Standards for Internationally Integrated Goods Markets* (Brookings, 1995).

20. See Geza Feketekuty, "Regulatory Reform and Trade Liberalization in Services," in Sauvé and Stern, eds., *GATS 2000*, pp. 85–111.

21. WTO, "Legal Services: Background Note by the Secretariat," S/C/W/43, July 6, 1998.

22. Here I put to one side the possibility that the private marginal product of lawyers to their clients exceeds the social marginal product of lawyers. This is a genuine issue de-pending upon the type of legal services that the lawyer provides, but no lawyer jokes, please.

23. See Daniel R. Fischel, "Multidisciplinary Practice," mimeo, University of Chicago, February 8, 2000.

24. This is the essential insight in Ronald Coase, "The Nature of the Firm," *Econom-ica*, vol. 4 (1937), p. 386.

COMMENT BY
David W. Leebron

Alan Sykes's chapter on efficient protection focuses on one major aspect of the relationship between efficiency and international trade rules. He asks whether the rules of the World Trade Organization ensure efficient protection, defined as achieving the minimum loss to economic welfare required to attain a politically necessary level of protection. His careful analysis concludes that, for the most part, WTO rules do encourage protection in its most efficient form.

I begin with some general observations about the relationship between efficiency and WTO rulemaking. Efficiency itself is not an articulated norm of the international trading system. The basic mechanism to encourage efficiency is to remove market distortions caused by "unjustified" regulation. This includes not only purely protectionist regulation (tariffs and de jure regulatory discrimination), but also regulation that effectively discriminates (de facto discrimination) in a way unnecessary to achieve legitimate regulatory purposes. Regulatory measures should be tailored closely to legitimate regulatory goals in order to avoid any unnecessary protectionist effect. To put it metaphorically, this tailoring or fit criterion requires that protectionist fat be trimmed from the regulatory meat. Alan Sykes turns his attention to a different norm. He suggests that regulatory fat, in the form of unnecessary and inefficient regulation, be trimmed from a politically necessary protectionist meat. He is undoubtedly right that this is one efficiency-encouraging aspect of the WTO regime, but I would hope, at this late stage of trade liberalization, that it is not the most important. Of late, most of the concern about the WTO has focused on the impact of its norms on domestic regulation, regulation that applies equally to domestic and imported goods.

The WTO, much more than the original General Agreement on Tariffs and Trade (GATT), subjects to review domestic regulations that may not be efficient. Expressed in this way, however, there is a geographic ambiguity in the notion of efficiency. Regulatory regimes that are "one-country" efficient or even multicountry efficient (countries that are members of a free trade area or a customs union, for example) may not be globally efficient. This notion is deeply problematic in a world that, at least nominally, maintains its respect for nation-state sovereignty. Assessing the efficiency of rules within a global context requires examining the cost side of the rules on

a worldwide basis and also somehow amalgamating globally diverse preferences. While I do not think any current WTO rules require that approach,
a globally oriented efficiency norm would. The geographic ambiguity of
the efficiency norm does not undercut the conclusion that removing "unnecessary" protection from domestic regulation will always be a move toward efficiency, both globally and for the importing country. The WTO
discipline on product regulation, for example, makes a significant contribution to achieving regulatory efficiency by requiring the elimination of
any distortions that result from discrimination between domestic and imported products, to the extent that such discriminatory regulation is unnecessary to achieve legitimate regulatory goals.

A more general efficiency norm would go beyond this mere trimming
of unjustified regulatory protection. To some degree, the favoring of international standards in the Agreement on Sanitary and Phytosanitary
Measures and the Agreement on Technical Barriers to Trade suggests a
move toward making efficiency judgments on a global rather than a
purely domestic basis. Yet if the international trade rules are designed to
create such efficiency gains, several kinds of distributive questions will
arise. First, as noted earlier, the globally efficient rules may not be locally
efficient, thus creating national welfare winners and losers. Second, and
more broadly, domestic and international claims will arise concerning the
distribution of those gains and losses. This is a question not of efficiency
but of equity.

Finally, procedural and institutional questions need to be addressed.
Professor Sykes's chapter is fairly abstract. Yet the problem of designing optimal rules is one of dealing with massive uncertainties about preferences,
costs, and benefits. Various regimes, with differing regulatory and geographic scope, may have different potential for achieving true regulatory
efficiency. In short, assuming some regulation is desirable (for example, to
deal with market failures and imperfections), who should regulate? Who
should review regulations for compliance with international trade norms?
Local regulatory authorities or courts may be the best regulators, given
their familiarity with local values. The adoption of international regulatory
norms requires some notion of "subsidiarity" if the best possible regulatory
results are to be achieved.

I turn now to the issue of "efficient protection." As Sykes recognizes,
this is an oxymoron. Protection distorts markets and results in inefficient
allocations of resources and products. Assume that for political reasons a
certain level of protection must be provided to a domestic industry. The

question Sykes asks is this: does the WTO minimize the costs of such protection by encouraging protection in its most efficient form?

This approach raises a serious problem of the second best. Protection itself is inefficient, and numerous other inefficient rules govern an industry. Therefore we really cannot be sure that a move from quotas to tariffs, for example, or from regulatory protection to tariffs, is a move toward greater welfare or efficiency.

For the most part Sykes adopts a static rather than a dynamic analysis. He asks whether some assumed stable form of protection is most efficient. The question we should ask is which forms of protection will, in a dynamic sense, lead ultimately to the least protection and hence the greatest efficiency. He does address the issue in terms of the dynamics of international trade negotiations: the transparency of tariffs and the comparative simplicity of most-favored-nation tariff negotiations (with the caveat of the free rider problem) will lead, he suggests, to greater liberalization. But we also need to examine carefully the dynamic effects of the form of protection on the domestic processes that produce economic protection in the first place. On a static basis tariffs may be more efficient than subsidies, as Sykes suggests, but subsidies are likely to be less politically stable than tariffs. Subsidies require government expenditure, whereas tariffs produce revenues on which the government may become dependent. Thus domestic pressures may help achieve the elimination of subsidies, whereas they are more likely to support the maintenance of tariffs. Similarly, quotas allocated to importers may be undesirable because they create an additional political group (quota owners) interested in maintaining those quotas.

In thinking about the "best" forms of protection, we should adopt a political economy analysis of protection rather than a pure economic analysis. Sykes refers to "politically essential" protectionist goals, but what is politically essential depends on the coalitions that form in favor of and against such protection, and the political and legal processes for enacting and challenging such protection. These will differ for different forms of protection (and for different legal and political processes for enacting and removing protection). We cannot assume that the statically efficient form of protection will be the form that most favors additional liberalization.

The transaction costs and the potential economies of scale of various forms of protection must also be considered. This is perhaps incorporated into the notion of "the amount of protection afforded." For example, the effect of a tariff is not only the percentage levy on the value of the goods, but also the transaction costs of processing and valuing the goods, which might be considerably less if goods entered free of any tariffs or other regulatory procedures. While tariffs have the advantage of not imposing a great barrier against entry (unlike regulatory compliance costs), they have the potential drawback of imposing the same marginal disadvantage regardless of the market share captured. More broadly, exporters can take actions and achieve innovations that would overcome some regulatory barriers. They can exercise political power to change the domestic regulation of their home country. But there is little they can do to reduce tariffs.

Sykes's caution about his general conclusions is well taken. As a theoretical and practical matter, it is difficult to conclude that any form of protection is efficient compared with any other, particularly if we take a dynamic rather than a static approach.

A good deal of his chapter is devoted to trade in services. Services is a complex area, which has raised new challenges for the international trade regime, challenges barely addressed by the General Agreement on Trade in Services (GATS). Because of the complexity of domestic regulatory regimes and the invisibility of services transactions, Sykes is skeptical that tariffication of the protection for services industries could be achieved. I am less skeptical, for two reasons. First, most taxation (at least in industrialized countries) is achieved through reporting mechanisms rather than actual inspection. So just as we can impose income or sales taxes on services transactions, we ought to be able to effectively impose tariffs, which are simply discriminatory taxes. Second, some sectors and some forms of service delivery are not "invisible," and hence could be subjected to tariffs relatively easily. A prime example is international shipping. In the many cases in which the provision of services requires a foreign presence and the use of immigrant employees, a discriminatory employment tax could be substituted for investment, establishment, and immigration barriers.

Sykes is certainly correct that those charged with negotiating and implementing the global trading system would benefit from a more careful analysis of the costs and benefits of different forms of protection for services, and that such analysis ought to be reflected in the structure of legal obligations under GATS. The "best" forms of protection for services might be different than for goods, and might differ from one type of service to another. One potential difference between services and goods is the relative ease with which importing states might be able to impose opaque protective measures. The complex regulatory structure of many services provides numerous opportunities for effective discrimination. Thus it might be desirable to tolerate such measures as long as they are made explicit as part of a scheduled set of commitments (or noncommitments, as the case may be).

Lastly, Sykes makes some remarks about lawyers and legal services. Here he oversimplifies the regulatory challenges posed by professional services. He moves beyond overtly discriminatory legislation to sweep away, in the name of efficiency, numerous if controversial aspects of regulation of legal services. His faith in the market seems complete, discounting the possibility that such regulation may achieve legitimate goals beyond the lawyer-client service relationship. Lawyers are an important part of regulatory structure, and the idea of professionalism incorporates the notion that a lawyer does not, and should not, solely serve the interests of her client. Leaving regulation to the market (that is, the transactions between lawyers and clients) eliminates the opportunity to correct certain externalities that unbridled service to the client might produce. The competence of lawyers is not simply a question of satisfying the demands of the client, but raises additionally issues of fidelity to law and the ideals of professionalism. I do not mean to defend such restrictions as the prohibition on interdisciplinary practice, but I do think the concerns about it cannot be waved off in deference to faith in markets. On the other hand, Sykes is clearly right that many restrictions serve only protectionist purposes, against both international and domestic competition.

One type of professional barrier common in legal services regulation is educational requirements. Sykes concludes that testing could substitute for educational requirements. While I must admit a good deal of self-interest in this question, it is not always the case that the goals of educational requirements can be measured by testing. Part of what goes on in a law school is, I hope, the inculcation of values, a sense of professionalism, and a broad familiarity with domestic legal culture. Limited time for testing makes it unlikely that testing can fully substitute for the educational process. That explains why, to take the bar exam, one must have attended and graduated from law school. Law schools must provide reasonable assurance that the students they graduate have indeed attended class. An educational requirement is akin to a production process method, as opposed to a performance standard. The latter are, as suggested in the international agreements governing goods, to be preferred, but in some cases performance requirements are not adequate substitutes for production requirements.

In sum, Alan Sykes offers a very useful framework for thinking about differing measures of protection and their welfare implications. As usual, he provides a penetrating analysis of economic consequences, while at the same time he is exceedingly careful in the conclusions that can actually be drawn. As he suggests, particularly in the area of services, further analysis and information are needed before conclusions can be reached on the optimal structuring of protection and the international legal agreements that seek to reduce it.

COMMENT BY
Motoshige Itoh

There are many kinds of protectionist policy instruments, including border restrictions, subsidies, and various domestic regulations. Removal of these instruments is desirable from an economic welfare viewpoint, but it is not politically realistic to remove them immediately in the face of political pressures for protection.

In his chapter Alan Sykes considers what WTO rulemaking is necessary to ensure that persistent protective measures cause no greater loss of economic welfare than is necessary to achieve protectionist goals that remain politically essential. For that purpose he introduces the concept of "efficient protection." A protectionist policy instrument is "most efficient" if it causes the least waste of resources, holding constant the amount of protection it affords.

I have difficulty when I apply Professor Sykes's static view to the dynamic process of liberalization. When one compares protectionist measures with respect to the least distortion in resource allocation, one must take into account not only the final static picture but also the process of liberalization and especially the speed of liberalization. Although border restrictions may be less resource wasting than domestic regulations, the removal of unnecessary domestic regulations is far more difficult than reducing border restrictions. The experience of liberalization under GATT is consistent with this point: reduction of border restrictions preceded the removal of various domestic regulations. The Japanese experience is instructive in three respects.

First, reducing border restrictions and removing domestic regulations are often complementary rather than alternative substitutes. The essential point is not whether border restrictions or domestic regulations are less distorting, but which, if removed first, is more effective in helping remove the other. The existing forms of domestic regulations are often the result of tough political struggles among domestic entities: one may call it some kind of political equilibrium among various domestic pressure groups.

Consider the notorious case of Japan's large-scale retail store law, which restricts the entry of large chain stores. This regulation obviously restricts the entry of foreign products as well as the entry of foreign retail stores. Local owners of small shops and large retail stores, both domestic entities, have been struggling to strengthen or weaken the regulation. The form of the regulation observable in the mid-1980s was the result of political equilibrium among these domestic entities. Changing the regulation is difficult without changes from outside to alter the equilibrium—either a new economic environment, macroeconomic change, or the entry of foreign firms that raise their voices to remove the regulation. The voices of domestic large retail stores, as well as consumers, were not enough by themselves to change the Japanese political equilibrium; the entry of foreign firms ("Toyzarus," in particular) was crucial. The lower the border restrictions, the more opportunities there will be for foreign participation in the domestic market and the greater the forces to remove protectionist regulations.

Second, it is far easier to remove border restrictions than to deregulate protective elements of domestic regulations. This is not only because negotiating domestic regulations is hard to do. It is also because identifying protectionist elements in domestic regulations is difficult. As Alan Sykes notes, domestic regulations—although they may protect against foreign firms—can have domestic reasons for their existence other than protection. It is not easy to identify in each regulation how serious the protective effect is. More opportunity for foreign participation through fewer border restrictions will reveal which regulations are, in fact, strongly protective. Trade liberalization under GATT started with the reduction of border restrictions, which actually highlighted the importance of domestic regulations as protectionist policies. It is very difficult to imagine that removal of domestic protectionist regulation preceded removal of border restrictions.

My third point relates to the political power of domestic pressure groups. Alan Sykes seems to assume that protectionist power will be kept at nearly the same level for some time. From this assumption comes his concept of efficient protection. It is important to note, however, that domestic protectionist pressure often weakens as liberalization proceeds. There is a simple economic reason for this. Take, for example, the case of the textile industry in Japan. The share of the industry in the national economy was quite high in the 1970s and in the first half of the 1980s. As a result, the political power of the industry was quite strong at that time. However, increased imports of textile products into Japan during the late 1980s and 1990s reduced the domestic industry's share of employment, output, and income. This made it more and more difficult for the domestic textile industry to maintain political influence, and the Ministry of International Trade and Industry (MITI) finally succeeded in changing long-standing textile policies. Increasing imports by reducing border restrictions contributed to weakening the political influence of the domestic industry.

A similar point comes from the case of agriculture in Japan. The influence of the sector is gradually declining as farmers' share of the population decreases. Various domestic regulations still protect against foreign firms, but these regulations have not attracted much attention, since foreign entry to the agricultural market in Japan is regulated considerably by border regulations. Under these circumstances, the most realistic liberalization scenario for this sector is the following: reduce border restrictions and increase imports first; then, if possible, repeal various protectionist domestic regulations in the face of increasing foreign participation and wait for the political influence of the sector to weaken.

Finally, let me reiterate that I agree with Alan Sykes's point that border restrictions and subsidies are often less distorting protectionist measures than various domestic regulations. If one draws a static picture of "politically efficient protection" under the presence of protectionist pressures, border restrictions and subsidies are less evil than protectionist regulations. However, when one considers the dynamic process and speed of liberalization, one may conclude that reducing border restrictions is far easier than removing protectionist domestic regulations. Reducing border restrictions is often effective in moving the political equilibrium toward deregulation of domestic measures and weakening the political influence of protectionist groups.

F. M. SCHERER

Part Two Summary

The United States and most of the rest of the world have come a long way in removing trade barriers. On this there is general agreement. But much remains to be done. That is where reasonable observers begin to disagree, on both the "how much" and the "how." There is near consensus on the industrial sectors with the greatest opportunities for further liberalization. Agriculture, textiles (because of the continuing Multi-Fibre Agreement restrictions), segments of transportation such as ocean shipping, government procurement, and other parts of the services sector head the list.

Jeffrey Frankel provides estimates, both from his own work and that of others, of the gains in income per capita that have been realized historically through increased trade and, prospectively, that might be achieved from plausible liberalization in the future. From computable general equilibrium (CGE) models, future worldwide gains of roughly $375 billion to $400 billion, or about 1.25 percent of the current world gross domestic product, have been projected. Frankel uses a more encompassing cross-sectional analysis of how trade affects incomes and takes other relevant variables into account. He estimates that a feasible 12 percentage point increase in U.S. imports plus exports as a percentage of GDP could, over a period of thirty years, raise income per capita in the United States by 4 percent.

The enrichment opportunities assumed by these models, as well as those that were not analyzed, come in several flavors. Computable general equilibrium models emphasize the classic allocative efficiency gains from trade (that is, the triangles formed when wedges intrude between demand and supply curves). Since the work of Arnold Harberger in 1954, if not from Alfred Marshall in 1890, economists have known that these "triangle" gains tend to be small.[1] More important, but requiring richer specification and data, are the "rectangles"—the reduction in cost of all traded and trade-impacted goods resulting from greater realization of scale economies, and the shedding of "fat" and rent-seeking outlays as a result of intensified competitive pressure. These are largely ignored by CGE models but are presumably captured by long-run cross-sectional studies like those of Frankel and David Romer.

Probably even more important are the gains that come from trade-induced technological change. One example is the increased specialization of research and development that was anticipated by Adam Smith and the increased likelihood or speed of breakthroughs when parallel R&D paths are pursued in numerous countries. Jeffrey Sachs argues that the gains from the more rapid advance and diffusion of technology are the most important. This is no surprise to some of us who have been studying the economics of technological change for several decades, but it is gratifying to see that the message is finally spreading into the disciplines of international trade and economic development.

Ignored in all the quantitative estimates are the benefits of increased product variety facilitated by trade. The gains to consumers enjoying a vast diversity of food, automobiles, home entertainment, and health care products, facilitated by the international division of labor, are plainly substantial. Economists are beginning to make progress in estimating their magnitudes,[2] but the new methodologies have not yet had much impact on quantitative international trade research.

Although it is clear that further payoffs from trade (and investment) liberalization are achievable, one can harbor doubts about the estimated magnitudes. Richard Cooper, for example, questions whether the measure emphasized by Frankel—imports plus exports divided by GDP—focuses properly on the smaller subset of tradable goods and services susceptible to liberalization. To his caveat I would add my own. Estimates from crossnational studies may be upward-biased for a nation like the United States, whose vast internal market offers richer opportunities for the division of labor and realization of scale economies than do much smaller national markets, and whose close proximity to the best-practice technological frontier means that productivity gains from improved technology come harder than for nations still operating some distance from the frontier. Despite these caveats, I believe that Frankel's estimates are not implausible, in part because they leave out some of the more important benefits from increased international trade.

Alan Winters emphasizes another opportunity: the gains that come when transitory or permanent emigration moves workers to locations where their productivity, all else equal, is higher than in their home nations. This applies not only to routine production activities but also to science and technology. The United States currently enjoys important benefits from the inflow of talented individuals supplementing its indigenous supply of software writers. Despite rapidly rising salaries in recent years, U.S. writers of software have been forthcoming in insufficient numbers to meet demand. Over a long period the United States has been blessed by an influx of immigrants who have made scientific contributions disproportionate to their share of the U.S. scientific and engineering work force.[3] These realities have implications for removing barriers to movement in what Adam Smith humorously called "the human luggage."[4] Currently debated is the question of increasing the number of H1B work visas and the possibility of making them permanent rather than temporary.

Granting that the United States and other nations can realize appreciable benefits from further trade (and immigration and investment) liberalization, the question remains: what strategies should be pursued to capture them? In his chapter Alan Sykes reminds us that we live in a second-best world—one in which all barriers to trade and mobility can scarcely be eliminated. He argues that the restrictions allowed to remain should be steered in least-distorting directions and that, once policies are chosen, they should be enforced assiduously. On the enforcement side, serious problems have arisen with the World Trade Organization's system. Uncorrected violations of the trading rules are punished by retaliatory tariffs that can hurt the offended nation as much as the offender. (Compensation, that is, agreements to relax some trade barriers in compensation for retaining other WTO-offending barriers, is used rarely.) Sykes suggests that adding fines and moral suasion to the arsenal of corrective weapons could lead to more effective enforcement of WTO decisions.

With respect to barrier removal strategies, Sykes argues forcefully in favor of tariffs over quotas—an emphasis consistent with the most recent GATT rules—and for greater transparency through publicly disclosed scheduling of the barriers that remain. I would like to have seen in his analysis more critical scrutiny of tariffized quotas, which have been used by the

United States recently as a substitute for GATT-disfavored quotas on sugar and softwood lumber imports. The only advantage of tariffized quotas is the possibility of reducing the tariff rates at some distant mañana. Absent a tariff approach, Sykes argues, there should be more stress on performance regulations governing the provision of services and less on micromanagement of how the services are rendered. David Leebron adds the important insight that nations targeting trade barriers for removal should consider not only which ones are most onerous at the moment, but also which ones will be most susceptible in the future to progressive phaseout.

The question of criteria for imposing tariffs following dumping judgments (Vinerian sales abroad at net prices lower than in the home market versus selling below "constructed value") is not addressed in part 2. But it is impossible to overlook the insidious impact of the constructed value approach on developing nations' opportunities for exporting their goods. Calling below-full-cost sales "dumping" makes exporting difficult for developing nations struggling to work their way down learning curves and realize scale economies. It also adds instability to their economic activity. Exporters must raise the prices of their products (riding up the left-hand branch of their short-run average total cost curves) when a recession occurs, while producers in the target market reduce prices, as the law of supply and demand dictates. The need for new WTO policies that are more rational and equitable is acute.

From his exalted position in a borderless heaven, Ray Vernon is without doubt unhappy that there was so little discussion of foreign direct investment (FDI) and the barriers, natural and artificial, that impede it. FDI has been growing more rapidly than international trade. It is one of the fastest means of transferring and adapting modern technology to developing nations; for nations with low savings rates, it can be an important supplement to indigenous capital formation. But its spread is far from even. Several dozen least-developed nations receive precious little FDI, in part because multinationals shun unstable governments.[5]

Foreign direct investment, to be sure, has limitations as a technology transfer mechanism. A rich quantitative study by Brian Aitken and Ann Harrison reveals that Venezuelan plants receiving FDI had higher productivity than their locally owned counterparts, but there was little evidence of spillover benefits to spatially or industrially proximate plants lacking FDI.[6] Ishtiaq Mahmood shows that technology transfer patterns differ widely among industrializing nations. South Korea and Taiwan have approached the technological frontier largely on the strength of efforts by domestic

companies, whereas the other Asian tigers have relied heavily on multinationals for their new technology (as evidenced by invention patents received in the United States).[7] Nevertheless, for nations lacking a strong
cadre of well-educated scientists and engineers, FDI may be the only game
in town. Removing barriers to it—those imposed deliberately by potential
recipient nations and those that are the inadvertent result of misguided domestic policies—should have high priority. On this I am confident that Ray
Vernon concurs.

Bobby Willig calls attention to the complementary role competition
policy can play in enhancing the liberalization of trade. Willig proposes,
among other things, the impossible dream: harmonizing the criteria applied to dumping with those used in antitrust analyses of predatory pricing.
Most instances of alleged dumping, Willig's research reveals, entail little
threat of market power increases sufficient to permit price raising when the
price-discriminating sales end. On a broader front, some have advocated
harmonizing competition policies across nations under the auspices of the
WTO (or, as suggested by a U.S. Department of Justice study group, under
a separate new world-competition-policy forum).[8] Willig's view reflects a
consensus that the world's nations are not ready for such an initiative. More
progress is likely toward limited objectives (for example, bilateral or plurilateral agreements to enforce domestic competition laws evenhandedly toward national and foreign enterprises). That cartels in international trade
have not faded into insignificance is shown by recent judgments and
record-breaking fines against the suppliers of vitamins, citric acid, lysine,
European cement, coated facsimile paper, and carbon electrodes. Working
groups at the Organization for Economic Cooperation and Development
and at the WTO have discovered noteworthy willingness among the industrialized nations to prosecute unauthorized cartels aggressively. Some are
convinced that competition policy initiatives can be particularly effective in
opening up national telecommunications markets.

Summing up, the efficiency session's wide-ranging discussion recalled
the wisdom in a poem written by the late Kenneth Boulding some four
decades ago:

> Four things that give mankind a shove
> Are threats, exchange, persuasion, love.
> Threats lead to manifold abuses
> In games where everybody loses.
> Exchange enriches every nation

But leads to dangerous alienation.
Persuaders seek to sway their brothers
But fool themselves as well as others;
And love, with longer pull than hate,
Is slow indeed to propagate.

Notes

1. Alfred Marshall, *Principles of Economics,* book 5 (London: Macmillan, 1890), chap. 12; Arnold C. Harberger, "Monopoly and Resource Allocation," *American Economic Review,* vol. 44 (May 1954), pp. 77–87.

2. Compare F. M. Scherer, "The Welfare Economics of Product Variety: An Application to the Ready-to-Eat Cereals Industry," *Journal of Industrial Economics,* vol. 28 (December 1979), pp. 113–34; and Jerry A. Hausman, "Valuation of New Goods under Perfect and Imperfect Competition," Working Paper 4970 (Cambridge, Mass.: National Bureau of Economic Research, December 1994).

3. Sharon Levin and Paula Stephan, "Are the Foreign Born a Source of Strength for U.S. Science?" *Science,* August 10, 1999, pp. 1213–14.

4. Adam Smith, *The Wealth of Nations,* book 1 (1776), chap. 8.

5. Howard J. Shatz, "The Location of U.S. Multinational Affiliates," Ph.D. diss., Harvard University, 2000, chap. 2.

6. Brian Aitken and Ann Harrison, "Do Domestic Firms Benefit from Direct Foreign Investment?" *American Economic Review,* vol. 89 (June 1999), pp. 605–18.

7. Ishtiaq Pasha Mahmood, "Technological Innovation in Asia and the Role of Business Groups," Ph.D. diss., Harvard University, 1999, chap. 2.

8. International Competition Policy Advisory Committee, "Final Report" (U.S. Department of Justice, Antitrust Division, 2000), pp. 279–80, 300–01.

PART THREE

Equity

ALAN V. DEARDORFF

8 | *Market Access for Developing Countries*

M ost scholars and policymakers today agree that the best strategy for a poor country to develop is to take advantage of international trade. In the past two decades one after another developing country saw the wisdom of this strategy and opened its markets to international trade and foreign direct investment (FDI). And yet, ironically, in spite of the approval that scholars from developed countries have accorded this change, the developed world has sometimes increased its own barriers to imports from these developing countries. A cynic might question whether the developed world really wants to see developing countries escape poverty. But I see this reluctance to embrace developing-country exports as, at least in part, a natural result of the dynamics of growth, of trade, and of the political economy of protection. It is in the nature of trade and specialization in the world today that developing countries can advance only by stepping on the heels of some of those in developed countries. That is, developing countries grow by expanding in industries that developed countries must then leave behind, and those whose interests are entrenched in those declining industries will inevitably, and to some extent successfully, seek protection. But this protection then denies critical market access to developing countries, slowing down their growth.

Conversations with Bob Stern on the topic of this chapter have been very beneficial. I thank him as well as Patrick Low and Craig VanGrasstek for their insights.

This chapter explores the reasons for this phenomenon loosely within the context of several models of international trade. It then notes some of its manifestations in the form of barriers to market access that have appeared during these decades of progress by developing countries. Finally, I speculate on how this problem is to be solved.

Theoretical Considerations

In its simplest form and in a simple world, economic progress need not have adverse effects on anyone, nor be resisted by anyone. In the Solow growth model, for example, savers accumulate capital and wealth, and by doing so they increase the wage of workers, whether or not the workers themselves engage in saving. The same would be true in a world of free neoclassical trade, as long as all countries are sufficiently similar in their factor endowments to have factor price equalization (FPE). Then any countries that grow faster than others will likewise accumulate wealth and force up the worldwide wage, raising per capita incomes even in those countries that do not manage to save.[1]

But that, most of us would agree, is not the world we live in. Instead, to the extent that the neoclassical (Heckscher-Ohlin, HO) model does describe the world, it is not one of FPE, but rather one in which factor endowments of different countries have become too diverse for FPE to be possible. In the terminology of the modern HO model, we are in a "multicone" equilibrium in which different groups of countries have different factor prices and specialize with free trade in different collections of goods.

In this multicone model, as economic growth in the poorer cone occurs, it expands its output into goods that were just marginally competitive in the richer cone, causing those industries there to contract and shut down. Someone will necessarily lose, the identity of the losers depending on the mobility of factors. If, instead, in the short run factors are industry specific, then those industry-specific factors in the declining industries will find their livelihoods undermined by trade with the advancing developing world. If factors are mobile across industries, then the shifting fortunes of industries based on factor intensities will cause the relatively scarce factors in the developed world to suffer decline in real wages. Either way, someone is worse off. The losers can be expected to resist this change by lobbying for protection. If they get it, market access for the growing developing world will be curtailed. In this particular model of trade and growth, there is a built-in dynamic: successful growth by the poor part of the world leads to restrictions of market access against it in the rich part of the world. Since those restrictions in turn make it that much harder for the poor countries to grow, there is a built-in bias against their catching up to the rich countries.[2]

Effects of Growth

Consider an HO model with two factors: labor and some sort of capital (human or physical). There are three goods: X, Y, and Z, with X the most labor intensive and Z the most capital intensive. Let there be two countries: North, with lots of capital, and South, with little. They are initially engaged in free trade. Perhaps South has just liberalized, as discussed earlier. Factor endowments differ sufficiently that FPE is not possible. Instead the initial equilibrium has different factor prices in the two countries, with South producing X and Y and North producing Y and Z. South exports X to North in exchange for Z, and the direction of trade of the good of intermediate factor intensity, Y, could go either way, depending on country sizes, demands, and the various factor ratios.

Now suppose that South accumulates a chunk of new capital. I will keep capital in North fixed, although it would be a minor variation on the argument to allow it to accumulate as well, so long as South accumulates relatively more. I will ask what happens, as a result, to all concerned.

Prices are going to change, of course, but to see how they will change, hold them fixed for a moment. Then South's growth will have the effects worked out by T. M. Rybczynski: its output of Y will increase and its output of X will decrease.[3] There will be no change yet, in the outputs of North, since we have not yet let prices change. Therefore, on world markets we will move from the initial equilibrium to situations of excess demand for X and excess supply of Y. There will also be some excess demand for Z as South spends part of its increased income on it. The prices of X and Z will therefore both rise compared with Y.

In the absence of any policy response, these price changes will restore market equilibrium, with South again just meeting the somewhat reduced world demand for X, and with North responding to the increased price of Z, relative to Y, by producing more Z. As for good Y, its output rose initially because of growth in South, but it now falls in both North and South with the price changes. The reduced price and increased world income ensure that the new equilibrium world output of Y is above its level before the growth occurred, with output in South increased by more than the fall in world demand and output in North. That is, there is a shift of resources in North away from producing good Y. North's industry Y contracts.

This contraction is the main focus of my argument because it will entail losses for somebody in North. Exactly who these losers are depends on the mobility of factors. I will consider two cases: the specific-factors case of mobile labor but immobile capital, and the HO case in which both factors are mobile across industries. Note that in both cases the responses of outputs in the two countries to the price changes mentioned earlier would be in the same direction (although of different magnitudes). Therefore, my conclusions about the changes in the new equilibrium are valid for both.

Considering first the specific-factors case, I let capital (of whatever type) be sector specific, perhaps representing a short-run inability to transform itself or retrain into a form needed for the expanding sector Z. Labor in North, assumed to be mobile although one could easily have parts of it be sector specific as well, is therefore drawn from the contracting sector Y to expanding sector Z by what would otherwise be a wage differential between the sectors. North's specific factor in sector Y, however, cannot move, and it suffers a loss in its factor payment as a result. That is, the return to specific capital in sector Y goes down, while the return to sector-specific capital in sector Z goes up. Both of these changes are close to unambiguous in real terms, North's owners of specific capital in sectors Y and Z being made worse off and better off respectively in terms of what they can buy of goods Y and Z.[4] As usual in a specific-factors model, the real return to the mobile factor, labor, is ambiguous, rising in terms of Y but falling in terms of Z.

If both factors are intersectorally mobile—which we may take as the case of a longer run—the Stolper-Samuelson results apply.[5] The rise in the relative price of good Z compared to Y ensures that in North, where both are produced, the factor used intensively in Z gains, while that used intensively in Y loses, both in real terms so long as we consider only these two goods. In this case, since Z is more capital intensive than Y, it is owners of capital that gain and owners of labor that lose, in terms of what they can buy of Y and Z.[6]

Realistically (if one can ask for that in a theoretical argument such as this), we may expect the world to be a hybrid of these cases: growth in South causes harm to some factors of production that are employed in North's contracting sector and cannot move quickly enough, and it causes harm to labor more generally in North, which is subjected to increased competition from the labor-abundant South. Ironically, this last effect is happening in spite of the fact that South is becoming *less* labor abundant, since it is accumulating capital. But South is still specialized in labor-intensive sectors, which means that its expansion of capital permits it to compete more vigorously with the most labor-intensive sector producing in North. That is, South is expanding into a sector that, for it, is relatively capital intensive, but from the point of view of North, this sector is still quite labor intensive. Therefore, the expansion causes the wage of labor in North to fall.

Naturally, there must be effects on the factor prices in South as well, although these are not the primary focus of my analysis. Here, too, we may consider specific factors and HO cases.

With specific factors, the addition to the capital stock of South would presumably have been installed entirely in the more capital-intensive sector, Y. At initial prices, this would raise labor's marginal product in sector Y, increasing the wage there, and drawing labor out of sector X and into sector Y. The return to sector-specific capital in X goes down as labor pulls out, while the return to capital in sector Y may rise or fall because of the conflicting effects of increased capital and increased labor there. However, as prices of X and Y now change—the price of X rising and that of Y falling—these changes are somewhat reversed. It is unclear, I think, just what the end result for any of these factor prices will be.

In the HO world with factor mobility, the forces of factor price equalization simplify things; at initial goods prices, factor prices cannot change at all with the accumulation of new capital. The only effects on factor prices occur with the price changes, which act to raise the real wage of labor and lower that of capital. Of course, this is not too surprising given that the country is accumulating more capital for a fixed labor force.

What is the net effect on the incomes of the two countries as a whole? This is not a simple question because of various terms-of-trade effects, and these depend in part on which country initially exports the good that both of them produce, Y. To avoid considering an unreasonable number of cases, I will make the very special but arguably neutral assumption that initially there is no trade in Y at all—not because there cannot be but because factor endowments happen to be such that both countries produce exactly what their own consumers demand. Therefore, the initial pattern of trade has South exporting only the most labor-intensive good, X, to North, in exchange for only the most capital-intensive good, Z. This will mean that the fall in the price of Y, which we found earlier, will have no terms-of-trade effects at all on either country. Of course, the reader should keep this in mind and recognize that under more general conditions the price change will cause an additional loss for whichever country exports good Y.

This simplifies things a bit, but not totally since the prices of both X and Z will rise as a result of the capital accumulation in South. The effect of this on the two countries' terms of trade therefore depends on which of these changes is larger. In general we cannot know, but I think that there is a presumption in favor of the relative price of X rising compared to Z. The reason is that, at initial prices, an excess demand for Z appears only because of the increased income in South, with no change in supply. But the excess demand for X appears not only because of the increased demand for X by South demanders, but also because of the decline in supply of X that happens when one or both factors (depending on whether it is the specific-factors or HO model) are withdrawn from its production. Differences in various demand elasticities could confound this conclusion, but nonetheless I will assume that the relative price of X rises compared to Z (and even more, of course, compared to Y).

With these quite special assumptions about changes in relative prices and their importance, the effects of South growth on national incomes are now unambiguous. South gains from its increased capital stock and then gains again as its terms of trade improve with the increased relative price of its export good, X. North, on the other hand, gains not at all at initial prices, since its production and the value of it are unchanged, and then North loses from this same worsening in its terms of trade.[7] So South gains, and North loses. Perhaps this is not entirely what you would have hoped, but remember that South was initially poor, and it remains so since I am assuming that the capital accumulation is nowhere near enough for it to catch up to North.

Effects of Politics

I turn now to what may happen to policies as a result of these changes. That takes me into the realm of the political economy of trade policy, an exciting area of research in which there are not yet tractable models on which most scholars agree. The state of the art, to my knowledge, is a 1994 publication by Gene M. Grossman and Elhanan Helpman, but it is from Grossman's 1998 comment that I infer that much more needs to be done.[8]

I will not attempt to model the politics myself but will simply assume that the aforementioned changes lead the North to implement a tariff on imports of good Y. I suggest several reasons why this could happen. I will *not* try to motivate the tariff by the loss in national income of North that was just noted. That was a somewhat special result depending on the assumed pattern of trade (or lack of it) in good Y, and in any case a tariff on good Y will not help North. It loses national income because the price of good X goes up, and although its market power may permit it to force that price back down a bit by placing a tariff on X, this would only unleash a tariff war to no purpose. In any case a tariff on Y would not help.

Rather, the reason for North's tariff on Y will be distributional: to protect those who lose, or lose most, from the expansion that has occurred in South. Who these are depends on assumptions about factor mobility, but the idea that the losers may be helped by a tariff does not. Whether factors are specific or mobile, the fall in prices of certain factors is a direct result of the increased imports of good Y and the accompanying fall in its price compared to Z within the economy of North. The owners of these factors and the policymakers who control trade policy know that.

Various institutional mechanisms are then possible that lead to a tariff. I begin with a cynical scenario: the losers from imports of Y may bribe the policymakers to provide a tariff.[9] Or the political process may permit the losers to achieve the same result less directly, by lobbying policymakers or by contributing to the election campaigns of those who promise a tariff. Or the losers themselves may constitute a majority of voters, and they can vote in the tariff on their own. Finally, the losers may need to do nothing at all and leave it to policymakers to respond to their plight out of sympathy, a possibility that underlies Max Corden's Conservative Social Welfare Function.[10] This last possibility underlies the safeguard clause of the World Trade Organization (Article XIX of the General Agreement on Tariffs and Trade), which permits a country to raise a tariff temporarily against any increase in imports that is perceived as causing sufficient injury.[11] Of course, the GATT does not permit the safeguards tariff to last indefinitely, but in practice countries have been adept at using antidumping and countervailing duties, especially the former, for what is arguably this purpose.

There are many ways that injury to factor owners in North may lead to protection, and I will simply assume that it happens. My purpose has not been to explain in any detail how protection comes about, just that it may well be a natural result of factor accumulation in the developing world. My next purpose is to examine its effects.

Effects of Protection

When North restricts its imports of good Y, the main effect is to lower the good's world price. North and South are assumed to be large enough to matter for world prices. Indeed North may have had an incentive to restrict trade before South ever grew. However, I assume that it did not do so, maybe because it recognized the harm this would do to the world, and even to itself if there were retaliation. Or perhaps it would have used protection but for the constraints of the WTO and GATT. In any case, North may not have been a significant importer of good Y before South grew, in which case restricting trade in Y would previously have done it no good.

But now the situation is different. South has grown, and North is importing Y, with the adverse consequences noted earlier for a portion of its population that it seeks to protect. North does this by restricting imports of good Y; its objective is to raise the price of Y on the domestic market. But because of North's size, it cannot help but lower the price of Y on the world market as well. This improvement in North's terms of trade occurs, but it is actually contrary to what North's government is trying to achieve, since it means that North's domestic price of Y rises by less than the tariff.

My concern is what this does to South. The further fall in the world price of good Y (recall that it already fell due to the growth itself) is, for South, a fall in the price of its capital-intensive good. Therefore, if factors are mobile, this price change will cause a further decline in the return to capital in South. Some decline was already expected, due to the capital accumulation, but now the response of North protecting its market causes the decline in the return to capital to be even larger. If factors are mobile in South, this effect will be felt throughout the economy. If they are not, the effect will be confined to sector-specific capital in industry Y. Either way, the return to the very investment that started this whole process is reduced.

At the same time, because this is a decline in South's terms of trade, its real national income as a country is reduced as well. Therefore, it is not just the return to capital as a privately owned factor that is undermined by North's protection. The overall social return to growth is also undermined. Not only has the particular episode of capital accumulation that I assumed at the start yielded a smaller benefit, the incentives for any further capital accumulation are reduced as well. Any way you look at it, South's attempt to grow, and to catch up with North in terms of per capita income, has been frustrated by North's protection of its own market.

The Lesson

In this particular theoretical framework, attempts by the poor countries of the world to escape poverty will stimulate protection in the rich countries, and this protection makes the escape from poverty more difficult. In this particular case, growth through capital accumulation expands the poor country's capacity to produce what are, for it, capital-intensive goods. But these same goods are at the labor-intensive end of the spectrum in the developed world, and the effect is thus to lower incomes in those labor-intensive industries. Because the effect is felt unevenly in the developed world, the pressure for protection is arguably larger than it would have been if spread more thinly across the whole population. And it also tends to be the poorer groups within the rich North that feel this effect, which increases even more the incentive for protection as a social policy.

The tendency for poor-country growth to cause rich-country protection arises in a variety of theoretical contexts and in the real world today. In the next section I will touch on the real world, but let me conclude this section by broadening the theoretical context.

First, I have described this phenomenon within a special model: a three-good, two-factor, two-country HO or specific-factors model without factor price equalization. In fact, the only one of these assumptions that I think is necessary is the absence of FPE. One could easily have more factors, goods, and countries, and the story could still be told, so long as the countries of the world are not so similar in their factor endowments that they can achieve the equilibrium of an integrated world economy and thus FPE. Without factor price equalization—that is, with multiple cones of diversification—development in the poor countries will inevitably mean expanding production in their most capital-intensive sectors, which are for them at the leading edge of industrialization. But these same sectors will be at the trailing edge of industrialization in the rich countries, and the expansion in the South will require their contraction in the North. This will have adverse consequences for precisely those factors in the North that are least well equipped to bear the loss. And it will lead to protection that to some extent blocks the progress of the developing South.

If there are many countries, there could be many cones, and the very poorest countries may stimulate protection—not in the richest countries—but in countries just a bit less poor than they are. Wherever a country lies in the path of economic development, it must tread on the heels of those just ahead of it in order to move forward, and those heels are likely to kick back, using trade protection, and make progress more difficult.

It is not only within a factor proportions model that this story might be told. It also fits well within what I take to be the product cycle model of Raymond Vernon.[12] In that model incomes rise from the advance of technology more than from capital accumulation, and the advance of technology takes the form of an unending stream of new products that are invented in the developed world. When first invented, these products can be produced only where they were invented, for a variety of reasons that gradually diminish in importance. Over time, new goods become old goods. The production of the old goods shifts to less advanced countries, which thus benefit with a delay from the expanding technology. And the now-old goods are replaced in the advanced countries by still newer goods that are more recently invented.

This is a wonderful story, and it describes a path for progress that seems to offer hope for the entire world. The problem is that advanced-country producers may be reluctant to quit producing new goods when they become old goods. Suppose that production of a new good requires a certain amount of product-specific investment, either in physical capital or in human capital. When the new good becomes an old good and the knowledge of how to produce it moves abroad, these investments become obsolete, and those who made them lose. Even if they knew in advance that this would happen, they still have an incentive to seek protection, if protection is available, and they will.

Therefore, within this version of the product cycle model, we see very much the same phenomenon that I described for the HO model. Here, too, developing countries advance by moving up a ladder of specialization, defined now by the newness of the goods that they produce rather than their capital intensity. In order to make progress, they must displace producers of the least advanced goods that are still being produced in the countries ahead of them. Those producers will suffer from this competition, and they will seek trade protection in order to avoid it, wherever possible.

Manifestations of Protectionism

The high tariffs in textiles and apparel, and the developed countries' great reluctance to reduce them, are probably the best manifestation of the phenomenon I have described. These are the first industries beyond handicrafts that developing countries try to establish as they industrialize, and therefore they should be the first industries that the developed countries move out of. But this movement has been resisted in virtually every advanced country. The Multi-Fibre Arrangement (MFA) carried this process a step farther and institutionalized it within GATT. The MFA departs slightly from the scenario I have described, however. Rather than a tariff, it uses quotas that are allocated to the developing countries. This serves to give them the rents from the quotas, and it removes the negative impact on their terms of trade. Nonetheless, it effectively stifles growth in these sectors. Ironically, the MFA creates entrenched property rights to export the limited amount of these products from countries, even after the countries have moved beyond them in their own development. This makes it that much harder for latecomers to economic development to establish a foothold in these industries.

Fortunately, many countries have succeeded in developing in spite of this, and as they have done so, their comparative advantage has progressed to more and more capital-intensive goods. For some years it has been the steel industry in the United States (even more than textiles and apparel) that has struggled most with import competition from some of the advanced developing countries. These steel producers have sought and found protection, most frequently by using the antidumping and countervailing duty statutes. Of course, these statutes require more than just import competition and injury: the imports must also be judged unfair by one of several definitions. But most observers agree that this is a formality that is easily satisfied, given the way the statutes are written and administered.

One might have thought, based on the theory here, that as the developing world advances, only those countries within it that are most advanced would pose a problem for the developed countries, just as the steel example suggests. Countries farther behind would be displacing industries that have long since disappeared from the most advanced countries, and resistance to them would be found mostly in developing countries that are just ahead of them. With that in mind, the recent opposition within the United States to giving small trade preferences to the poorest countries of Africa is surprising. These countries are so far behind the United States economically that it is hard to imagine that they pose a competitive threat to anyone in America. Nonetheless, the U.S. textile unions have mounted an effective campaign against this initiative. Apparently, if protection of declining industries is sufficient, they never disappear from countries that should have left them far behind. Declining industries can create resistance to development by even the poorest of countries.

"Globalization" has raised many concerns. One big concern is that wages and employment of developed-country workers are being reduced by competition with the developing world. Fortunately, this concern has not yet led to any increase in actual protection, as far as I know. But it has contributed to the protests against the WTO, and it may have helped prevent a new round of negotiations to reduce tariffs from getting under way. It has recently appeared as resistance to admitting China to the WTO. And it promises to continue to impede expansion of the NAFTA to include other developing countries.

What to Do

The lesson is not just that countries protect against imports. We knew that. It is that progress by developing countries leads rather naturally to increases in protection, which in turn render that progress more difficult. The process works through normal economic mechanisms and through politics: countries try to protect those within their societies who are being hurt. We should not expect it to be otherwise, no matter how much we may deplore it. Instead, what we need to do is to seek institutional mechanisms that will assist development while recognizing the reality of developed-country resistance to it.

Furthermore, although I have not stressed it as much as perhaps I should, those protected in developed countries from the competition with developing countries tend to include those who are already near the bottom of the developed-country income distributions. Not all owners of factors in labor-intensive industries are poor, of course—but many are workers with limited skills and low wages. As long as they are working, they are much better off than the workers in developing countries whose competition they fear. But they are surely among those whom income redistribution policies ought to help, not hurt, within the developed world. So to some extent, what we face is a trade-off between helping our own poor and helping the world's poor.

Indeed, the tendency to use protection in this situation is a natural response to exactly this trade-off, given the high weight that countries naturally place on their own people in preference to others. Protection against imports from developing countries does not necessarily mean that we do not want to help them, but rather that we also want even more to help our own poor.

The world as a whole, however, must treat all poor as its own, and one purpose of international institutions must be to ensure that. It is the responsibility of the WTO to prevent rich countries' trade policies from tilting too far in favor of their own people and against the world's, even when it is their poor whom they are trying to help. That is why the WTO must hold the line against increases in protection, even if they are motivated by what seem to be legitimate concerns of domestic income distribution.

Unfortunately, it is not obvious that the WTO is doing a very good job of this. By that I do not mean to criticize the Safeguards Clause, the purpose of which is explicitly to buffer adverse income shocks due to import competition. If the only use of trade policy for such purposes were under it, then I think we would be in pretty good shape. The problem is that countries rarely use the safeguards clause at all, and instead have found so many other ways to protect declining industries. The expanding use of anti-dumping, the MFA, and the carve-out of agricultural policies have all permitted countries to protect against imports from developing countries far beyond what the world's conscience should permit. The Uruguay Round promised progress in eliminating the MFA, and it made a first step toward controlling agricultural protection, but even these promises have been disappointing in their implementation. And anti-dumping was not made any less destructive.

So what can we do? We can continue, of course, to resist protection in all of these and other forms, and we can push to strengthen the international institutions that support this aim. But more important, recognizing that at least some protection arises from a legitimate need, we must seek other ways to meet that need and thus lessen the pressure for protection.

That is, to the extent that developing countries do advance, it is true that they will displace workers and firms in developed countries. Many of these are among the poor of the developed countries, or at least they are by the time this happens to them. The developed countries therefore need to have better arrangements to assist these people.

I am led, therefore, to an argument for a familiar and never very successful policy: trade adjustment assistance (TAA). We need it now, more than ever, not just for the recipients of the assistance but also for the developing world whose progress will be blocked by protection if we do not find some other way to help those who compete with developing country exports. Indeed, because the need for TAA is larger than just the interests of developed countries, perhaps our international institutions—the WTO and the World Bank most likely—should be putting pressure on developed countries to implement such policies more effectively. The safeguards clause, for example, could require that any use of a tariff for safeguards purposes must also be accompanied by some form of TAA.

Of course, TAA programs have been notorious for their ineffectiveness. Therefore, we also need to find ways to improve them. Considering how important they seem to be in principle, it is appalling that they have not gotten more creative scholarly attention. I was slightly encouraged, a few months ago, by news reports that the Bradley presidential campaign was proposing a program of wage insurance for trade-impacted workers. But of course the Bradley campaign ended, and I have seen no more mention of this or any other ideas along these lines. I hope that will change.

Notes

1. Increased saving by one country or a group of countries will lower per capita incomes only in countries that have more than the world average stock of capital per capita.

2. See Alan V. Deardorff, "Developing Country Growth and Developed Country Response," Discussion Paper 462 (University of Michigan, Research Seminar in International Economics, August 14, 2000).

3. T. M. Rybczynski, "Factor Endowments and Relative Commodity Prices," *Economica,* vol 22 (1955), pp. 336–41.

4. Real wages in this model must also take account of good X, which is not produced in North. In this case, since the price of X goes up as resources are pulled out of its production by South's growth, the real decline in the return to sector-specific capital in North's Y remains unambiguous. It is possible, but unlikely, that the sector-specific capital in Z may also lose from this price increase. The reason that both may lose is that North as a whole is experiencing a worsening of its terms of trade.

5. Alan V. Deardorff, "Overview of the Stolper-Samuelson Theorem," in Alan V. Deardorff and Robert M. Stern, eds., *The Stolper-Samuelson Theorem: A Golden Jubilee* (University of Michigan Press, 1994), pp. 7–34.

6. Again, the rise in price of X means that the loss of labor is even greater, while the gain to capital can potentially be reversed.

7. This conclusion may seem to contradict Paul R. Krugman, who answered "no" to the question of his title, "Does Third World Growth Hurt First World Prosperity?" *Harvard Business Review* (July–August 1994), pp. 113–21. In fact, although Krugman looked at several models, he never really addressed this question in this model. The closest he came, in a model without FPE, was to ask about the effects of trade, not growth, and there he only cited the empirical answer of Robert Z. Lawrence and Matthew J. Slaughter, "International Trade and American Wages in the 1980s: Giant Sucking Sound or Small Hiccup?" *Brookings Papers on Economic Activity, 2:1993,* pp. 161–226.

8. Gene M. Grossman and Elhanan Helpman, "Protection for Sale," *American Economic Review,* vol. 84 (September 1994), pp. 833–50; Gene M. Grossman, "Comments on Conference Version of Paper," in Alan V. Deardorff and Robert M. Stern, eds., *Constituent Interests and U.S. Trade Policies* (University of Michigan Press, 1994), pp. 57–61.

9. Or even more cynically, I could say the losers threaten to discontinue bribes if the policymakers do not provide a tariff.

10. W. M. Corden, *Trade Policy and Economic Welfare* (Oxford: Clarendon Press, 1974).

11. Alan V. Deardorff, "Safeguards Policy and the Conservative Social Welfare Function," in H. Kierzkowski, ed., *Protection and Competition in International Trade* (Blackwell, 1987).

12. Raymond Vernon, "International Investment and International Trade in the Product Cycle," *Quarterly Journal of Economics,* vol. 80 (May 1966), pp. 190–207.

COMMENT BY
Craig VanGrasstek

Alan Deardorff addresses one of the classic questions in the political economy of trade policy: Will established producers act to limit the opportunities of newcomers? He contends that although "developing countries grow by expanding in industries that developed countries must then leave behind," the entrenched interests in the developed countries' "declining industries will inevitably, and to some extent successfully, seek protection." If the governments of developed countries grant these demands, the aspirations of the developing countries will be thwarted.

This explanation misses some key developments in trade policy. While tariffs and quotas are still important, the more relevant question today is whether and on what terms the existing trade barriers will be reduced or removed. An updated version of Raymond Vernon's product-cycle paradigm shows why some residual protection persists, and why policymakers are increasingly prone to choose the "second-best" option of regional trade agreements and preferential trade programs, rather than universal and nondiscriminatory free trade.

The Product Cycle and Its Implications

Vernon's product-cycle paradigm suggested that an industry's competitiveness would go through a predictable series of stages. The cycle began when "U.S.-controlled enterprises generate new products and processes" and then "introduce these products or processes abroad through exports." These same firms establish subsidiaries abroad "when their export position is threatened," but eventually they lose their oligopolistic advantage altogether.[1] While Vernon's main objective was to explain the causes and consequences of foreign investment, the stages also implied that an industry's perspective on trade policy would evolve. Industries can be expected to favor open markets when they are competitive and to favor protection when they are not. Deardorff's analysis is largely consonant with this cycle.

I would suggest two adjustments to the points raised by both Vernon and Deardorff. The first concerns the policy question, which for Deardorff appears to be: "Will developed countries respond to increased competition from developing countries by erecting new barriers to trade?" I would ask instead, "How will the interests of declining industries affect the pace and form of new trade liberalization?" While it may be useful to assume that the two countries in the model "are initially engaged in free trade," it is equally parsimonious and more realistic to begin with the assumption that trade restrictions already exist. World Trade Organization (WTO) rules are not so watertight as to prevent countries from imposing any new restrictions on trade.[2] But I quarrel with the assumption that increased import competition will "lead the North to implement a tariff on imports."[3] The track record for both legislated protection and safeguards cases suggests that protectionist industries have had little success in winning support from government.[4] Markets are much more open today than they were in decades past, and the rules are more enforceable.

I also suggest that the range of options not be limited to a stark choice between "free trade" or "protection." Beyond the obvious point that there are many degrees of openness, discrimination is an equally important consideration. Here the rules of the General Agreement on Tariffs and Trade (GATT) and WTO have been permissive. Free trade agreements and customs unions are allowable exceptions to the general rule of universal most-favored-nation treatment, and preferential trade programs such as the Generalized System of Preferences (GSP) are granted waivers. While each of these options provide for more liberal trade, they are widely seen as a second-best alternative to nondiscriminatory liberalization. Discrimination is also a natural consequence of the product cycle.

Vernon's benign view of the product cycle was in the tradition of Joseph Schumpeter, who believed that a combination of entrepreneurial innovation and periodic depressions are engines of progress.[5] A free-trading country would regularly produce a new crop of innovators, while firms that lost their competitiveness would either find new lines of work or be swept away when the business cycle swung downward. This Darwinian optimism is challenged, however, if firms and workers in a declining industry refuse to go quietly into that good night. Deardorff's analysis falls into this second category, concluding that declining industries will demand and receive protection.

In the third alternative that I offer here, the product cycle encourages both liberalization and discrimination. Vernon was right that distressed industries do not face a simple choice between *extinction* (giving way to more competitive rivals) and *survival* (protectionism) but have the third option of *evolution.* They can evolve by moving some or all of their production offshore and become multinational producers. What Vernon did not recognize was that this mid-range option might encourage a similarly hybrid set of policy preferences in which industries favor a discriminatory approach to trade liberalization. A multinational producer will be much more favorably disposed toward open markets than a "mature" domestic industry but will not inevitably be a paragon of free-trade purism. These producers may perceive a strong incentive to support discriminatory options that create sanctuary markets at home or abroad.

Discriminatory Options for Industries in Transition

Viewed in the aggregate, changes in the competitive position of domestic industries clarify the "big picture" of an evolving U.S. trade policy. Largely in response to shifts in the interests of domestic industries, the United States moved from nondiscriminatory protection (1816–1933) to discriminatory liberalization (1934–42), to a period of nondiscriminatory liberalization since 1942 that, beginning in the mid-1960s, has also seen a growing number of discriminatory agreements and programs. When viewed at the industry level, these changes help to explain the specific policy options that individual industries favor.

Even when it is granted, protection may only slow the rate of decline. When faced with the alternative of extinction, many firms will consider the switch to multinational production. Vernon correctly predicted this move, but he did not anticipate the consequences that it might have for the trade policy preferences of multinational producers. Some of them indeed favor a policy of pure free trade, but others prefer more targeted initiatives that favor the countries where they invest their capital, source their materials, or export their finished products. Through both nonreciprocal trade preferences and the negotiation of reciprocal free trade agreements, discrimination creates new opportunities to manipulate trade rules for the benefit of specific U.S. industries. These discriminatory arrangements are now a key part of a multitiered trade regime in which "normal" treatment is now the exception rather than the rule. Just under half of all imports in 1999 originated in countries that have nothing but permanent normal trade relations (formerly known as most-favored-nation treatment) with the United States.[6] All the rest came from countries that were either denied this treatment or enjoyed preferential access.

Preferential trade programs and discriminatory agreements offer new opportunities for the manipulation of rules on behalf of specific U.S. industries. These instruments can limit the extension of preferential treatment to those countries that host their offshore investments, while keeping imports from third countries subject to the existing tariff rates. Some industries take the further step of seeking more specific rules of origin (ROOs). These are the rules by which a product is deemed eligible for preferential treatment. Some programs have fairly simple and standard ROOs, such as the Generalized System of Preferences (which generally requires that at least 35 percent of the value of an import originate in the beneficiary country), but the ROOs for the more generous programs are often predicated on the inclusion of U.S. materials.

Consider how the evolving preferences of the U.S. automotive industry helped to shape three sequential North American trade agreements: the Auto Pact negotiated with Canada in 1965, the U.S.-Canada Free Trade Agreement in 1988, and the North American Free Trade Agreement (NAFTA) in 1993. Each successive agreement further manipulated the rules to restrict trade from nonparticipating countries and prompted a significant reordering of trade flows in automotive products. As of 1999, Canada was by far the largest trading partner of the United States in this sector, and Mexico came in third, behind Japan. This reordering is a good deal for Detroit: The United States exported 53 cents' worth of automotive products to its two North American partners for every dollar's worth of automotive products that it imported from them, but a dollar's worth of automotive imports from Japan meant just 5 cents worth of automotive exports. These comparisons may mean little to free traders, but they have great persuasive power for neo-mercantilists in government and industry.

Trade in the textile and apparel sector shows how preferential trade programs can be manipulated to encourage coproduction, especially in regions that are politically friendly to the United States and economically tied to the U.S. industry. For the past two decades, U.S. textile trade policy has been based on a direct relationship between the degree of preferential treatment that is extended to a trading partner and the requisite level of U.S. content in the imported merchandise. Under nonpreferential rules, the country of origin is the one in which a garment is assembled. In order to benefit from preferences, a garment generally must incorporate U.S. materials. These programs have had the intended effect: The Western Hemisphere now accounts for a larger share of U.S. textile and apparel trade than does Asia. For every dollar's worth of textile and apparel products imported from countries in the Western Hemisphere in 1999, the United States exported to them 55 cents' worth of fabric, partial made-ups, and finished goods. By contrast, the United States exported just 4 cents' worth of product to Asia for every dollar's worth of textiles and apparel imported from that region.

Conclusion

These brief illustrations show how import competition does not inevitably lead to demands for protection. A widening circle of industries in decline has found that a combination of foreign investment and discriminatory trade arrangements can give them a means of surviving the competitive challenge. It is well beyond the limited aims of this comment to delve into the extensive debate over discriminatory trade agreements as a second-best alternative to nondiscriminatory liberalization, but it is quite clear that discriminatory trade programs and agreements are more susceptible to capture by special interests than are multilateral agreements. For good or for ill, they are an increasingly important aspect of the U.S. trade regime, and they are useful to those industries that find themselves at the hazardous part of the product cycle.

Notes

1. Raymond Vernon, *Sovereignty at Bay: The Multinational Spread of U.S. Enterprises* (Basic Books, 1971), p. 66.
2. Ibid., p. 3.
3. Ibid., p. 9.
4. My calculations from U.S. International Trade Commission data show that petitioners have succeeded in winning import protection in only twenty-three of the seventy cases considered in the quarter century since enactment of the current safeguards law (section 201 of the Trade Act of 1974).
5. Joseph A. Schumpeter, *The Theory of Economic Development* (Harvard University Press, 1936).
6. All trade data here are calculated from the trade database of the U.S. International Trade Commission.

ANDRÉ SAPIR

9 | Who's Afraid of Globalization? Domestic Adjustment in Europe and America

> The political problem of mankind is to combine three things:
> Economic Efficiency, Social Justice, and Individual Liberty.
>
> JOHN MAYNARD KEYNES, *Essays in Persuasion*

Imagine the following situation: On the one hand, the sole political super-power and the biggest, most dynamic economy on earth; on the other, a collection of fifteen countries struggling to attain international political status and to cure a serious case of Eurosclerosis. One would think the former, a "new economy," would gleefully embrace the current wave of globalization, and the latter, an "old economy" with a per capita GDP lower by one-third, would resist it forcefully. In fact, America, more than Europe, appears to ponder whether globalization has gone too far and to suffer from globaphobia.[1]

The main opposition to globalization in the United States and in Europe comes from labor, which claims that international economic integration is largely responsible for the recent deterioration of its economic and social condition. Since the mid-1970s, the United States, where wages are relatively flexible, has seen rising wage disparity between skilled and unskilled workers and falling real wages for large segments of the labor force. Between 1973 and 1997, the median real weekly earnings of male full-time workers fell from $700 to $600 in constant 1997 dollars.[2] By contrast, Europe, where wages are relatively rigid, has undergone rising unemployment, with little or no downward pressure on wages (except in the United Kingdom). Between 1973 and 1997, the unemployment rate in the European Union (EU-15) jumped from less 3 percent to nearly 11 percent.[3]

Trade economists have examined two channels through which globalization might affect labor market conditions in the United States and Europe: one is increased competition with low-wage countries, resulting in lower demand for unskilled labor; the other is increased international competition in product and capital markets, resulting in more elastic labor demand.

Discussion about the first channel usually starts from the observation that the demand for unskilled labor has fallen considerably on both sides of the Atlantic since the mid-1970s. This phenomenon is attributed either to competition from unskilled labor-abundant developing countries (one of the facets of globalization) or to skill-biased technological progress, both of which have rapidly increased during the past two decades. All trade economists agree that both factors have played a role in the demise of unskilled workers, but most conclude that the latter is far more important. The common wisdom is that trade accounts for about 20 percent of the rising wage inequality in the United States and roughly the same percentage of the increasing unemployment in Europe.[4] Dissenting voices, however, claim that technological change cannot be treated entirely independently from trade; therefore, trade accounts for a bigger fraction of the deterioration in labor's condition than is usually assumed.[5]

But the plight of labor in the United States and in Europe is not limited to unskilled workers. Moreover, globalization encompasses other aspects of international economic integration besides trade, in particular international investment. Hence the second channel. The story told convincingly by Dani Rodrik is that increased trade and capital mobility make the demand for the services of immobile workers more elastic. In his words, "the services of large segments of the population can be more easily substituted by the services of other people across national boundaries."[6] In this view globalization implies that workers lose bargaining power and incur, at least in the United States, where labor markets are flexible, greater instability in earnings and hours worked in response to shocks. For Americans "who lack the skills to make themselves hard to replace," Rodrik notes, globalization means "greater insecurity and a more precarious existence."[7]

Thus *prima facie* academic evidence supports the popular view that globalization (increasing international economic integration of product and capital markets) contributes to the waning fortune of American and European workers: declining wages and rising job insecurity in flexible

America and growing unemployment under rigid labor market conditions in Europe.[8]

The different economic environment in Europe and the United States, "social protection versus economic flexibility," provides a potential clue to the puzzling divergent attitudes of American and European labor toward increased international economic integration.[9] In the United States declining wages and rising job insecurity have clearly produced an anxious "median voter." By contrast, in Europe the "median voter" has been largely spared from growing unemployment; the burden has fallen mainly on the young and women, while older workers have exited the labor market thanks to generous early retirement programs.[10]

The first part of this essay examines whether the European social protection system can take the credit for having insulated much of the European citizenry from the negative impact of globalization. Three issues are analyzed: the nature of globalization in Europe; European social policy in relationship to economic integration, and its contrast with U.S. trade adjustment assistance programs and liberalization initiatives; and the sustainability of the European model in the face of increasing international economic integration.

My focus then shifts to international labor mobility, the grand absentee of the current wave of globalization.[11] Here is a topic where phobia runs high on both sides of the Atlantic, with probably a clear advantage this time to Europe. The fear of the American median voter toward immigration is probably rooted in the same cause as his or her globaphobia: declining wages and rising job insecurity. By contrast, Europeans seem ready to accept increasing international economic integration of product and capital markets, as long as labor mobility is kept out of the picture.[12] One reason may be the European social protection system, which helps cushion against the negative impact of globalization. In the case of massive labor flows, however, this system may be viewed as unsustainable. In this part of the chapter I analyze the policy of European countries toward labor migration and its relationship to social protection.

Trade

Let me start with a mea culpa. I am just as guilty as any other trade economist of having a tendency to concentrate on the gains from trade and simply ignoring that some individuals, usually workers, may also incur pains from trade. The potential costs to labor from trade liberalization are of two kinds: permanent income loss and temporary adjustment costs. The extent of these costs depends on the source of gains from trade (comparative advantage or economies of scale) and on labor market institutions.

Consider first the effect of trade on labor's income. Under perfect competition in all product and factor markets, and with different factor endowments across countries, trade liberalization is likely to be detrimental to (unskilled) workers in industrial countries, where (unskilled) labor is relatively scarce.[13] However, since countries enjoy overall gains from trade, there is the possibility of winners compensating losers, which raises the crucial issue of redistributional mechanisms. By contrast, if countries are sufficiently similar and there are important scale economies, so lowering trade costs gives rise to increased intra-industry trade, both scarce and abundant factors are likely to gain from trade.[14]

These results may not hold if labor markets are distorted by relative wage rigidity or monopoly power on the part of labor. The impact of wage rigidity on labor depends on whether trade is inter- or intra-industry. In the comparative advantage case, rigid wages imply that trade integration has little or no effect on relative output prices, which translates into little or no Stolper-Samuelson effect and a fall in employment.[15] By contrast, in the intra-industry trade situation, even if wages are totally rigid, every factor could still gain from trade liberalization, and employment could remain unaffected.

The impact of union monopoly power on wages also depends on the nature of trade. Robin Naylor constructs a model that shows that the direction of the effects of falling trade costs on wages varies according to whether trade is inter- or intra-industry.[16] With interindustry trade, a fall in the costs of international trade leads unions to reduce wage demands. On the other hand, when trade is primarily intra-industry, increased trade makes unions more assertive in bargaining for higher wages.

The effect of trade on labor adjustment costs is closely related to the previous discussion. When economic integration leads to an expansion of intra-industry trade, labor faces relatively few adjustment costs, since there is no sectoral, and probably little geographical, reallocation of resources. When the lowering of trade costs generates interindustry trade, however, labor needs to be reallocated across sectors and across regions since many sectors tend to be geographically concentrated. Obviously, the greater the rigidity of wages, the lower the reallocation of labor across sectors and regions, hence the lower the adjustment cost but the higher the cost of unemployment.

The cost to labor from increased international economic integration is likely to vary across countries depending on three factors: the nature of trade, the type of labor market institutions, and the kind of redistribution and adjustment mechanisms. Despite similar increases in the degree of international economic integration, the United States and the European Union differ sufficiently in all three dimensions to explain the different reactions of labor to globalization.

Trade Openness and the Nature of Trade

Exposure to trade has always been far greater in Europe than in the United States. In 1960 the degree of trade openness (exports plus imports divided by GDP) stood between 20 and 30 percent in France, Germany, Italy, and the United Kingdom—the four largest European economies—with considerably higher levels in smaller countries.[17] By contrast, in the United States, international trade amounted to barely 7 percent of GDP. In the next forty years, exposure to trade increased significantly on both sides of the Atlantic, reaching between 40 and 50 percent in the large European countries and nearly 20 percent in the United States. The main driving force behind this dramatic change was the steady removal of trade barriers. This was accomplished not only through successive negotiations on the General Agreement on Tariffs and Trade (GATT) and the World Trade Organization (WTO) but also through regional efforts in Europe (with the widening and deepening of the European Union and the spread of regional trade arrangements between the EU and its neighbors) and in America (with the formation of the Canada-U.S. Free Trade Agreement and the North American Free Trade Agreement).[18]

Behind the apparent similarity of Europe and the United States in the rise of trade openness, there are, in fact, two important differences in the nature of the process of international economic integration between the two areas. First, as figure 9-1 demonstrates, the increase in trade openness in France and Germany between 1960 and 1998 was entirely an intra-EU phenomenon.[19] At the end of the 1990s, the exposure of these two countries to trade with countries outside the group of fifteen nations that today constitute the European Union was the same as it had been in 1960.[20] A similar picture holds for the other countries in the European Union. For EU-15 as a whole, trade openness increased from 30 percent to 50 percent between 1960 and 1998, with the share of extra-EU trade in GDP remaining constant around 20 percent.[21] However, the trend changed during the

Figure 9-1. *Trade Openness: France, Germany, and the United States,*
1960–98[a]

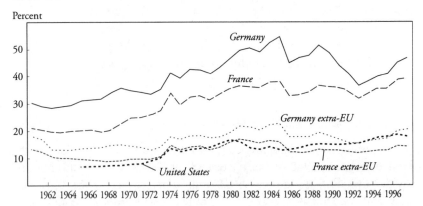

Percent

Source: Author's calculations based on data from Eurostat (the Statistical Office of the European Communities).
a. Exports plus imports as share of GDP.

1990s. Between 1993 and 1998, the degree of trade openness in France
(and in the EU-15 as a whole) increased by 8 percentage points, of which
5 points came from increased intra-EU trade (completion of the Single
Market Program and enlargement) and 3 points from increased extra-EU
trade (especially with the countries of central and eastern Europe). At the
same time, trade openness increased by 10 points in Germany, with an
equal contribution of intra- and extra-trade. (This reflects Germany's role
as the main trading partner of the countries of central and eastern Europe.)

Second, the increase in trade openness of European countries has resulted in intra-industry trade (IIT) specialization. I have computed an
index of intra-industry trade for the EU-15, France, Germany, and the
United States based on the work of Herbert Grubel and P. J. Lloyd.[22] All
data used for the calculation of the indexes are at the three-digit Standard
International Trade Classification (SITC-Rev. 3) level and are subsequently
aggregated using the procedure of Grubel and Lloyd in order to obtain
country indexes. Only trade in manufactured goods (SITC 5-8, minus 68)
is taken into consideration. The index can vary between zero and one. A
value of zero would suggest that there is no intra-industry trade, whereas
as value of one would indicate that all trade is intra-industry.

Table 9-1 reports values of the IIT index computed for the EU-15,
France, Germany, and the United States, with respect to different trading
partners and for the period 1989 to 1998. For Europe, the level of intra-

Table 9-1. *Intra-Industry Trade: France, Germany, and the United States with Various Partners, 1989 and 1998*

Partner	1989				1998			
	France	Germany	EU-15	United States	France	Germany	EU-15	United States
Intra-EU	0.80	0.71	0.69	. . .	0.86	0.78	0.73	. . .
World[a]	0.66	0.53	0.56	0.64	0.69	0.60	0.62	0.68
Rich neighbor[b]	0.68	0.66	0.61	0.68	0.62	0.66	0.59	0.63
Poor neighbor[c]	0.46	0.35	0.39	0.66	0.52	0.56	0.52	0.57
Dynamic Asian economies[d]	0.33	0.30	0.31	0.37	0.44	0.44	0.42	0.48
China	0.11	0.10	0.10	0.11	0.23	0.22	0.21	0.12

Source: Author's calculations based on Eurostat data.

a. For EU countries, all countries beyond the EU.

b. For the EU, EFTA (Switzerland, Norway, Iceland, and Liechtenstein); for the United States, Canada.

c. For the EU, Poland, the Czech Republic, Slovakia, Hungary, Romania, Bulgaria, Albania, Latvia, Lithuania, Estonia, Slovenia, Croatia, Bosnia-Herzegovina, Serbia, and FYROM; for the United States, Mexico.

d. Singapore, Taiwan, Hong Kong, South Korea, Thailand, and Malaysia.

industry trade is significantly and consistently higher within the EU than for extra-EU trade. This obviously reflects the fact that factor endowments are much more similar within the European Union than between the EU and third countries. Between 1960 and 1998, most of the increase in trade openness of France, Germany, and the EU-15 in general was accounted for by intra-EU trade; therefore, the IIT indexes suggest that the trade liberalization has been relatively painless for EU countries. This message echoes the early work of Bela Balassa. In 1966 he found that the establishment of the Common Market resulted primarily in intra-industry trade, where "the income redistributional effects . . . are expected to be smaller than in the traditional [interindustry] case."[23] By contrast, trade liberalization may have been more painful during the 1990s, when a significant portion of the increase in trade openness was taken by extra-EU transactions, particularly to and from central and eastern European countries.

In the United States the level of intra-industry trade is fairly high as well, about halfway between the levels recorded in Europe for intra- and extra-EU trade. It is unlikely, therefore, that the difference in intra-industry trade explains why Europe and America have reacted differently to globalization.

Labor Market Institutions

Given the plethora of writings on the subject, there is little need to dwell on the greater rigidity of labor markets in Europe than in the United States. A useful summary of the literature is provided by Marco Buti, L. R. Pench, and Paolo Sestito, who examine the role of labor market institutions in some detail.[24] Using data from various studies by the Organization for Economic Cooperation and Development, the authors plot for each OECD country the combination of employment protection legislation (EPL) strictness, and unemployment benefit (UB) generosity, on what they refer to as the "workers' protection" space. They observe that all European Union countries (with the exception of the United Kingdom) choose a much higher degree of protection than do the other OECD countries, with the United States ranking last on both dimensions. At the same time they find that different groups of countries in the European Union choose different combinations of EPL strictness and UB generosity in order to achieve similar levels of worker protection. Scandinavian countries tend to go for liberal labor market regulations and generous unemployment compensation, whereas Mediterranean countries tend to choose the opposite combination; France, Germany, and the other EU countries occupy an intermediate position.

One of the features that distinguishes European and U.S. labor market institutions is the centralization of wage bargaining, which results in the compression of relative wages across skills, sectors, and regions. With rigid wages, a shift in demand, such as globalization that favors skilled workers, new sectors, or perhaps new regions, tends to produce unemployment among unskilled workers and in older sectors and regions. It also means that insufficient resources are shifted between sectors and regions. A clear indication of Europe's problem can be seen from data on sectoral specialization. There is a significant gap between the European Union and the United States in the share of employment in services. In 1997 services accounted for 73 percent of U.S. employment but only 65 percent in the European Union.[25] By contrast, industry absorbed 30 percent of those employed in the EU compared with only 24 percent in the United States.[26] Moreover, within the manufacturing sector, Europe tends to specialize much more than the United States in traditional areas, characterized by relatively low demand, and much less than the United States in the more dynamic, information and communication technology sectors.[27]

Adjustment and Redistribution Mechanisms

Globalization may have affected labor somewhat more in America than in Europe due to differences in the nature of trade and in the type of labor market institutions. Ultimately, however, the (real or perceived) cost of globalization borne by labor is also a function of the available adjustment and redistribution mechanisms.

In the United States various programs have been established in response to the fear of trade liberalization voiced by labor. The Trade Adjustment Assistance (TAA) program, established under the Trade Act of 1962 authorizing the United States to participate in the Kennedy Round, is the federal entitlement program for workers affected by trade liberalization. Initially meant to provide income support to those who lose their jobs because of trade negotiations, the TAA program was amended by the Trade Act of 1974 to aid workers who lose their jobs or whose hours of work and wages are reduced as a result of increased imports. The program assists workers who have been certified by their local state labor department as having been adversely affected by increased imports; these workers receive services to help them prepare for and obtain alternative employment. In

1993, when the North American Free Trade Agreement was approved by the U.S. Congress, the NAFTA-Transitional Adjustment Assistance (NAFTA-TAA) program was introduced to provide benefits to workers negatively affected not only by imports from Canada or Mexico, but also by the relocation of plants to these countries.

The stated purpose of TAA and NAFTA-TAA is to assist certified individuals to return to "suitable employment," defined as work of a substantially equal or higher skill level than the person's previous job and that pays not less than 80 percent of the previous wage. In other words, the programs try to reduce temporary adjustment costs incurred in the generally efficient U.S. labor market, not compensate (possibly) permanent income losses. Thus the activities of TAA and NAFTA-TAA focus on career counseling, training, job search, and relocation. Income support, known in both programs as trade readjustment allowances, is available for fifty-two weeks after a worker's unemployment compensation benefit is exhausted (at the end of the twenty-sixth unemployment week) and while the worker participates in an approved full-time training program.

Given the role of the North American Free Trade Agreement in the U.S. debate on globalization, it is useful to focus for a moment on the NAFTA-TAA program. By July 1999, roughly 240,000 workers had been certified under it—an average of fewer than 4,000 workers a month over sixty-five months.[28] While this figure is small compared with the 110 million workers in the U.S. labor force or the total number of long-term displaced workers (about 175,000 a month in the mid-1990s), its potential impact on the public debate should not be underestimated.

There are several reasons. First, the number of certified workers is only a fraction of the number of workers who filed a petition to participate in the program. Second, labor unions play an important role in the process of petition and certification. Unionization increases the probability that an adverse NAFTA-related impact will result in a program application. Hinojosa-Ojeda and others note that given the advocacy role of unions, the high percentage of union involvement in NAFTA-TAA certifications is not surprising. Union petitions made up 22 percent of all the petitions that were certified but accounted for 31 percent of certified workers, a far higher union rate than that which prevails generally in the United States.[29] Finally, the U.S. Department of Labor, which administers the program, is probably adding fuel to the public debate with a NAFTA-TAA fact sheet posted on its website. "If Imports from Canada or Mexico Cost You Your Job," the site proclaims, "Apply for NAFTA-Transitional Adjustment Assistance." The exact same remarks hold for the Trade Adjustment Assistance program, which certifies about two-thirds as many workers as does NAFTA-TAA.[30]

Organized labor in the United States promotes trade adjustment programs and helps to implement them, yet it strongly opposes globalization. I propose the following explanation for this seeming paradox. When the Trade Adjustment Assistance program was created in 1962, the United States traded very little internationally and imported virtually no manufactured goods from low-income countries. In those days trade liberalization imposed little cost on labor. Import surges were mainly cyclical phenomena, only giving rise to temporary adjustment costs. Indeed, until 1981 the program provided mainly income support to workers on temporary layoff (usually in the steel sector); eventually these workers returned to their previous employer. As the degree of trade openness of the United States increased, and trade-induced layoffs became more permanent, TAA evolved into a program aiming at finding jobs in other sectors and regions. Accordingly, in the late 1980s, training became required for certified workers to receive extended income support, a condition also found in the NAFTA-TAA program introduced in 1994.[31] During the 1990s, trade openness and manufactured imports from low-income countries increased substantially, thereby adding permanent income losses to temporary adjustment costs. Yet Trade Adjustment Assistance remains the only response.

Recognizing the fundamental shortcoming of the program, Gary Burtless and others in 1998 recommended that adjustment assistance be complemented with an explicit compensation mechanism. They argued that the basis for compensation of trade-displaced workers should be the difference between what the workers earn in their new job and what they earned previously. Workers would be compensated for half their loss in earnings, and the compensation would last for a limited period (two to three years). Although an improvement on TAA, the scheme of Burtless et al. is still far removed from full income compensation. Like TAA, it belongs more to the realm of efficiency than equity.[32]

In Europe there is no similar program. More broadly, there is no EU social program specifically designed to deal with the fears and costs of trade liberalization. I see two reasons for this contrasting situation with the United States.

First, all EU members are countries with large welfare states. The welfare state in Europe is not only much larger than in the United States; it also is more equity oriented and less efficiency oriented than the U.S. welfare state. Unquestionably, Europe's social policy has been much more effective than America's in limiting income inequality and poverty. In the mid-1990s, the ratio between the share of income accruing to the highest decile and the share earned by the lowest decile was equal to 17 in the United States compared with an EU average of 8.[33] At the same time, 17 percent of the U.S. population lived in households with an income below the 50 percent median income level; the equivalent share in the European Union was generally less than 10 percent.[34] On the other hand, America's social policy has certainly been much more successful than Europe's in ensuring an efficient use of labor. During the late 1990s, income per capita in the United States was 50 percent higher than in the European Union, not because of higher labor productivity but because of a higher employment rate—the result of lower youth unemployment and higher participation of older workers.

Second, the integrationist ideology of the European Union and its executive body, the European Commission, clearly precludes a website proclaiming "If the Single Market Costs You Your Job . . . Apply for Trade Adjustment Assistance." Moreover, the 1957 Treaty of Rome, the founding document of the European Union, recognized that the abolition, between member countries, of obstacles to freedom of movement for goods, services, capital, and persons needed to be accompanied by social reforms. The treaty called for a two-pronged social policy: the approximation or harmonization of social provisions among member countries; and the establishment of a European Social Fund (ESF) to improve employment opportunities for workers in the Common Market by increasing their geographical and occupational mobility.

The fund has undergone many phases throughout its history. During the first phase (1958–71), it provided grants for vocational training and resettlement to workers suffering a temporary drop in wages during restructuring operations of their enterprises. Although the texts made no explicit link between restructuring and the Common Market, the intention was clear. Thus the ESF was rather like the TAA program in the United States, except that governments, rather than individuals, applied for funding. During this phase, the fund had little role to play in the adjustment process since, as noted by Balassa, "there are no examples of declining manufacturing industries in any of the member states, nor have they experienced a wave of bankruptcies. Indeed, the number of bankruptcies has fallen since the Common Market's establishment, and there is little evidence of frictional unemployment."[35]

During this first phase, the budget for the European Social Fund remained extremely modest. As the unemployment situation gradually deteriorated inside the European Union, the fund grew substantially, concentrating mostly on vocational training for young people. New changes were introduced in the late 1980s, after the entry of Portugal and Spain in the European Community (EC), and in 1995, after the accession of Austria, Finland, and Sweden. Since 1995, the fund has been allocated into six objectives, of which two (receiving 10 percent of the funds) are connected to industrial restructuring.[36] Wisely, I think, no distinction is made between the sources of restructuring. The purpose is to adapt to economic changes, regardless of whether the cause is (intra- or extra-EU) trade liberalization or technological progress. Hence trade adjustment assistance, as such, is totally absent from the current European landscape.

With regard to European economic integration and social harmonization, two periods can be distinguished.[37] Before the mid-1980s there was little or no demand for social harmonization between member states. The main reason was that the EC was fairly homogeneous. Member countries had similar factor endowments, which meant that trade was mainly intra-industry, and adjustment costs were limited. Moreover, social policies were fairly similar across EC countries.

A clear shift in the direction of social harmonization occurred in the mid-1980s as a result of three factors. The first and foremost was the enlargement of the European Community to include Portugal and Spain, two countries with substantially lower labor costs than the old members. The southern enlargement raised the possibility of increased interindustry trade and rising adjustment costs; it also brought up the specter of "social dumping" in high-income northern countries. The second factor was the Single Market Program, which was designed to eliminate the remaining barriers to free circulation of products and factors within the Community. The last factor was the high unemployment and stagnating real wages in the EC. Despite much effort, however, little in the way of actual social harmonization was achieved.

Labor Mobility

There is an intense economic and political debate raging across Europe about migration policy. As the *Economist* succinctly put it: "Foreigners are streaming into the EU in search of jobs. They are often vilified, but they are increasingly necessary."[38]

During the 1960s and early 1970s, the six members of the European

Community opened their doors to large numbers of guest workers from (northern and southern) Mediterranean countries. In 1970 Germany granted nearly 500,000 work permits to recruits from Greece, Portugal, Spain, Turkey, and Yugoslavia. The inflow was abruptly interrupted in 1973 in the wake of the oil crisis. Thereafter, virtually no new permits were awarded to foreign workers, but those who were in the EC were able to settle permanently and to bring their relations. During the 1990s, the raising of the Iron Curtain and events in Yugoslavia unleashed a new flow of migrants into the European Union, usually illegal workers or asylum-seekers.

Meanwhile, inside Europe, migration flows dwindled. When Greece acceded to the European Community in 1981 and Portugal and Spain entered in 1986, high-income members feared that freedom of movement of workers, a principle enshrined in the Treaty of Rome, would result in large migratory movements from these traditional labor-sending countries. Consequently, the free movement of workers was banned during a transition period, which expired in 1988 for Greece and in 1991 for Portugal and Spain. However, there was virtually no increase in migration from these countries after the transition period.

Two principal reasons explain the fall of migration within Europe in spite of its enlargement to low-income countries.[39] The first is the rapid increase in income and employment opportunity in southern Europe, partly aided by massive EU transfers financed by the Structural Funds. The second factor is the increased generosity of the welfare state in these countries.[40]

The current debate on migration in Europe pits the vast majority of citizens, who tend to perceive immigrants as "welfare-scroungers, job-snatchers and threats to stability," against a small, enlightened group, which claims that "Europe needs more immigrants."[41] This positive attitude stems from the emphasis on two developments: the rapid aging of Europe's population and growing labor shortages in specific activities or countries. Estimates by the United Nations' Population Division indicate that, at current birth and death rates, the European Union would need 1.6 million immigrants a year in order to keep its working-age population stable in the next fifty years. Holding the ratio of workers to pensioners constant would require an additional inflow of 12 million workers each year. In addition to helping finance Europe's welfare state, immigrants would "inject into stale, aging countries fresh vitality, fresh energy and an uncommon willingness to work hard at . . . the sorts of jobs Europeans are increasingly unwilling, or ill-equipped to do."[42]

Clearly, the welfare state plays a central role in the political economy of migration in Europe.[43] Two economic factors are likely to shape the attitude of European citizens toward migrants: whether the migrants are substitutes or complements; and whether they are net contributors to or beneficiaries of the welfare state. Divide European citizens into three categories: capital owners, skilled workers, and unskilled workers. And consider four types of immigrants: (1) unskilled guest-workers, that is, temporary migrants without relatives; (2) unskilled permanent migrants with relatives; (3) illegal unskilled workers; and (4) asylum-seekers.

During the 1960s and early 1970s, migrants belonged entirely to category (1). They were complements to native capital owners and skilled workers but substitutes for unskilled natives. However, the latter probably benefited from the fact that guest-workers were net contributors to the welfare state. Therefore, migration, on the whole, was welcomed by natives.

During the remainder of the 1970s and throughout the 1980s, migrants gradually shifted to category (2). Native capital owners were still better off with migrants, but the position of skilled and unskilled workers shifted from what it was in the earlier period. Unskilled workers were now clearly opposed to migrants on economic grounds as the migrants were joined by their relatively numerous relations and became net beneficiaries of the welfare state. The position of skilled workers was probably ambiguous: they were still complements to the migrants, yet they were feeling the pinch of social transfers.[44] Altogether, therefore, the attitude of natives toward migrants was probably divided.

Since the early 1990s, all four categories of migrants have been present in Europe. The main contingent belongs to category (2), but there are also some guest-workers as well as large numbers of illegal workers and asylum-seekers from central and eastern Europe. The impact of illegal workers on natives is the same as the impact of guest-workers on natives except in two regards. First, illegal workers' wages are lower than natives' wages, so they probably compete more fiercely with native unskilled workers than in the case of guest-workers. Second, illegal workers (and their employers) do not pay social security contributions. Therefore, native unskilled workers are likely to be hurt by illegal unskilled workers on both counts. The impact of asylum-seekers is the same for all natives, since they are usually not allowed to work. They are simply social welfare recipients. All in all, therefore, these short-term economic considerations go a long way in explaining the majority opinion of Europeans that immigrants are "welfare-scroungers and job-snatchers."[45]

Figure 9-2. *Share of Foreign Workers in the Labor Force, EU Total and Member States, 1998*

Percent

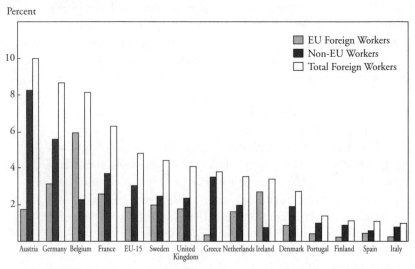

Source: Author's calculations based on Eurostat data.

In the remainder of this section, I examine the link between migration and unemployment.

There is a vast body of literature examining the impact of migration on wages and unemployment. Contrary to the literature on trade and labor, which is largely dominated by trade economists, studies about the effects of migration on domestic labor markets are written mostly by labor economists. In the United States the leading contributor has repeatedly argued that massive immigration of unskilled workers depresses the wages of native unskilled workers. He advocates a reduction in the level of immigration and a shift in its composition toward more skilled workers.[46]

In Europe most of the empirical work on the effects of migration on domestic labor markets focuses on Austria and Germany, the two countries with the highest share of foreign workers in the labor force. In 1998 foreign workers accounted for 10 percent of the labor force in Austria and 9 percent in Germany compared with an average of roughly 5 percent for the EU-15 (figure 9-2). Moreover, the share of non-EU foreign workers in Austria and Germany was, respectively, 8 percent and 6 percent compared with an average in the European Union of only 3 percent. According to the literature summarized by Rudolf Winter-Ebmer and Klaus F. Zimmer-

Figure 9-3. *Unemployment Rates for Foreigners and Nationals, EU Total and Member States, 1998*

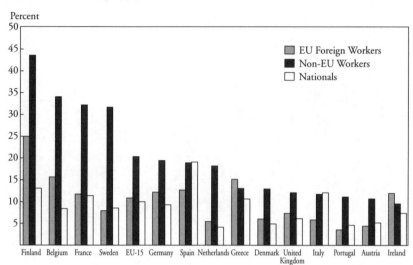

Source: Author's calculations based on Eurostat data.

mann, immigration of non-EU nationals produces negative effects on native employment and wages in Austria but has no significant effect on the German labor market.[47]

The effects of migration on labor markets will not be addressed here. I turn instead to the different incidence of unemployment among national and foreign workers.

Figure 9-3 presents publicly available but little-known data on unemployment rates in EU countries in 1998 broken down between nationals, EU foreigners, and non-EU foreigners.[48] It reveals two important features. First, for the European Union as a whole, the unemployment rate for non-EU foreigners was twice the unemployment rate for nationals or EU foreigners. By contrast, in the United States the unemployment rate among persons born abroad was only 25 percent higher than the unemployment rate among those born in the country.[49] At the same time, however, the unemployment rate for blacks was twice that of whites, a constant feature of the U.S. economy for many years.[50] The disparity among unemployment rates in the European Union probably reflects in part cross-country differences in educational attainment between nationals and EU foreigners, on the one hand, and non-EU foreigners, on the other. The persistence

Figure 9-4. *Unemployment Rates for Non-EU Foreigners Relative to Total Unemployment Rates, EU Member States, 1983–98*[a]

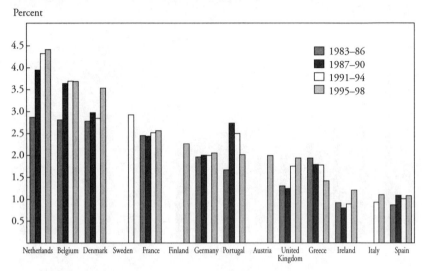

Percent

Source: Author's calculations based on Eurostat data.
a. Data for the full period are not available for Sweden, Finland, Austria or Italy.

of unemployment differentials among blacks and whites with similar levels of education suggests that racial discrimination may be at work in the United States. Similarly, the higher rate of unemployment among non-EU foreigners may reflect discrimination in EU labor markets.

The other central finding is the considerable variance in the situations of EU countries. In Finland, Belgium, France, and Sweden, the unemployment rate for non-EU foreigners was much above the EU average (30 to 45 percent compared with 20 percent), but the unemployment rate for nationals was either slightly below or slightly above the EU average (8 to 13 percent compared with 10 percent). In Italy and Spain, and to a lesser extent in Greece and Ireland, unemployment rates were roughly similar for nationals and non-EU foreigners.

Figure 9-4 uses the ratio of the unemployment rate for non-EU foreigners to the total unemployment rate to tell the same story in a slightly different way. The ratio is presented for four subperiods: 1983-86, 1987-90, 1991-94, and 1995-98. Countries with high ratios (3 or above) are the Netherlands, Belgium, and Denmark, with Sweden not far behind. Countries with low ratios (around 1) are Ireland, Italy, and Spain. Those with average ratios (between 1.5 and 2.5) include France, Finland, Germany, Portugal, Austria, the United Kingdom, and Greece. The composition of

Figure 9-5. *Generosity of the Welfare State and Unemployment Rates, EU and the United States, mid-1990s*

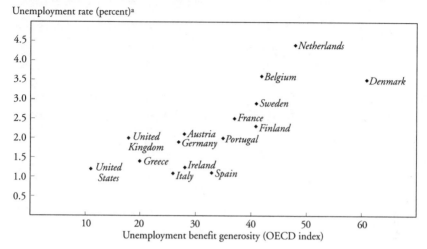

Unemployment rate (percent)ᵃ

Source: Author's calculations based on data from the Organization for Economic Cooperation and Development.
a. Non-EU foreigners/total unemployment rate, average 1995–98.

the three categories has remained fairly stable throughout the entire period from 1983 to 1998.

The country grouping suggests that countries with the most generous welfare state may also be those countries where the unemployment rate of non-EU foreigners most exceeds the total unemployment rate. I offer two reasons for this. First, countries with generous welfare states may be those that most attract secondary migrants (that is, family members of immigrant workers). Whereas primary migrants, usually settled guest-workers, may be expected to have unemployment rates no higher than those of nationals, the same may not be true of their relatives for a variety of reasons. Second, countries with generous social transfers are likely to have large public sectors where employment is typically restricted to nationals or EU foreigners.

Figure 9-5 shows the relationship between the generosity of the welfare state (measured by the OECD index of unemployment benefit generosity, slightly modified by Buti, Sestito, and Pench)[51] and the unemployment rate for non-EU nationals relative to the total unemployment rate (average for 1995 to 1998). The figure plots values for the United States and for all EU-15 countries except Luxembourg. A clear positive relationship exists between welfare state generosity and the incidence of unemployment for

Table 9-2. *Determinants of Unemployed Incidence among Foreign Workers Relative to Total Labor Force, 1995–98*[a]

Variable	EU-14	EU-14 plus Australia, Canada, and United States	
α	1.225	1.242	1.226
	(0.591)	(0.713)	(0.571)
	[0.065]	[0.107]	[0.055]
β	0.049	0.040	0.047
	(0.011)	(0.013)	(0.011)
	[0.001]	[0.008]	[0.001]
γ	0.448	0.409	0.449
	(0.099)	(0.118)	(0.096)
	[0.001]	[0.005]	[0.001]
δ	−2.171	−2.374	−2.338
	(0.748)	(0.889)	(0.713)
	[0.016]	[0.020]	[0.009]
ε		−1.363	−3.987
		(0.452)	(1.014)
		[0.011]	[0.002]
φ			−1.472
			(0.531)
			(0.018)
Adj. R^2	0.852	0.788	0.864
Observations	14	17	17

a. Table reports result of the following OLS regression:

$$UFT = \alpha + \beta UBEN + \gamma \log(FORRATE) + \delta \log(PARTRATE) + \varepsilon ACU$$
$$+ \varphi ACU * \log(FORRATE) + \eta.$$

See text for description of all variables. Standard errors are given in parentheses, and p values in brackets.

non-EU foreigners. The coefficient of correlation between the two indicators equals 0.76 for the fourteen EU countries and increases slightly when the United States is added to the sample.

Table 9-2 presents regression results that confirm the relationship between the generosity of the welfare state (*UBEN*) and the unemployment rate for non-EU nationals relative to the total unemployment rate (*UFT*) in a multifactor setting. I control for two factors. The first is the share of non-EU foreigners in the total population (*FORRATE*). This variable is meant to test the discrimination hypothesis that the higher the non-EU foreign population relative to the total population, the higher the incidence of the unemployment rate among non-EU foreign workers relative to the total unemployment rate.[52] The second control variable is the participation rate (labor force divided by population) among non-EU foreigners (*PARTRATE*). The assumption is that the incidence of unemployment among non-EU foreigners is lower in countries where the participation rate is higher (that is, when foreigners are mostly primary rather than secondary migrants).[53]

The regression results are surprisingly good, given that the sample includes only fourteen observations. The three independent variables explain 85 percent of the variance of the dependent variable. The main finding concerns the impact of the generosity of the welfare state on the unemployment rate for non-EU nationals relative to the total unemployment rate. The (highly significant) coefficient of *UBEN* indicates that a 10 percentage point increase in the index of benefit generosity results in an increase of 0.5 in the unemployment ratio. Adding Australia, Canada, and the United States (*ACU* = 1) to the sample does not affect the coefficient of *UBEN*.[54] There are, however, two important differences between the two subsamples that show up in other coefficients. First, the constant is much lower for Australia, Canada, and the United States, which reflects the fact that the unemployment ratio averages about 1 for these countries compared with 2 for the members of the European Union. Second, the coefficient of *FORRATE*, the share of (non-EU) foreigners in the total population, is positive for the EU countries but negative for Australia, Canada, and the United States. The reason may be the following differences between the two groups. On average, the share of foreigners in the population is 10 percentage points higher in Australia, Canada, and the United States than in the European Union. Moreover, migrants are much more skilled in Australia, Canada, and the United States than they are in the EU.

To summarize, the unemployment rate among non-EU foreigners is significantly higher than the total unemployment rate in most EU countries, sometimes even by a factor 3 or 4. There is strong evidence that this situation is partly linked to the generosity of the welfare state and to the importance of secondary or second-generation migrants. Let there be no misunderstanding: I claim only that cross-country differences in the unemployment rate among migrants tend to be positively correlated with cross-country differences in welfare generosity. Part of the reason may be that countries with generous welfare states have a large share of public jobs, and these jobs are restricted to nationals. The response to this potentially explosive situation both politically and socially is simple: Europe needs to make more efforts to integrate the immigrants in its population and unleash their productive potential.

Conclusion

The emergence of "one world," where goods, services, and capital flow almost freely thanks to the elimination of regulatory barriers and the advent of the information revolution, has brought unprecedented wealth to Europe and America. At the same time, however, labor has fared relatively poorly on both sides of the Atlantic: declining wages and rising job insecurity in America and growing unemployment in Europe. Whereas economists continue to argue about whether trade or technological change is the main culprit behind the waning fortune of labor, ordinary citizens tend to see the two as simply different facets of globalization. To them, it makes no difference whether economists label flows of goods or services as trade, and flows of ideas passing through the Internet or multinational corporations as technological change. Both constitute globalization.

I have attempted to show that the political economy of domestic adjustment to globalization is different in Europe and America. In the United States, where markets operate efficiently, globalization generated more wealth but also more income inequality and adjustment problems than in Europe. The median voter lost wages and experienced rising job insecurity. Both resulted in labor's fierce opposition to globalization. In Europe, where the welfare state is more generous and markets are less efficient, globalization generated less wealth but also less income inequality and adjustment than in the United States. The European median voter suffered relatively little. Unemployment increased, but its effect fell mainly on "outsiders": the young and immigrants. Accordingly, organized labor in Europe voiced less opposition to globalization than in America.

This is the essential question: Can current responses to the challenge of globalization be sustained? In America the challenge is to ensure a better distribution of income and a decrease in poverty. In Europe the challenge is to prevent the demise of welfare states that are confronted with rising demands and dwindling resources. Possibly, both the United States and Europe have entered a new era in which permanently higher GDP growth is, finally, reversing the decline of wages in America and the fall in employment rates in Europe. If so, the question simply disappears. But what if the worst of globalization is not over? What if trade and technological change continue to threaten the situation of the median voter in America or the sustainability of the welfare state in Europe? There is a broad consensus in Europe that the welfare state must be reformed for efficiency as well as budgetary reasons.[55] Aging and further economic integration in Europe are expected to increase the gap between social expenditures and revenue, if current benefit levels and eligibility rules remain unchanged. Demographic scenarios forecast a dramatic increase in the ratio of pensioners to workers during the next fifty years in Europe.[56] Much sooner than that the Economic and Monetary Union (EMU) is likely to increase the demand for social transfers—through greater competition in product and capital markets and ultimately greater pressure on labor markets—and to reduce the collection of taxes needed to finance them because of greater mobility of financial and human capital. Given the current high level of taxation in Europe, raising taxes is probably not a politically viable option. This leaves two options. One is to adjust social expenditures downward. The other is to employ more migrant workers by attempting to lower the unemployment rate among the current population of immigrants.

Notes

1. Dani Rodrik, *Has Globalization Gone Too Far?* (Washington: Institute for International Economics, 1997); and Gary Burtless and others, *Globaphobia: Confronting Fears about Open Trade* (Brookings, 1998).

2. Council of Economic Advisers, *Changing America: Indicators of Social and Economic Well-Being by Race and Hispanic Origin* (Executive Office of the President, 1998).

3. European Commission, *Statistical Annex of European Economy, Autumn 1999* (Brussels: Directorate General for Economic and Financial Affairs, 2000).

4. See William R. Cline, *Trade and Income Distribution* (Washington: Institute for International Economics, 1997); and Mathias Dewatripont, André Sapir, and Khalid Sekkat, eds., *Trade and Jobs in Europe: Much Ado about Nothing?* (Oxford University Press, 1999).

5. In particular, see Adrian Wood, "How Trade Hurt Unskilled Workers," *Journal of Economic Perspectives*, vol. 9 (1995), pp. 57–80; and Rodrik, *Has Globalization Gone Too Far?*

6. Rodrik, *Has Globalization Gone Too Far?* p. 4.

7. Ibid., p. 27.

8. The distinction between labor markets that are flexible in the United States but rigid in Europe is common throughout the literature on globalization and labor, although admittedly the distinction is oversimplified. See Stephen Nickell, "Unemployment and Labor Market Rigidities: Europe versus North America," *Journal of Economic Perspectives*, vol. 11 (1997), pp. 55–74.

9. See R. M. Blank, ed., *Social Protection versus Economic Flexibility: Is There a Trade-off?* (University of Chicago Press, 1994).

10. In the European Union in 1997 the unemployment rate of young persons (younger than 25) was 21.1 percent compared with a total unemployment rate of 10.6 percent. At the same time, the EU-15 employment rate for men ages 25 to 54 was 86 percent (89 percent in the United States), 37 percent for individuals ages 15 to 24 (52 percent in the United States), and 36 percent for individuals ages 55 to 64 (57 percent in the United States). The employment rate for women ages 25 to 54 was 63 percent (74 percent in the United States).

11. This is in sharp contrast to the wave of globalization during the forty years or so before World War I.

12. This is very clear in the ongoing debate about the eastern enlargement. Public opinion in the European Union remained largely indifferent to the free trade agreements with central and eastern European countries. The possibility of free labor movement, however, is prompting expressions of profound dissatisfaction.

13. W. F. Stolper and P. A. Samuelson, "Protection and Real Wages," *Review of Economic Studies,* vol. 9 (1941), pp. 58–73.

14. See Elhanan Helpman and Paul R. Krugman, *Market Structure and Foreign Trade: Increasing Returns, Imperfect Competition, and the International Economy* (MIT Press, 1985), chap. 9.

15. Paul R. Krugman, "Growing World Trade: Causes and Consequences," *Brookings Papers on Economic Activity, 1:1995,* pp. 327–77. The effect on relative prices depends on the extent of wage rigidity. Relative prices are constant if relative wages are fixed.

16. Robin Naylor, "Union Wage Strategies and International Trade," *Economic Journal,* vol. 109 (1999), pp. 102–25, and Naylor, "Endogenous Determination of Trade Regime and Bargaining Outcome," paper prepared for the Trade and Labour Market Adjustment Conference, University of Nottingham, Centre for Research on Globalisation and Labour Markets, March 27–28, 1999.

17. I agree with Richard Cooper that this traditional measure of trade openness is open to criticism.

18. There have been four enlargements of the European Union: in 1973 (Denmark, Ireland, and the United Kingdom), in 1981 (Greece), in 1986 (Portugal and Spain), and in 1996 (Austria, Finland, and Sweden). The EU was deepened by the completion of the Single Market in 1993. On the EU and regional trade arrangements, see André Sapir, "EC Regionalism at the Turn of the Millennium: Towards a New Paradigm?" in P. Lloyd and C. Milner, eds., *The World Economy: Global Trade Policy 2000* (Oxford: Blackwell, forthcoming).

19. The same holds for Italy and the United Kingdom and for the smaller EU countries. These countries are not shown in figure 9-1 in the interest of clarity.

20. About 15 percent in France and 20 percent in Germany.

21. The evolution of trade openness for EU-15 (not shown in figure 9-1) is almost the same as for Germany. There was, however, a major difference in the decline of trade exposure following German reunification. Trade openness decreased from 52 percent in 1989 for West Germany to 37 percent in 1993 for unified Germany (see figure 9-1), but only from 47 percent for the EU-15 (excluding East Germany) to 40 percent for the EU-15 (including East Germany).

22. Herbert Grubel and P. J. Lloyd, *Intra-Industry Trade: The Theory and Measurement of International Trade in Differentiated Products* (London: Halsted Press, 1975).

23. Bela Balassa, "Tariff Reductions and Trade in Manufactures among Industrial Countries," *American Economic Review,* vol. 56 (1966), p. 472.

24. Marco Buti, L. R. Pench, and Paolo Sestito, "European Unemployment: Contending Theories and Institutional Complexities," Policy Papers 98/1 (Florence: European University Institute, Robert Schuman Centre, 1998).

25. The gap is even more striking if public administrations are excluded from services. In this case the share of employment in services is 69 percent in the United States and only 58 percent in the EU-15.

26. European Commission, *Employment Rates Report 1998* (Brussels: Directorate General for Employment and Social Affairs, 1999).

27. In 1997 the European Union accounted for 40 percent of the EU-Japan-U.S. triad GDP but only 26 percent of the production of ICT goods. See *Information Technology Outlook 2000*, draft, DSTI/ICCP/IE(99)5 (Paris: Organization for Economic Cooperation and Development, 1999).

28. R. Hinojosa-Ojeda and others, "The U.S. Employment Impacts of the North American Integration after NAFTA: A Partial Equilibrium Approach," research report NAID-RR-010-00 (University of California at Los Angeles, North American Integration and Development Center, 2000). See also (http://naid.sppsr.ucla.edu).

29. Ibid.

30. According to H. D. Samuel and others, "Strengthening Trade Adjustment Assistance" (n.d.) (www.econstrat.org/taa.htm), the number of workers certified for benefits in 1997 was 60,000 under TAA and 90,000 under NAFTA-TAA. The actual number of benefit recipients is far lower than these figures because workers were able to obtain alternative employment very rapidly or did not meet eligibility requirements.

31. See G. K. Schoepfle, "U.S. Trade Adjustment Assistance Policies for Workers," in Alan V. Deardorff and Robert M. Stern, eds., *Social Dimensions of U.S. Trade Policy* (University of Michigan Press, 2000).

32. Burtless and others, *Globaphobia*.

33. See World Bank, *World Development Indicators 2000* (Washington, 2000).

34. See Organization for Economic Cooperation and Development, *Trends in Income Distribution and Poverty in the OECD Area*, DEELSA/ELSA/WP1(99)15 (Paris, 1999).

35. Balassa, "Tariff Reductions," p. 472.

36. Since 1988, the four EU Structural Funds have accounted for one-third of the EU budget. In the late 1990s, the ESF amounted to 30 percent of the Structural Funds or 10 percent of the EU budget. With a total EU budget reaching about 1.2 percent of GDP, the ESF amounted to 0.12 percent of the gross domestic product of the European Union, certainly not a trivial figure.

37. André Sapir, "Trade Liberalization and the Harmonization of Social Policies: Lessons from European Integration," in Jagdish N. Bhagwati and R. E. Hudec, eds., *Fair Trade and Harmonization: Prerequisites for Free Trade?* vol. 1 (MIT Press, 1996).

38. *The Economist*, May 6, 2000.

39. For alternative explanations, see P. Braunerhjelm and others, "Integration and the Regions of Europe: How the Right Policies Can Prevent Polarisation," Monitoring European Integration 10 (London: Center for Economic Policy Research, 2000).

40. Social transfers, as a percentage of GDP, increased between 1970 and 1995 from 9 to 16 percent in Greece, 7 to 15 percent in Spain, and 4 to 15 percent in Portugal.

41. *The Economist*, May 6, 2000.

42. Ibid.

43. On the link between the welfare state and migration, see Assef Razin and Efraim Sadka, "Tax Burden and Migration: A Political Economy Perspective," Working Paper 9778 (Washington: International Monetary Fund, 1997); and Dietmar Wellisch and Uwe Walz, "Why Do Rich Countries Prefer Free Trade over Free Migration? The Role of the Modern Welfare State," *European Economic Review,* vol. 42 (1998), pp. 1595–612.

44. I am assuming that skilled workers contribute far more to the welfare state than do capital owners.

45. See Assef Razin and Efraim Sadka, "Migration and Pension," Working Paper 6778 (Cambridge, Mass.: National Bureau of Economic Research, 1998). They show that although unskilled migrants are net beneficiaries of the welfare state and may induce adverse effects on natives in a static model, they are likely to benefit all natives in an overlapping generation model with pensions.

46. See, for instance, George J. Borjas, *Heaven's Door: Immigration Policy and the American Economy* (Princeton University Press, 1999).

47. Rudolf Winter-Ebmer and Klaus F. Zimmermann, "East-West Trade and Migration: The Austrio-German Case," in Riccardo Faini, Jaime de Melo, and Klaus Zimmermann, eds., *Migration: The Controversies and Evidence* (Cambridge University Press, 1999), chap. 11.

48. I am grateful to Eurostat, the Statistical Office of the European Commission, for providing the data.

49. There are no statistics on unemployment rates broken down by nationals and foreigners for the United States.

50. See Council of Economic Advisers, *Changing America.*

51. Buti, Pench, and Sestito, "European Unemployment."

52. *FORRATE* ranges from less than 1 percent in Finland, Ireland, Italy, Portugal, and Spain to between 6 and 8 percent in Austria and Germany.

53. *PARTRATE* ranges from about 40 percent in Belgium and the Netherlands to more than 75 percent in Austria and Sweden.

54. *ACU* is a dummy variable equal to 1 for Australia, Canada, or the United States.

55. See Marco Buti, Daniele Franco, and L. R. Pench, eds., *The Welfare State in Europe* (Cheltenham: Edward Elgar, 1999).

56. The projected increase is from 0.4 in 2000 to 0.7 in 2050.

COMMENT BY
Richard N. Cooper

André Sapir's well-argued chapter contrasts developments in the United States and Europe over the past two decades—growth in employment in the United States, with low measured productivity growth (until the late 1990s), and rising unemployment in Europe (until the late 1990s), with rising measured productivity. The chapter corresponds with my general sense of what has been happening, but several of the empirical propositions on which Sapir relies for his basic theme cause me some uneasiness. I will take up four points about data and economic assumptions and conclude with general observations.

First, Sapir relies on the alleged decline in real wages in the United States, at least until the mid-1990s. The most widely cited statistic, average weekly earnings of nonsupervisory workers in private U.S. nonagricultural sectors, corrected for inflation, did show a decline of 14 percent over the period 1970 to 1996, an extraordinary event during a quarter century of economic growth.[1] This figure supported the widespread claim in the early 1990s that "our grandchildren will be worse off than we are."

I say "alleged decline" since this figure badly needs to be reconciled with another one: real per capita consumption in the United States rose by 76 percent, 2.2 percent a year, during the same period of time. Extraordinary contortions are required to reconcile these two figures. Indeed, in the end they cannot be reconciled: one or both of them must be wrong. My candidate is the real earnings figure.

As so often, the explanation is complicated, involving both concept and measurement. Over this quarter century the American economy experienced higher rates of participation in the labor force, especially by women, and a decline in the share of children in the population. Civilian employment relative to population grew by 24 percent. Nonwage income, especially but not exclusively pension income, grew relative to wage income (disposable income/wages rose by 17 percent). The savings rate declined by a measured 5 percentage points. Allowing for these factors *implies* an increase in the average real wage of 16 percent—34 percent above the official figure.

The official weekly wage figures have several known downward biases to them that are usually ignored. First, the wage figure excludes fringe benefits, especially health care, which since 1970 have been increasingly shifted from wage-earners to insurers. Second, the series covers hours paid rather than hours worked, thus excluding the substantial increase in paid vacations. Third, the series excludes bonuses. Fourth, the series was broadened over time to include many small, low-wage firms. Thus the data have been improved, but the series records excessively high average wages thirty years ago, imparting a downward bias to recorded changes in average wages. Taken together, these factors are quantitatively significant.

Moreover, while the official wage series covers "production and non-supervisory" workers, which in principle covers most American nonagricultural, nongovernment employment, excluding managers, in actual fact (due to reporting errors) many high-paying nonsupervisory workers that are not covered by the U.S. Fair Labor Standards Act are probably excluded. Furthermore, the "real" wage is calculated using a price index with a widely known mistake in it, due to incorrect measurement of housing costs. The error was corrected in 1983, but not for preceding years, leaving it 6 percent too high in 1996 compared with 1970. And it makes no allowance for the widely acknowledged upward bias in the U.S. consumer price index, by perhaps 1 percent annually according to the Boskin Report. Allowing for that alone would raise the real wage a further 30 percent over the 1970-96 period. But there is a great difference between acknowledgment of a bias and meticulous correction of it. (Corrections amounting to 0.45 percent a year have been made recently.)

When all these factors are put together, the evidence is overwhelming that the average American worker is materially much better off than he (or she) was thirty years ago. Statements to the contrary, both in Europe and in the United States, are badly misinformed.

Second, Sapir assumes that the wage structure in Europe is considerably more rigid than it is in the United States. That assumption may well be correct, but it needs to be examined. In trying to understand some of the phenomena that engage Sapir, I calculated that the average wage of U.S. workers in the textile, apparel, and leather (TAL) industries, heavy with low-skill workers, declined by 8 percent relative to the average wage in manufacturing between 1980 and 1990, a period of rapid growth of imports of manufactured goods from developing countries. Over the same period the relative TAL wage declined by 10 percent in Italy, 6.6 percent in Britain and Germany, and 6.3 percent in the Netherlands (but only 3.8 percent in Spain and 1.3 percent in France).[2] These figures suggest that wage structure in some European countries is not notably more rigid than in the United States.

Third, Sapir is rightly interested in the "exposure to trade" of a country and then conventionally but erroneously measures that by taking a ratio of exports plus imports to GDP. If we must choose a single measure, it should be the ratio of tradable goods and services to GDP, where "tradable" is defined by reference to each country's import regime. (Many EU agricultural goods are not "tradable" because their production and sale within the EU is insulated from world market developments.) This ratio, like Sapir's, must have risen over time, thanks to successive rounds of multilateral trade liberalization and to the emergence of many developing countries as exporters of manufactures. But this ratio should be similar for the European Union and the United States, despite the lower level of observed U.S. trade. Indeed, because of agriculture, the United States may well have a greater "exposure to trade." Residents of New England experience rises in the world price of oil, and it makes no difference to them whether the oil comes from Texas or Venezuela or Nigeria.

Fourth, we should not fall into the too easy assumption that increases in intra-industry trade require markedly less adjustment than do increases in interindustry trade, measured at the three-digit level, which is relatively coarse for most economic activities in highly developed economies. Unskilled workers, by definition, lack specialized skills and can therefore move among economic sectors with relative ease (from apparel manufacturing, for example, to retail trade). It is displaced highly specialized workers that experience difficulty finding new jobs with comparable working conditions, and their specialties are likely to be considerably finer than the three-digit industry level.

The fiercest resistance to imports into the United States, especially manufactures from developing countries, has come from textile and apparel workers and firms, from steel workers and firms, and from workers in the automobile industry. Steel and auto workers can be called aristocrats among U.S. manufacturing workers. Both represented at one time the country's high-prestige industry, and (for particular historical reasons unrelated to productivity) received wages far above average. Steel and auto workers stand to lose from increased competition from any source and find it politically easier to attack imports. Labor union leaders and certain groups of highly paid specialized workers have led the protectionist cause, and any general explanation of U.S. labor resistance to "globalization" must focus on the interests of union leaders and on these particular workers, at least as much as on more general structural factors.

In evaluating economic systems, one needs to look at the total system, not just selected pieces of it such as the social safety net. In particular, the U.S. "labor market" seems to do well at placing people in new jobs, whether new entrants or recently displaced workers. The average period of unemployment in the United States is six weeks, and less than 15 percent of the unemployed have been unemployed for longer than twenty-seven weeks. Total U.S. employment increased by 16 million (13 percent) over the 1990s, and total job creation was perhaps twice that, compensating for the millions of particular jobs eliminated during this period.

Thus an active labor market compensates partially for the relatively frugal social safety net (by continental European standards), with only 26 weeks of unemployment compensation (except in a recession) and public assistance based on a demonstration of need, administered by the states.

Foreign trade is small potatoes when it comes to disturbing modern economies, compared with technological change. Employment in the U.S. coal industry, for instance, declined by 60 percent since 1980, even though coal production and exports rose. Trade adjustment assistance in the United States, which has had its ups and downs, addresses dislocations created by increased imports. The European social safety, as Sapir points out, is not similarly specialized; it covers workers dislocated for whatever reason. On structural analysis, that fact alone suggests that European labor should be less resistant to job-disturbing technical change and industrial innovation than is American labor. Is it so?

Notes

1. Real hourly earnings fell less, by 8 percent, because of a decline in the average number of hours worked each week.

2. Richard N. Cooper, "Foreign Trade, Wages, and Unemployment," in Herbert Giersch, ed., *Fighting Europe's Unemployment in the 1990s* (Berlin: Springer, 1996), p. 111.

COMMENT BY
Dani Rodrik

Ray Vernon was an iconoclast for whom scholarly fashions never held much attraction. That is, of course, what made him a visionary: his pioneering studies of the multinational enterprise, comparative political economy, and what we today call globalization anticipated the flourishing academic work in these areas by a decade or two. His intellect and scholarly curiosity were matched by a distinguished career in the real world, spanning both the private and public sectors.

Nuanced analysis, attention to cultural and historical context, skepticism of grand theories, and distrust of statistical evidence were the hallmarks of Ray's scholarly approach. For a conventional economist, this could be frustrating. I remember trying to convince him of some new econometric finding or the relevance of a theoretical model, only to encounter his bemused smile. Invariably, time proved kinder to his skepticism than to my gullibility.

Ray was a charming man, but he could be intimidating. I know this all too well since my initial foray into research took place under his auspices. In 1977 I was a shy undergraduate at Harvard looking for a job. Ray had a large research operation based at the Harvard Business School. After I was successfully screened by his research assistants, I had my first meeting with him. He asked me how much international economics I had studied. I mumbled that I knew something about multinational companies. His reply continues to ring in my ear: "You *think* you know!" His point, was not to put me down but to warn me against overconfidence. He taught me a lasting lesson about the kind of scholar he was. No matter what the theories of the day say, our tendency is to think we know more than we really do.

When I returned to Harvard as an assistant professor at the Kennedy School, I taught a course with him entitled "Economics and Enterprise in International Affairs." The thought of teaching with Ray was frightening. He did not make matters easy for me: he attended each of my lectures, and after a couple of classes began to openly disagree with some of the things I was saying. My anxiety, however, soon gave way to enjoyment as we developed a pattern of friendly debate. Students, I was told, had a great time watching the two of us argue. Ray held strong opinions, but he was not close-minded. What made arguing with him fun was the ever-present chance that you could actually change his mind.

This chapter by André Sapir is very much in the tradition of Ray Vernon. It focuses on the differences between the United States and Europe (a question of long-standing interest to Ray) and on the political economy of international trade and immigration. I now address a few of the questions stimulated by André Sapir's essay.

First, is there a significant difference in popular attitudes toward globalization in these two advanced regions of the world? To answer this question, I turned to a recent survey conducted by the Program on International Policy Attitudes at the University of Maryland and to the World Values Survey, coordinated by the University of Michigan. On balance, Americans tend to have a more favorable view of globalization than the British, the French, and the Germans (but not the Italians). On the other hand, they are less positive on foreign investment and tend to ascribe greater responsibility to trade for job loss. The latter is remarkable in view of the much smaller imports-to-GDP ratio in the United States.

Second, do European and U.S. trade differ in their adjustment and distributional costs? Sapir points to the greater share of developing countries in U.S. trade. He also suggests that the intra-industry nature of much of intra-European trade (the major source of trade expansion in Europe) is responsible for the "painless" trade liberalization in Europe. With regard to the relative magnitude of adjustment costs, what matters is not the share of developing-country trade in total trade, but its share in the overall activity in the economy (that is, GDP). Measured against GDP, trade with developing countries has increased somewhat more rapidly in Europe during the 1990s. It actually stands at a higher level than in the United States. (11.0 percent compared with 9.3 percent).

It is also not necessarily the case that adjustment costs are lower with intra-industry trade (IIT). In the standard models, what IIT does is to shift resources (labor and capital) across plants and firms rather than across sectors. But in the real world, workers who are displaced incur hefty wage losses, even when they are re-employed in similar occupations in the same industry. The most likely reason is that job-specific skills account for a substantial part of compensation. Under these conditions, one should not read too much into the share of IIT as an indicator of adjustment costs.

So how does Europe differ from the United States? First, there seems to be much greater sensitivity to environmental and biosafety issues in Europe. It would be interesting to explore why. Second, there is considerably less opposition to trade from labor unions in Europe. As Sapir discusses, European-style social protection, much more ambitious and effective than the trade-adjustment assistance in the United States, probably has something to do with this.

To me, the most interesting question posed by European integration is the following: How did Europe manage to integrate economically to such an extent without running into domestic political trouble? As I have indicated, the standard answer based on intra-industry trade does not provide a satisfactory account. The story needs to be augmented by at least three other features of the European landscape:

—relative uniformity in social protection around a high level;

—compensation through cross-border transfers to underperforming regions (structural and social funds); and

—an overarching legal system that enforced market integration (the European Court of Justice).

None of these would have been possible in the absence of institutional and legal harmonization alongside trade liberalization. This provides an important lesson about globalization: economic integration can go far only if it is accompanied by institutional convergence. The international reach of markets is limited by jurisdictional boundaries and the diversity of institutions.

I conclude with four points. First, it is not clear that globalization is in more trouble in the United States than it is in Europe. Second, the greater opposition by labor in the United States than in Europe has less to do with the nature of trade than with the absence of a coherent strategy of social protection (against employment, health, and income risks). Third, the European "model" of integration—with its uniformly high system of social protection—has enabled greater economic integration within Europe than might have been possible otherwise. Fourth, immigration (from non-EU countries) and capital mobility (within the European Union) pose dangers to the existing EU model, insofar as they undermine the financing base of social protection. I believe Ray would have been in agreement with these points, although I am sure he would have disputed the manner by which I arrived at them.

DAVID DOLLAR

10 | *Fostering Equity through International Institutions*

In chapter 5 Jeffrey Sachs points out that technology and technological development play critical roles in economic growth, an idea with which most development economists would agree. What is new is the argument that a key reason for poverty in the developing world is the lack of relevant technologies that poor countries need to raise productivity and build human capital: "Occasionally, the needed technologies are available from the outside world, but the countries are too poor to purchase them or license them at needed scale. Too often, the technologies do not yet exist in appropriate form and the impoverished markets of the poor countries offer scant market incentives for the needed research and development," he writes. The solution in his view is international policies that "foster new technologies for development, as well as long-term innovative capacity in the poor countries."

No doubt we can think of specific development problems where new technologies would make a large difference. It is misleading, however, to suggest that a lack of appropriate technologies is the main problem holding back poor countries. Many developing countries are not taking advantage of easily available technologies (in agriculture, in manufacturing, in health areas) because of poor policies and ineffective government bureau-

The views expressed in this chapter are those of the author and do not necessarily reflect official views of the World Bank.

cracies. Without better economic institutions and policies in these countries, new technologies would make little difference.

A somewhat different framework for thinking about globalization and international equity would include three elements. The first is openness to foreign trade and investment, which leads to more rapid growth. The effect is arguably larger in developing countries than in developed ones. From a purely economic point of view, developing countries would be better off with "unilateral trade disarmament" than with the very high levels of protection that were common through the 1980s and that persist in some developing countries today. What about the effect of trade on the poor within countries? Trade liberalization inevitably affects the distribution of income among factors of production. In the short run there are winners and losers. But, a priori, it seems extremely unlikely that these changes would generally take the form of greater household income inequality (that is, be biased against the poor). What happens to the household distribution depends on what factors a country has and how they are owned among households. It would be remarkable if trade liberalization everywhere tended to increase household income inequality, and yet that is one of the firm beliefs of the antiglobalization crowd. Fortunately, good data on income distribution are now available for a large number of developing countries (and developed ones too, of course). It simply is not true that more trade openness is associated with greater income inequality. There are countries such as the United States where more trade has gone hand in hand with greater inequality (although there is extensive literature disputing whether there is much of a *causal relationship* there). But there are lots of examples of developing countries participating more in international trade while household inequality remains stable or even declines. Happily, this is the case for the best-known low-income reformers (India, Ghana, Uganda, Vietnam). Thus, for the truly poor countries, there is powerful evidence that trade raises incomes of the poor.

Second, in our zest we have oversold the benefits of trade openness *by itself*. Poor countries need supporting institutions and public services to benefit strongly from openness. If existing firms cannot get reliable power, or decent human capital, or goods through customs without a series of payoffs, the benefits of relaxed trade rules will be small. More important, if the regulatory framework makes it virtually impossible to start new firms, or for old ones to go out of business, the benefits of openness that come through enhanced competition will be muted. We need to combine multilateral trade liberalization with help to developing countries to identify the supporting institutions and policies that they need to get the maximum benefit from openness. Technology policy is one of the areas in which countries need reform and assistance but by no means the only area.

Third, the global community has taken the wrong political-economy approach to promoting openness in the developing world. The rich countries did not bring the developing countries into the General Agreement on Tariffs and Trade (GATT) and the World Trade Organization (WTO) as full partners. On the one hand, they gave exemptions to developing countries that allowed them to maintain high levels of protection (the worst "favor" we ever did them); on the other hand, they maintained protections in agriculture and textiles that were particularly damaging to poor countries. At the same time, the conditionality of the International Monetary Fund (IMF) and World Bank was used to arm-twist developing countries into opening their trade regimes. This package has been a disaster, fostering suspicion and hostility in developing-country governments and civil societies. Much of the developing world's hostility toward openness is connected to this failed approach to promoting it.

Globalization *is* good for the poor. Jeffrey Sachs is right that it could be made a lot more beneficial for poor countries and poor people, and developing technologies to address tropical problems would help. However, the benefits of openness would also be strengthened if the interests of developing countries were better reflected in WTO negotiations (notably better rich-country market access for the low-income countries), and if rich countries and multilateral agencies helped poor countries put in place necessary supporting institutions and policies. From a political point of view, we need to shift from arm-twisting countries to reform via adjustment programs to treating them more as equal partners in the governance of the international trade system. The failure of the past approach has left a legacy of mistrust. Change will not be easy, but a new approach is essential if polarization into two worlds is to be avoided.

Openness, Growth, and Inequality

One of the most widely held beliefs among development economists is that openness to trade accelerates growth in poor countries. The higher growth rate may occur only during a transition phase to a new steady state, but the transition period apparently lasts for two or more decades. Therefore, it is reasonable to refer to this as an acceleration of growth and not merely as a short-term adjustment to a higher income level.

The belief that openness to trade accelerates growth in poor countries is based on case studies; firm-level evidence that trade liberalization leads to more competitive product markets in which more productive firms expand; and cross-country statistical analysis.[1] Ross Levine and David Renelt's important work has taught everyone to be cautious about the latter type of evidence.[2] There are quite a few public institutions and policies that are correlated with higher growth rates: measures of the rule of law, indicators of macrostability, the size of government as proxied by government consumption, and indicators of the extent of trade barriers (high barriers correlate with low growth). These "good policies" are highly correlated among themselves. Levine and Renelt show that there is a severe multicollinearity problem if all of these policies, and other country characteristics commonly used in the empirical growth literature, are pulled into a regression together.

Francisco Rodriguez and Dani Rodrik make a Levine-Renelt-type critique of empirical growth papers that found a correlation between trade openness and growth.[3] By adding additional variables to the analysis, they show that t-statistics on trade policy measures can be reduced to insignificant levels. Their critique, however, ignores the fact that trade openness tends to go hand in hand with other good policies (such as macrostability), which is surely not a coincidence. Furthermore, T. N. Srinivasan and Jagdish Bhagwati have criticized the Rodriguez and Rodrik paper for ignoring the case study evidence—a key underpinning of the widely held belief that trade openness is good for development.[4] Since 1980 India, China, Mexico, Uganda, and Vietnam have lowered trade barriers (either reducing tariffs or joining the World Trade Organization, or both). During the 1980s and the 1990s, while OECD growth rates were slowing down, growth rates in all of these countries accelerated.

There has been extensive work on the relationship between trade openness and growth but much less work on the relationship between trade openness and inequality, primarily because distribution data for many developing countries were not available until recently. In the current debates about globalization, one of the most popular beliefs is that openness typically leads to higher income inequality. In an influential article in *Foreign Affairs*, Jay Mazur asserts that "globalization has dramatically increased inequality between and within nations."[5] The liberalizing developing countries named above are all growing faster than the OECD world, and hence there is *declining inequality* between those developing countries and the first world. What about within-country inequality?

To test a number of popular hypotheses about inequality, Aart Kraay and I collected household income distribution data from more than eighty countries.[6] We estimate an equation for average income of the bottom 20 percent of the income distribution (our definition of "the poor") as a function of per capita income (an endogenous variable) and a host of other institutions and policies, including several related to globalization. This estimation is formally almost equivalent to estimating an equation for income inequality as measured by the Gini coefficient. We do the estimation in both levels and differences and get consistent results.

First, in general, there is no systematic relationship between the growth rate and changes in inequality. On average, income of the poor rises proportionally with growth of per capita income. Of course, in some cases growth is more "pro-poor" and in others less "pro-poor." Openness to foreign trade or foreign capital cannot explain any of this variation. In other words, it is simply not true that more participation in trade or openness to capital flows is related to growing inequality. Consider the prominent developing-world liberalizers noted earlier. China certainly had growing inequality in the 1990s, during its opening. But Mexico and Uganda had small declines in the Gini coefficient, and India and Vietnam had no significant changes.

If we think about the factor-proportions model of international trade, we would expect trade opening to alter the distribution of income among factors. It would be remarkable, however, if this led in every country to higher inequality in household income. The effect on factor income will be different in different countries depending on what factors are abundant. Then the effect on household income distribution will depend on how factors are owned among households. Thus from theory one would expect the effect on household income distribution to be quite different in different countries; that is what we find in the data. Furthermore, and quite encouraging, is the fact that changes in Gini coefficients tend to be small.

Vietnam provides a concrete example of what I am talking about. In the case of Vietnam we have particularly good data, because a careful household survey was done at the beginning of liberalization (1992), and then the same 5,000 households were surveyed six years later. Of the poorest 5 percent of the income distribution in 1992 (really poor rural households), 98 percent had higher consumption six years later. For the lower income groups more generally, per capita income rose to the same extent as the country's per capita income (roughly doubling in six years). Since liberalization meant higher rice prices for farmers (the vast majority of the poor) and more manufacturing jobs to take pressure off agricultural employment, it had quick and dramatic effects on the prosperity of the poor.

The Importance of Complementary Institutions and Policies

While the evidence is clear that openness is good for poor countries and poor people, it is also true that the international institutions have oversold the benefits of trade liberalization. Good policies tend to go together as do bad policies. This correlation makes it hard to estimate precisely what is likely to happen if a country changes only one policy. Furthermore, it is easy to make the mistake of ascribing to open trade policy what is really the benefit of overall good policy.

Kenya's experience is a concrete example of the importance of moving on different policy fronts at the same time. The data show a decline in Kenya's trade-weighted average tariff rate from 41.0 percent in 1980 to 13.5 percent in the late 1990s. It is hard to know for sure if Kenya has liberalized trade because in many developing countries the truly big distortions are licensing schemes and other nontariff barriers whose magnitudes are hard to measure. But let us assume for the sake of argument that Kenya did liberalize its trade regime. What has been the result? The actual volume of trade relative to GDP has not changed over the past twenty years, and Kenya's growth rate remained around zero in the 1980s and 1990s. (For the world as a whole, the trade-to-GDP ratio has gone up; for the liberalizers noted earlier it has gone up dramatically: Vietnam, for example, saw trade to GDP rise from 0.58 in the late 1980s to 1.59 in the second half of the 1990s, an extraordinarily high level for a country of 75 million people.)

Why might liberalization not have led to more trade and higher growth for Kenya? The answer potentially can be found in other institutions and policies of the country. A firm-level study found that foreign-owned plants, working with the same capital and labor, produced 200 percent more product in Thailand than in Kenya in the mid-1990s.[7] The same firm-level survey data provide a glimpse into why. It takes longer to clear goods through customs in Kenya than in Thailand; corruption and poor rule of law appear to be a more serious problem; infrastructure is deficient; and in general Kenya maintains a lot of inefficient government regulation that harasses private firms.

Intuitively, more access to the global economy is not going to make much difference if there are ineffective government services and over-regulation of entry and exit. Openness to trade is just one of a number of important public institutions and policies that are necessary for efficient investment and growth in poor countries.

Obviously, the extent to which developing countries create relevant technologies (technologies for agriculture and health, especially) will affect their rate of development. But, equally obviously, the economic institutions and policies in these countries will matter as well. In many cases poor countries are not utilizing existing technologies. It is a cliché—but nevertheless true—that for about 75 cents per person poor countries can implement a whole set of important health interventions. It is not uncommon for low-income countries to receive $40 to $50 per capita each year in foreign aid—a net figure after any official debt service payments. Despite all of these resources, many countries do not implement the simple health packages. Clearly, there is some failure of public institutions and policies. With such institutions and policies in place, why would we expect new technologies to be used any more effectively?

Addressing the HIV-AIDS problem is another good example. There are proven approaches involving public education and distribution of condoms, and countries such as Uganda have used these approaches to dramatically reduce the spread of HIV. But many other low-income countries are not using the existing knowledge.

Political Economy of Reform

When GATT was established after World War II, many former colonies were allowed to join on preferential terms. This permitted developing countries to operate within the GATT system yet maintain high tariffs and highly restrictive trade practices. It was common in the developing world to have complicated licensing schemes that made the allocation of imports a de facto planning decision. In light of the evidence about the benefits of exposure to international competition and international markets, it was unfortunate that poor countries were allowed this leeway, which in fact worked against their own economic interests. Their lack of genuine participation in GATT also tended to push their legitimate trade interests to the side. Products important to developing countries, including agriculture and clothing, have yet to see fully liberalized markets in OECD countries.

Although to a large extent the wealthy countries did not rely on the GATT mechanism to negotiate entry to developing-world markets, those same countries did increasingly rely on the Bretton Woods institutions to encourage trade liberalization in the developing world. The World Bank was not always pro-trade: it financed a lot of state-owned, import-competing investment in low-income countries in the 1960s and 1970s. The failure of those projects was an important factor spurring the Bank to re-evaluate its policy advice.[8] At the same time intellectual contributions by Bela Balasssa and Anne Krueger influenced the institution as well. By the mid-1980s the World Bank and the IMF were putting a lot of emphasis on trade liberalization in their policy advice and in their conditionality.

Conditionality, however, has not been effective in generating policy reform. Many of the adjustment programs supported by the Bank and the Fund failed because the key policy conditionalities were not implemented. In Africa about half of the adjustment programs failed; globally the failure rate was about one-third in the 1980s. The success or failure of these reform programs can be predicted by underlying political-economy factors.[9] Success is more likely with new governments, democratically elected ones, and in less polarized societies. On the other hand, variables under the control of the donors (size of the loan, number of conditions, resources devoted to preparation and supervision) have no systematic relationship with success or failure of reform. Thus the evidence suggests that reform, when it occurs, is primarily driven by the domestic political economy and by factors outside of donors' control. Conditionality cannot make a reformer out of a government with little inclination or domestic support in that direction.

Kenya provides a concrete example. The same measures (for example, agricultural price liberalization) appeared in one structural adjustment program after another in the 1980s. The measures were not carried out, the money was disbursed, and the same measures appeared as conditionality in the next adjustment loan.[10]

This conditionality approach to promoting trade liberalization had several negative consequences. First, a lot of money went into poor policy environments that in the end did not reform, in retrospect a clear waste of resources. Second, the conditionality approach to spurring policy reform created suspicion about the promoted policies. In successful reform countries such as Uganda, India, China, and Vietnam, the governments and different elements of society came to embrace open markets because of the visible failure of the closed strategy. In many other low-income countries, the government took half-hearted measures toward trade reform because of external pressure but lacked a deep conviction that these measures would actually be good for the economy. Conditionality is not a substitute for conviction and may actually hamper its development. It is a natural human reaction to rebel against measures that are imposed upon you by an outside source.

These findings suggest a different role for aid in promoting development in poor countries. Where we see governments pursuing macro and trade reforms, we should provide financial assistance to accelerate their growth and to help finance the kinds of complementary institutions and policies that I highlighted in the previous section. For the recalcitrant governments, we need to step back, reduce financing, and rely on policy dialogue and analysis rather than on heavy-handed conditionality.

Fostering Equity through International Institutions

Participation in the global economy is generally beneficial to poor countries and poor people within those countries. The benefits of globalization for poor countries could be greatly enhanced through

—More attention to developing-world concerns within the WTO framework, especially improved access to OECD markets for agriculture and light manufactured products;

—More research into health and agricultural technologies relevant to poor tropical countries along the lines recommended by Sachs; and

—More and better managed foreign aid to support poor countries to put in place the institutions and policies that complement openness: rule of law and functioning police and judiciaries; sustainable macroeconomic policies (which will require debt relief for some highly indebted countries); and effective public services in education, health, and infrastructure.

The demonstrators in Seattle were right to fear an increasingly polarized world between rich and poor, but wrong in their analysis. Globalization is not creating this dichotomy. Rather, globalization creates the potential to overcome the dichotomy. It is nonparticipation in globalization that is creating the dichotomy, so the answer is not to stop globalization, which would be impossible anyway. Developing-country societies need to take the initiative to integrate with the world economy, and the international community should support that integration through the kinds of measures enumerated earlier. Without such an effort, an increasingly polarized world is a certainty.

Notes

1. Jagdish Bhagwati, *Foreign Trade Regimes and Economic Development* (Cambridge, Mass.: Ballinger, 1978); Jeffrey D. Sachs and Andrew Warner, "Economic Reform and the Process of Global Integration," *Brookings Papers on Economic Activity, 1:1995,* pp. 1–118.

2. Ross Levine and David Renelt, "A Sensitivity Analysis of Cross-Country Growth Regressions," *American Economic Review,* vol. 84, no. 4 (1992), pp. 962–83.

3. Francisco Rodriguez and Dani Rodrik, "Trade Policy and Economic Growth: A Skeptic's Guide to the Cross-National Evidence," Working Paper W7081 (Cambridge, Mass.: National Bureau of Economic Research, April 1999).

4. T. N. Srinivasan and Jagdish Bhagwati, "Outward-Orientation and Development: Are Revisionists Right?" mimeo, Yale University, Department of Economics, 1999.

5. Jay Mazur, "Labor's New Internationalism," *Foreign Affairs* (January–February 2000), pp. 79–93.

6. David Dollar and Aart Kraay, "Growth *Is* Good for the Poor," mimeo, World Bank, Research Department, 2000.

7. David Dollar and Albert Zeufack, "Manufacturing Productivity in Kenya and Thailand: A Firm-Level Analysis," mimeo, World Bank, Research Department, 2000.

8. Jonathan Isham and Daniel Kaufmann, "The Forgotten Rationale for Policy Reform: The Impact on Projects," *Quarterly Journal of Economics,* vol. 114, no. 1 (1999), pp. 149–84.

9. David Dollar and Jakob Svensson, "What Explains the Success or Failure of Structural Adjustment Programs?" *Economic Journal,* vol. 110 (October 2000), pp. 894–917.

10. Paul Collier, "The Failure of Conditionality," in C. Gwin and J. Nelson. eds., *Perspectives on Aid and Development* (Washington: Overseas Development Council, 1997).

DEBORA SPAR

Part Three Summary

The preceding chapters on equity share two rather striking points of agreement: first, that equity is important, however it is defined; and second, that trade is good. The authors also agreed that the conduct and expansion of international trade affect equity in important ways. Beyond that, however, the chapters produced more questions than answers. How, in fact, does trade affect equity? And what sectors are affected?

More specifically, the chapters seem to suggest four broad questions. The first is the empirical question of whether or not inequities even exist. Richard Cooper, for example, emphatically challenged the conventional wisdom in the United States that we have had rising inequity. André Sapir and Dani Rodrik explored how we look at the differences between the United States and the European Union—regions for which we have very good statistics—and examined what these differences may mean in terms of both economic structures and attitudes toward them. If we put these contributions together, then, they suggest that some very basic empirical issues still remain on the table.

A second question concerns the extent to which trade is responsible for whatever inequities may exist. As Richard Cooper noted, there was until recently an entire cottage industry devoted to trying to figure out how much blame should be placed on trade for inequity. To a large extent, people have tired of that discussion and moved on, but a great deal of empirical work still needs to be done. Would it not be possible at least to produce some consensus about what kinds of trade lead to what kinds of inequities? We could focus, for example, on the particular characteristics of commodity-based trade, or of manufacturing. We could look at the impact of North-South trade, as opposed to North-North. And we could begin to develop some broad map of the conditions under which problems are most likely to arise. For there are doubtless a wide range of conditions under which there simply is no problem: trade does what we all want it to do, and we do not have to worry about inequities. Separating that out would be useful and would give policymakers more empirical evidence about the likely impact of various types of trade policy.

A third question concerns the likely response over time to the inequities —or perceived inequities—created by trade and liberalization. As Craig VanGrasstek noted, different industries are likely to react in different ways. In addition, we also need to differentiate industry from labor, and industries that have participated in foreign direct investment from those that have not. We need to understand what nongovernmental organizations are doing, and how various groups in society are likely to respond to their own vision of inequity.

George Soros's crazy word *reflexivity* may apply here. Soros describes how a process in motion will affect its own environment and thus its outcome. He is talking in particular about the stock market, and about how individuals' response to the market is what shapes it. I see elements of that same phenomenon here. Nongovernmental organizations (NGOs) put pressure on the World Trade Organization, which then responds in a certain way, changing both trading patterns and the NGOs' view of them. In order to affect that process in a positive way, however, we need to understand all of the pieces I just laid out. This is what Ray Vernon used to do: he looked at what actually happens when multinationals go out and invest and trade. This kind of empirical work would be hugely helpful in elucidating the debates before us.

The final question I address concerns the role of the International Monetary Fund (IMF) and the World Bank. Based on others' comments and my own experience, I am convinced that the Bank and the IMF have been more sorely beaten up than just about any other institutions. They are deeply flawed institutions, to be sure, but also deeply self-critical ones. In that context, I find it intriguing to watch other economists rush to criticize the Bank. For the irony is that the Bank has hardly been alone in its policy prescriptions. Indeed, its focus on macroeconomic stabilization has been largely supported by most mainstream economists (at least until quite recently) and by all those who happily belonged to the Washington Consensus. And thus an apt analogy may be made to the weather: everybody talks about it, but nobody does anything.

I conclude, therefore, where David Dollar left off. The World Bank is a political institution, as are most international organizations. Like them, it is responsive and responsible to a wide range of constituencies and can only operate through a political process. Our job as academics is to provide the hard evidence that will allow the World Bank to make both its political and economic decisions as wisely as possible.

PART FOUR

Legitimacy

ROBERT HOWSE
KALYPSO NICOLAÏDIS

11 | *Legitimacy and Global Governance: Why Constitutionalizing the WTO Is a Step Too Far*

Increasingly, scholars and even some politicians have articulated the challenge of global economic governance in constitutional terms. While the General Agreement on Tariffs and Trade (GATT) lent itself to being viewed as a structure to facilitate mutually self-interested bargains between sovereign states, its successor, the World Trade Organization (WTO), is often claimed to be performing constitutional functions or to be an incipient global economic constitution. Its legitimacy will be enhanced, it is surmised, by transforming the WTO treaty system into a federal construct. Descriptively, the proponents of a constitutional understanding of the WTO point to the new dispute settlement mechanism. This binding, juridically rigorous mechanism provides for virtually automatic authorization of countermeasures in the case of noncompliance. Proponents also point to the explicit role such tribunals play in balancing competing public values (economic efficiency versus health and safety goals, for instance) in the scrutiny of domestic regulation.[1] Normatively, the proponents of a constitutional understanding of the WTO aspire to greater legal certainty for private economic rights against the risk of depredation of powerful domestic interest groups. There is, however, a minority position that sees the ultimate implication of WTO constitutionalism as

The authors thank Thomas Cottier, Steve Charnovitz, Robert Hudec, Andrew Hurrell, Petros Mavroidis, Eric Stein, Alec Stone Sweet, and J. H. H. Weiler for inspiring discussions on this topic.

the transformation of the WTO into a progressive economic regulator, bringing into the WTO social rights, environmental and developmental concerns, realizing distributive justice at the global level, so as to make the WTO a transnational economic constitution for *all* the people.[2]

The connection between constitutionalism and legitimacy is a complex one. In the short run, at least, the application of the language of constitutionalism to WTO is likely to exaggerate the hopes of globalization's friends that economic liberalism can acquire the legitimacy of higher law—irreversible, irresistible, and comprehensive. At the same time, it is likely to exacerbate the fears of the "discontents" of globalization that the international institutions of economic governance have become a supranational Behemoth, not democratically accountable to anyone.[3]

The proposed adoption of a "constitutional" mode of thinking for the WTO system has important practical or policy implications. The first, and central implication is what is loosely called "direct effect"—constitutional norms are rights, and therefore the WTO system should evolve to a point where individuals rather than states can rely on directly enforceable WTO law. Moreover, appeal should be possible not only before WTO dispute settlement panels or appellate bodies, but also before domestic courts. Second, constitutional law is generally regarded as higher law, with a presumption against the change of basic structures. Constitutionalizing discourse tends to serve a "door closing" function against claims that the WTO has gone too far (in areas such as food safety and intellectual property rights, for example) and may need to be scaled back to give greater scope for democracy at the national level. Third, by characterizing the WTO treaty system as a constitution, one transforms its character from that of a complex, messy negotiated bargain of diverse rules, principles, and norms into a single structure. Individual elements become less easily contestable. The WTO becomes reified as something one is either for or against.

We argue that the legitimacy of the multilateral trading order requires greater democratic contestability and a more inclusive view of those who are entitled to influence the shape of the system. "Constitutionalization" of the WTO will only exacerbate the legitimacy crisis or constrain appropriate responses to it.

We discuss two different models or views of WTO constitutionalism. The first is the economic liberalism or (as some would say) libertarianism model. The WTO constitutional function is viewed in terms of a precommitment by which politicians tie their hands in such a manner as to resist the depredation of economic rights by domestic interest groups that demand rent-conferring interventionist and protectionist government. This model is articulated most explicitly by Ernst-Ulrich Petersmann.[4] It is inspired by an economic liberal reading of European integration, according to which activist judicial review, on the basis of broad or expandable treaty commitments to economic mobility, drives European integration largely irrespective of political dynamics. Constitutionalism is viewed as the means of placing law, or the rule of law, above politics. WTO constitutionalism is a solution to the limits of domestic constitutionalism in achieving such a result with respect to *economic* rights—limits that are attributed to the "capture" of domestic politics by "special interests." In short, a constitutionalized WTO attempts to place economic freedom above politics, but just the reverse is necessary to address the legitimacy crisis of the multilateral trading order. More politics is needed, not less.

The second view of WTO constitutionalism is more philosophically or ideologically modest. It identifies constitutionalism with the adjudication of competing values in WTO dispute settlement.[5] Trade-offs between, say, freer trade and protection of human health and safety are to be struck in light of the WTO "constitution," the principles of trade liberalization taken as constitutional norms, rather than in the framework of international law. Economic freedom is understood as the *telos* of the WTO. Competing human values enter into the picture as narrow and carefully policed exceptions or limits to the overall constitutional project of freer trade.

Here also, we argue that just the opposite response is needed if the legitimacy of the World Trade Organization is to be preserved and enhanced. We endorse the approach taken by the WTO Appellate Body in the interpretation of WTO rules that engage competing or divergent human values. Instead of presupposing that the treaty text is animated by a constitutional *telos* of freer trade or looking primarily within the WTO for the relevant structural principles, we emphasize the importance of non-WTO institutions and norms in treaty interpretation that represent values other than free or freer trade. Thus we advocate a kind of diffuse externalization of what Thomas Cottier identifies as the constitutional dimension.[6]

The European Union can be an inspiration in this matter if we were to apply at the global level a kind of subsidiarity adapted to the structure of the international system. This includes "horizontal" subsidiarity—deference to non-WTO international institutions and norms. The dispute settlement organs of the World Trade Organization must display considerable deference to substantive domestic regulatory choices as well as defer to other international regimes that represent and articulate such values, whether in respect to health, labor standards, the environment, or human rights. To the extent this occurs, the WTO need not have the kind of legitimacy that it would require if it were to act as the final authority in the prioritization of diverse human and societal values.

The chapter is divided into three main parts. The first explains why the traditional conception of the GATT as a mutually self-interested bargain between states has become problematic as a basis for the WTO's legitimacy. The second part critiques "constitutional" approaches to the WTO. These approaches misapply the EU experience and draw the wrong lessons for WTO governance. Finally, we sketch out alternative, nonconstitutional approaches to reviving the multilateral trading system as an interstate bargain. They vindicate the original ideals of the GATT founders in a vastly changed world through three strategies for WTO governance: institutional sensitivity, political inclusiveness, and top-down empowerment. We believe that this is the most promising route to recovering the spirit of "embedded liberalism" that characterized the postwar era and underpins the success of European integration.

From Interstate Bargaining to Constitutionalism: Embedded Liberalism in Disrepair

Of all the postwar economic institutions, the multilateral trading order seems to be the one most amenable to explanation and justification in terms of "cooperation under anarchy."[7] Other multilateral institutions (the World Bank, the International Monetary Fund, and specialized agencies of the United Nations) more easily appear as projections of the U.S. pro-interventionist, post–New Deal constitutional order.[8] GATT, however, was born from the failure of an ambitious project for a global trade regulatory agency, the International Trade Organization (ITO). At the start it was little more than a bare-bones structure for progressive negotiated reduction of tariffs on a reciprocal basis among sovereign states— subject to most-favored-nation and national treatment rules. The story of how the GATT evolved beyond its modest beginnings has often been told.

The Underlying Assumptions of Embedded Liberalism

The theory of comparative advantage suggests that unilateral free trade is normally the first-best policy for every country. Yet asymmetric distributive consequences internationally and domestically, combined with the lack of adequate compensatory mechanisms in either sphere, leads to resistance to liberalization and protectionist pressures by certain types of economic actors. The postwar GATT system can be seen as a set of commitments not to resort to protectionist measures in response to such pressures, which is only sustainable if predicated on the assumption that a wide range of alternative policy responses is available and legitimate. This includes the recognition that adjustment pressures might be such that, at least in the short term, some scope for recourse to trade-restrictive discriminatory policy instruments might be needed.

Thus there was no requirement to eliminate tariffs at any given rate or pace. Allowance was made for temporary, balance-of-payments-based import restrictions (Articles XII–XV), for safeguards in response to the injury to domestic industries from sudden surges of imports (Article XIX), and for negotiated rebalancing of concessions (Article XXVIII). The National Treatment obligation, Article III, was a means of preventing member states from instituting discriminatory domestic policies that would distort competition between domestic and imported products (in other words, cheat on the negotiated bargain), not a mechanism for liberalization, per se. At the same time, the dispute settlement practices developed out of the general language in Article XXIII of the 1947 GATT identified instances of cheating on the trade liberalization bargain, thereby sustaining member states' confidence that defection from the cooperative equilibrium could be clearly and rapidly ascertained and appropriately sanctioned by allowing withdrawal of concessions.

Furthermore, even discriminatory domestic policies might be permitted if they did not entail *arbitrary* or *unjustified* discrimination and could be linked, more or less tightly, to superior public policy goals such as the protection of human life or health, the conservation of exhaustible natural resources, or the protection of public morals (Article XX). Such a form of multilateralism, molded by domestic requirements, rather than the other way around, is what John Ruggie has aptly called embedded liberalism.[9]

The Embedded Liberalism Bargain under Stress

The embedded liberalism bargain came under sustained stress in the 1970s as the gold standard collapsed, and with it the structure for managed macroeconomic adjustment foreseen by the Bretton Woods system. The 1970s recession and mounting intellectual as well as practical (stagflation) challenges to the Keynesian consensus led to microeconomic interventions and trade restrictions—"voluntary" export restraints negotiated under threat of unilateral action—of dubious legality under GATT.[10] For various reasons, the safety valves for adjustment written explicitly into the agreement did not prove to have the appropriate kind of flexibility to deal with the political economy of adjustment in the 1970s.[11]

As for the domestic microeconomic interventions, especially subsidies but also technical regulations, they challenged the stability of GATT's non-discrimination norm as a means of distinguishing normal legitimate domestic policies from cheating on the trade liberalization bargain.[12] By the end of the 1970s it was evident that the postwar multilateral trade liberalization needed fine-tuning in order to sustain a cooperative equilibrium. The problem, at least for the United States, was no longer that the rules of the game did not ensure adequate scope for domestic adjustment. In fact, the normative basis for interventionist adjustment policies was put in question by the moral laissez faire outlook of the ascendant political right, abetted by widely accepted "public choice" accounts of interventionism as the payment of rents to concentrated, entrenched constituencies.

Beyond the Border: Economic Liberal Ideology and the New Negotiating Agenda

The focus then shifted from trade measures to the inherent worth of interventionism, and from liberalization bargains under diffuse reciprocity to competition between policy norms. The multilateral rules of the game had enabled Germany and Japan, America's wartime enemies, to compete successfully in the U.S. market for industrial products; they had also enabled the newly industrializing countries to compete successfully in highly labor-intensive industries such as textiles. America faced many barriers worldwide to exploiting its apparent comparative advantage in knowledge-intensive industries and services. Intellectual property was largely unprotected in many countries. Competition in network service industries, such as telecommunications and financial services, was severely restricted; in many industries byzantine and archaic regulatory requirements existed. In many cases, a business presence in the other country was necessary, and American firms faced severe foreign investment restrictions. These disparate nontariff barriers had to be eliminated.[13]

This new agenda became the core of the Uruguay Round agreements, concluded in 1993, but it would prove a greater threat to the sustainability of the multilateral trading system than any of the adjustment pressures of the 1970s. The new WTO rules, while clearly enhancing market access for some, have much more ambiguous welfare effects, both domestic and global, than the traditional GATT rules constraining tariffs, quotas, and discriminatory domestic regulations. Take the case of intellectual property protection. For developing countries in particular, it is easy to imagine how the gains in terms of incentives to efficient innovation from enhanced patent protection will be far outweighed by the welfare losses to consumers deprived of affordable generic pharmaceuticals. Some countries gain from increased patent protection and some lose; aggregate welfare may increase or decrease.[14]

The WTO rules in the areas negotiated in the Uruguay Round contain a balance of rights and obligations that, when interpreted carefully, still permit a great deal of regulatory diversity. There is a nonconstitutional or nonconstitutionalizing way of applying these rules: they can be applied within the framework of general international law and not in light of a telos of economic liberalism as the constitutional concept of the WTO. However, it is also true that the spirit in which the rules were made at the time reflected overenthusiasm for economic liberal ideology, not mere trade liberalization, as the basic economic objective of the system. This explains why the new system could easily appear to create higher law rather than simply treaty law.[15]

The developing countries did, formally, sign on to the new system. Why did they do so, if it was not unquestionably welfare enhancing? First, due to the debt crisis in the 1980s, many of these countries had been required to engage in unilateral trade and microeconomic policy reform as a condition for IMF support for debt rescheduling. Second, there was the notion that while developing countries might "lose" from some of the agreements, they gained from others, such as commitments to agricultural and textiles trade liberalization. Linkage politics in the Uruguay Round may even have convinced their leaders that the overall package was in their interest since there was little way to tell. What if it turns out that gains (say from textiles or agricultural trade liberalization) are proving elusive for certain countries, while costs (say, from implementing obligations under the General Agreement on Trade in Services or on Trade-Related Aspects of Intellectual Property Rights) are proving greater than expected? The bargain becomes highly unstable.

"Trade and . . . ": The Left Strikes Back with its Own
Beyond-the-Border Agenda

Two developments in the past decade contributed significantly to the challenge to embedded liberalism, as its meaning became subverted to underpin a multilateral order apparently hostile to social noneconomic values. At the beginning of the 1990s, GATT dispute settlement panels had to examine certain kinds of measures that did not fit within the normal, postwar model of domestic policy interventionism yet did not resemble old-style protectionism either. Two GATT panels had to decide the legality of a U.S. trade embargo against tuna fished in a manner that killed dolphins at high rates. Because they extended a domestic scheme to imports, the measures in question did not arguably constitute discrimination against imports. Yet the scope for domestic policy intervention that attached to the postwar embedded liberalism bargain did not necessarily encompass actions of this nature (actions to influence behavior or at least address various noncommercial consequences of behavior) outside the boundaries of the intervening state. Nor did it expressly exclude them.

Sorting out how to deal with such measures within the embedded liberalism bargain while preserving the centrality and coherence of the non-discrimination norm is not an insuperable intellectual challenge.[16] In contrast to the approach of the panels in the *Tuna-Dolphin* cases, the Appellate Body of the WTO in the *Shrimp-Turtle* case accepted the view that such measures could be justified under Article XX of GATT, subject to the conditions of the "chapeau" of Article XX, in particular, that they not be *applied* in such a way as to constitute arbitrary or unjustified discrimination. But the GATT panels in *Tuna-Dolphin* were not up to it and instead read into GATT various kinds of limitations on such measures that would exclude them entirely from the legitimate scope for domestic policy intervention. To many, the panels had blown up what they had been trying to preserve—the notion of trade liberalization as consistent with deep regulatory diversity, accommodating a full range of noneconomic public values.

A second set of developments—fallout from the debt crisis of the 1980s—also put pressure on the embedded liberalism bargain. Many developing countries removed or modified restrictions on foreign investment and other domestic policies that were disincentives to foreign capital, either because of IMF conditionality or because attracting new equity investment from abroad seemed the only plausible means of financing economic growth. Fears of "social dumping" by developing countries, and as a consequence, fears of a "race to the bottom" among domestic laws, became prominent in the developed world. The developed countries would not be able to sustain high environmental and labor standards, or rates of taxation needed to finance the redistributive policies of the welfare state, if they had to compete with developing countries for the location of capital invest-

ment. The empirical evidence for a race to the bottom has been highly contested among economists, yet this does not make such fears go away.[17]

Whatever its analytical merits, the race to the bottom gave a new, nonprotectionist foundation to traditional "level-playing-field" concerns about
fair trade. It put in question the sustainability of the legitimate policy interventionism that was the domestic side of the embedded liberalism bargain.
Furthermore, the race to the bottom conjured up images of the kind of beggar-thy-neighbor competition that the international side of the embedded
liberalism bargain was aimed at constraining.

In this context, the new social movements protesting in Seattle were
not necessarily contradicting themselves when they called for both global
standards in certain areas (environment, labor) and the protection of local
standards in others (food, culture, intellectual property). Both sets of demands reflected unease at the increasingly "disembedded" character of the
international liberal order, fears that either lack of international minimum
standards or imposition of foreign standards threatened the sustainability
of the domestic social contract under conditions of globalization. The
stability of the bargain that underpinned the postwar model of embedded
liberalism had been subverted by the combination in the last two decades
of domestic ideological change, economic forces, and international policy
prescriptions. The bargain needed to be revisited.

Responses to the Legitimacy Crisis: The Fallacy of Constitutionalism

To many, the WTO in its present form constrains some domestic policies too tightly while not constraining others tightly enough. In response
to such criticisms, no one has provided a persuasive overarching rationale
to explain the choice for embodying intellectual property rights in a trade
agreement but not labor rights, for instance. Certainly, neoclassical trade
economics does not offer the basis for such a choice. It is not surprising,
under these circumstances, that a constitutional route to the legitimization
of WTO rules and institutions would prove attractive. Especially to those
well accustomed to the "madhouse" of contemporary trade politics and less
accustomed to the complexities of constitutional politics, this option may
seem to offer greater stability.

Constitutionalization means different things to different people. In
traditional terms it refers to a constitutional moment, which defines the

founding or refounding of coherent polities or nations. This is not what advocates of WTO constitutionalism have in mind. Instead, some simply seek the constitutionalization of market access rights, while others seek to redefine the regulative functions and the organizational structures of the WTO as a global federal system.

The "Libertarian Constitutional" Alternative

If the World Trade Organization can be understood as a charter of economic rights, conferring enforceable claims on nongovernmental actors, then balancing the welfare effects of its rules on different groups and different countries over time seems unnecessary. The complex welfare effects of beyond-the-border trade rules need not create significant challenges for democratic legitimacy, nor even be the subject of explicit democratic deliberation. Constitutionalism is often said to be about principle, not policy; rights, not interests. Thus according to Petersmann, "The time has come to recognize that human rights law offers WTO rules moral, constitutional and democratic legitimacy that may be more important for parliamentary ratification of future WTO Agreements than the traditional economic and utilitarian justifications."[18] When a WTO dispute settlement panel invalidates an environmental protection scheme, the panel can be understood, not as replacing the policy balancing of domestic democratic institutions with its own policy balancing (environmental benefits versus trade costs and benefits), but rather as enforcing a higher legal norm with which *all* domestic policy balancing must be consistent.[19] WTO members must protect intellectual property rights, for example, not because doing so necessarily maximizes global or domestic welfare (in many cases it may be welfare reducing for a given polity), but because these are private rights, with a moral foundation independent of predicted welfare effects. In this view, the WTO, with its binding system of dispute settlement, already provides far more effective protection for individual rights than do the human rights organs of the UN institutions.[20]

Why would states agree to the protection of individual rights at the international level, when in many cases they are not recognized in their own domestic constitutions? Kant saw a transnational constitution as possible only once the members of the juridical union had themselves adopted domestic liberal republican constitutions.[21] Petersmann suggests there are forms of hands-tying or precommitment that are not possible at the domestic level but can be effective at the international level. A government acting in the public interest may make effective precommitments at the international level that tie its hands; these precommitments impose a new set of costs (retaliation from trading partners, in particular) on giving in to rent-seeking demands for protection.[22] This may seem to beg the question of how the constituencies that will lose once the government ties its hands would permit hands-tying in the first place. Here the nature of international trade negotiations provides an answer: the prospective benefits from reciprocal liberalization bring new constituencies that have an interest in increased access to foreign markets and the government can depend on these new constituencies to counterbalance the impact of constituencies seeking rents from interventionist government policies. Thus negotiated trade liberalization provides opportunities for the protection of economic rights against interest group depredation that are not available within the domestic political process.

In our view this approach underestimates the conditions under which hand-tying can be made legitimate in the WTO context. Jon Elster has recently reconsidered the complexities of understanding constitutional arrangements in terms of such precommitments since "in politics, people never try to bind themselves, only to bind others."[23] What Petersmann characterizes as the precommitment of a public-interest-motivated government to tie its own hands in the future is really a commitment to tie the hands of its political opponents and the groups they represent should they win a democratic victory. As Elster describes, at the level of domestic constitution-making, an important hedge against the antidemocratic feature of hands-tying is to require extraordinary levels of democratic consent in the first place to the rules that will tie the hands of future governments. Examples include referenda, supermajority votes, and elected constitutional assemblies. But judging hand-tying through WTO law against this standard puts into high relief the questionable democratic *bona fides* of WTO rules. Domestic deliberation on these rules is perfunctory and constrained by information and agency costs. This process produces a mass of general and often ambiguous rules. Their effects cannot easily be debated intelligently ex ante in national legislatures, and they must be accepted or rejected as a single package.[24]

Of course, in the embedded liberalism view, GATT itself could be understood as hand-tying. But the same democratic difficulties did not arise. The rules could rightly be understood as providing sufficient leeway for adjustment policy, and regulatory diversity generally, so that the domestic policy sphere could address the claims of all constituencies through nontrade measures. Liberals such as Petersmann are consistent: they are confident that economic rights reflect the public interest because they believe legitimate public goals can be achieved adequately and most *efficiently* in a manner that does not violate these rights. If the government intervenes in a protectionist manner or excessively interferes with these rights, this is because of public choice considerations. Ultimately, this is little more than "disembedded liberalism" in pseudo-Kantian dress. This approach may have had merit in the crusade against border measures, but it cannot easily be applied to the new rules about intellectual property, food safety, technical standards, and the like. Yet it is above all these new rules that call for a "constitutional" justification.

Furthermore, Petersmann claims that "the dynamic functions of human rights and fundamental citizen rights have prompted many courts (notably in Europe) to adopt functional and teleological interpretations that have progressively extended individual freedoms across frontiers and beyond more narrow interpretations. The jurisprudence of the EC Court of Justice, on the free movement of goods, services, persons, capital and payments, illustrates the legal, political and economic importance of individual rights and of their judicial protection for international economic integration."[25]

Petersmann fails to draw the right lessons from the EU experience. Economic rights have not been justified on their own merit but framed by the Court as a by-product of the pursuit of a "common good," a single market in Europe. If the teleology needs to be collective goals rather than individual wants in the EU context (in order to justify encroachment of trade on competing collective values), on what basis are we led to believe that individual rights would do more for legitimacy at the global level? To the extent that there are inferred individual economic rights in the European Union, history has shown that they cannot occupy the field and benefit from a monopoly on constitutional status. When the European Court of Justice stated that it was balancing individual rights against the interests and policies of governments, it did so in the name of social rights, not market access rights.[26] Constitutionalization was made acceptable in Europe by characteristics whose functional equivalent cannot be obtained at the WTO level, including the complex relationship between constitutional politics and legislative politics in the European Union. The EU process of constitutionalization turned from the first to the second model because constitutionalism based solely on economic libertarianism did not provide the kind of democratically grounded flexibility that allows for cycles of centralization and decentralization in the regulation of free trade.

The European "Federal Vision" Alternative

The second model inspiring a WTO constitutional project is an idea akin to evolutionary federalism, advocated by those who call for a shift from current international law to a new "global law." Such a law would define and integrate a series of legitimate goals and entrust to the World Trade Organization the task of interpreting and enforcing these goals.[27] This vision, more than the idea of libertarian precommitment, is based on a standard conception of the constitutional trajectory of the European Union.[28]

The European example is obviously appealing to WTO constitutionalists. Although some of the founders of the European project, such as Jean Monnet and Robert Schumann, might have discerned at the outset a constitutional *telos*, European constitutionalism appears to have evolved organically. J. H. H. Weiler observes: "The Community was conceived as a legal order founded by international treaties negotiated by governments of States under international law and giving birth to an international organization. The constitutionalism thesis claims that in critical aspects the Community has evolved and behaves as if its founding instrument were not a treaty governed by international law but, to use the language of the European Court, a constitutional charter governed by a form of constitutional law."[29]

Particularly persuasive to proponents of WTO constitutionalization is the European Court's transformation of the European treaty system into a constitutional order. In the Uruguay Round the GATT membership rejected the invitation to reconceive the WTO system in constitutional terms (that is, as an autonomous level of governance), despite proposals to create regulatory powers in the WTO.[30] Lawmaking in the WTO was to remain consensus-based interstate bargaining. No autonomous or independent lawmaking or regulating institution was created within the organization. On the other hand, the Uruguay Round produced a dispute settlement of a judicial sort, whose workings were made largely independent of the political choices of the membership. The European example suggests that a conventional treaty regime, once endowed with a judicial mechanism for interpretation and enforcement, can be converted by degrees to a genuine constitutional order.

The European Union, however, possessed the prerequisites for these developments that the WTO lacks. The Treaty of Rome conferred upon European Community institutions the explicit power, in the case of regulations, to create law that was directly applicable in the member states (Article 189). Implicit in the treaty was an idea of *federal* governance transcending the confederal notion of a pact among sovereigns to merely pool, or limit, exercises of sovereignty as among each other. A direct relationship was created between the individual and the orders of governance established by the treaty. The logic of applying the ideal of the rule of law to that direct relationship was a doctrine of direct effect that was extended beyond the limited, special case of regulations.

By contrast, according to a recent unappealed panel decision, "neither the GATT nor the WTO has so far been interpreted by GATT/WTO institutions as a legal order producing direct effect. Following this approach, the GATT/WTO did *not* create a new legal order the subjects of which comprise both contracting parties or Members and their nationals."[31] To this passage, the panel added a cautious footnote. In some instances the only way of effectively implementing a WTO obligation to other members might be to create court-enforceable rights for individuals within the domestic legal system in question. The individuals in question would have these rights, not by virtue of a direct relationship to an autonomous WTO legal order, but simply as an inference from the requirements of treaty compliance.

In the European Union the legitimacy of judicial rulings on the application of domestic regulation had been predicated upon the existence and development of a political and administrative system for "compatibility assessment and enforcement." This includes the institutional foundations for mutual regulatory monitoring, which enabled the legislative and administrative process to take over from the judiciary in sensitive areas of economic integration.[32] Thus the ambitious interpretation of direct effect by the European Court of Justice helped establish the credentials of the Council, and particularly the Commission, as autonomous institutions of governance, encouraging them, at least indirectly, to deliver on the promise of a federal level of governance implicit in the Treaty of Rome. But such a promise does *not* exist in the WTO treaties. If the dispute settlement organs were to create such expectations among the citizens of member states, they would likely undermine the legitimacy of the WTO system as a whole, making it seem to promise something that it does not have the institutional structure to deliver. Proponents of constitutionalization argue that this is precisely why an institutional structure appropriate to constitutional status needs to be created at the WTO, as trade liberalization "inherently starts to require, rely upon and develop positive integration."[33]

Although WTO law allows for the *constraint* of policies that interfere with the trading rights of members, there are no institutional arrangements that provide for the creation of new, agreed policies that can rebalance such trading rights with other legitimate policy objectives. An aggressive, constitutionalizing reading of trading "rights" by the WTO dispute settlement organs would necessarily have a libertarian bias in the case of the WTO, while in the EU context it could be taken as a challenge and even a mandate to the Commission and the Council to perform their responsibilities for positive integration. It may be argued that other international forums exist for positive integration. Indeed, in the WTO's Sanitary and Phytosanitary Agreement (on food safety measures) and the Technical Barriers to Trade Agreement, there is a formal link between WTO rules and harmonization in some of those forums. However, they do not make up part of the purported constitutional order of the WTO and their existence precisely points to the need for greater openness to other institutions and forums on the outside, rather than a notion of normative self-sufficiency implied by the constitutional idea.

In response to these objections, constitutionalization driven by the judicial branch of the WTO could be recommended as a strategy for building pressure for treaty amendments (that is, the creation of an explicit level of federal governance at the WTO, with the regulatory powers required for positive integration). But this is unlikely to happen, and legitimacy difficulties would arise if it were to happen. We need only consider developments in the European Union. Europeans became conscious that the Community institutions were behaving as an autonomous federal order of governance, acting directly on the citizens of member states. These developments display the danger of, in Weiler's words, "adopting constitutional practices without any underlying legitimizing constitutionalism."[34]

Some would argue that a direct relationship between the federal level of governance and the individual implies a direct *democratic* relationship and that the European Parliament—if given the appropriate powers— could play this role. Although the option of a directly elected WTO Parliament is far removed, a first step might be to facilitate the participation of national parliamentarians in the World Trade Organization. One must take seriously, however, the critique that in Europe the European Parliament is not effective in creating a direct democratic relationship between the European level of governance and individual citizens because there is no European *demos* or democratic community whose considered will the Parliament can express. The communitarian Right maintains that a democratic community must be constituted on the basis of a *Volk* (in other words, united by subpolitical or prepolitical bonds such as religion, race, and culture), a condition that does not or cannot hold at the European level. We are skeptical of this view for many reasons but rejecting it does not dispense with the need to articulate the civic conditions of a democratic community based on a deliberative public sphere.[35] At a minimum this requires, as Eric Stein recently articulated, "a certain community of a common good and common expectations of the people that bridge the cultural differences."[36] While some suggestions as to how to build such a community within Europe could be applied to the WTO—for instance, Weiler's notion that the deliberations of the European institutions be put on the Internet—the two projects are still incommensurable.[37]

Finally, it may also be a condition of a democratic community that it shares equitably the benefits and burdens of the common community project, particularly as deeper integration reveals more sharply the skewed distribution of benefits and burdens. The evolution of the European Union in the 1980s and 1990s showed clearly how every bargain over economic liberalism needed to be accompanied by side payments to regions, groups, and countries in order to be sustainable. Member states of the European Union have become irreversibly committed to a pervasive program of European economic integration whose very success is now confronting national welfare states with the same kind of regulatory competition that had impeded the development of social policies in the American states.[38] As a result, democratic legitimacy cannot be ensured under conditions of regulatory competition short of a proactive engagement on the part of the federal level to allow states to deliver on their welfare function. One cannot underestimate the distance between members of the WTO on the appropriate conception of distributive justice, if any, to govern the operations of the multilateral trading system. A large part of the membership is opposed to the WTO having any social agenda. These members also are not seriously seeking to address the issue in other international institutions. Unlike the old GATT or the European Union today, the WTO does not have decision-making structures that easily allow for variable geometry, or what the Europeans call integration "*à deux ou à multiples vitesses*." The divergence of values and circumstances among WTO members is, however, immensely greater than that among the member states of the European Union. The WTO's commitment to universalism does not square easily with this condition of WTO membership: not merely the recognition of a set of common values but a definite reflection of those values in the domestic legal system of all members.

Nonconstitutional Means of Strengthening the WTO: A Model of Global Subsidiarity

Imposing the constitutionalist spirit on the World Trade Organization is not the answer. Rather, the spirit of embedded liberalism needs to be recovered and reinterpreted under the new conditions of globalization. Again inspiration can come from the European Union, not in its constitutional guise, but by incorporating some of the institutional and political features associated with subsidiarity. A model of global subsidiarity can help take into account the process dynamics and the kinds of conflicts present in the WTO and assumed away by constitutionalism. Such a model can suggest functional equivalents to traditional "safeguards" for the state while acknowledging other legitimate loci of governance than the state.

A model of global subsidiarity would incorporate throughout the workings of the WTO three basic principles: institutional sensitivity, political inclusiveness, and top-down empowerment. We now examine each of them in turn.

Institutional Sensitivity

The core of the principle is the most straightforward understanding of subsidiarity, namely, sensitivity to the superior credentials that other institutions of governance may have in addressing the substantive value trade-offs entailed in domestic measures that the WTO dispute settlement organs are, necessarily, required to review from the perspective of WTO rules on trade.[39] This includes deference to the states themselves. But deference in WTO treaty interpretation needs to be expanded to issue-area regimes, such as international environmental, health, and labor regimes.

Yet institutional sensitivity is not mere deference: it is consistent with strict scrutiny of national compliance with general trade regime norms such as nondiscrimination, and especially procedural norms such as transparency and due process in the formulation and implementation of policies. Here the WTO dispute settlement organs *are* the institutions of superior competence.

Institutional sensitivity may also entail deference to the political processes of negotiations on the part of the judiciary, either with regard to bilateral disputes or multilateral rulemaking. An example is the *Kodak-Fuji*
ruling, where a WTO panel refused to invoke the general "non-violation
nullification and impairment" clause in GATT to stretch the existing regime to include restrictive business practices. This ruling reflected sensitivity to the fact that extension of WTO rulemaking to the antitrust field
is the subject of intense and controversial negotiations among members.

Provisions of the WTO agreements that are not easily understood as
a straightforward "win-win" deal for all members need to be interpreted in
a manner sensitive to the inadequacy of constitutional sources of legitimacy *within* the WTO system. Already the Appellate Body has substituted
for such sources; it has placed WTO law in the framework of general international law—externalizing, as it were, the constitutional dimension. In
the *Beef Hormone* case, it questioned an interpretation by the panel of a requirement that members (in this case the European Union) not take trade
restrictive sanitary and phytosanitary measures unless they are "based on"
international standards. The Appellate Body, in a more lenient interpretation of the implied obligations, upheld the crucial legitimizing role of the
negotiated text, reflecting as it does a "delicate and carefully negotiated
balance . . . between these shared, but sometimes competing, interests of
promoting international trade and of protecting the life and health of
human beings."[40] Such "testing" of their view of purpose against the exact
words used in the treaty should continue to provide interpreters with a
necessary safeguard against the importation of a single purpose into a legal
text crafted to balance diverse, and possibly competing, values.[41]

Reference to interpretative norms of general public international law
enhances the legitimacy of the dispute settlement organs in adjudicating
competing values; the norms are not specific to a regime that has traditionally privileged a single value, that of free trade.[42] In *Shrimp-Turtle,* assessing
the alleged "unjust" or "arbitrary" nature of U.S. measures, the Appellate
Body did not simply invent its own limitation on unilateralism as a means
of protecting the environmental commons, as had been done by the *Tuna-
Dolphin* panels. Instead, it referred to a baseline in international environmental law, that contained in the Rio Declaration. Principle 12 of the Rio
Declaration called for the avoidance of unilateral measures, preferring a solution based on consensus whenever possible. Thus the Appellate Body
could find that the failure of the United States to negotiate seriously with
the complainants to achieve a consensus-based solution, while having al-

ready negotiated successfully with other members, constituted "unjustified" discrimination (paras. 168–72).

However subtly the dispute settlement organs apply the tools of institutional sensitivity, the most delicate interpretation of such rules will not legitimately resolve the dispute in some cases. The *Beef Hormone* case is one
example. Neither European noncompliance in this case nor U.S. insistence
on retaliation signals a wavering commitment to a cooperative equilibrium
in international trade. Rather, the trading system has not evolved to the
point where such disagreements can be legitimately resolved above (domestic) politics. In a case like this, the outcome of noncompliance can be system
supporting, avoiding inordinate pressure on rules that do not yet have an institutional context that would confer on them the legitimacy needed for supremacy. However, in order to forestall escalation, the parties, we suggest,
should seek "no fault" alternatives to retaliation, such as negotiated rebalancing of concessions. Finally, the progress made on the directions for reform discussed earlier should strongly determine the speed with which
further economic-liberalism-oriented negotiations are undertaken, whether
in competition policy, domestic regulation in services, rules on intellectual
property protection, or investment. This might mean a standstill on some
significant new disciplines until the legitimating structures "catch up."
Time may bring about the necessary convergence in regulatory perspectives
and new, legitimate institutions and norms of global governance. Progressive liberalization of trade need not come to a complete halt. There remain
many traditional discriminatory trade barriers, including high tariff barriers
in some sectors and various forms of agricultural protection, that it would be
clearly welfare enhancing to reduce or remove, within the classic model of
multilateral bargaining. Moreover, states may legitimately choose to embark
on exercises of regulatory cooperation and mutual recognition for the purpose of plurilateral liberalization, under the express conditions that they respect procedural obligations of openness and inclusiveness as outlined
below.

Political Inclusiveness

The second guiding principle that can serve as a model for global subsidiarity is political inclusiveness. As Robert Keohane and Joseph Nye explain in chapter 12 of this volume, international regimes like the trade
regime were conceived as decomposable hierarchies governing specific issue
areas, and they were designed to keep out the public as well as officials from

other branches. The undoing of the embedded liberalism bargain suggests that this club paradigm needs to be adapted.

At the national, level the WTO can encourage greater inclusiveness in trade policymaking, thus strengthening indirect accountability. National citizens, groups, or parliaments can participate more meaningfully in trade policy decisionmaking under obligations of domestic consultation. At the *supranational* level, it has become much harder to pretend that governments adequately represent all relevant interests in a given trade issue. There are epistemic communities, transnational issue networks, and global advocacy NGOs that do not find any adequate point of entry at the domestic level. But for a long time this kind of inclusiveness is bound to fall short of the direct democratic relationship required for constitutionalization. As long as one understands the nonconstitutional role of participatory opportunities in dispute settlement (*amicus* type intervention, right to attend hearings, and so on), one need not, and should not, view such opportunities as the first step toward private rights of action. Similarly, participatory opportunities in political debates need not be understood as rights of representation.

In addition, the WTO could enhance *transnational* inclusiveness in domestic rule-making processes.[43] To this end, the Uruguay Round created contact points and inquiry points through which information about trade-relevant domestic regulations is disseminated by the WTO. This approach needs to be generalized through an obligation of transparency in domestic processes borne by the members themselves. More radically, obligations of inclusiveness could be applied in certain areas to earlier stages of law and regulation making, whereby calls for input would have to be issued in areas of extraterritorial effect. The same applies to bilateral or plurilateral deals where inclusiveness calls for an emphasis on due process elements of WTO rules with regard to rights of access to negotiations conducted between small groups of countries as in the case of mutual recognition agreements.[44]

Top-Down Empowerment

Finally, the permissive interpretation of embedded liberalism needs to be supplemented by a proactive interpretation that lays some of the responsibility on the global community to help states fulfill the functions that the original bargain was meant to protect. Globalization has made it more complicated for some states to deliver the goods that citizens have come to expect of them, or at least for many states to recast or redesign the domestic social bargain to respond effectively to the new pressures and opportunities of globalization.[45] It is because the state is still the greatest buffer against the effects of globalization that the more open countries are also the biggest welfare states.[46]

Here again, the WTO may be able to borrow from the EU experience. Fritz Scharpf and others have proposed implementing a "European law of unfair competition."[47] Why not create such a law at the global level to curb extreme instances of social or environmental dumping or of tax competition? And why not introduce differentiated applicability of such a law depending on the level of development or the type of actor? It may enhance the legitimacy of the system to require multinational corporations to apply minimum social standards across countries before this is required from local producers. Differentiated applicability, opt-outs for very poor or underdeveloped countries, will ensure that such a regime does not amount to a surreptitious harmonization of domestic policies or the imposition of a paradigm of global distributive equity, both of which require, to be legitimate, federal democratic governance. In other words, we can address the race to the bottom concern within the embedded liberalism model, whose major function is to provide constraints against beggar-thy-neighbor interstate competition. Some of the poorest countries in the world may not accept being so constrained, perhaps quite justifiably, but there is little empirical evidence that the importance of these countries in global markets is such as to induce movement downward of regulatory standards elsewhere. On the other hand, a major player in the global marketplace that refused to be so constrained would bear a heavy burden of proof that it was not simply a free rider (a holdout from a bargain with widespread benefits). Thus we could envisage a plurilateral code at the WTO on environmental and social dumping. Adherence to the code would not be a requirement of membership in the WTO. And existing benefits under the WTO system would not be conditioned on joining the code.

When the WTO envisages obligations with real financial consequences, it needs to support state efforts to adjust to those obligations. The European proposal for a joint WTO-World Bank-IMF institutional entity to examine the social clause issue should be seen in this context, while operationalizing the kind of regime linkages called for by political sensitivity. Again, we do not see such an initiative in constitutional terms, but as a means of returning to the adjustment focus of the embedded liberalism bargain while adapting the methods to very different global financial arrangements than those presupposed by the Bretton Woods system. Here, the role of financial assistance should be be viewed as based on conditionality—the imposition of a model of governance on the country concerned—but rather as underpinning the political economy of a world trading system based for the forseeable future on mutually beneficial interstate bargains.

Conclusion

In this chapter we have addressed the challenge of recovering the spirit of embedded liberalism under conditions radically different from those at its inception. We have criticized the use of the European Union as a model for constitutionalizing the WTO, not to belabor the self-evident point that the two settings are too different to warrant a direct (albeit partial) transfer in mode of governance, but to highlight the critical political assumptions behind constitutionalization. If all of our proposals were fully realized, especially those on inclusiveness and deliberative democracy, we might bring about the very conditions for global democratic federalism that we have been arguing are structurally incompatible with the multilateral trading system. It might further be argued that with enough subsidiarity of the right kind(s), some of the normative objections to a world state or government, based on concerns about democratic deficits, the destruction of desirable human diversity, and the risk of technocratic tyranny, might no longer have significant weight. Indeed, the guidelines that we have suggested, all in some way, could ultimately result in creating some of the conditions for constitutionalism in the long run. Integration of human rights and environment into WTO law as higher norms that shape and limit specific trade liberalization commitments would certainly give it more of the kind of normative structure consistent with constitutional status. There is force in these claims, and certainly we do not wish to foreclose the possibility that the conditions for a legitimate global federal government might eventually emerge. At that point one would need to reassess the whole problem of globalization and the political *sine ira illi studium*. Indeed, in terms of achieving some kind of overlapping consensus about the future direction of the multilateral trading system, this self-limiting feature of our critique of constitutionalization bears an advantage. To those already committed to the ultimate goal of WTO constitutionalism, we would say that the best means of attaining it are nonconstitutional—means that have legitimacy on their own terms within a revised understanding of the embedded liberalism bargain.

Notes

1. Thomas Cottier, "Limits to International Trade: The Constitutional Challenge," in P. Stepan, ed., *American Society of International Law: Proceedings of the 94th Meeting* (Washington: ASIL, 2000).

2. G. R. Shell, "Trade Legalism and International Relations Theory: An Analysis of the World Trade Organization," *Duke Law Journal,* vol. 44, pp. 829–927.

3. Cottier, "Limits to International Trade."

4. Ernst-Ulrich Petersmann, "Trade Policy as a Constitutional Problem: On the Domestic Policy Functions of International Rules," *Aussenwirtschaft,* vol. 41, pp. 405–39.

5. Cottier, "Limits to International Trade."

6. Ibid.

7. Robert Keohane, *After Hegemony: Cooperation and Discord in the Modern World Economy* (Princeton University Press, 1984); Kenneth Oye, ed., *Cooperation under Anarchy* (Princeton University Press, 1985); Robert Axelrod, *The Evolution of Cooperation* (Basic Books, 1980).

8. A. M. Slaughter, "Regulating the World: Multilateralism, Internationalism, and the Projection of the New Deal Regulatory State," in Robert Howse, ed., *The World Trading System: Critical Perspectives on the World Economy* (Routledge, 1998).

9. "The task of postwar institutional reconstruction . . . was . . . to devise a framework which would safeguard and even aid the quest for domestic stability without, at the same time, triggering mutually destructive external consequences that had plagued the interwar period. This was the essence of the embedded liberalism compromise: unlike the economic nationalism of the thirties, it would be multilateral in character; unlike the liberalism of the gold standard and free trade, its multilateralism would be predicated upon domestic interventionism. If this was the shared objective of postwar institutional reconstruction for the international economy, there remained enormous differences between countries over precisely what it meant and what sorts of policies and institutional arrangements, domestic and international, the objective necessitated or was compatible with. This was the stuff of the negotiations on the postwar international economic order." John G. Ruggie, "International Regimes, Transactions and Change: Embedded Liberalism and the Post-War Economic Regimes," *International Organization,* vol. 36 (1982), pp. 195–232.

10. See Jagdish Bhagwati, *Protectionism* (Cambridge University Press, 1988).

11. M. J. Treblicock, M. A. Chandler, and Robert Howse, *Trade and Transitions: A Comparative Analysis of Industrial Policies* (Routledge, 1990).

12. Daniel Tarullo, "Beyond Normalcy in the Regulation of International Trade," *Harvard Law Review,* vol. 100 (1987), pp. 546ff.

13. William Drake and Kalypso Nicolaïdis, "Ideas, Interests and Institutionalization: 'Trade in Services' and the Uruguay Round," *International Organization,* vol 46 (Winter 1992), pp. 37–100.

14. Alan Deardorff, "Should Patent Protection Be Extended to All Developing Countries?" *World Economy,* vol. 13 (1990), pp. 497ff.

15. This is notwithstanding the fact that the texts lend themselves to a wide array of interpretations. See Kalypso Nicolaïdis and Joel P. Trachtman, "From Policed Regulation to Managed Recognition: Mapping the Boundary in GATS," in Pierre Sauvé and Robert Stern, eds., *Services 2000: New Directions in Services Trade Liberalization* (Brookings, 2000).

16. See Kalypso Nicolaïdis, "Non-Discriminatory Mutual Recognition: An Oxymoron in the New WTO Lexicon?" in Thomas Cottier, Petros Mavroidis, and P. Blatter, eds., *Regulatory Barriers and the Principle of Non-Discrimination of World Trade Law: Past, Present and Future* (Michigan University Press, 2000.)

17. Jagdish Bhagwati and Robert Hudec, *Fair Trade and Harmonization* (MIT Press, 1996).

18. Ernst-Ulrich Petersmann, "Human Rights and International Law in the 21st Century: The Need to Clarify Their Interrelationships," *Journal of International Economic Law,* vol. 4, no. 3 (2001).

19. J. Dunoff, "The Death of the Trade Regime," *European Journal of International Law,* vol. 10 (1999), pp. 733–62.

20. Petersmann, "Human Rights and International Law."

21. Hedley Bull, "Society and Anarchy in International Relations," in Henry Butterfield and Martin Wight, eds., *Diplomatic Investigations* (London: Allen and Unwin, 1966); M. Wight, "An Anatomy of International Thought," *Review of International Studies,* vol. 15 (1987); A. Hurrell, "Kant and the Kantian Paradigm in International Relations," *Review of International Studies,* vol. 16 (1990), pp. 183–205; and H. Reiss, *Kant's Political Writings* (Cambridge University Press, 1970).

22. Petersmann, "Human Rights and International Law."

23. Jon Elster, *Ulysses Unbound* (Cambridge University Press, 2000), p. ix.

24. See E. Benvenisti, "Exit and Voice in the Age of Globalization," *Michigan Law Review,* vol. 98 (1999), p. 200; Marco Bronckers, "Better Rules for a New Millennium: A Warning against Undemocratic Developments in the WTO," *Journal of International Economic Law,* vol. 2 (1999), p. 547.

25. Petersmann, "Human Rights and International Law."

26. European Court of Justice, *Wachauf* v. *Germany* (Case 5/88) [1989] ECR 2609 [1991].

27. Cottier, "Limits to International Trade."

28. We recognize that those advocating the European analogy do not deny the obvious point that the WTO is different from the EU. But their methodological premise relies on two types of arguments. First, this is an evolutionary process: the WTO is simply at the point of the EU in the early 1960s. Second, even while the two are different, many of their institutional and procedural features are functionally equivalent. On the first point, we argue that the EU was different at birth and thus cannot be emulated on path dependency grounds. On the second point, we show that such functional equivalence does not obtain.

29. J. H. H. Weiler, "The Transformation of Europe," *Yale Law Journal,* vol. 100 (1991), p. 221.

30. John Jackson, *Restructuring the GATT System* (London: Royal Institute of International Affairs, 1990).

31. *United States—Sections 301–310 of the Trade Act of 1974*, Report of the Panel, 1999, para. 7.72.

32. Kalypso Nicolaïdis, "Mutual Recognition of Regulatory Regimes: Some Lessons and Prospects," *Regulatory Reform and International Market Openness* (Paris: Organization for Economic Cooperation and Development, 1996).

33. Cottier, "Limits to International Trade."

34. J. H. H. Weiler, *The Constitution of Europe* (Cambridge University Press, 1999), p. 298. Indeed building on this formula, one could say that what the constitutional enthusiasts for the WTO draw from their reading of the European experience is that one can *create* the underlying legitimizing constitutionalism that the WTO now needs (given the problems with the embedded liberalism—interstate bargaining model) only if constitutional practices are boldly asserted at the WTO.

35. See the chapters by S. Choudhry and D. Lacorne in Kalypso Nicolaïdis and Robert Howse, eds., *The Federal Vision: Legitimacy and Levels of Governance in the US and the EU* (Oxford University Press, 2001).

36. Eric Stein, "Panel Statement on Democracy without a 'People'," paper delivered at the meeting of the European Studies Association, Pittsburgh, June 1999, p. 10.

37. Weiler, *The Constitution of Europe*, pp. 351–52.

38. Fritz Scharpf, *Governing in Europe: Effective and Democratic?* (Oxford University Press, 1999).

39. Robert Howse, "Adjudicative Legitimacy and Treaty Interpretation in International Trade Law: The Early Years of WTO Jurisprudence," in Jospeh H. H. Weiler, *EU, WTO and NAFTA: Towards a Common Law of Economic Integration?* (Oxford University Press, 2000).

40. *EC—Measures Concerning Meat and Meat Products (Hormones)*, Report of the Appellate Body, n. 76, paragraph 177.

41. As Cass Sunstein notes in the context of domestic public law adjudication, "statutory terms—not legislative history, nor legislative purpose, nor legislative 'intent'—have gone through the constitutionally specified procedures for the enactment of law. Largely for this reason, the words of a statute provide the foundation for interpretation, and those words, together with widely shared conventions about how they should be understood, often lead to uniquely right answers, or at least sharply constrain the territory of legitimate disagreement. Resort to the text also promotes goals associated with the rule of law: the statutory words are available to affected citizens, and it is in response to those words that they can most readily order their affairs. An emphasis on the primacy of the text also serves as a salutary warning about the risks of judicial use of statutory purpose and of legislative history, both of which are . . . subject to interpretive abuse." Cass Sunstein, *After the Rights Revolution: Reconceiving the Regulatory State* (Harvard University Press, 1990), p. 114.

42. Peter Nichols discusses some of the GATT-specific interpretive canons that evolved before the WTO adoption of customary interpretive rules in public international law: for instance, that exception to trade liberalizing obligations is to be interpreted narrowly, and whenever an exception is at issue the party that seeks to invoke it bears the burden of proof that it meets the specific criteria for the exception. Clearly, in both these cases, these canons assume the primacy of trade liberalization as a value in treaty interpreta-

tion. Peter M. Nichols, "GATT Doctrine," *Virginia Journal of International Law,* vol. 36 (1996), pp. 434–35, n. 73.

43. For a discussion in the EU context, see "Conclusion" in Nicolaïdis and Howse, *The Federal Vision.*

44. Nicolaïdis, "Non-Discriminatory Mutual Recognition."

45. P. Hirst and G. Thompson argue that globalization does not necessarily diminish the regulatory and redistributive capacities of the state but puts pressure on the traditional social bargains that define how those capacities are exercised. Depending on the nature of the polity, it may be very difficult to recast such bargains so as to make the state effective again under the new conditions of globalization—although there are some success stories (for example, the Netherlands) that suggest that this will not always be the case. See P. Hirst and G. Thompson, *Globalization in Question: The International Economy and the Possibilities of Governance,* 2d ed. (London: Polity, 1999), esp. ch. 6, "Can the Welfare State Survive Globalization?"

46. Dani Rodrik, *Has Globalization Gone Too Far?* (Washington: Institute for International Economics, 1997).

47. Scharpf, *Governing in Europe.*

COMMENT BY

Steve Charnovitz

Robert Howse and Kalypso Nicolaïdis analyze the constitutional discourse regarding the World Trade Organization, rejecting it in favor of a nonconstitutional perspective. Whether or not the WTO is thought of as a constitution, four key relationships need to be considered: (1) the WTO and the laws of its member states, including issues of federalism and deference, (2) separation of powers inside the WTO, (3) the WTO and other international law, including conflicts of law, and (4) the WTO and the individual. The authors explore these relationships, and I would like to build on their points.

Constitutional Models

To attain a better model for understanding the WTO, commentators are engaging more in constitutional discourse. Howse and Nicolaïdis examine two such models of WTO constitutionalism. The first they call libertarian constitutionalism. The second they call the European federal vision. They conclude that both are inadequate.

In libertarian constitutionalism, politicians see the WTO as a way of tying their hands to resist domestic interest groups that demand rent-seeking, protectionist behavior by the government. Thus the WTO pact is as much vertical as it is horizontal.

The authors raise several problems with the libertarian constitutional model. One is that it seems antidemocratic. Another is that the underlying value judgments may not be right. The authors also object to the way that WTO constitutionalists use the European Union as a model. The WTO constitutionalists see the constraints in EU law but miss the social community that enables those constraints.

The other model critiqued is the European federal vision, in which the WTO gradually evolves into a constitutional system. The authors pose doubts about this path for the WTO. For unlike the European Community, the WTO has no provision for domestic effect of regulations and no interaction between national courts and WTO tribunals.

The Global Subsidiarity Alternative

The final section of the chapter presents the authors' answer for recovering the spirit of "embedded liberalism." They propose a model called global subsidiarity, which has three main principles. First, the WTO should manifest institutional sensitivity to national regulatory choices and to other international regimes. Second, the WTO should promote the principle of political inclusiveness at the national and international levels. Third, the WTO should empower global subunits, including states, by fulfilling the conditions necessary for governments to carry out their international obligations. My assessment begins with a general comment on the entire exercise and then discusses the four WTO relationships just noted.

WTO Exceptionalism

Analysts should be cautious about formulating any theory of the WTO that is detached from other international organizations.[1] The WTO has made many advances from the General Agreement on Tariffs and Trade (GATT), but it is not fundamentally a different species from other treaty-based organizations. In thinking through international constitutionalism, it is helpful to do so in a comparative manner. As Ray Vernon taught us:

> With economic interactions between national economies growing at a breathtaking pace, it is apparent that international cooperation among national governments will be essential in a wide range of activities, from controlling the environment to maintaining the probity of securities markets. There is a race between constructing the international regimes that can master some of the consequences of the dizzying growth in international linkages, and coming to terms with interests within the United States that have the power to thwart any constructive response.[2]

This passage points to two key realities. One is that a range of international regimes will be essential to achieve needed international cooperation. The other is that there will be tension between each regime and domestic interests at the national level. Thus, in trying to solve the problems of the trading system, we should look to other regimes for useful insights.

Deference to National Decisionmaking

Howse and Nicolaïdis argue that "WTO dispute settlement organs must display considerable deference to substantive domestic regulatory choices." Let me mention two concerns that I have with this analysis. First, it is not clear why WTO tribunals should show deference. Most people do not favor such deference in other international regimes. For example, when the International Labor Organization found that Myanmar had violated the Convention on Forced Labor, no one said to be deferential to Myanmar's regulatory choices. Similarly, when the parties to the Convention on International Trade in Endangered Species found that Burundi was flouting the convention's rules on ivory, no one recommended deference to Burundi's choices. So why should WTO rules be more softly applied? Once a specific discipline becomes a treaty obligation, there may not be much space for deference.

Second, the authors focus only on the WTO judiciary but do not consider sensitivity to states in relation to the WTO executive. Director-General Mike Moore has been an activist executive in his first year on the job. To give one example, Moore visited the United States in May 2000—at a time when a controversial congressional vote was pending on the normalization of trade relations with China—and spoke in favor of approving the legislation.[3] For an international civil servant to intervene in domestic politics is unusual. But Moore weighed in on the important issue in dispute. At the time the legal implication of a negative vote was hotly contested; the legislators opposed to normal relations were arguing that a long-standing U.S. trade agreement with China would guarantee that China's commitments in the accession negotiations would apply to the United States. Yet the director-general lent the weight of his office to the pro-normalization side of the debate by averring that "American business and workers will only get these [trade] benefits if Congress votes for permanent trade relations with China."

Separation of Powers

Constitutions typically provide for a separation of powers between the executive, legislative, and judicial branches. The authors encourage deference by the WTO judiciary to the political processes of negotiations. A healthy constitution requires the engagement of all three branches of government. Otherwise, the roles of the branches will overgrow and interfere with one another. As John Jackson has noted, the weak legislative capacity of the WTO puts a great deal of strain on the Appellate Body.[4]

WTO and Other International Law

Howse and Nicolaïdis suggest that the WTO draw on and defer to other international regimes and be sensitive to the "superior credentials" that other institutions of governance may have. They also point to the need for "institutionalized linkages between segmented regimes."

In my view this relationship is the key challenge for the trade regime and one it is failing to meet. After six years in operation, the WTO General Council has not granted observer status to the UN Environment Programme. Similarly, the Secretariat of the Biodiversity Convention has not received observer status in the WTO Council dealing with patenting.

The WTO and the Individual

Howse and Nicolaïdis make two distinct recommendations with respect to political inclusiveness. The first is that the WTO "play a role in enhancing obligations of transnational inclusiveness in domestic rulemaking processes." They point to an example of this in the WTO requirements for enquiry points.

They can strengthen their thesis by noting the numerous provisions in the WTO that require national governments to give private economic actors an opportunity to participate in domestic decisionmaking.[5] For example, the Agreement on Subsidies and Countervailing Measures requires governments to inform interested parties (such as an exporter or trade association) before making countervailing duty determinations; the intent is to give time for such parties to "defend their interests."[6] The champions of the WTO missed an opportunity to show how it can push governments to guarantee procedural rights to individuals.

The second recommendation is that governments should facilitate greater access to WTO processes for nongovernmental organizations (NGOs). I agree with this recommendation and with the authors' statement that such opportunities "need not be understood as rights of representation." The rationale for NGO participation is not that NGOs represent constituents in the same way that elected officials do. Instead, NGOs should be able to participate to enrich the debate and to help authoritative decisionmakers reach the best conclusions.[7]

In allowing NGOs to offer amicus briefs, the Appellate Body has moved the WTO ahead of other international courts that often reject amicus briefs. This development is particularly interesting because the WTO governments would not have taken this step on their own. It occurred as a judicial decision reminiscent of the way that the European Court of Justice provided for procedural rights.

The crude version of WTO constitutionalism promotes the wrong prescription in seeking to tie the hands of politicians so that they will not succumb to bad ideas from interest groups. Yet the right way to defeat bad ideas is with better ideas. Just as national democracy entails participation and debate at the domestic level, so too democratic global governance entails opportunities for participation by national and transnational NGOs. Politicians should act and decide as a result of listening to a vigorous, competitive debate. It is illusionary to think that good economic policy can be ensured by having the decisionmakers of today tie the hands of (or lock in policies for) the decisionmakers of the future. Sustainable policies require renewed political support.

The recent WTO Section 301 panel, perhaps recognizing the hollowness in conventional images of the WTO, called our attention to the needs of individual traders. According to the panel, the multilateral trading system is "composed not only of States but also, indeed mostly, of individual economic operators."[8] One might doubt that the panel accurately states the international economic law of today, but I predict that it foresees the international law of tomorrow.

Notes

1. For examples of analysts who view the WTO as conceptually different from other international treaties and organizations, see John O. McGinnis, "The Political Economy of Global Multilateralism," *Chicago Journal of International Law,* vol. 1 (2000), pp. 381–99; William H. Lash III and Daniel T. Griswold, "WTO Report Card II," briefing paper, Cato Institute, May 2000.
2. Raymond Vernon, "The U.S. Government at Bretton Woods and After," in Orin Kirshner, ed., *The Bretton Woods–GATT System: Retrospect and Prospect after Fifty Years* (Armonk, N.Y.: M. E. Sharpe, 1996), pp. 52–67.

3. Mike Moore, "The WTO and the New Economy," speech to the National Foreign Trade Council, New York, May 22, 2000; "WTO DG Moore Urges Passage of PNTR for China" (www.wto.org/english/news).

4. John H. Jackson, "International Economic Law in Times That Are Interesting," *Journal of International Economic Law,* vol. 3 (March 2000), pp. 3, 8.

5. See Steve Charnovitz, "The WTO and the Rights of the Individual," *Intereconomics,* vol. 36 (March–April, 2001), p. 98.

6. Agreement on Subsidies and Countervailing Measures, art. 12.8. Another provision states that governments shall permit "representative consumer organizations" to provide relevant information (art. 12.10).

7. See Steve Charnovitz, "Opening the WTO to Nongovernmental Interests," *Fordham International Law Journal,* vol. 24 (November–December 2000), p. 173.

8. World Trade Organization, "United States—Sections 301–10 of the Trade Act of 1974, December 22, 1999," WT/DS/152/R, paragraph 7.76. See also paragraphs 7.73, 7.86, 7.90.

COMMENT BY

Gary N. Horlick

Critics who spread tales of the World Trade Organization as a global tyrant ask whether further constitutionalization is necessary to address a formal legitimacy deficit in the organization. Robert Howse and Kalypso Nicolaïdis pull the debate back into a more rigorously analytical form. They conclude that constitutionalization is neither feasible nor advisable at this moment, and they offer an alternative method of legitimacy building: adapting the European Union model of subsidiarity to a global context. Adjusting the institutional mission statement to be more politically sensitive and inclusive, the authors suggest, might appease some popular critics.

My comment concentrates on a different dimension of legitimacy—popular legitimacy driven by the perception of success. In other words, is the WTO seen to work? A popular perception of success provides a basis for political leaders to seek further liberalization if they so choose. This author considers the current crisis of popular legitimacy to be in good part the result of a gap between the actual and perceived success of the WTO system.

One way institutions develop popular legitimacy is to make people better off. Thus Howse and Nicolaïdis begin their analysis with a description of the mutually self-interested bargain on which the legitimacy of the General Agreement on Tariffs and Trade (GATT) was founded.[1] After the Uruguay Round, this win-win bargain became "unstuck," they suggest, because all countries did not benefit from each individual piece of the agreement. The authors therefore offer a new basis for popular support: "subsidiarity adapted to the structure of the international system." They attempt to reconstitute the original postwar embedded liberalism agreement by institutionalizing layers of deference to national and alternative supranational institutions. Their approach, however, is problematic if it supposes that once the formal elements of inclusivity and transparency are incorporated into the WTO system, popular legitimacy will automatically follow and with no loss of the benefits of the current system. Popular legitimacy, unlike formal legitimacy, is based on the perception of benefits for its members.

I wish to thank Lisa Pearlman of Harvard Law School for clarifying and refining my initial paper. I remain fully responsible for the views and any errors expressed here.

The GATT/WTO has been and continues to be successful. An important part of the postwar world economic system, it has met the basic human needs (such as better nutrition and health) of billions of people, and it has started to meet many of their aspirations (including higher wages, better rights for workers, and better environmental protection in precisely those countries that opened the most). The dynamic effect of freeing up markets, and the more direct effects of lowering trade barriers, are important engines for ongoing economic expansion.

While, as Howse and Nicolaïdis note, each individual component of the Uruguay Round agreements is arguably not win-win, the agreement as a whole continues to work, including for the United States. Academic studies estimate an annual GDP gain for the United States of $27 billion to $37 billion from the Uruguay Round.[2] Thus, if nowhere else, the WTO should enjoy popular legitimacy in the United States. In fact, despite the noisy anti-WTO protests in Seattle in 1999, a recent poll found that 50 percent of Americans approve of the work of the organization.[3]

The most serious effect of these attacks in terms of popular legitimacy is that they have fostered a perception problem: 22 percent of the U.S. population agree that "the WTO is a huge secretive international organization and powerful bureaucracy that tells countries how to run their economies, serves the interests of large, multinational corporations, and threatens a country's sovereignty by interfering in its national law-making."[4] The 50 percent who agree "that the WTO provides a forum for member countries to conduct trade negotiations, handles trade disputes, monitors national trade policies, and provides training for developing countries on trade and regulatory matters" are being drowned out by a louder minority.

One reason for the success of interest groups at undermining the popular legitimacy of the WTO may be quite simple—while the WTO works out the kinks in a fairly new arrangement, it has not had time to advertise its record of success. The key to sustaining its hard-earned legitimacy is first to continue its current success: the multilateral negotiation of lower, not higher, trade barriers. There are plenty of traditional tariffs to be lowered (for example, agriculture, textiles, glass and chinaware, and footwear). Continuing success will also require further classic trade liberalization, such as reducing barriers to trade in services, extending General Agreement on Trade in Services (GATS) coverage, cleaning up the mess of antidumping law, and refining the subsidies and safeguard rules.[5] Most important, the record of success must be publicized by business groups, which often assume the inevitability of the current trading environment provided by

WTO rules, and by politicians (in the United States, especially those with the "bully pulpit" of the White House). Unseen success begets little popular legitimacy.

As Howse and Nicolaïdis recognize, it could be counterproductive to include "new areas," such as competition, labor, or the environment, on the current negotiating agenda of the WTO. Reluctance to take on these sectors is less an acknowledgment of questionable formal legitimacy than recognition of a political reality that could undermine the quest to maintain popular legitimacy.

The practical obstacles to a successful negotiation of international competition rules and procedures within the next few years seem daunting. However, work on competition policy can still be carried out, even beyond bilateral cooperation agreements. The sole published attempt at a comprehensive international competition agreement, the so-called Munich Draft, was attacked by hordes of critics, which suggests that what we need is more drafts (and fewer concept papers) to study, criticize, and synthesize, after which a productive negotiation may be possible.

Advocates of including labor rights and environmental protection measures in the WTO are following a path trod by the services and intellectual property industries. Labor and environment groups express frustration with existing forums and view the availability of trade sanctions as a prized tool to enforce labor and environmental agreements. But including these rules simply to make use of the trade sanction punishment threatens the basis of the formal and popular legitimacy of the organization—its success at lowering trade barriers. There is a practical reason for not including in the WTO labor rights and environmental protection rules (assuming they would raise living standards). It is that enforcement of those rules might destroy the foundation of the organization advocates count on to do the enforcement without achieving the desired result.

These issues also threaten the perception of mutual benefit because there will always be the suspicion that interest groups in developed countries (whether labor unions or nongovernmental organizations funded by or allied to them) are more interested in preventing import competition and *increasing* unemployment in poor countries, than in improving working and living standards of workers in poor countries. Living standards and environmental protection are, however, matters closely tied to popular legitimacy. A trading system that is seen as driving down the living standards of workers around the world, rather than improving them as the WTO has done, will have no popular legitimacy.

When considering health, safety, labor, and environmental standards, advocates of uniform WTO standards should realize that all countries, not only developed country politicians and activists, will get a "vote" in setting the rules.[6] Such rules will likely be different than some activists would favor. International popular legitimacy demands rules that allow all countries, especially developing ones, to see the benefits of the WTO agreements in the way the United States has.

As Victoria Curzon notes, while the protesters ("ethical protectionists") make weak arguments when viewed from an empirical economic perspective, they use the media skillfully to exploit the moral sensibilities of heretofore "rationally ignorant consumers." Indeed, they have changed the stage on which trade liberalization occurs. Henceforth, she explains, international trade policy will be worked out in the public eye.[7] If this is to be the case, those who understand the benefit of the continued opening of markets must learn to make their arguments outside of academic classrooms and closed negotiating sessions and in the public eye.

Governments and individuals who understand the benefits of the system must stay firm on the path that has led to the current successes, and advertise these successes in order to shore up the popular legitimacy of the WTO system. There is no reason why there should be any gap (even 22 percent) in the popular legitimacy of an institution that is working as well as the WTO.

Notes

1. In a system of comparative advantage, each country should unilaterally benefit from the liberalization of trade barriers.

2. "The WTO and U.S. Economic Growth," March 2, 2000 (www.ustr.gov/new/wtofact2.html).

3. EpicX MRA Nationwide Survey on Trade, May 2000.

4. Ibid.

5. Conventionally, this has been done through "rounds." It is common to criticize rounds for taking too long, although much of the eight-year length of the Uruguay Round reflects the political unwillingness of Europe and Japan to accept liberalization of trade in agriculture. The complaints about comprehensive rounds should be taken with a grain of salt when offered by governments or industry advocates whose real goal is to exclude from negotiations their own protectionist barriers. In any event, the alternative—sectoral negotiations such as the successful reduction of barriers in the Information Technology Agreement, financial services, and telecoms—seems to have run its course and is no longer

politically acceptable to the vast majority of WTO members (and may have had the perverse effect of reducing or eliminating the support by the beneficiaries of those reductions for more general trade liberalization rounds).

6. For example, the European Union can have EU-wide rules because each member state has votes. The North American Free Trade Agreement, however, cannot have NAFTA-wide rules unless Mexico and Canada are given a vote in setting U.S. environmental laws. If the WTO were to take up the question of environmental regulation, U.S. environmental groups could well find themselves much in the same position as the U.S antitrust agencies facing negotiation of global competition rules.

7. Victoria Price Curzon, "Putting Ethical Protectionism and Its Proponents in Perspective" (Cordell Hull Institute, forthcoming).

ROBERT O. KEOHANE
JOSEPH S. NYE JR.

12 | The Club Model of Multilateral Cooperation and Problems of Democratic Legitimacy

Multilateral cooperation was remarkably extensive, indeed unprecedented, in the latter half of the twentieth century. After World War II a compromise was struck in rich countries that John Ruggie has termed *embedded liberalism*.[1] Increasing economic openness became politically feasible in a democratic era through the development of the welfare state, and through a set of international regimes for finance and trade that accommodated the welfare state.

Until the end of the 1970s, what Fred Hirsch called "the missing legitimacy for a predominantly capitalist system in conditions of universal political participation" was provided by Keynesian policies that were tolerant of inflation. International regimes in this period "served the second-best objective of the liberal community, of maintaining an open international economy at whatever inflation rate [had] to be accepted to attain this."[2] Inflation eventually rose to the point where it caused political disaffection, and since the 1980s governments of the advanced capitalist economies have emphasized price stability. Legitimacy at the domestic level has apparently been maintained in these countries, judging from the lack of large-scale protests and the maintenance in power of governments—whether nominally of the Left or the Right—dedicated to preservation of a market system. Such legitimacy has different sources in different countries: in the United States, economic growth; in continental Europe, the preservation of a social safety net despite substantial unemployment; and in Japan, the maintenance of a still

prosperous and orderly, if stagnant, political economy. In any event, the collapse of socialism in the Soviet Union, and the serious constraints on the expansion of the welfare state resulting from global competition, have
reinforced the dominant position of liberal capitalism.[3]

Until recently, the international regimes for trade and money that
made this system work were largely invisible to publics. We will character-
ize them as following a "club model" of institutions. As these institutions
have become more important and their membership more diverse, they
have become more controversial. The Seattle demonstrations against the
World Trade Organization (WTO) in November 1999 and the Washington protests in April 2000 against the International Monetary Fund (IMF)
and World Bank are examples. The classic political issue of legitimacy,
within the context of democratic norms, has been insistently raised. The
club model has come under challenge.

In this essay we consider descriptive and normative aspects of legitimacy as it relates to international institutions, particularly to the WTO.
First we describe the club model and how, in a stylized sense, it has operated
for the past half-century on issues such as international trade. After distinguishing between adversary and unitary democracy, we consider the ways
in which international organizations such as the WTO experience a "democratic deficit." Issues of transparency and participation are examined, but
we emphasize the *insufficient politicization* of these organizations—their
lack of effective politicians who link organizations to constituencies. Then
a more detailed normative analysis of democratic legitimacy is offered. The
legitimacy of institutions is affected on the "input" side—in particular,
through procedures for accountability—and on the "output" side in terms
of effectiveness. The chapter concludes with steps that the WTO and similar international organizations might take to enhance their legitimacy in a
world infused by democratic norms.

The Club Model of Multilateral Cooperation

International institutions have facilitated cooperation by reducing
the costs of making agreements, through established rules and practices, and
by providing information, particularly about the extent to which governments were following these rules.[4] Beginning with the Bretton Woods conference of 1944, key regimes for governance operated like clubs. Cabinet
ministers or the equivalent, working in the same issue-area, initially from a

relatively small number of relatively rich countries, got together to make rules. Trade ministers dominated the General Agreement on Tariffs and Trade (GATT); finance ministers ran the IMF; defense and foreign ministers met at the headquarters of NATO (the North Atlantic Treaty Organization); central bankers convened at the Bank for International Settlements (BIS). They negotiated in secret, then reported their agreements to national legislatures and publics. Until recently, they were largely unchallenged.

Using Herbert Simon's terminology these traditional international regimes can be described as "decomposable hierarchies."[5] In the decomposable hierarchy model of international regimes—characteristic of the second half of the twentieth century, at least in formal terms—international regimes, with particular states as members, were established to govern "issue-areas," defined in terms of clusters of issues. In this respect they were hierarchic: governments collaborated to make binding rules. Some of these regimes were open to universal membership, others were selective or required meeting a set of standards imposed by the original participants. The regimes, thus defined by membership and issues, were "decomposable" from the rest of the system, in the sense that they operated without close links to other regimes in other issue-areas. Their members constructed rules—traditional international law or established but less obligatory practices known as "soft law"—to govern their relationships within the issue-area.

The club model was very convenient for officials negotiating agreements within issue-areas since in two ways it kept outsiders out. First, officials in other government bureaucracies and in international organizations in different issue-areas were excluded from the negotiations. Environmental, labor rights, and finance officials did not participate on a regular basis in WTO negotiations. In general, they did not object to their exclusion. After all, they were able to exclude outsiders from their own negotiations. Second, the public was confronted with a series of *faits accomplis,* making domestic politics easier to manage. It was difficult for outsiders to understand the actual positions taken in negotiations, how firmly they were held, and the bargaining dynamics that produced compromises; therefore, it was hard to hold negotiators accountable for their actions. From the standpoint of negotiators oriented toward reaching solutions, these were positive features of the negotiating situation. They could develop close working relationships with their colleagues from other countries, limiting the disruptive force of parochial concerns emanating from domestic politics. Keeping their internal deliberations confidential was in their collective interest. Under such conditions, as Michael Zurn comments, the opportunity for "strategic manipulation of information is wide open to decision-makers."[6]

Under the club model a lack of transparency to functional outsiders was a key to political efficacy. Protected by the lack of transparency, ministers could make package deals that were difficult to disaggregate or even sometimes to understand. For instance, after the U.S. Congress deconstructed the trade agreements made during the Kennedy Round (1967), implementing unilateral modifications to bargains that had been reached, America's trade partners demanded modifications in internal U.S. practices as a condition for the next trade round. The political response in the United States was a "fast-track" procedure, agreed to by Congress, that limited congressional power to pick apart agreements. In effect, Congress agreed to "tie itself to the mast" as it sailed past specific protectionist sirens.

As Robert Hudec points out in his comment on this chapter, Congress has voted many times for such procedures since its disastrous experience of unfettered participation in earlier years, culminating in the Smoot-Hawley tariff of 1930. It agreed to immunize international bargains from disaggregation in return for European, Japanese, and Canadian willingness to negotiate further reductions in trade barriers. Cooperation on international trade benefited, but the influence of labor unions and environmentalists was reduced by the practice. They have reacted strongly against it and the associated international institutions.

From the perspective of multilateral cooperation, the club model can be judged a great success. The world seems more peaceful, more prosperous, and even somewhat cleaner, at least on some environmental issues, than it would have been without such cooperation.[7] Admittedly, integration was often relatively shallow. The easier problems were tackled first. High rates of observed compliance with treaties do not necessarily indicate that noncompliance was a trivial problem.[8] Furthermore, the progress in institutional authority that did occur—as in the move from GATT to the WTO—was hardly the result of a sudden conversion of governments to the view that international law should prevail over national interests. As Robert Hudec has observed, the willingness of governments to negotiate the more precise rules and more authoritative procedures of the WTO stemmed from the U.S. threat unilaterally to impose trade restrictions under Section 301 of its trade act:

> The change in position seems to have been a choice between two evils: between an almost certain legal meltdown if the United States were to carry out its new Section 301 instructions, and a very serious risk of legal failure, in the somewhat more distant

future, if GATT adopted a dispute settlement procedure that was more demanding than governments could obey. In these circumstances, the fact that GATT governments chose the later option does not mean that they were confident it would work.[9]

The club model of cooperation, as illustrated in the Uruguay Round, had a political logic of its own. The governments of advanced capitalist countries understood that their electorates would hold them responsible for the results of trade negotiations. Liberalization would produce overall gains for the economy and for the electorates, but in the absence of compensation, protectionist interests "can be expected to resist, desperately and justifiably, their unhappy economic fate."[10] These groups, whose interests are more concentrated than those of consumers, could derail liberalizing trade measures unless they were "paid off" with rents from "voluntary" export restraints or subsidies of one type or another. In the United States each administration seeking liberalization bought off enough protectionist sectors (for example, textile manufacturers in the 1960s and 1970s) to pass liberalizing legislation.[11]

Negotiations in each trade round were tedious and fraught with anxiety for liberal trade forces. Yet they increased openness. Each round decreased the political weight of protectionist interests and increased the influence of their export-oriented opponents and of multinational firms allied with export interests.[12] As globalization progressed, the pro-liberal forces became more concentrated, since the largest firms in each country were highly multinational. The core political fact creating protectionism— that protectionist domestic producers were more concentrated than the far more numerous but less concentrated consumers—had been reversed. Exporters and multinationals were much more concentrated than the smaller and more scattered import-competing producers. Hence liberalizers were playing a winning game in which each round of liberalization strengthened their own coalitions, and weakened their opponents', for the next round.

Armed with stronger mandates as a result of liberalizing domestic coalitions, the governments could negotiate with one another on the basis of reciprocity. Reciprocity took two complementary forms: specific reciprocity, since very precise deals were built into the agreements at the end of each trade round, and diffuse reciprocity, the belief that in the end everyone would benefit from liberalization, even if not all of the specific deals worked out as expected.[13] The result was a series of liberalizing trade agreements between the inauguration of GATT in 1948 and the completion of the Uruguay Round in 1994.

If the "club pattern"—under which small numbers of rich-country trade ministers controlled the agenda and made deals—were to continue in trade, so could this spiral of liberalization. However in a dialectical fashion, the club arrangements are, we believe, being undercut by their success. Specifically, we can point to four reasons for the weakening of the old club system of trade politics.

First, increasing trade made publics more sensitive to further concessions. During the 1960s, 1970s, and 1980s, trade liberalization had been facilitated by the fact that substantial barriers to trade remained. Toronto still trades ten times as much with Vancouver as it does with Seattle, proportionate to the size of the latter two markets.[14] The barriers that produce this effect may be, in Richard Cooper's words, "political and psychological" more than natural in a geographical sense.[15] Yet from a political economy perspective, they created what could be termed a "useful inefficiency" that provided a buffer for domestic political differences while allowing openness to the global economy. Adjustment is an economic good but a political bad: it causes distress to many people, usually including potentially influential constituents of politicians. It is difficult to force adjustment quickly; hence barriers that reduce the pressure, or slow down the process, are often politically welcome. It has therefore been fortunate for politicians, although lamented by economists, that national borders matter so much for trade. The persistence of these barriers to both trade and capital movements, whether due to policy or psychology, helps to explain why national policy automony in fiscal and regulatory policy has not disappeared.[16]

With time and market integration, this useful inefficiency is being gradually eroded. Trade-to-GDP ratios are significantly higher than they were before the 1990s. Capital moves much more freely across borders than it did then. Sensitivity has increased during the last thirty years and can be expected to continue to do so. Inceased sensitivity creates the potential for greater public pressure on policy.[17]

The second development that seems to have undercut the club system is that developing countries are demanding greater participation in policy-making. Their leaders are often ambivalent about the regimes, suspicious about the implications of rich-country leadership, and resentful of club rules, made by the rich, that they did not help to establish. Current hopes for a revival of serious negotiations on trade depend, in part, on developing countries' agreement to new rules. Many of these countries have been excluded from the club-like negotiations of the WTO. Early in 2000 India's commerce and industry minister complained that only about thirty countries were authorized to participate in the WTO's consultative process in Seattle at the end of November 1999. That process, he declared, "eliminated 100-plus countries from any participation at all, and some could not even enter the premises" where the negotiations were taking place.[18]

Governments of developing countries have their own agendas for trade negotiations, which are at odds both with the agendas of rich governments and with the agendas of rich-country nongovernmental organizations (NGOs). At the same time, the developing countries do not want to destroy the club; they want to join it and have more power within it. The challenge they pose is not to the legitimacy of the club concept per se but to its implementation. They are not pressing for the inclusion of environment ministers or nongovernmental actors. On the contrary, they have led the opposition to such changes. They are happy to have an intergovernmental club of trade ministers. The problem they pose is their number. As Harlan Cleveland once put it, how do you get everyone into the action and still get action? In principle, representative working groups with transparent processes might help to alleviate developing countries' concerns about legitimacy if such processes could be worked out.

Third, globalization has led to proliferation of nonstate agents, including business firms, business associations, labor unions, and NGOs; clamoring to make their voices heard, they have broadened the agenda of the WTO from trade policy.[19] During the 1990s, the number of international NGOs grew from 6,000 to 26,000, ranging in size from the Worldwide Fund for Nature with 5 million members to tiny network organizations.[20] The Seattle meetings of the WTO demonstrated the variety of such organizations and the intensity of members' feelings about the real or imagined links between trade and issues such as labor rights and environmental protection. Seen from a trade-specific transgovernmental perspective, the WTO is a club of trade ministers working with rules that have served well in that issue-area. But issue linkages ("trade and . . ." issues) are more problematic. Environment and labor ministers, for example, do not have a seat at the table. In other words, some relevant publics have no direct voice— only an indirect voice through national legislatures and executives.

The demonstrators at Seattle, incoherent and self-interested though they were, had a point. They wanted more direct access to the arena where their interests were being affected. In principle, this could be solved by linkages between the WTO and other international organizations, such as the UN Environment Program (UNEP) or the International Labor Organization (ILO). These organizations, however, do not have direct authority over trade policy, nor do they have as strong constituencies as does the WTO. Of course, there was not a single consistent NGO position at Seattle on these issues. Some NGO demonstrators wanted to weaken the World Trade Organization to protect sovereign regulation of the environment; others wanted to borrow the power of the organization to overcome sovereign regulation of labor conditions.

Nongovernmental organizations and their networks should not be viewed as a monolithic opposition to unitary states. On the contrary, different NGOs will participate in different transnational-transgovernmental coalitions with governmental officials, often pitted against other transnational-transgovernmental networks with different purposes.[21] Mixed or trisectoral coalitions are becoming more common in world politics. Agents will be connected to one another in networks and will work through competing and cooperating coalitions, but none of the components will be subordinate to another. Trade politics will be less dominated in the future by multilateral intergovernmental cooperation within a "decomposable" issue-area. The involvement of NGOs, the formation of transnational-transgovernmental networks, and linkages among issues are inherently connected.

This evolving pattern of transnational linkage politics intersects not only with the old club politics but also with the increasing assertiveness of governments of developing countries. At Seattle pressure from nongovernmental organizations, including politically influential U.S. trade unions, led President Bill Clinton to demand that labor standards be incorporated in the WTO's trade agreements, and even to threaten sanctions to enforce them.[22] The reaction of India's commerce and industry minister was not only firm but scornful: "The threat of sanctions," said Murasoli Maran, "was the last straw. It was a nakedly protectionist act by a clique of developed countries behaving like a 'kangaroo court'."[23] Seattle made very clear the difficulties that a combination of heterogeneous state objectives, and activism by NGOs, can create for international trade negotiations.

The fourth force undermining the club system is the spread of democratic norms to more and more countries and attempts to implement them at the international level. There is more to the Seattle and Washington protests than the "protest envy" of young people whose parents demonstrated against the Vietnam War. Behind the protesters' annoyingly naïve characterizations of the WTO, IMF, and World Bank, and their frequent failure to understand even elementary economics, lies a deep concern with democratic procedures. When asked, students involved in these protests may concede ignorance on how the World Bank is organized or whether it has changed its policies to help the poor. Pressed on their economics, and on issues of fact, they come back to their normative base: global institutions are "undemocratic." Lori Wallach attributes half the success of the Seattle coalition to the notion that "the democracy deficit in the global economy is neither necessary nor acceptable." When it was pointed out that Mike Moore was appointed by democratically elected governments, she replied, "Between someone who actually got elected, and the director general of the WTO, there are so many miles that, in fact, he and his staff are ac-countable to no one."[24] This claim is debatable, but many social demo-crats in Europe claim that international institutions do not meet the procedural standards of democracy, particularly that of transparency.[25]

All of these pressures on international institutions are, ironically, re-flections of their success. If international institutions were unimportant, as so-called "realists" claimed until recently, no one would care about their legitimacy.[26] But it is now recognized that the policies of the IMF, the World Bank, and the WTO make a difference. Hence they are judged not only on the results that these policies yield, but also on the procedures by which the policies are developed.

In the rest of this chapter, we focus on issues of democratic legitimacy raised by the pluralization of trade politics and the spread of democratic norms. These raise more novel questions of political theory than do the demands of governments of developing countries to have their voices heard within the club. In what sense does the club model of international regimes fail to meet democratic standards? Insofar as it does fail, what changes toward greater democracy would be feasible? And what trade-offs—for instance with liberalization and international cooperation in general—could be expected as democratization increased? Our interpreta-tion of an actual political-economic problem—the endangered legitimacy of international political-economic institutions, including trade institu-tions such as the WTO—leads us to reconsider democratic theory as it may apply to issues of international governance.

Adversary Democracy and Unitary Democracy in Global Institutions

In a book written right after the last great period of "creedal passion," Jane J. Mansbridge explored two types of democracy, which she called "adversary" and "unitary."[27] Adversary democracy assumes conflicting interests and employs established procedures to make decisions in the face of such conflicts. Unitary or direct democracy assumes that people have the same interests but may not know, individually, what is best to do. Face-to-face deliberation, as in the New England town meeting, is, in this view, the democratic way to reach decisions.[28] Mansbridge asks how both forms of democracy could be employed in a large country such as the United States. Admitting the decisionmaking advantages of adversary democracies, she asks her readers to appreciate the values of equal respect, or equal status, of unitary democracy. "The task confronting us," she says, "is to knit together these two fundamentally different kinds of democracy into a single institutional network that can allow us both to advance our common interests and to resolve our conflicting ones."[29]

Knitting these two forms together is a daunting task, and one that the United States certainly has not managed to accomplish in any coherent fashion. Indeed, participation in civil society in the United States, on a wide variety of dimensions, decreased during the second half of the twentieth century.[30] At the international level, with 6 billion people in the world, unitary or direct democracy appears a utopian dream. Nevertheless, adversary democracy does not have the inherently normative appeal that direct democracy often has.

One way to address the problems of democratic practices at the international level would be to apply an analogy between domestic and international politics.[31] International institutions would be viewed as if they were national institutions writ large. This perspective makes some sense for the European Union, which has extensive authority and elaborate institutions, including a parliament and a European Court of Justice. It is not surprising that Europeans have taken the lead in the debate on transparency, accountability, and the so-called democratic deficit, or that their chief target has been the European Union. Indeed, as Martin Wolf has commented, "if a country organized like the EU were to apply for membership, it would be rejected because it is not a democracy."[32] The mass resignation in March 1999 of the European Commission, under pressure from the European Parliament, is indicative of moves toward a European Union that may look more like a democratic federal state than it does now. Such an entity is unlikely to meet the standards of unitary democracy, although it may increasingly meet those of adversary democracy.

Direct democracy is more an impulse than an actual set of institutions. At an international level it would be utopian to suggest that anything like it is remotely feasible. However, its ideals should be kept in mind. They lie behind the protests against international institutions.

Transparency and Participation in the WTO

Whether global regimes have a democratic deficit is more ambiguous than whether the European Union has one because the domestic analogy is less plausible for global regimes. Indeed, one could ask, "What's the fuss?" International institutions are weak relative to the governments of rich, powerful states. They operate formally according to democratic principles of delegation. And increasingly the WTO, in particular, conforms to the rule of law. We examine these three defenses of international institutions before taking a closer look at problems of transparency and participation in the WTO.

No international institution operating on a global scale has anything like the authority of the European Union, much less that of a state. Among international organizations, the WTO stands out as having quite authoritative and precise rules, and a relatively good record of eventual compliance with those rules by governments. So far, through diplomatic finesse and compromise the WTO has avoided outright refusals. The U.S. Helms-Burton legislation, for instance, did not lead to a formal case at the WTO, precisely because both the United States and the EU feared that any decision by the WTO against the United States could lead to an anti-WTO backlash in this country. The WTO decisions on beef hormones and bananas strained EU support for the WTO, and the WTO decision on U.S. export-tax benefits for corporations strained corporate support for the organization in the United States. The authoritative dispute settlement procedures of the WTO were, as Hudec has argued, a gamble. Despite successes so far, it remains unclear whether the WTO will have the ability to implement decisions that are strongly opposed by powerful states or the European Union.

The WTO-centered trade regime is strong compared with other international regimes. It compares favorably with the nonregime for exchange rates, with the fragmented international environmental regimes, and with the very weak regimes for international labor standards. The nominally central international organizations for environment and labor—the United Nations Environment Program and the International Labor Organization—are ineffective compared with the WTO. However, the reason for the WTO's relative strength is not that it has a powerful bureaucracy. On the contrary, the WTO has a weak bureaucracy that is kept on a short leash by its 135 member states. It has a secretariat of about 500 and a modest budget of $80 million. It decides by consensus, not by majority voting, and the autonomy of its management is much less than that of the IMF or the World Bank. The WTO must be highly responsive to the (mostly) elected governments of its member states.

The success of the WTO is not attributable to its organizational strength but to the fact that its dispute settlement procedures provide space for both diplomatic settlements and national democratic processes while still protecting the system of world trade. As in the case of Helms-Burton, diplomatic agreements can head off the appointment of a panel. After a panel ruling, the losing government typically appeals to the Appellate Body, which is certain to take into account political constraints and potential opposition when making its final decision. If pressures within a democracy cause a country to derogate from its agreements, the WTO does not have the authority (unlike the European Court of Justice) to enforce its rulings through national courts. What it can do is to authorize others to punish the noncompliant country and provide some measure of compensation. Instead of forcing its wishes on recalcitrant governments, the WTO serves the political function of a "circuit breaker" against a downward spiral of retaliation. Better for the lights to go out than for the house to burn down. Better to make concessions to the domestic politics of trade than to precipitate tit-for-tat retaliation, making everyone worse off. In a world of shallow integration, escape clauses and procedures are wise institutional arrangements. An overly legalistic WTO would be in danger of being both rigid and brittle.

The negotiations of the World Trade Organization meet democratic principles insofar as member governments are democratic. Negotiators are appointed by governments, and the final agreements must be ratified through domestic procedures. Representative government always relies on delegation. Rousseau and subsequent advocates of direct democracy have railed against representative government as keeping people "in chains," but no one has figured out how to make unitary democracy work at a scale larger than the city-state. Admittedly, even though international organizations are ultimately accountable to (mostly) democratically elected member governments, the international bureaucrats are more remote than national bureaucracies, and the chain of connection to elections is more indirect. But the chain of connections between elections and the actions of an under-secretary of the Treasury, an independent congressional commission, or a federal court is at least as indirect, and they are rarely accused, except by utopians, of being, for that reason, undemocratic.

The WTO also conforms better to the rule of law than did the GATT. Its Appellate Body set out detailed rules of procedure at the outset, and its opinions have included more rigorous legal analysis than was customary in GATT.[33] Compared with traditional diplomatic negotiations, the WTO's procedures are perfectly lucid. Democracy is not identical to the rule of law but certainly depends on it; in this regard also the WTO could be considered a democratic advance on its predecessors.

So what is the problem? From one democratic perspective, the WTO is almost the ideal design of an international institution. The international bureaucracy is weak; the organization is responsive to (mostly) elected governments. The escape clauses and dispute settlement procedures allow domestic political processes to prevail when severely challenged by international integration without at the same time destroying all rules and procedures. Thus the WTO contributes to the preservation of the embedded liberal bargain that has allowed the welfare state and increasing economic openness to co-exist.

The critics, however, have been emphasizing a different set of issues: direct participation and accountability. They see closed clubs indirectly linked to popular demands by long and opaque chains of delegation. Later in this paper we will address in more depth what we think *accountability* means and how it relates to legitimacy. Here we focus on three specific sets of issues: (1) a lack of transparency in the WTO process; (2) barriers to the participation of interested groups, who will clamor to be allowed in until institutional changes are made; and (3) the absence of politicians with ties both to the organization and to constituencies.

Transparency

Delegates to WTO bargaining sessions, though instructed and accountable to elected officials in democracies, often act in the privacy of the clubs built around their issues and related institutions. It is difficult independently to check their claims about how hard they bargained for particular advantages. Negotiators know how to "wink"—to signal when they are only going through the motions or wish to use a demand as a bargaining chip for something else. If outsiders cannot see the winks, they have a hard time judging how well they were represented in the process. Indeed, the opacity of the negotiations, taking place among club members behind closed doors, may facilitate intergovernmental bargaining.

WTO dispute settlement procedures have not been very transparent, although this is gradually changing. It was feared that transparency would lead governments to behave in more adversarial ways in order to appeal to domestic audiences. Lack of transparency and restrictions on participation adversely affect the public legitimacy of the WTO since, in accordance with democratic norms, "the public at large simply does not trust the honesty and legitimacy of secret proceedings."[34] It is therefore not surprising that even before the Seattle events, the United States was pressing to open panel and Appellate Body proceedings to the public, and for the right of private parties to submit briefs to panels and the Appellate Body.

U.S. institutions that are deliberately insulated from elections—in particular, the Supreme Court and the Federal Reserve Board—routinely publish their deliberations or opinions, so that not only the results, but the reasoning and disagreements involved, can be publicly known. These institutions are held accountable through criticisms by professional networks, such as legal scholars writing in law journals and economists writing scholarly articles and offering opinions in the public media. Without transparency, these means of accountability would be eviscerated.

Transparency does not imply governance through elections, as the examples of the Supreme Court and the Federal Reserve Board show. Transparency does mean that the arguments and reasoning on trade rules, and the adjudication of those rules, are made public. Democratic societies demand this of institutions that allocate values profoundly affecting people's lives.

Participation

In representative democracies, participation is channeled and in many ways limited, but some opportunities are available to make one's views known. In the U.S. Congress, for instance, hearings open to spokespeople from a variety of groups in part satisfy demands for participation. With respect to rulemaking in the WTO, only idealistic proponents of unitary democracy would demand that the public be allowed into the negotiating rooms where deals are being made. The consequences for trade liberalization of doing this would probably be grave. But allowing a certain number of observers and press at the Council meetings is a different matter. In addition, the WTO could consider the possibility of institutionalizing public hearings on trade policy—now limited to national forums. Particularly through the worldwide web, the WTO could reach out to individuals and groups around the globe to solicit their views. The perception that the WTO is an institution open to participation, rather than a closed bureaucracy, could be an asset to the organization in democratic societies.

In dispute settlement, a key demand is equal treatment. Under the current system, states are formally gatekeepers to the WTO process, but they often have incentives to open the gates to powerful actors (such as firms and industry groups) within their societies. GATT, as Hudec has shown, became more legalized and dealt with more cases, even before WTO came into effect.[35] Trade lawyers not working for governments, or for powerful clients with access to governments, claim that they are unfairly disadvantaged by not being able to see what happens behind closed doors. On the other hand, opening the adjudicatory process to nongovernmental organizations could disadvantage governments of poor countries, which may lack the high-powered legal resources to compete with well-funded environmental organizations and trade unions from rich countries. As is so often the case, struggles over "fair procedures" reflect underlying struggles over substance—"who gets what?" Charges of unaccountability and lack of democracy are often used as instruments to pry open access or to cry "foul" when one has lost on the merits.

Opening up the WTO's dispute settlement proceedings could have far-reaching consequences. There are systematic differences between "international" and "transnational" modes of dispute resolution.[36] In international dispute resolution, access to the adjudication process is limited to states, whereas in transnational dispute resolution, nonstate parties can bring cases and file briefs. International dispute resolution is epitomized by the International Court of Justice (ICJ); transnational dispute resolution, by the European Court of Justice (ECJ). The major apparent consequence of differential access is that transnational dispute resolution is much more expansive than international dispute resolution. The ECJ has become an authoritative interpreter of EU law. Its opinions are regularly incorporated into the decisions of national courts. This dynamic of expansion is fueled by a de facto alliance between plaintiffs and their lawyers, on the one hand, and the Court, on the other. Ready access to a tribunal creates cases—without which, courts wither on the vine. When these cases are decided and the decisions enforced, future plaintiffs are encouraged to bring more cases, and a spiral of positive feedback ensues. By contrast, a much smaller proportion of ICJ member states accepts its compulsory jurisdiction than did so in 1945, undermining the authority of the ICJ.[37]

If the WTO became open to cases brought by nonstate actors, would it be strengthened, as the ECJ has been? In the WTO, ambiguous formal rules have to be interpreted by panels and the Appellate Body in order to make them operational. The extent of this interpretation is such that, in effect, rules are being made through the Dispute Settlement Mechanism rather than in negotiations among governments.[38] When a smiliar process occurred in the EU, the ECJ was able to draw on support from national courts that enforced ECJ decisions. Since national courts were enforcing ECJ decisions, their own governments could not rely on extralegal measures. Instead, they "were forced to frame their response in terms that could persuade a legal audience, and thus they became constrained by the legal rules of the game."[39] By contrast, WTO rulings are not enforced by national courts but rely on governments' political decisions to comply. The Appellate Body of the WTO does not have nearly as much elite or public support as the ECJ, which claims to speak for the idea of European union and the rule of law. Hence it would be much easier for a disgruntled government to raise a political challenge against the Appellate Body than for governments to challenge the authority of the ECJ.

Politicians and Constituencies

The club model helps to overcome deadlock that accompanies the diffusion of power. Club-based intergovernmental organizations (IGOs) can move incrementally and gradually reinterpret their mandates insofar as their secretariats and leading states can build alliances with crucial private-sector and third-sector actors. But they cannot make large formal moves forward without a broad consensus about their proper purposes or without political institutions that can give them definitive guidance based on a wide expression of social views. As a result of the constraints and opportunities that they face, international organizations, like the WTO, tend to be dominated by small networks of professionals who can modify their informal rules and practices and sometimes develop a body of case law. Indeed, there is a danger of overreliance on judicial practices as a way to duck difficult political bargaining, with the effect of a hollowing out of institutions.

What is missing? The legitimating activity of broadly based politicians speaking directly to domestic publics. The absence of effective political leadership may have mattered less in the past when issues were less linked. Trade ministers' accountability to parliaments was sufficient to provide legitimacy. But with the linkage of issues, politicians are needed who can link specific organizations and policies with a broader range of public issues through electoral accountability. Someone has to take responsibility for making judgments about the relative importance of issues, and how to manage the trade-offs between them. And in a democratic society, politicians who take this responsibility have to be held accountable for their actions. Indeed, their very accountability is a source of credibility and strength, since policy pronouncements, for accountable officials, are potentially costly, rather than being mere "cheap talk."

If constituents have confidence in their elected officials, they are more likely to support policies endorsed by those officials, even if they do not understand the specifics of the policies. Politicians intermediate between organizations and constituencies in civil societies, strengthening the legitimacy of organizations in return for ensuring that constituencies have influence over the organizations' policies.

The lack of intermediating politicians is the most serious democratic deficit of international organizations in general and the WTO in particular. Lack of transparency and deficiencies of participation are relatively easy to fix, but without responsible politicians, "solving" these problems could create deadlock as more and more heterogeneous actors compete for publicity and over policy.

To enhance democratic accountability, the WTO would require a strong office of director-general—a move that would surely be resisted by many governments. But having an institutionally empowered director-general would not be sufficient. Somehow that director-general would have to become accountable to organized constituencies within the organization. In other words, the functional equivalent of political parties would be needed to perform the functions of interest aggregation and organization of debate that parties perform in democracies. Having done so, the director-general might have a fighting chance to compete with other political entrepreneurs for influence, and somehow to integrate a variety of concerns (trade liberalization, environmental protection, labor rights, protection for groups disadvantaged by liberalization) in a single policy matrix.

Merely to state the conditions is to suggest how utopian such a prospect is. The notion that functional equivalents of political parties will emerge, on a global basis, to represent constituencies with similar interests boggles the mind. Even in Europe, with all the successes of the European Union, there are no genuinely transnational political parties, only coalitions among generally like-minded parties in a weak European Parliament. The idea of a WTO parliament is likely to prove even more illusory, although inclusion of more parliamentarians in national delegations might help to sensitize trade officials to the need for public legitimacy. However, such modest measures will not correct the central legitimacy problem of the WTO: the absence of politicians to intermediate between policymakers and constituencies.

Conclusion

We have only managed to state the problem, not to provide a solution. The problem is how to increase transparency and accountability, while enhancing international cooperation and achieving some degree of policy integration. At a minimum, the goal is to reach agreements without subjecting all deals to deconstruction and unwinding. But social globalization, reflected in the explosion of NGOs, works against careful integration in the absence of collective identity. It will remain easier to pick packages apart than to put them together.

Democracy, Legitimacy, and Accountability

We turn now to some broader reflections on issues of legitimacy and accountability in international organizations. Democracy is government by officials who are accountable to the majority of the people in a jurisdiction, albeit with frequent provisions for supermajority voting and protections for individuals and minorities. For democracy to work well, "the people" have to regard themselves as a political community. Who are "we the people" when there is little sense of political identity or community, and the political world is organized largely around a system of unequal states? In a nondemocratic world in which international institutions merely facilitated interstate cooperation, such a question would be irrelevant. But in the contemporary world, democratic norms are increasingly applied to international institutions as a test of their legitimacy. If international institutions are to be legitimate, therefore, their practices and the results of their activities need to meet broadly democratic standards. But as noted earlier, the domestic analogy does not apply, since the world as a whole lacks a coherent public, a corresponding public space for discussion, and institutions linking the public, through elections, to governing organizations.

Democratic governments are judged both on the procedures they follow (inputs) and on the results they obtain (outputs). Despite having been, in several dimensions, quite an effective president, President Richard Nixon was forced to resign because he violated the law. Conversely, President Clinton's successes in managing the economy, and the high level of public appreciation of his performance in this realm, helped to rally support for him during the impeachment process in 1998. Both inputs and outputs affect legitimacy at the international level as well, and it is useful to consider them separately.

Inputs: Procedures and Accountability

On the input side, the key issue is one of accountability. In democracies, publics hold elites accountable for their actions through elections, which can result in removal from office. Accountability is by no means perfect: governing elites can sometimes manipulate publics, by controlling the agenda, through campaign spending, or otherwise. But the competition of elites provides some assurance that in the long run governments cannot defy the strongly felt will of a majority. "The democratic method," declared Joseph Schumpeter in 1942, "is that institutional arrangement for arriving at political decisions in which individuals acquire the power to decide by means of a competitive structure for the people's vote."[40]

International institutions lack the essential feature that makes democracy possible and that, in democracies, facilitates accountability: an acknowledged public operating within a political community in which there is a general consensus on what makes public decisions legitimate. What are the boundaries of the relevant electoral constituencies in which votes are held? If the moral claim for democracy rests on the worth and equality of individuals, then a basic rule is one person: one vote. One state: one vote is not democratic because a Maldive Islander would have 1,000 times the voting power of a citizen of China. On the other hand, a cosmopolitan view that treats the globe as one constituency implies the existence of a political community in which citizens of 198 states would be willing to be continually outvoted by a billion Chinese and a billion Indians. As Pippa Norris has shown, there is no evidence that national identities are changing in a manner that would make that feasible for a long time to come.[41] In the absence of such a community, the extension of domestic voting practices to the world scale would make little normative sense, even if it were feasible. Meaningful voting and associated democratic political activities occur within the boundaries of nation states that have democratic constitutions and processes. Minorities are willing to acquiesce to a majority in which they may not participate directly because they feel they participate in some larger community. Such a sense of community is clearly absent at the global level and creates severe normative as well as practical problems for the input side of global democracy.

However, as we have noted, accountability is not ensured through elections alone. Indeed, it is a multidimensional phenomenon. We can distinguish electoral accountability and nonelectoral accountability. At the interstate level, three types of mechanisms strengthen electoral accountability.[42] First, state control, through chains of delegation, can strengthen accountability. At the same time it can ensure that sufficient transparency exists so that members of the public can judge whether their government, operating within the international institution, is carrying out its mandate. It is not inherently any more undemocratic for the U.S. president to delegate authority to the U.S. trade representative to negotiate at the WTO than for the president to delegate authority to the attorney general to deal with organized crime. As long as the public knows what actions the delegated agent took, it can reward or punish the president and his party for its deeds. The key is transparency.

The second means of increasing the democratic accountability of international institutions is to strengthen mechanisms of domestic accountability. Indeed, many of the problems of aggregating interests and responding to different constituencies must be handled at the domestic level where democratic electoral procedures make sense. For instance, Denmark's parliament has developed procedures that give it much more information than is available to other parliaments in Europe about its government's actual policies within the European Union. The Danish government is therefore much more accountable, for better and worse, to its parliament for its actions within the European Union than are other member governments.[43] The third mechanism is to increase legislative control over policy at the supranational level, although this has been accomplished only through the European Parliament and, there, only in a rather halting and limited way.

Voting, delegation, and parliamentary action are not the only ways in which democratic governments are held accountable to publics. There are also important nonelectoral dimensions to accountability. Many democratic theorists would argue that elections, and the long shadows that elections cast, do not exhaust the voice that people should have on issues that affect their lives. Intensity of feeling also matters; and people should be able to exercise voice in the long intervals between elections, even if their representatives do not speak up on their behalf. The mechanisms of adversarial democracy stretch from polls to protests.

The boundaries for this nonelectoral type of input are less clearly defined than are those of electoral politics. A public space is an identifiable set of issues within a communicative environment in which people can speak to one another in comprehensible ways. The public is the group of people who communicate and agitate over their shared externalities in that space—sometimes at a local level and sometimes at transnational levels. In this sense of shared externalities and a degree of shared understanding, there may be some global publics even if there is no global community. NGOs contest and ally with each other and with parts of governments to set agendas and press for preferred actions by governments. The media play an important role as a target for NGO action and as a means to hold NGOs to some standards of accountability.

Another form of nonelectoral accountability is achieved through professional norms and transnational networks. As Arthur Applebaum has argued, professional ethical standards can be used to hold adversaries accountable.[44] Lawyers care about the opinion of the bar; academic economists about their standing in the eyes of some colleagues. Epistemic communities increasingly take the lead in raising the issues and constructing the domestic and transnational conversations necessary to create a public space.[45] They keep governing elites accountable in the same way in which networks of legal scholars or economists make the Supreme Court or the Federal Reserve accountable: through reasoned criticism and discussion rather than through elections.

Third, markets provide nonelectoral accountability. Obviously, people have unequal votes in markets depending upon the wealth they bring to the table. Thus competitive markets are not a form of pure democratic accountability. Nonetheless, corporations and governments that fail to perform well are held accountable through markets in ways that are often more rapid and effective than through electoral practices. Rating agencies help to consolidate and publicize a number of market judgments about firms. Governments that are closed and corrupt find it more difficult to attract capital and maintain the confidence of transnational investors. Firms whose goods are made in sweat shops may be held accountable to consumers through publicity and boycotts.

The problem of accountability for governance at the international level is not the complete absence of mechanisms for accountability. The problem is that the mechanisms are *disarticulated*. In a well-functioning domestic democracy, political inputs—popular activity, media attention, interest group lobbying, parties, elections, and formal legislation—are articulated together. There is a clear pathway by which laws can be created; and when laws are enacted, regular procedures and organizations exist to implement, amend, and change those laws. This is the procedural basis for democratic legitimacy. Internationally, however, the link between popular activity and policy is severely attenuated.

In a well-functioning domestic democracy, popular politics and the organization of interest groups lead through fairly well-defined pathways to legislation and to the implementation of such legislation. Since governing elites work hard to anticipate reactions to their actions, through such pathways, the effects of anticipated criticisms and electoral consequences can be even more important than ex post punishment. These connections are lacking at the international level. Intergovernmental organizations that make binding rules often lack the democratic legitimacy that comes from having transparent procedures, institutional arrangements that facilitate accountability, and activities by politicians seeking reelection by appealing to publics. At the same time, the private and NGO sectors that agitate political issues internationally do not have any greater claim to democratic legitimacy. Despite their claims to represent civil society, they tend to be self-selected and often unrepresentative elites. The disjunction between international arrangements facilitating such public involvement and multilateral cooperation on binding decisions causes disputes over legitimacy and dangers of stalemate in intergovernmental institutions. This disjunction cannot be solved simply by adopting the domestic voting model at a global level. On the input side, mechanisms for accountability exist, but they are not joined into a coherent system with mutually reinforcing components.

Outputs: Effectiveness

The legitimacy of governments is not determined solely by the procedures used on the input side. Substantive outputs also matter. Citizens are concerned about issues of security, welfare, and identity. When these substantive outputs are missing, procedural democracy on the input side is often not sufficient. Conversely, however, their past successes on the output side may give them some space for reform.

Effectiveness enhances legitimacy in both "macro" and "micro" ways. On the macro side, the overall accomplishments of an international regime in producing a collective good may be appreciated. The eradication of smallpox by the World Health Organization gave the WHO substantial legitimacy for being effective in dealing with global health problems, whereas its slowness in focusing on AIDs may have had the opposite effect. Critics of the IMF's performance in the world economic crisis of 1997–99 emphasize how much worse the crisis was because of the fund's misguided actions.[46] Defenders of the IMF, on the other hand, argue that its actions, while leading to pain at the time, account for the rapid recovery after 1998 in most of Asia. They seek to turn the crisis into a success for the IMF, enhancing its legitimacy.[47]

On the macro side, the legitimacy of the WTO rests on its fostering of trade liberalization. Since trade liberalization has been a fairly consistent policy of most rich-country governments during the past half-century and recently a policy of many developing countries as well, WTO's dedication to trade liberalization probably enhances its legitimacy. Trade liberalization is regarded as being a good thing. Hence being "on the side of the angels" may have conferred some legitimacy on the WTO even in the absence of procedures ensuring transparency and participation.

At the micro level, the activities of international organizations build coalitions of individuals, firms, or groups that support them out of self-interest. For many international organizations, such coalitions are weak because the beneficiaries of the organization's actions are weak and fragmented or because the organizations are easy scapegoats for domestic politicians. Insofar as the World Bank seeks to help the poor, it ensures that it will have a weak political base, since neither powerful transnational capitalist interests, nor the governments of many developing countries, give priority to the interests of the poor in their own policies or lobbying. For the IMF, the micro-political problem is that its strong medicine usually is administered after the government of the country—through either political opportunism or incompetence—has made substantial policy blunders. Blaming the IMF is the obvious strategy for politicians seeking to avoid being held accountable for their own failed policies.

At the micro level, the WTO has one advantage over the World Bank and the IMF, since the WTO has a powerful constituency: multinational corporations that seek to expand their own exports and investments abroad. These firms, and related industry associations, have influential voices in policy councils at home and strong interests in continued liberalization. By and large, they have prevailed over labor unions that have advocated protectionism. Hence the WTO should have some coalitional support against more generalized, and symbolic, criticisms that focus on the input side—on accountability. If appealing changes can be made on the input side, the WTO may be able to recover more readily than international organizations that have less to show for their efforts.

Suggestions about Legitimacy

There are vast differences in political context between domestic and international governance. Therefore, a more appropriate measure for judging democratic legitimacy is needed than the so-called democratic deficit based on the domestic analogy. The literature based on the European Union with its close links to the domestic analogy is not well suited to global institutions, for reasons given earlier. Nor will new theories based on the potential for direct voting in cyberdemocracy be sufficient. One can imagine technology making it possible for the votes of vast numbers of people to be collected easily in frequent plebiscites, but in the absence of community it is more difficult to envisage the effective processes of deliberation that would make such voting meaningful. With time such obstacles may be overcome and practices gradually develop, but even under the most optimistic assumptions, genuinely global public space is a long way off.

Another optimistic view is that transgovernmental relations, or "government networks," will help to solve problems of global governance. Transgovernmental networks (such as the Basle Committee of Central Bank Governors of rich countries or the International Organization of Securities Commissioners) act informally, aided by strong personal contacts among participants. They can often operate more quickly and effectively than formal bodies. However, they are not open to a broad range of participants, they are often secretive, and they are typically accountable to only a few relatively powerful elites. As Anne-Marie Slaughter has pointed out, "the informality, flexibility, and decentralization of networks mean that it is very difficult to establish precisely who is acting and when."[48] Hence serious issues of accountability arise. Nevertheless, as she argues, the critics often miss several key points: legitimacy may derive from performance as well as process; governmental networks typically operate through persuasion rather than authoritative decision; and these networks may actually empower democratic politicians and their governments, by promoting cooperation among them, when the alternative could be leaving decisions to markets.

Another possibility is to supplement the work of the WTO with what Wolfgang Reinicke calls "trisectoral networks" of governments, multilateral organizations, and nongovernmental groups, both profit and nonprofit. For example, the World Commission on Dams consists of twelve members, four each from the public, private, and nonprofit sectors. It has been analyzing the effects of large dams and developing a set of standards for dams that it recommends to governments and the Bank.[49] One could imagine creating a similar group to work through some of the thorny issues of the club model and the trade regime. It is unlikely that states will turn over major decisionmaking activities, creating hard law, to transgovernmental and trisectoral networks, but what Sylvia Ostry calls "hybrid governance" involving such networks is likely to be an increasingly important part of the global policy process.[50] Insofar as it is effective, hybrid governance will be welcome as a supplement to other forms of governance. The legitimacy of government and trisectoral networks, however, will depend on whether they produce widely accepted outcomes and whether their processes appear sufficiently transparent and accountable to elites and publics in civil society.

As experiments continue with governance and trisectoral networks, it will be important to develop more modest normative principles and practices to enhance transparency and accountability—not only of IGOs but of corporations and NGOs that constitute global governance today. For example, increased transparency advances accountability, but transparency need not be instantaneous or complete. Consider the delayed release of Federal Reserve Board hearings or the details of Supreme Court deliberations. Similarly, accountability has many dimensions, only one of which is reporting up the chain of delegation to elected leaders. Markets aggregate the preferences (albeit unequally) of large numbers of people, and both governments and transnational corporations are accountable to them. Professional associations create and maintain transnational norms to which IGOs, NGOs, and government officials can be judged accountable. The practice, by nongovernmental organizations and the press, of "naming and shaming" of transnational corporations with valuable brand names also provides a sort of accountability. Similarly, Transparency International's naming and shaming of governments engaged in corrupt practices helps create accountability. While trisectoral cooperation and government networks can be productive, competition among sectors and among networks continues to be useful for transparency and accountability.

Greater cooperation with nongovernmental organizations might alleviate concerns about the World Trade Organization's accountability. For example, some NGOs might be given observer status at WTO Council meetings where rules are discussed. It would be problematic, however, to give NGOs the right to participate in trade bargaining sessions, since consummating deals often requires a certain degree of obfuscation of the trade-offs being made. The greater intensity of activity by groups threatened by losses, than by groups likely to reap gains, could foster deadlock.[51] A greater role for NGOs in the World Trade Organization has its own problems. For one thing, many developing countries would object to it, not only because of their devotion to the doctrine of sovereignty, but also because the preferences of NGOs (mostly from rich countries) are opposed to developing countries' interests. In addition, there is the problem of the lack of transparency and accountability of the nongovernmental organizations themselves. In principle, the World Trade Organization could set requirements of transparency of budgets and membership for NGOs that wish to participate, and as more of them develop in the South, the opposition of the developing countries may diminish.

The World Bank has been relatively successful in working with nongovernmental organizations. More than seventy NGO specialists (mostly from technically proficient organizations) work in the Bank's field offices. "From environmental policy to debt relief, NGOs are at the center of World Bank policy," the *Economist* noted. "The new World Bank is more transparent, but is also beholden to a new set of special interests."[52] Environmental NGOs have played effective roles at UN conferences. It was notable in April 2000 that Oxfam, an active NGO, did not participate in the demonstrations against the World Bank, declaring instead that it sought to continue to promote reform of the Bank rather than to agitate for its dissolution.

Whether involving—or co-opting—selected nongovernmental organizations would work for the World Trade Organization is an open question. Their democratic legitimacy is not established simply by their claims to be part of civil society. The legitimacy of favored NGOs could be called into question by co-optation, and excluded NGOs are likely to criticize those that are included for "selling out." Political battles among nongovernmental organizations will limit a co-optation strategy. Nonetheless, some form of NGO representation in the institutions involved in multilateral governance, and in particular the WTO, could help to maintain their legitimacy.

Conclusions: The WTO, Legitimacy, and Governance

The compromise of embedded liberalism created a social safety net in return for openness. Although successful in the second half of the twentieth century, it is under new pressure today. That compromise was the basis for Bretton Woods institutions that (along with other regimes) employed the club model to govern decomposable issue-areas in world politics. Now the club model is under challenge. Rulemaking and rule interpretation in global governance have become pluralized. Rules are no longer a matter for states or intergovernmental organizations alone. Private firms, NGOs, subunits of governments, and the resulting transnational and transgovernmental networks play a role as well. Any sustainable pattern of governance will have to institutionalize channels of contact between international organizations and constituencies within civil society. The international regimes, broadly conceived, must be political rather than technocratic. They must be linked to legitimate domestic institutions.

The club model, instead of being discarded entirely, requires modification. As a general precaution, it will be important not to put more weight on such institutions than they can bear. Rather than pursue strong institutions to foster deep integration at the global level, it is more appropriate to pursue an image of what we have elsewhere called "networked minimalism."[53] Multilateral institutions do not compete so much with domestic institutions as rely on them. They will only thrive when substantial space is preserved for domestic political processes—"subsidiarity" in the language of the European Union. By allowing domestic politics to sometimes depart from international agreements without unraveling the whole system of norms, the WTO provides a helpful model. Putting too much weight on international institutions before they are sufficiently legitimate to bear it is a recipe for deadlock, disruption, and failure.

In a world of active NGOs and strong democratic norms, more attention will have to be paid to issues of legitimacy. Some of these issues can be addressed at the level of the multilateral organization's own practices. But as Robert Hudec rightly emphasizes in his comment, in this volume, the prime components of democratic legitimacy will remain at the domestic level. Unless domestic processes are viewed as legitimate, the regimes that rest on those domestic processes will not be viewed as legitimate.

At the domestic or international levels, legitimacy should not be viewed solely in terms of majoritarian voting procedures. Many parts of the American constitution (such as the Supreme Court) and political practice would fail that test. Democratic legitimacy has a number of sources, both normative and substantive. Legitimacy in international regimes depends partly on effectiveness. Insofar as legitimacy depends on processes, accountability is central. Accountability need not take place exclusively through delegation from elected national governments with parliamentary oversight. Arrangements to ensure other forms of participation from civil society, ranging from protests to the involvement of NGOs in decisionmaking and dispute resolution, can enhance accountability. Markets and professional networks also play a role. Whatever form accountability takes, transparency will be crucial to ensure that accountability is meaningful.

In the absence of political institutions linking governance organizations with constituencies, the legitimacy of global institutions will probably remain shaky for many decades. Indeed, the political base of intergovernmental organizations and international regimes may be so weak that effective international cooperation on trade will decline or even collapse into deadlock. But the costs of deadlock would be high. If deadlock is to be avoided, international organizations such as the WTO will need to become more, rather than less, political. They must balance greater transparency and participation with opportunities for closer ties between public leadership and constituencies. A bewildering array of interests need to be aggregated in ways that are democratically acceptable. Devising effective and legitimate international institutions is indeed a crucial problem of political design for the twenty-first century.

Notes

1. John G. Ruggie, "International Regimes, Transactions and Change: Embedded Liberalism in the Postwar Economic Order," in Stephen D. Krasner, ed., *International Regimes* (Cornell University Press, 1983).

2. Fred Hirsch, "The Ideological Underlay of Inflation," in Fred Hirsch and John Goldthorpe, eds., *The Political Economy of Inflation* (London: Martin Robertson, 1978), pp. 284, 278.

3. For different views on the situation facing contemporary social democracy in western Europe, see Geoffrey Garrett, *Partisan Politics in the Global Economy* (Cambridge University Press, 1998); and Torben Iversen, *Contested Economic Institutions: The Politics of Macroeconomics and Wage Bargaining in Advanced Democracies* (Cambridge University Press, 1999).

4. Robert O. Keohane, *After Hegemony: Cooperation and Discord in the World Political Economy* (Princeton University Press, 1984).

5. Herbert A. Simon, *The Sciences of the Artificial*, 3d ed. (MIT Press, 1996), pp. 197–207.

6. Michael Zurn, "Democratic Governance beyond the Nation State: The EU and Other International Institutions," *European Journal of International Relations*, vol. 6, no. 2 (2000), pp. 183–222.

7. Peter M. Haas, Robert O. Keohane, and Marc Levy, eds., *Institutions for the Earth: Sources of Effective Environmental Protection* (MIT Press, 1993).

8. George W. Downs, David M. Rocke, and Peter N. Barsoom, "Is the Good News about Compliance Good News about Cooperation?" *International Organization*, vol. 50, no. 3 (1996), pp. 379–406.

9. Robert E. Hudec, "The New WTO Dispute Settlement Procedure: An Overview of the First Three Years," *Minnesota Journal of Global Trade, Inc.*, vol. 8, no. 1 (1999), p. 14.

10. Ronald Rogowski, *Commerce and Coalitions: How Trade Affects Domestic Political Alignments* (Princeton University Press, 1989), p. 172.

11. Vinod Aggarwal, *Liberal Protectionism: The International Politics of Organized Textile Trade* (University of California Press, 1985).

12. See Rogowski, *Commerce and Coalitions*; and Helen V. Milner, *Resisting Protectionism: Global Industries and the Politics of International Trade* (Princeton University Press, 1988).

13. Robert O. Keohane, "Reciprocity in International Relations," *International Organization*, vol. 40, no. 1 (1986), pp. 1–27.

14. John Helliwell, *How Much Do National Borders Matter?* (Brookings, 1998).

15. Richard N. Cooper, *The Economics of Interdependence: Economic Policy in the Atlantic Community* (McGraw-Hill, 1968), esp. chap. 4 and p. 173.

16. See also, Geoffrey Garrett, *Partisan Politics in the Global Economy* (Cambridge University Press, 1998), p. 183.

17. Cooper pointed out in his classic study that increasing sensitivity not only increased the likelihood of imbalances in international payments, but would make such imbalances easier to deal with, since small policy changes would have larger effects. From an economic standpoint, therefore, increasing sensitivity could be a policy advantage. Nevertheless, from a political perspective, increasing sensitivity subjected policymakers to more pressures for accountability. See Cooper, *Economics of Interdependence*, p. 77.

18. Murasoli Maran, interviewed in the *Financial Times*, February 2, 2000, p. 5.

19. Wolfgang H. Reinicke, *Global Public Policy: Governing without Government* (Brookings, 1998).

20. *The Economist*, December 11, 1999, p. 21.

21. Robert O. Keohane and Joseph S. Nye Jr., *Transnational Relations and World Politics* (Harvard University Press, 1972).

22. *Financial Times*, December 2, 1999, p. 1.

23. *Financial Times*, February 2, 2000, p. 5.

24. "The FP Interview: Lori's War," *Foreign Policy*, no. 118 (Spring 2000), pp. 37, 47.

25. Zurn, "Democratic Governance." Zurn seeks to refute the arguments of social democrats such as Claus Offe that international and supranational institutions are undemocratic and therefore their further growth should be resisted.

26. John J. Mearsheimer, "The False Promise of International Institutions," *International Security*, vol. 19, no. 3 (1994–95), pp. 5–49. For responses, see *International Security*, vol. 20, no. 1 (1995).

27. Jane J. Mansbridge, *Beyond Adversary Democracy* (1980; University of Chicago Press, 1983). On "creedal passion," see Samuel P. Huntington, *American Politics: The Promise of Disharmony* (Cambridge, Mass.: Belknap Press, 1981).

28. Unitary democracy has a clear affinity with Jurgen Habermas's theory of communication, in which the persuasiveness of speech acts depends on the intersubjective ties between speaker and listener, as well as on the propositional content of the speech. See Jurgen Habermas, *Communication and the Evolution of Society*, translated by Thomas McCarthy (Beacon Press, 1979), chap. 1.

29. Mansbridge, *Beyond Adversary Democracy*, p. 7.

30. Robert D. Putnam, *Bowling Alone: The Collapse and Revival of American Community* (Simon and Schuster, 2000).

31. The term "domestic analogy" is used with a different meaning from ours by Hedley Bull, *The Anarchical Society: A Study of Order in World Politics* (Columbia University Press, 1977).

32. Martin Wolf, "Europe's Challenge," *Financial Times*, January 6, 1999, p. 12.

33. Hudec, "The New WTO Dispute Settlement Procedure," p. 28.

34. Ibid., p. 45.

35. Hudec, "The New WTO Dispute Settlement Procedure."

36. Robert O. Keohane, Andrew Moravcsik, and Anne-Marie Slaughter, "Legalized Dispute Resolution: Interstate and Transnational," *International Organization*, vol. 54, no. 3 (2000), pp. 457–88. Daniel Esty, "Non-Governmental Organizations at the World Trade Organization," *Journal of International Economic Law*, vol. 123 (1998).

37. Stephen Schwebel, "The Performance and Prospects of the International Court of Justice," in Karl-Heinz Boeckstiegel, ed., *Perspectives of Air Law, Space Law and International Business Law for the Next Century* (Köln: Carl Heymanns Verlag, 1996).

38. This point was made by Sylvia Ostry at the conference where an earlier version of this chapter was presented. See Ostry's chapter in this volume.

39. Karen J. Alter, "Who Are the 'Masters of the Treaty'? European Governments and the European Court of Justice," *International Organization*, vol. 52, no. 1 (1998), p. 123.

40. Joseph S. Schumpeter, *Capitalism, Socialism, and Democracy* (1942; Harper Torchbook edition, 1962), p. 269. For a sophisticated analysis of input and output legitimacy in Europe, see Fritz Scharpf, *Governing in Europe* (Oxford University Press, 1999).

41. Pippa Norris, "Global Governance and Cosmopolitan Citizens," in Joseph S. Nye Jr. and John Donahue, eds., *Governance in a Globalizing World* (Brookings, 2000).

42. Here we rely on a synthesis by Professor Anne-Marie Slaughter of a number of points made by herself and others at a conference on accountability and international institutions, Duke University, May 7–8, 1999.

43. Lisa L. Martin, *Democratic Commitments: Legislatures and International Cooperation* (Princeton University Press, 2000).

44. Arthur Applebaum, *Ethics for Adversaries: The Morality of Roles in Public and Professional Life* (Princeton University Press, 1999).

45. Peter M. Haas, "Introduction: Epistemic Communities and International Policy Coordination," *International Organization,* vol. 46, no. 1 (1992), pp. 1–36. See also Margaret E. Keck and Kathryn Sikkink, *Activists beyond Borders: Advocacy Networks in International Politics* (Cornell University Press, 1998).

46. For a particularly biting critique, see Joseph Stiglitz, "The Insider: What I Learned at the World Economic Crisis," *New Republic,* April 17, 2000, pp. 56–60.

47. Reply to Stiglitz by Rudiger Dornbush, *New Republic,* May 29, 2000, pp. 4–5.

48. Anne-Marie Slaughter, "Governing the Global Economy through Government Networks," in Michael Byers, ed., *The Role of Law in International Politics: Essays in International Relations and International Law* (Oxford University Press, 2000), pp. 193–94.

49. Wolfgang Reinicke, "The Other World Wide Web: Global Public Policy Networks," *Foreign Policy,* no. 117 (Winter 1999–2000), pp. 44–57.

50. See Sylvia Ostry's chapter in this volume.

51. For an interesting discussion of the effects of information on trade negotiations, see Judith Goldstein and Lisa L. Martin, "Legalization, Trade Liberalization, and Domestic Politics," *International Organization,* vol. 54, no. 3 (2000), pp. 603–32.

52. "The Non-Governmental Order," *The Economist,* December 11, 1999, p. 21.

53. Robert O. Keohane and Joseph S. Nye Jr., "Governance in a Globalizing World," in Nye and Donahue, *Governance in a Globalizing World.*

COMMENT BY
Robert E. Hudec

Legitimacy is a term typically associated with the exercise of power. In this essay two kinds of exercise of power are discussed in connection with complaints about the legitimacy of the World Trade Organization: (1) the exercise of power by the WTO itself, often referred to as global governance; and (2) the role of the WTO as part of the political decisionmaking process that directs the exercise of power by national governments. Legitimacy complaints assume a different character depending on the kind of power being exercised. Since affected constituencies are different, those who have standing to complain in each case will be different. Likewise, the criteria will differ by which the legitimacy of each kind of power is judged. Responsibility for correcting problems falls upon different institutions, and the corrective measures needed to maintain legitimacy vary.

Robert Keohane and Joseph Nye primarily focus on the exercise of power by the WTO. A sharper focus on legitimacy as it relates to the political decisionmaking process of national governments would be useful.

The best way to present the domestic political aspect of challenges to the WTO's legitimacy is to consider the origins of the "club model" of international cooperation. The watershed event in modern trade policy in the United States was the Tariff Act of 1930, known popularly as the Smoot-Hawley Tariff. The 1930 act began as a bill to increase tariffs on agricultural products to protect against low prices on the world market. It ended as a logrolling jamboree that increased U.S. tariffs pretty much across the board to one of the highest levels in U.S. history. Whatever its merits, Smoot-Hawley was a classic example of direct democracy at the national level because every producer interest seeking protection from foreign competition seemed to find sympathetic hearing from someone of influence in the Congress.

The Smoot-Hawley tariff was the last tariff written by the U.S. Congress. It retired from the tariff-writing business just four years later, when it enacted the Reciprocal Trade Agreements Act of 1934. This act granted the president time-limited authority to reduce tariffs by up to 50 percent, merely by "proclaiming" the new rates, whenever that was "necessary or appropriate" to carry out bilateral trade agreements negotiated in accordance with the act's procedures.

The impact of the Reciprocal Trade Agreements Act on the political decisionmaking process was a quite deliberate part of the reasons for enacting it. The Smoot-Hawley experience had persuaded the Congress that the political forces drawn into play over issues of U.S. tariff policy were too unruly to produce sound tariff policy. The Congress wanted to insulate itself from the direct pressure of those political forces. Internationalization of the problem was one way to do this. To be sure, the idea of negotiating reciprocal tariff concessions altered the very nature of substantive policy issues by attaching foreign market access as a benefit to justify U.S. tariff reductions. But the change in the structure of the political decisionmaking process was equally important. The negotiating approach would give Congress a plausible ground for saying that it no longer could legislate about individual tariffs because they were the subject of ongoing negotiations with other countries. It would also give Congress a ground for accepting the result as a package of advantages that could not be broken. Finally, the fact that the final decision was cast as an international obligation would give a plausible reason for not considering proposals to reverse the tariff-reducing decision in the years that followed. While international commitments do not raise trade policy decisions to constitutional status in the sense of the Treaty of Rome or even the U.S. Constitution, they do make them more difficult to reverse than ordinary legislation.

A second Smoot-Hawley type of experience occurred when the General Agreement on Tariffs and Trade (GATT) began to negotiate nontariff barriers during the Kennedy Round negotiations from 1963 to 1967. As part of the Kennedy Round agreement, the United States agreed to change certain U.S. regulatory laws that were creating nontariff barriers. Lacking advance authority to change U.S. regulatory laws, the United States negotiated on an *ad referendum* basis, agreeing to seek congressional action to change the laws after the negotiation. The Congress refused to enact the necessary legal changes, thereby breaking the package deal. Once again, as in 1934, it was perceived that traditional methods of enacting legislation were not compatible with sound trade policymaking. Requiring ad referendum legislative proposals to run the gauntlet of congressional committee procedures would give individual committees and committee chairs the ability to pick apart the negotiating package. According to the executive branch, such item-by-item review would make it impossible for the U.S. government to negotiate on nontariff barriers because other governments were saying they could not negotiate on that basis. In response, the Congress adopted the fast-track legislative approach for approving trade agreements. This restructured the political decisionmaking process so that

Congress would be forced to vote on the entire package, and its vote would be a simple up or down vote without amendment. As in the case of the Reciprocal Trade Agreements Act, the fast-track legislation was a way of insulating the negotiated agreement from the direct political pressures of the normal legislative process. The insulation was not quite as protective as that provided by the Reciprocal Trade Agreements Act, but the up-or-down, single package approach did make it difficult for opponents to attack any single part of the trade agreement.

As the story of the Smoot-Hawley reforms and the fast-track reforms show, many of the WTO's "anti-democratic" characteristics are deliberate efforts by governments to limit certain forms of political access to the trade policy decisionmaking process. At one level, these limitations were considered necessary to achieve the international cooperation the government believed valuable in trade policy matters. These limitations were also thought necessary to sound trade policy decisions, in much the same way good monetary policy, some say, requires shielding central banks from the political forces of day-to-day legislative politics.

This domestic political dimension of the WTO's processes offers a second way of looking at complaints about the organization's legitimacy. Most of the complaints are addressed to the WTO as if it were a freestanding institution that asserted its own powers of governance. The kind of domestic political decisions just described remind us that the structure of the WTO can also be viewed as an ingredient of the domestic decisionmaking process of national governments. Complaints about the structure may also be complaints by citizens about the way their own government makes trade policy.

Complaints concerning the legitimacy of national policymaking are not quite the same as complaints about the legitimacy of "governance" by the WTO. The criteria of legitimacy vary according to which of these two perspectives is involved. Framed in terms of the WTO's power to govern, the legitimacy issue imposes a rather high barrier against acceptance of what the WTO does. In a world of sovereign national states the existence of supranational governance authority that impinges on national sovereignty is usually viewed as a transfer of power that requires special justification. If, on the other hand, the WTO is viewed merely as an instrument of national policymaking, the issue becomes whether policymaking through the particular processes of the WTO meets the standards of legitimacy that national governments must meet when they exercise power. The criteria of legitimacy for national governments tend to be more complex and ultimately less rigorous. National governments begin with the base of demo-

cratic legitimacy supplied by their constitutional structure of governance—
in the case of the Reciprocal Trade Agreements Act, the fact that legislation
was passed by a democratically elected legislature in open debate. In addition, since the governing power of national governments is considered a
given, the question of their legitimacy is usually a question of alternatives:
are there other ways of doing business that can strike a better balance between effectiveness and democratic legitimacy? And finally, since the domestic decisionmaking process as a whole has to be considered, the answers
available to deal with complaints include changes in the domestic side of
international processes, such as changes in the participation requirements
of the U.S. fast-track law.

Consequently, it is important to be clear about which of these two
sorts of legitimacy is at issue. Once that distinction is clear, it is necessary
to look again at which of the two types of legitimacy is in fact relevant to
complaints against the WTO. The key issue is whether the WTO is really
a separate institution of governance to which higher standards of legitimacy must be applied. And that issue, in turn, depends on whether the
WTO really does exercise power of its own—that is, power that is outside
the control of the governments upon which it is employed. Most critics
who argue that the WTO must meet higher, "governance" standards of legitimacy do not confront this issue head on. To the extent they do, the
well-informed critics usually concede that the WTO does not "govern" in
the true sense of the word, but then they go on and apply the higher standard anyway. The issue cannot be finessed in this way.

The World Trade Organization is a member-driven organization, and
the force of its orders is the product of a process in which governments
agree to participate and which they ultimately control. Unless that fact can
be disproved, I cannot see any basis for asking the WTO to meet the legitimacy standards of an institution with powers of governance. As the
WTO stands today, its actions deserve to be treated as activities of individual national governments—activities of concern only to the citizens of
the government in question and subject only to the standards of legitimacy
applicable to the exercise of power by that government.

The Smoot-Hawley story illustrates a second point about the standards of legitimacy applied to national governments. It underlines the rel-
ativity of those legitimacy standards. The political decisionmaking process
established by tariff negotiations under the Reciprocal Trade Agreements
Act was a good deal less legitimate than the decisionmaking in negotiations under today's WTO. Tariff negotiations in the 1930s, 1940s, 1950s,

and 1960s were much less transparent than WTO negotiations today, and there was no legislative review of such deals, not even a fast-track ratification process. The Reciprocal Trade Agreements Act was repeatedly reenacted, and the decisionmaking process it authorized eventually resulted in the virtual elimination of most industrial tariffs. Why wasn't the legitimacy of this relatively closed process of domestic decisionmaking not more successfully attacked during those years?

Keohane and Nye observe that no one seemed to notice what the GATT was doing from 1948 until the late 1980s or early 1990s. I do not believe that explanation captures the full story. A large number of producer interests were adversely affected by the negotiations under the Reciprocal Trade Agreements Act. Producers were paying attention, and their direct economic interests gave them a stake at least equal in intensity to the stake of the well-known NGOs in the controversial issues of today. Moreover, these producer interests exercised a fair amount of political power from 1934 to the mid-1960s. They failed to halt the process but not because they failed to notice. They were simply unable to mount a really serious threat to GATT-based decisionmaking.

The producer interests failed because there was broad agreement on the goals of tariff reduction. Even before it was passed, the Smoot-Hawley tariff was widely regarded as a major blunder. The catastrophic world depression that followed sealed its fate. Although not a cause of the depression of the 1930s, the Smoot-Hawley tariff certainly aggravated its effects by setting off a chain reaction of protectionist measures around the world that reduced world trade by at least a third. The result was a broad consensus that Smoot-Hawley tariff rates had to be reduced. Because of that consensus, protectionist producer interests were unable to complain about being shut out of direct participation in the negotiating process. The end more or less justified the means. Of course, the means themselves were not totally lacking in claims to democratic legitimacy: they were adopted in open debate by a democratically elected Congress fourteen times over a fifty-two year period. Perhaps more accurately, at the margin the end justified the means.

The procedural components of legitimacy complaints—lack of transparency, lack of participation—are not absolutes. When good policy seems to require it, they have been overridden in the past, and they will be again in the future. The WTO's critics have had traction, some say, because the problems of substantive policy they reflect are of concern to large numbers of people. Even so, governments must confront the more detailed issues of

how much is to be paid for what improvements. The answers to those policy questions will guide the answers to today's complaints about the legitimacy of the WTO.

Underlying the present substantive discord are "trade and . . ." issues
different in kind from the trade-only issues that confronted the early
GATT. Accordingly, different decisionmaking processes are needed to deal
with these new issues in a legitimate manner. There is, of course, an understandable tendency by critics of the WTO to claim that the values they
represent are of a higher order than the values involved in early trade policy
decisions. Earlier decisions on tariffs and other border measures involved
merely economic interests, they claim, whereas present issues involve
health, safety, the environment, and human rights. This distinction is too
facile. The claims of protectionist interests involved plenty of noneconomic values—the suffering of the workers being thrown out of work and
the decimation of communities dependent on these noncompetitive firms,
for example.

The "trade and . . ." issues are encountering more popular opposition
than the trade-only issues, and there may in fact be a need for better processes of decision to take that into account. But this will be a political judgment, not a moral one.

COMMENT BY
Daniel C. Esty

Trouble looms for the international trading system, as embodied in the World Trade Organization (WTO). Although some commentators dismiss the emblematic rioting in the streets of Seattle during the WTO's 1999 Ministerial Meeting as mere "noise," a "signal" can be extracted from the current difficulties of the trade regime—centered on a crisis of legitimacy. Robert Keohane and Joseph Nye make a similar point in their chapter. Keohane and Nye's overarching description is compelling, but their diagnosis of the WTO's legitimacy problems is less convincing. More importantly, their prescription—a world made safe for national democracies through a retreat from globalization and an acceptance of shallower economic integration—strikes me as inadequate. While acknowledging the serious "democratic deficit" that must be overcome to establish real WTO legitimacy, I argue that the future of the trade regime rests on broader foundations than the global popular sovereignty that Keohane and Nye suggest would be required. In particular, the legitimacy of a governing body in the modern world derives interactively from the degree to which it reflects the will of a political community (in the spirit of Rousseau) and the reason or rationality of the outcomes it generates (in the Kantian tradition).[1] If the right path forward is chosen, the WTO could regain its footing.

Beyond the Club Model

As Keohane and Nye note, the club model trade regime has persisted because it has delivered on its mission. The WTO (and its forerunner, the General Agreement on Tariffs and Trade) have an enviable half-century record of accomplishment. Throughout this period, the trade regime's low profile and obscure workings have been seen as an asset. The WTO may represent the high-water mark of twentieth-century technocratic decisionmaking.[2] It also reflects belief in a governance model centered on bureaucratic rationality.[3] Just as the American people have seemed happy to leave domestic economic decisions to Federal Reserve Board Chairman Alan Greenspan, many believe that, to the extent international economics and trade policymaking are a science, we do best to rely on technical expertise such as that in the staff and national delegations at the WTO.

But this club model no longer represents a viable management structure. The trade regime's legitimacy has been broadly called into question. Where authority and acceptance are founded on efficacy, not popular sovereignty, perceived good performance becomes the touchstone of ongoing legitimacy. In this regard the international trading system has been attacked from several directions.

First, because of the WTO's raised profile, the trade cognoscenti can no longer gather quietly in Geneva or elsewhere and hammer out major trade agreements. Post-Seattle, the whole world is watching. The club model's closed-door approach to decisionmaking, which insulated trade policymaking from the protectionist pressures of domestic politics, has impeded popular understanding and support. Lacking any real appreciation for how the trade regime works, much of the public sees the WTO as a "black box" and suspects that multinational corporations and other insiders are taking advantage of their access to the levers of power within the system.

When the trade community alone assessed the WTO's outputs, the performance reviews were quite positive. But the traditional international regime centered on "decomposable hierarchies" has begun to break down.[4] United by a common vision of a world of liberalized trade, a commitment to well-defined core principles (for example, nondiscrimination), and common traditions of education (particularly an emphasis on economics and a belief in open markets), the trade community sees the WTO's virtues. The broader public and political community that now stands in judgment on the WTO does not, however, share this cultural affinity and understanding. As a result, the WTO's representativeness has been called into question, the organization's performance rating has fallen, and its legitimacy has begun to erode.

Simultaneously, the trade system's ever-broader reach has undermined the WTO's efficacy-based claim to legitimacy. As Keohane and Nye note, the seeds of the organization's current troubles were planted in the furrows of its recent success. Because the international trade regime developed a reputation for effectiveness, increasing numbers of people began to see the WTO as an important point of policy leverage. Environmentalists have focused on "greening the GATT" because they see no international environmental bodies of comparable strength available to advance their agenda.[5] Similarly, a wide range of conflicts that involve trade (but other policy domains as well) have been settled within the confines of the WTO because of the vitality of its dispute resolution procedures. A number of

these matters (protecting dolphins and sea turtles or implementing the re-
formulated gasoline provisions of the U.S. Clean Air Act of 1990) led the
WTO to make judgments beyond its core competence. As the trade system's reach has extended so has unhappiness about trade goals trumping
policy aims in other arenas, such as the environment. Simply put, the
WTO's claim to legitimacy based on bureaucratic rationality gets strained
by its efforts to make "trade and . . ." decisions.[6]

Acceptance of a decisionmaking process based on delegation to bureaucratic experts can only persist if the decisions appear to be technical in
nature and undergirded by science. But the WTO has indisputably moved
beyond the narrow realm of trade economics. Its policies impinge on other
realms and clearly involve value judgments. The scope for action provided
by a presumption in favor of technocratic rationality has therefore been
lost. Insofar as the trade agenda intersects with other policy domains, such
as environmental protection, trade science cannot be counted upon to reconcile appropriately the competing policy goals that are at play.

As legitimacy based on rationality erodes, demands for legitimacy
based on democracy mount. But the former virtues of the WTO have become serious detriments. The exclusion in Seattle of most developing-
country representatives from the green rooms where an inner circle of
key countries did the real negotiating raised hackles among many delegates. Similarly, the WTO's long-standing exclusion of nongovernmental
organizations (NGOs) from its decision processes has become a bone of
contention. In addition to developing-country negotiators and NGOs,
government officials representing various issue areas (environment ministers, for example) sat on the sidelines at the Seattle convocation feeling excluded. Their distress at being marginalized broadened the fissures in the
old issue-based hierarchical regime.

As economic integration advances, it inevitably touches upon more issues and competing values.[7] Much of the WTO's recent trouble can be
traced to the trade community's failure to recognize the implications of a
shift away from shallow integration based on tit-for-tat tariff reductions. A
deeper integration program with a rule-based regime for managing economic interdependence demands concomitant political integration. Keohane and Nye recognize this economics-politics connection but believe that
a buffer exists, permitting substantial domestic political differences to persist and insulating politicians from the pressures of globalization. But economic integration and political integration are more intertwined than
Keohane and Nye suggest. For the public to be comfortable opening mar-

kets to goods from other jurisdictions, people must sense that these jurisdictions share their core values. At the same time, broader economic ties
often lead to shared values, creating a stronger sense of community, which
makes the public more willing to accept deeper economic integration. Narrow integration limited to the economic realm cannot be sustained. The
faltering Asia-Pacific Economic Coordination (APEC) process demonstrates this reality.

The protestors in the streets of Seattle had at least one thing right: the
WTO matters. In many respects the trade regime stands at the center of the
globalization process in general and the emerging structure of global governance in particular. And while there have been a series of rounds of multilateral trade negotiations over the past fifty years, the Millennium Round
that was meant to be launched at Seattle had a palpably different purpose:
the identification of rules and procedures to manage economic interdependence. In important respects the Seattle negotiations signaled the opening
of a Global Constitutional Convention. Obviously, this "constitutional"
process—defining core principles, establishing procedures, and creating institutions to manage interdependence—will involve decades or even centuries of discussions and refinements. Nevertheless, the WTO mission
must be understood as an exercise in regime building with profound effects
for every person on the planet.

An Alternative Model of Legitimacy

Keohane and Nye trace the legitimacy crisis at the WTO to a lack of
political accountability. While they acknowledge that "democratic governments are judged both on the procedures they follow and on the results
they obtain" and accept that "accountability is not ensured only through
elections . . . and is a multidimensional phenomenon," Keohane and Nye
conclude that "only politicians, with ties both to constituencies and to
governmental organizations, can create the linkages that make accountability real." I see a more granular world where legitimacy is not simply a
function of political will and decisionmaking by majority vote. Institutions win credibility and authority, in part, because of their capacity to deliver good results. While Keohane and Nye conclude that the WTO suffers
from a fatal democratic deficit based on its lack of political intermediaries
accountable to a political community, I see more hope. I find their suggestion that the best answer to the WTO's legitimacy crisis lies in a step

back from full-scale globalization based on the presumed dominance of nation-states to be both descriptively incomplete and normatively unsatisfactory.

As Stephen Kobrin notes, "territorial sovereignty is not historically privileged," and the centrality of the nation-state continues to crumble on many fronts.[8] Invigorating global-scale decision processes is a better strategy than retreating to a world of shallow integration (the possibility of which seems unrealistic). We need systematic reforms leading to a more transparent international trading regime that promotes vigorous dialogue and debate and has its legitimacy established on a broader, not narrower, base of international politics. While Keohane and Nye argue that there is no worldwide political community, I would counter that their world view fails to encompass today's multitier political reality, in which most individuals' sense of self builds on affiliations beyond the nation state. In a world where people identify with a set of communities, some of which are issue oriented rather than geographic, it is possible to envision a strengthened global governance structure, including a World Trade Organization, with firmer foundations of democratic legitimacy.

A degree of legitimacy can also be obtained from the broader structure within which a decision process is embedded. The legitimacy of the World Trade Organization could be enhanced, for example, by lodging the trade regime within a global-scale system of checks and balances. Although Keohane and Nye (and Robert Hudec in his commentary) seem to fall back on reliance on an international regime configured around the nation-state, I believe that we should build a multitier governance structure, including a more robust international regime, that can support globalization in its many facets. A multidimensional and multilayered governance system promises not only to deliver better results with regard to international-scale policy challenges but also to improve national-scale decision processes through greater policymaking "competition" both horizontally (among entities at any one level) and vertically (between levels of government).[9]

Conclusion

Wistfulness about the disappearance of the club model and of the postwar economic order and its implied shallow integration should be put aside. Such a vision is dated and undesirable. Instead, the WTO must be seen as a central element of the emerging international regime. We should acknowledge the challenge of defining the core principles, rules, and procedures for managing interdependence. Getting the structure of this new international regime right, including its limitations, is important. Indeed, reserving space for domestic political processes and judgments is critical to the success of global governance, just as the vitality and durability of the U.S. federal system depend on the Constitution's delegation of important powers to the states. But it would be a mistake to think that the future of the international economic regime would be on solid footings if we simply made domestic political processes work better and relaxed the drive for improved global institutions. In the end, while it is useful to have escape clauses as a safety valve for the national pressures that inevitably arise within the trading system, a more promising answer to the demands of domestic politics is a better functioning international regime. Revitalizing the WTO—making the organization more *democratic* and more *rational*—must therefore be seen as a high priority.

Notes

1. Paul Kahn, "Reason and Will in the Origins of American Constitutionalism," *Yale Law Journal*, vol. 98 (1989), pp. 449–517; Daniel Bodansky, "The Legitimacy of International Governance: A Coming Challenge for International Environmental Law," *American Journal of International Law*, vol. 93 (1999), pp. 596–624; Thomas M. Franck, *The Power of Legitimacy among Nations* (New York: Oxford University Press, 1990).

2. Steve Charnovitz, "The World Trade Organization and Social Issues," *Journal of World Trade*, vol. 28 (October 1994), pp. 17–34; Robert Howse, "The House That Jackson Built: Restructuring the GATT System," *Michigan Law Review*, vol. 20 (1999), pp. 2329–57.

3. Gerald E. Frug, "The Ideology of Bureaucracy in American Law," *Harvard Law Review*, vol. 97 (1984), pp. 1277–1388; Paul Kahn, *Reign of Law: Marbury v. Madison and the Construction of America* (Yale University Press, 1997); Max Weber, "The Profession and Vocation of Politics," in Peter Lassman and Ronald Speirs, eds., *Political Writings* (Cambridge University Press, 1994); James Q. Wilson, *Bureaucracy: What Government Agencies Do and Why They Do It* (Basic Books, 1989).

4. Herbert A. Simon, *The Sciences of the Artificial*, 3d ed. (MIT Press, 1996).

5. John J. Audley, *Green Politics and Global Trade: NAFTA and the Future of Environmental Politics* (Georgetown University Press, 1997). See also Daniel C. Esty, *Greening the GATT: Trade, Environment, and the Future* (Washington: Institute for International Economics, 1994).

6. Jeffrey L. Dunoff, "'Trade and': Recent Developments in Trade Policy and Scholarship —and Their Surprising Political Implications," *Northwestern Journal of International Law and Business*, vol. 17 (Winter-Spring 1996–97), pp. 579–74.

7. Andre Dua and Daniel C. Esty, *Sustaining the Asia Pacific Miracle: Environmental Protection and Economic Integration* (Washington: Institute for International Economics, 1997), pp. 109–10, 120–27.

8. Stephen Kobrin, "Back to the Future: Neomedievalism and the Postmodern Digital World Economy," in Aseem Prakash and Jeffrey A. Hart, eds., *Globalizaiton and Governance: An Introduction* (Routledge, 1999), p. 364.

9. See Daniel C. Esty, "Toward Optimal Environmental Governance," *New York University Law Review,* vol. 74, no. 6 (1999), pp. 1495–574; Daniel C. Esty and Damien Geradin, "Regulatory Co-opetition," *Journal of International Economic Law,* vol. 3, no. 2 (2000), pp. 235–55.

FRIEDER ROESSLER

13 | *Are the Judicial Organs of the World Trade Organization Overburdened?*

Under the General Agreement on Tariffs and Trade of 1947 (GATT), all decisionmaking authority was attributed to (and then delegated by) a single organ, the Contracting Parties acting jointly.[1] This organ also settled disputes on the basis of proposals by independent panels. The framers of the Agreement Establishing the World Trade Organization (WTO Agreement), however, carefully negotiated a more complex institutional structure under which separate judicial and political bodies are empowered to take binding decisions that confirm, define, or alter the rights and obligations of Members. In a manner akin to the *trias politica* of modern states, decisionmaking in the WTO is divided between

—the membership of the WTO acting under the amendment and other rulemaking provisions of the WTO Agreement (the "legislator");

—the political organs of the WTO, such as the Committee on Regional Trade Agreements, the Committee on Subsidies and Countervailing Measures, the Safeguards Committee, and the Committee on Balance-of-Payments Restrictions (the "executive authorities"); and

This paper is a modified version of "The Institutional Balance between the Judicial and the Political Organs of the WTO," in Marco Bronckers and Reinhard Quick, eds., *New Directions in International Economic Law: Essays in Honour of John H. Jackson* (Boston: Kluwer Law International, 2000), pp. 325–45.

—the judicial organs of the WTO, in particular the panels, arbitrators, and the Appellate Body, pursuant to the WTO Understanding on Rules and Procedures Governing the Settlement of Disputes (DSU).

National legal systems have developed a multitude of doctrines to ensure that the judicial powers do not assume functions of the other branches of government. In the United States, for example, the Supreme Court developed the *Chevron* doctrine, which instructs the courts to defer to an administrative agency's interpretation of the law if the statute in question is ambiguous and the agency's interpretation is "reasonable."[2] Certain government actions in antidumping and countervailing duty cases are reviewed by the Court of International Trade only to determine if they were "arbitrary, capricious, an abuse of discretion or unlawful."[3] The federal courts of the United States have also developed doctrines preventing the courts from intruding on the president's conduct of foreign affairs.[4] The purpose of all these forms of judicial restraint is to ensure that the institutional balance between the judicial and administrative organs of the U.S. government established by the Constitution or by legislation is not upset.

Like modern states, the WTO must ensure that its judicial organs exercise their powers with due regard for the jurisdiction assigned to the other parts of its institutional structure. This chapter examines the jurisprudence of GATT and the WTO on the relationship between the general dispute settlement procedures and the special review procedures for balance-of-payments measures and regional trade agreements. Two recent rulings of the WTO Appellate Body shifted the resolution of delicate political disputes from the executive to the judicial organs of the WTO.

In a national system of law, courts cannot develop jurisprudence inconsistent with the will of the legislature. If a court's interpretation of a law is unacceptable to the legislature, a new law overriding the interpretation can be adopted. The possibility of reversal by the legislature confers democratic legitimacy upon the decisions of the judicial organs. This chapter examines the WTO procedures to amend WTO law and concludes that these procedures make a prompt legislative response targeted to an individual judicial decision close to impossible. This imposes responsibilities on the WTO judge that should be borne by the WTO legislator and undermines the effectiveness and legitimacy of the dispute settlement process.

Institutional Balance between the WTO's Judicial and Executive Organs

The first extensive GATT Council discussions on the relationship between the procedures under Article XXIV:7 for the review of regional trade agreements and the dispute settlement provisions of Article XXIII were held in 1982. The United States had requested the establishment of a panel to examine the tariff preferences granted by the European Economic Community (EEC) to Mediterranean countries within the framework of association agreements.[5] After long consultations, a GATT panel on *European Community—Tariff Treatment on Imports of Citrus Products from Certain Countries in the Mediterranean Region* was established. This panel found that

> examination—or re-examination—of Article XXIV agreements was the responsibility of the Contracting Parties. In the absence of a decision by the Contracting Parties and without prejudice to any decision the Contracting Parties might take in the future on such a matter, the Panel was of the view that it would not be appropriate to determine the conformity of an agreement with the requirements of Article XXIV on the basis of a complaint by a contracting party under Article XXIII:1(a). . . . [T]his should be done clearly in the context of Article XXIV and not Article XXIII, as an assessment of all the duties, regulations of commerce and trade coverage as well as the interests and rights of all contracting parties were at stake in such an examination and not just the interests and rights of the contracting party raising a complaint.[6]

The same issues arose in the proceedings of the panel on *EEC—Member States' Import Regimes for Bananas*. The EEC claimed that its tariff preferences for bananas, which were granted under the Lomé Convention, were justified by Article XXIV and that this convention could be examined only under the procedures of Article XXIV:7 of GATT.[7] The panel concluded that, faced with the invocation of Article XXIV, it first had to examine whether this provision applied to the agreement in question.[8] It determined that the provision did not apply, because it provided only for one-sided preferences by the EEC. The EEC could therefore not invoke Article XXIV as a legal justification for its preferences. The panel thus found a way to protect the complainant's rights while respecting the competence of the Contracting Parties under Article XXIV:7.

Equally controversial was the issue of whether panels may review balance-of-payments measures. The issue arose when Australia, New Zealand,

and the United States each requested the establishment of a panel to examine Korea's import restrictions on beef notified under Article XVIII:B. Several GATT Members felt that the panel procedures could not be used as a substitute for the consultation process in the Committee on Balance-of-Payments Restrictions (BOP Committee) and that these panels should not be established; others considered the resort to Article XXIII to be an unconditional right. Three panels on *Korea—Restrictions on Imports of Beef* were eventually established.[9] The controversy on this issue continued in the proceedings before them.[10] The panels concluded that the BOP Committee had already determined the legal status of the restrictions imposed by Korea and they could therefore base their decision on the determination made by that committee.[11]

No GATT panel has decided to determine the overall consistency of a regional trade agreement with Article XXIV, or the balance-of-payments justification of measures notified under Article XII without a prior determination of the BOP Committee. Panels have consistently left these matters to bodies composed of the representatives of the contracting parties.

Institutional Balance under the WTO Agreement

During the Uruguay Round, the United States proposed, together with Canada, that matters left unresolved by the BOP Committee could be settled under the normal dispute settlement procedures:

> The consulting contracting party or affected contracting parties can, if they wish, attempt to resolve the question in the Council. *Alternatively, affected contracting parties can, if they wish, pursue the matter through normal GATT dispute settlement procedures pursuant to Articles XXII and XXIII.*[12]

This proposal was not taken over into WTO law. Instead, the following compromise language was included in the footnote to the Understanding on the Balance-of-Payments Provisions of GATT 1994 ("BOP Understanding"):

> Nothing in this Understanding is intended to modify the rights and obligations of Members under Articles XII or XVIII:B of GATT 1994. The provisions of Articles XXII and XXIII of GATT 1994 as elaborated and applied by the Dispute Settlement

Understanding may be invoked with respect to *any matters arising from the application of* restrictive import measures taken for balance-of-payments purposes.

This clarifies that the invocation of the DSU must relate to "matters arising from the application of" balance-of-payments measures. The ordinary meaning of the term *application* is "a specific use or purpose for which something is put" and "applicability in a particular case."[13] This suggests that panels can make findings only on the consistency of specific measures imposed for balance-of-payments purposes, not however on their overall balance-of-payments justification.

The only other reference to the application of measures is contained in paragraph 12 of the Understanding on the Interpretation of Article XXIV of GATT 1994 ("Understanding on Article XXIV"), which reads as follows:

The provisions of Articles XXII and XXIII of GATT 1994 as elaborated and applied by the Dispute Settlement Understanding may be invoked with respect to *any matters arising from the application* of those provisions of Article XXIV relating to customs unions, free-trade areas or interim agreements leading to the formation of a customs union or free-trade area.

The institutional balance between the political and judicial organs of the WTO reflected in the footnote to the BOP Understanding is the balance that has emerged in practice. The BOP Committee has not examined the application of individual measures but has focused on their overall balance-of-payments justification. A panel's examination of whether the application of a specific balance-of-payments measure is consistent with the various WTO agreements therefore does not encroach upon the competence of the BOP Committee as it has effectively been exercised. Furthermore, the footnote reflects the fact that, while the application of individual trade measures imposed for balance-of-payments reasons is subject to clear WTO rules and therefore capable of resolution by a panel, there are no internationally agreed standards for assessing the adequacy of monetary reserves. A panel that determines the overall balance-of-payments justification of trade measures therefore acts in a complete normative vacuum.

The same is true for the distinction made in the Understanding on Article XXIV between matters arising from the application of the provisions on regional trade agreements and matters relating to the overall justification of such agreements. The WTO Committee on Regional Trade Agreements (CRTA) is not expected, and is not equipped procedurally, to examine whether all the individual measures taken within the framework of a regional trade agreement conform to the WTO agreements. On the other hand, since each regional trade agreement affects the overall trade policy of Members, the consistency of that policy cannot be appropriately addressed in disputes between individual Members. The Contracting Parties have deliberately never defined the degree of trade integration required by Article XXIV, and a panel that rules on this matter would be acting without any prior normative guidance. Moreover, a complaint may be brought under the DSU only against one of the parties to a regional trade agreement, and since the DSU does not recognize the status of co-defendant, the other parties to the agreement can be deprived of all active participation in the proceedings.[14] Here, too, it makes sense to distinguish between the panel's examination of individual measures taken within the framework of a regional trade agreement and the examination of the overall justification of such an agreement, entrusted to the CRTA.

Institutional Balance in WTO Jurisprudence

At the request of India, a panel ruled in 1999 on Turkey's restrictions on imports of textiles and clothing products from India (*Turkey—Textile Products*).[15] These restrictions were introduced in the context of a trade arrangement that Turkey described as an agreement providing for the completion of the EC-Turkey customs union. Concurrently, another panel considered the balance-of-payments justification of India's import restrictions (*India—Quantitative Restrictions*).

PANEL REPORT ON TURKEY. Turkey claimed that the panel appointed to rule on *Turkey—Textile Products* was not competent to examine the restrictions imposed on imports from India. It was not the panel's task, it said, to substitute itself for the CRTA. The panel "could not rule on the legality of the measures forming the object of the complaint in the absence of agreed conclusions on the consistency of the Turkey-EC Agreements with Article XXIV."[16] In response, the panel argued that

> panels have jurisdiction to examine "any matters 'arising from' the application of those provisions of Article XXIV." For us this confirms that a panel can examine the WTO compatibility of one or several measures "arising from" Article XXIV types of agree-

ment. . . . Thus *we consider that a panel can assess the WTO compatibility of any specific measure adopted by WTO Members . . . on the occasion of the formation of a customs union*. . . . CRTA has been established, *inter alia*, to assess the GATT/WTO compatibility of regional trade agreements entered into by Members, a very complex undertaking which involves consideration by the CRTA, from the economic, legal and political perspectives of different Members, of the numerous facets of a regional trade agreement in relation to the provisions of the WTO. It appears to us that *the issue regarding the GATT/WTO compatibility of a customs union, as such, is generally a matter for the CRTA* since . . . it involves a broad multilateral assessment of any such customs union, i.e. a matter which concerns the WTO membership as a whole.[17]

PANEL REPORT ON INDIA.   While the proceedings on *Turkey—Textile Products* were under way, the panel on *India—Quantitative Restrictions* examined whether it was competent to rule on the balance-of-payments justification of India's restrictions. The panel concluded that the reference to the "application of" measures in the footnote to the BOP Understanding did not curtail its competence in any way: "The 'application' of a measure would thus refer to the fact that a measure is in use. The terms . . . therefore simply refer to the fact that a measure is applied for balance-of-payments purposes."[18]

The panel on *India—Quantitative Restrictions* also rejected the proposition that the provisions allocating competence to panels had to be interpreted in the light of the provisions allocating competence to the BOP Committee:

The role of panels is defined in Article 3.2 of the DSU which provides that the dispute settlement system "serves to preserve the rights and obligations of Members under the covered agreements, and to clarify the existing provisions of those agreements in accordance with customary rules of interpretation of public international law." *Panels are in all instances required to make an objective assessment of the facts of the case and apply the relevant WTO provisions to those facts.*[19]

India urged the panel to take into account the fact that the Understanding on Article XXIV qualified the access to the DSU with terms similar to those contained in the footnote to the BOP Understanding. The panel rejected this argument: "The phrase 'the application of those provisions of Article XXIV' plainly means 'the implementation of the provisions of

Article XXIV . . .' and does not allow for a distinction such as the one proposed by India."[20]

Two WTO panels, meeting concurrently, thus arrived at an entirely different conclusion on the relationship between the judicial and the political organs of the WTO in their interpretation of the terms "any matters arising from the application of . . . ." The two panel reports were appealed, giving the Appellate Body the opportunity to resolve the contradiction.

APPELLATE BODY RULINGS ON TURKEY.   In the Appellate Body's proceedings on *India—Quantitative Restrictions*, India argued that, if the panel's interpretation of the terms in the footnote of the BOP Understanding was correct, the terms would be deprived of their meaning or effect.[21] This was inconsistent with the principle of interpretation recalled in the Appellate Body's report on *Japan—Taxes on Alcoholic Beverages*, which states that

> A fundamental tenet of treaty interpretation flowing from the general rules of interpretation set out in Article 31 is the principle of effectiveness (*ut res magis valeat quam pereat*). [O]ne of the corollaries of the general rules of interpretation in the Vienna Convention is that *interpretation must give meaning and effect to all the terms of the treaty.*[22]

The Appellate Body did not agree with India that "under the Panel's interpretation, the words 'matters arising from the application of' would have no meaning at all and would be read out of existence. These words reflect the traditional GATT doctrine that, with the exception of mandatory rules, only measures that are effectively applied can be the subject of dispute settlement proceedings."[23]

Having found that the footnote to the BOP Understanding does not curtail the panels' competence, the Appellate Body's remaining task was to determine the relationship between the DSU provisions creating and defining the competence of panels (and conferring procedural rights on the complainant) and the equally valid provisions creating and defining the competence of the BOP Committee and the General Council (and conferring procedural rights on the defendant). Three options to resolve this issue were in theory available:

—First, the provisions allocating competence to the judicial organs of the WTO (and consequently the rights of the complainant under the DSU) prevail completely over the provisions assigning competence to the political organs (and hence the procedural rights of the defendant under other WTO agreements).

—Second, the competence of the political organs is exclusive.

—Third, a balance between the competence of the judicial organs of the WTO and that of its political organs should be attained by the exercise of judicial restraint (and with it a balance between the rights of the complainant under the DSU and the rights of the defendant under other WTO agreements).

The Appellate Body chose the first option. It ruled that the panel's competence "to review all aspects of balance-of-payments restrictions should be determined in the light of Article XXIII of GATT, as elaborated and applied by the DSU, and of footnote 1 to the BOP Understanding."[24] If panels refrained from reviewing the justification of the balance-of-payments restrictions, the Appellate Body explained, "they would diminish the explicit procedural rights of Members under Article XXIII and footnote 1 to the BOP Understanding, as well as their substantive rights under Article XVIII:11."[25]

Neither Turkey nor India appealed the ruling of the panel on *Turkey— Textile Products* regarding the competence of panels to determine the overall consistency of regional trade agreements. Neither party presented arguments on this issue to the Appellate Body. Nevertheless, the Appellate Body ruled on this issue.

The basic conclusion of the panel on *Turkey—Textile Products* was that Article XXIV cannot be interpreted to permit Members to form a customs union to impose otherwise prohibited import restrictions:

> We consider that the wording of Article XXIV does not authorise a departure from the obligations contained in Articles XI and XIII of GATT and Article 2.4 of the ATC . . . . [P]aragraphs 5 and 8 of Article XXIV provide parameters for the establishment and assessment of a customs union. . . . These provisions do not, however, address any specific measures that may or may not be adopted on the formation of a customs union and importantly they do not authorise violations of Articles XI and XIII, and Article 2.4 of the ATC. Moreover, . . . paragraph 6 of Article XXIV provides for a specific procedure for the renegotiation of tariffs which are increased above their bindings upon formation of a customs union; no such provision exists for quantitative restrictions. To the Panel, if the introduction of WTO inconsistent quantitative restrictions were intended to be negotiable on the formation of a customs union, it would seem odd to us that an explicit procedure would exist for changes in GATT's preferred form of trade barrier (i.e., tariffs), while no procedure would be provided for negotiation of compensation connected with imposition of otherwise GATT inconsistent measures.[26]

The Appellate Body reversed this finding and ruled that Article XXIV *can* provide a justification for quantitative restrictions in situations in which the formation of a customs union would be prevented if such restrictions were not imposed. This view was based on Article XXIV:5: "the provisions of this Agreement shall not prevent . . . the formation of a customs union."[27] The Appellate Body does not reveal under which circumstances the obligation to not impose a quantitative restriction might be deemed to prevent the formation of a customs union. "We make no finding," it says, "on the issue of whether quantitative restrictions found to be inconsistent with Article XI . . . will *ever* be justified by Article XXIV. We find only that the quantitative restrictions at issue in the appeal in this case were not so justified."[28]

Having determined that Article XXIV can justify quantitative restrictions, under as yet undefined circumstances, the Appellate Body then declares that panels are duty bound to examine the overall consistency of a customs union with Article XXIV of GATT, if the provision is invoked as a justification for inconsistencies with other provisions:

> Article XXIV may justify a measure which is inconsistent with certain other GATT provisions. However, in a case involving the formation of a customs union, this "defence" is available only when two conditions are fulfilled. First, *the party claiming the benefit of this defence must demonstrate that the measure at issue is introduced upon the formation of a customs union that fully meets the requirements of sub-paragraphs 8(a) and 5(a) of Article XXIV.* And, second, that party must demonstrate that the formation of that customs union would be prevented if it were not allowed to introduce the measure at issue. Again, *both* these conditions must be met to have the benefit of the defence under Article XXIV. *We would expect a panel, when examining such a measure, to require a party to establish that both of these conditions have been fulfilled.*[29]

This ruling logically implies that panels are competent to examine the overall consistency of a regional trade agreement, a point on which the Appellate Body leaves no doubt by adding:

> We are not called upon in this appeal to address this issue, but we note in this respect our ruling in *India—Quantitative Restrictions on Imports of Agricultural, Textile and Industrial Products* on the jurisdiction of panels to review the justification of balance-of-payments restrictions under Article XVIII:B of the GATT 1994.[30]

The Appellate Body recognizes that the terms "matters arising from the application of," to be given meaning and effect, must be interpreted as a qualification of the right to resort to the DSU. According to the Appellate Body, their implication is that "only measures that are effectively applied can be the subject of dispute settlement proceedings."[31] The Appellate Body, however, does not indicate any reason why the drafters of the BOP Understanding and the Understanding on Article XXIV would have wanted to establish the requirement of effective application *only* with respect to balance-of-payments measures and regional trade agreements. This idea does not appear in the documents leading to the adoption of the BOP Understanding and the Understanding on Article XXIV, and it is difficult to conceive of a rationale for distinguishing balance-of-payments measures and measures taken under regional trade agreements from other measures in this respect.[32]

Whatever the correct interpretation of "application of," the question remains whether the DSU provisions assigning competence to panels can be interpreted as overriding the provisions of other agreements assigning competence to the WTO's political bodies. It is recognized in international law that "as a general rule, any body possessing jurisdictional powers has the right in the first place itself to determine the extent of its own jurisdiction."[33] When an organ of the WTO determines its own jurisdiction, it thus exercises its right to interpret the provision of the WTO Agreement conferring authority upon it. In doing so, it must, pursuant to Article 31 of the Vienna Convention on the Law of Treaties, take into account not only the terms of the provision attributing powers to it but also the context in which this provision appears. That context comprises those provisions of the WTO Agreement that attribute related powers to other bodies. An analysis of the terms of those jurisdictional provisions may lead the WTO organ to the conclusion that not only it but also other organs could claim jurisdiction over the matter at issue. Such a conflict must be resolved in good faith in the light of the institutional structure that the framers of the WTO Agreement have established to realize the purposes of the WTO. The principles of interpretation of the Vienna Convention of the Law of Treaties thus suggest that the judicial organs of the WTO cannot determine their jurisdiction exclusively on the basis of the provisions of the DSU.

Article 3:2 of the DSU states the obvious, namely that the complainant's rights under the DSU cannot diminish the rights of the defendant under other WTO agreements. The procedural rights of Members under the DSU are thus clearly subsidiary to those conferred by the WTO agreements: a complainant may resort to the DSU only to enforce the obligations of the defendant under other WTO agreements, not to diminish the rights of the defendant under those agreements. This implies that a panel cannot determine its jurisdiction in a manner that diminishes those rights. Article 3:2 of the DSU obliges the panel to exercise judicial restraint whenever a WTO Member attempts to resort to the DSU for the purpose of negating another Member's procedural rights under another WTO agreement.

It is extremely important to observe this principle in WTO law. Each of the WTO organs charged with making legal determinations operates within a different legal framework. Moving an issue from one organ to another can profoundly change the procedural and substantive rights of the Members involved. With respect to balance-of-payments measures, for example, the procedures under Article XVIII:12(c) permit the membership of the WTO as a whole, acting through the BOP Committee and the General Council, to examine, with the assistance of the IMF, the measures notified by one Member under Article XVIII:B. By contrast, the rulings of the Dispute Settlement Body emerge from a proceeding in which only the facts and claims submitted by the parties to the dispute are considered; the results are binding only on the parties to the dispute. Furthermore, if the restrictions of the Member consulting with the BOP Committee are not, or are no longer, justified, the General Council may, upon the recommendation of the BOP Committee, specify a period for their removal or approve a time schedule for their removal. Balance-of-payments measures are in place—legally—for long periods of time, and their phased removal is therefore appropriate to permit economic operators to adjust. In contrast, Articles 19:1 and 21 of the DSU are designed to deal with measures that were never legal and that should therefore be removed promptly. Shifting the resolution of a dispute on the balance-of-payments measures from the BOP Committee to a panel thus changes fundamentally the balance of rights and obligations under Article XVIII:B.

APPELLATE BODY RULINGS ON INDIA. The panel on *India—Quantitative Restrictions* found that making the "panel track" available to Members for the determination of the balance-of-payments justification of measures affects neither the institutional balance between panels and the BOP Committee nor the procedural rights of the consulting Member. "Even if this Panel were to decide that India's measures are not justified," it said, "nothing would prevent the Committee and the General Council from reaching different conclusions on the basis of new, different facts, in which case the Council could take a decision on a phase-out period under paragraph 13 of the 1994 Understanding on Balance-of-Payments Provisions."[34] The Appellate Body similarly concluded that

> recourse to the dispute settlement procedures does not call into question either the availability or the utility of the procedures under Article XVIII:12 and the BOP Understanding. . . . We are cognisant of the competence of the BOP Committee and the General Council with respect to balance-of-payments restrictions under Article XVIII:12 of the GATT 1994 and the BOP Understanding. However, we see no conflict between that competence and the competence of panels.[35]

The panel and the Appellate Body are formally correct: a "panel track" does not impinge on the right of the BOP Committee to take decisions. They do not consider, however, that the legal alternatives formally available in one forum can be curtailed, and even reduced to inutility, by the creation of new legal opportunities in another. In the BOP Committee, as in any other WTO body, reaching a consensus takes place in the shadow of the procedural alternatives available in the absence of a consensus. These alternatives can effectively dictate the outcome of that process.

The events preceding the United States' complaint against India's balance-of-payments restrictions demonstrate this point. In May 1997, after the International Monetary Fund had found that India no longer had any balance-of-payments problems justifying import restrictions, India notified the BOP Committee of its intention to remove the restrictions. India presented a time schedule for the elimination and progressive relaxation of the remaining restrictions in accordance with paragraph 13 of the BOP Understanding.[36] By November 1997 India had agreed with its main trading partners on a time schedule of six years, a period in line with past practices. Only the United States refused to accept the plan. The declared strategy of the United States was to block the consensus in the BOP Committee and to invoke the Dispute Settlement Understanding so as to deprive India of the benefit of the provisions of Article XVIII:B and the BOP Understanding that apply to the phased removal of balance-of-payments measures. It is true, of course, that the United States's initiation of the DSU procedures did not formally curtail the right of the BOP Committee to recommend a formal approval of India's phase-out plan. However, convinced that the option of the "panel track" was available to it, the United States refused to cooperate in the committee's decisionmaking under paragraph 13 of the BOP Understanding.

The application of the balance-of-payments provisions involves "difficult economic judgments on which reasonable minds can differ," writes John H. Jackson. Therefore, "the efforts to bring about compliance with these obligations have been primarily ones of persuasion, negotiation and international pressure rather than analytical legal exercises designed to establish breach of legal obligation."[37]

This approach has worked well in practice. Since the introduction of flexible exchange rates, the industrialized countries have practically ceased resorting to trade measures for balance-of-payments purposes. The number of developing-country Members consulting in the BOP Committee has now dwindled to *five*. There is no case in the history of GATT and the WTO where a consensus in the BOP Committee was blocked by the consulting country. The consensus tradition consequently did not prevent the enforcement of the rights under Articles XII and XVIII:B. The approach to balance-of-payments issues that has evolved over a half a century does not require radical change. The objectives of the WTO would not be better served if these delicate issues were submitted entirely to the rigidities of a judicial proceeding.

Balance-of-payments measures and regional trade agreements have one common feature: in order to be WTO-consistent, they must be applied across most sectors. For a balance-of-payments measure to be consistent with paragraph 4 of the BOP Understanding, it must be used to control the general level of imports and not for the protection of individual sectors. Similarly, a regional trade agreement, to be consistent with Article XXIV:8 of GATT 1994, must cover substantially all the trade between the territories of its parties. A panel that determines the overall consistency of balance-of-payments measures or regional trade agreements passes judgment on an entire trade regime. There are no agreed standards for determining the adequacy of monetary reserves, and the scope of trade integration required by Article XXIV has deliberately been left undefined. Therefore, the panel must pass its judgment without having received any normative guidance from the WTO membership. Essentially, it is engaging in a legislative or political task. If the panel's ruling is not implemented, it becomes a license to retaliate of enormous proportions.

The view reflected in the consistent practice of the Contracting Parties was that the dispute settlement system would be overburdened if it were used to resolve conflicts of this nature. The adoption of the DSU led to a clear separation between the judicial and the political organs determining the legality of trade measures. The now independent judicial or-

gans should be even more cautious than the Contracting Parties were and
therefore refrain from using their interpretative power to confer decisionmaking authority upon themselves—authority that the Members of the
WTO have explicitly assigned to bodies composed of Members.

General Observations

The Appellate Body would be well advised to exercise caution and cir-
cumspection when asked to make the same legal determination that a political body of the WTO is empowered to make. This is particularly true
when neither the WTO agreements nor the practices that evolved under
GATT provide the Appellate Body with any normative guidance. Its aim
should be to reconcile the objectives of the DSU (and the procedural rights
of the complainant under the DSU) with the negotiated, legitimate policy objectives reflected in the assignment of jurisdiction to political organs
of the WTO (and the procedural rights of the defendant under WTO
agreements other than the DSU). In the case of balance-of-payments
measures, the overall objective of a panel's examination should not be to
make *de novo* or in anticipation an assessment equivalent to the assessments the BOP Committee and the IMF are to make. The panel should
merely determine whether the measure at issue, given the margin of appreciation of the BOP Committee and the IMF, can be approved by them.
This approach would protect Members against invocations of the balance-
of-payments provisions that are made in bad faith *and* preserve the discretion of the BOP Committee.

In the case of regional trade agreements, the Appellate Body should
exercise judicial restraint in a similar fashion. It should normally limit its
examination to whether the specific measures implementing the agreement are consistent with the WTO agreement and whether the agreement
as a whole can be justified under Article XXIV. This approach would ensure that the DSU procedures protect Members against an abusive invocation of Article XXIV.

Institutional Balance between the WTO's Judicial and Legislative Organs

Under GATT 1947, the rulings and recommendations of panels became binding upon the parties to the dispute only after they were adopted
by the GATT Contracting Parties. Theoretically, adoption of panel reports

by a simple majority of the votes cast would have been possible. In practice, all reports were adopted by consensus. Not only the parties to the dispute but also third parties could, and occasionally did, block the consensus. The GATT panels proposed, the Contracting Parties disposed.[38]

Under GATT 1947, if the Contracting Parties found a panel ruling unacceptable, for whatever reason, they refused to adopt it. This ensured that the final control over the determination of obligations under GATT rested with those that were bound by them, and it gave panel rulings legitimacy and normative force, including rulings based on creative interpretations advancing the objectives of GATT. This dispute settlement system had the obvious disadvantage that the respondent in a dispute could block its proper functioning. Moreover, it permitted the Contracting Parties to refuse the adoption of one interpretation without adopting another. As a result, normative voids were created and legal uncertainty ensued.

With the establishment of the World Trade Organization, fully automatic dispute settlement procedures, and a standing Appellate Body as the supreme judicial organ, replaced GATT's consensus-based system of dispute settlement. The DSU makes it seem as if Members are closely involved in all important decisions. The Dispute Settlement Body (DSB), an organ composed of the representatives of all the Members, establishes the panels, adopts the rulings of the panels and the Appellate Body, and authorizes sanctions for noncompliance.[39] However, the DSB *must* establish the panels, adopt the panel and Appellate Body reports, and authorize sanctions, unless there is a consensus not to do so. Such a negative consensus, of course, can be achieved only if the complainant and the respondent agree that the matter submitted to the DSB should no longer be pursued through the WTO dispute settlement procedures. However, the parties to a dispute in any case have the right to settle at any time.[40] For these reasons the involvement of the WTO's executive branch in the dispute settlement process is a formality without any legal consequences for the DSB or the parties to the dispute.

Unlike the membership of GATT, the membership of the WTO can refuse to adopt reports with undesired interpretations of a provision. It also can amend, modify, or reinterpret the provision interpreted by the judicial organ. Under current procedures the legislative response of the WTO membership could theoretically take the form of (a) an amendment of the text of provision, (b) a waiver from the obligations under the provision, or (c) the adoption of an authoritative interpretation of the provision.

The basic voting requirements for amendments under the WTO Agreement are the same as under GATT 1947: an amendment of most

WTO provisions enters into effect upon acceptance by a two-thirds majority. An amendment binds only those WTO Members that have accepted it.[41] Decisions to amend the DSU must be made by consensus; in other words, they can be adopted only if no Member formally objects.[42] There is no way to amend the text of a provision of a WTO agreement with effect for all Members unless all Members consent to the amendment.

Waivers were adopted under GATT 1947 by a two-thirds majority of the votes cast, comprising at least one-half of the GATT contracting parties.[43] Since negative votes were rare, the consent of one-half of the contracting parties was the minimum requirement for a waiver. Under WTO law, a waiver requires the consent of three-fourths of the WTO Members.[44] In practice, waivers are accorded by consensus decisions of the General Council and are therefore not granted if a WTO Member present at the Council meeting formally objects. Furthermore, waivers may now be granted only for a specified period of time, and they must be periodically reviewed.[45] Waivers therefore do not lend themselves to permanent, generally applicable modifications of WTO law.

Authoritative interpretations, which could be adopted under GATT 1947 by a simple majority of the votes cast,[46] require the consent of three-fourths of the Members under the WTO.[47] A three-fourths majority is extremely difficult to obtain since over one-fourth of the Members do not actively participate in the work of the WTO. No interpretations have been adopted so far. Presumably, interpretations, like waivers, would be adopted by consensus. Therefore, the procedural obstacles to a reversal of an Appellate Body decision through the adoption of an authoritative interpretation are enormous.

The WTO's amendment, waiver, and interpretation procedures, which have been the subject of lengthy negotiations, protect the sovereignty of WTO Members. They make it nearly impossible to adjust the rules of the WTO to new circumstances, however. The fear of being bound by majority decisions adopted by the political organs of the WTO was greater than the fear of being bound by decisions adopted by its judicial organs. Members' only remaining legislative response to judicial decisions is to replace the WTO Agreement with a new treaty. This, however, is a step with far-reaching consequences that can realistically be expected only in the framework of negotiations covering as many subjects as the Uruguay Round. A targeted legislative response to individual Appellate Body decisions is well nigh impossible. Members, eager to protect their sovereignty against each other, ended up surrendering it to the judicial organs of the WTO.

The normative force of a GATT panel ruling rested primarily on its endorsement by the community of trading nations. The rulings of the panels and the Appellate Body of the WTO are binding without such an endorsement and therefore lack that source of legitimacy. Creating the possibility of a legislative response would confer democratic legitimacy, and greater normative force, upon the decisions of the WTO judge.

The lack of a potential legislative response imposes legal constraints and extralegal burdens on the judicial organs of the World Trade Organization. It forces the WTO judge to exercise extreme caution in determining the scope of obligations. This can discourage creative interpretations furthering the objectives of the WTO or even provoke excessive judicial economy amounting to a denial of justice. Furthermore, it forces the WTO judge to take into account the political acceptability of the rulings and their impact on the balance of advantages accruing to Members under the WTO. This may require the WTO judge to take into account extralegal considerations that normally are addressed by the political organs of the WTO. Legal inconsistencies and an unequal treatment of large and small Members may result.

Conclusions

The question raised in this chapter's title must be answered affirmatively. The judicial organs of the WTO are overburdened as a result of their own decisions and because procedures permitting a legislative response to their rulings are lacking.

The Appellate Body ruled that panels are competent to determine the overall consistency of balance-of-payments measures and regional trade agreements. The judicial organs of the WTO thus gave themselves the power to make the same legal determinations that the WTO Agreement assigns to the Committee on Balance-of-Payments Restrictions and the Committee on Regional Trade Agreements. The Appellate Body invoked as the legal basis for this far-reaching ruling the DSU provisions defining the competence of panels. However, the purpose of the complex institutional structure established by the WTO Agreement is to divide decisionmaking power between different organs—executive, legislative, as well as judicial. Each organ of the WTO must determine its jurisdiction with due regard for the powers conferred on the other organs and resolve conflicts of jurisdiction in a manner that reconciles those objectives to the maximum. The ruling of the Appellate Body will require the WTO judicial organs to arbitrate on the legal status of entire trade regimes without any normative guidance and to hand out licenses to retaliate of enormous proportions. Moreover, they must conduct this arbitration in the framework of a legal proceeding between individual WTO Members in which all legitimate interests are not represented. For instance, they would have to examine a complaint against one party to a free trade area without all parties to that area present because current procedures do not provide for the status of co-respondent.

The World Trade Organization's amendment, waiver, and interpretation procedures protect the sovereignty of Members but render a targeted legislative response to individual judicial decisions well nigh impossible. The Members of the WTO, eager to protect their sovereignty against each other, surrendered it to the judicial organs of the WTO. Creating the possibility of a legislative response would confer democratic legitimacy, and hence greater normative force, upon the decisions of the WTO judicial organs. The lack of a potential legislative response forces the WTO judge to exercise extreme caution in determining the scope of obligations, which can discourage creative interpretations furthering the objectives of the WTO or even provoke excessive judicial economy amounting to a denial of justice. Most important, the inability of the WTO membership to modify the consequences of judicial rulings effectively transfers to the judicial organs the responsibility to ensure the political acceptability of their rulings. This may require them to take into account factors and circumstances that should be addressed by the political organs of the WTO.

Notes

1. Article XXV of GATT.

2. See Steven P. Croley and John H. Jackson, "WTO Dispute Panel Deference to National Government Decisions: The Misplaced Analogy to the U.S. Chevron Standard-of-Review Doctrine," in Ernst-Ulrich Petersmann, ed., *International Trade Law and the GATT/WTO Dispute Settlement System,* Studies in Transnational Economic Law 11 (Boston: Kluwer Law International, 1997), pp. 198–99.

3. On the judicial review of administrative action in the United States, see John H. Jackson, William J. Davey, and Alan O. Sykes, *Legal Problems of International Economic Relations,* 3d ed. (West, 1995), pp. 157–61. The United States's practice is reflected in Article 17:6(i) of the Antidumping Agreement.

4. Quoted from Jackson, Davey, and Sykes, *Legal Problems of International Economic Relations*, p. 151.

5. C/M/159–62.

6. GATT 1947 document L/5776, p. 81. The report was not adopted.

7. DS32/R, circulated on 3 June 1993, p. 81.

8. Paras 158–59. The report was not adopted.

9. BISD 36S/268, adopted on 7 November 1989.

10. BISD 26S/279–89.

11. BISD 36S/302–03 (footnote omitted). Emphasis added.

12. *Proposal by Canada and the United States,* Multilateral Trade Negotiations, The Uruguay Round, Group of Negotiations on Goods (GATT), Negotiating Group on GATT Articles (MTN.GNG/NG7/W/72, 15 June 1990). Emphasis added. The first attempt to modify the procedures for the review of balance-of-payments measures was made by the United States in 1954. (See GATT document W.9/73.)

13. See para. 5.58 of the panel report.

14. In the panel proceedings on *Turkey—Textile Products,* Turkey claimed that India's complaint should be rejected because it had not been brought simultaneously against Turkey's customs union partner, the European Community. The panel found no legal basis supporting this claim but decided to seek factual and legal information from the EC pursuant to Article 13.2 of the DSU (WT/DS34/R, paras. 3.26, 4.1, and 9.3).

15. *Turkey—Restrictions on Imports of Textiles and Clothing Products* (WT/DS34/R).

16. Para. 6.133.

17. Paras. 9.48–9.52 (footnotes omitted).

18. *India—Quantitative Restrictions on Imports of Agricultural, Textile and Industrial Products* (WT/DS/90R), para. 5.58.

19. Para. 5.87 (footnote omitted).

20. Para. 5.70.

21. WT/DS90/AB/R, para. 18.

22. WT/DS8, 10, and 11/AB/R, p. 12.

23. Para. 93.

24. Para. 83.

25. Para. 102.

26. Para. 9.189.

27. Para. 57.

28. Para. 65.

29. Para. 58. Emphasis added. The Appellate Body's brief report does not address the panel's detailed demonstration that none of the recognized principles of interpretation could possibly justify the conclusion that Article XXIV:5 can give Members forming a customs union the right to impose restrictions on imports from third countries. Article XI does not oblige Members to impose quantitative restrictions and therefore can never constitute a legal obstacle to the formation of a customs union. Only Article I of GATT and the other most-favored-nation provisions of GATT can prevent the formation of a customs union in a legal sense because no customs union can be formed without measures contrary to these provisions. The Appellate Body's ruling implies that Article XXIV may justify quantitative restrictions during the formation of a customs union if there are practical obstacles to their removal.

30. Para. 60 (footnote omitted). In the Appellate Body proceedings on *India—Quan-*

titative Restrictions, India had referred to the several GATT panel reports and the report of the panel on *Turkey—Textile Products* as precedents supporting the conclusion that the balance-of-payments justification of import restrictions should not be reviewed by panels. The Appellate Body dismissed these precedents as irrelevant on the ground that the question before it was limited to that of the jurisdiction of panels with respect to balance-of-payments measures (para. 100). In the obiter dictum quoted earlier, however, the Appellate Body declares—without further explanation—that its ruling on the jurisdiction of panels regarding balance-of-payments measures is also relevant for determining their jurisdiction on regional trade agreements. In neither of its reports does the Appellate Body provide a rationale for its conclusion on the competence of panels to determine the overall consistency of regional trade agreements with Article XXIV.

31. Para. 93.

32. The distinction made by the Appellate Body is without legal consequence. Under Article XVI:4 of the WTO Agreement, Members must ensure the conformity of their domestic law with the provisions on balance-of-payments measures. Furthermore, Article XVI:3 of the WTO Agreement provides that the general requirement of Article XVI:4 overrides any conflicting requirement in the provisions of the agreements annexed to the WTO Agreement. Article XVI:3 and 4 make clear that laws, regulations, and administrative procedures on balance-of-payments measures—before they are effectively applied—could be subject to dispute settlement proceedings. The Appellate Body, contrary to its own jurisprudence, thus interpreted the terms of a heavily negotiated treaty provision in a manner that deprives them of any effect.

33. *Interpretation of the Greco-Turkish Agreement of December 1st, 1926*, PCIJ Rep. 1928, series B, no. 16, p. 20. See also the *Certain Expenses Case*, in which the Court concluded that each organ of the UN "must, in the first place at least, determine its own jurisdiction" (ICJ Rep. 1962, p. 168).

34. Para. 5.93.

35. Paras. 102 and 103.

36. WT/BOP/R32, pp. 11–15.

37. John H. Jackson, *World Trade and the Law of GATT* (Indianapolis: Bobbs-Merrill, 1969), p. 682.

38. See *Understanding Regarding Notification, Consultation, Dispute Settlement and Surveillance*, adopted 28 November 1979 (BISD 26S/210–18).

39. See Articles 6, 16, 17, and 22 of the DSU.

40. See Article 3:6 of the DSU.

41. The Ministerial Conference may decide that those WTO Members who have not accepted a particular amendment "shall be free to withdraw from the WTO or remain a Member with the consent of the Ministerial Conference" (Articles X:1 and 3 of the WTO Agreement). This diplomatically formulated grant of the power of expulsion existed under Article XXX:2 of GATT 1947 but was never used.

42. Article X:8 of the WTO Agreement.

43. Article XXV of GATT.

44. Article IX:2 of the WTO Agreement.

45. Article IX:3 and 4 of the WTO Agreement.

46. Jackson, *World Trade*, pp. 132–36.

47. Article IX:2 of the WTO Agreement.

COMMENT BY

William J. Davey

It is critical for the World Trade Organization to ensure a proper balance between its judicial and political organs, a matter that requires particular attention because of the relative strength of its dispute settlement mechanism. This balance is best achieved through means that do not call into question the role of WTO dispute settlement in ensuring the effective recognition and enforcement of WTO Members' rights and obligations. To the extent any imbalance exists or threatens to develop, the already existing powers of the political organs to control the judicial organs should be improved.

My comments on Frieder Roessler's chapter are organized in two parts. First, I discuss the two areas that he highlights: the exceptions for balance-of-payments measures and regional trading arrangements. It is my view that WTO Members did agree that disputes involving those exceptions could be submitted to the dispute settlement system. That basic decision made by Members should be accepted by panels and the Appellate Body. By doing so, they do not upset but reinforce the balance of rights and obligations in the WTO. Second, I consider ways in which the WTO's political organs control its judicial organs and whether changes are necessary in that regard.

Balance-of-Payments and Regional Trading Exceptions

The panel in the *India—Quantitative Restrictions* case carefully considered whether WTO dispute settlement panels should determine the justification of balance-of-payments restrictions in a specific case in the absence of decision on that issue by the WTO Committee on Balance-of-Payments Restrictions (BOP Committee). [1] In light of standard principles of treaty interpretation, the panel concluded that it should do so, and the Appellate Body upheld that decision.

The proper basis for interpreting treaty text is the ordinary meaning of the text. The specific WTO rules that deal with the issue of dispute settlement in cases arising under the GATT balance-of-payments and regional trading exceptions are similar and worded quite broadly. One text authorizes consideration under WTO dispute settlement procedures of *"any mat-*

ters arising from the application of restrictive import measures taken for balance-of-payments purposes" and the other authorizes consideration of "*any matters* arising from the application of those *provisions of Article XXIV* relating to customs unions [emphasis added]."[2] The ordinary meaning of the emphasized text (especially that referring to Article XXIV) clearly demonstrates that there is a broad grant of authority to dispute settlement panels to consider issues related to the underlying basis for invocation of the two exceptions.[3]

WTO rules were not intended to restrict the power of panels as compared to GATT practice. Although the 1989 panel on *Korea–Balance-of-Payments* took into account past action by the BOP Committee, it also made its own independent determination of Korea's balance-of-payments situation as of the time of the panel proceeding.[4] In addition, it explained how review by the committee and a dispute settlement panel were not mutually exclusive.[5]

More important, consideration in dispute settlement proceedings of such issues as the justification of balance-of-payments restrictions does not upset the political-judicial balance within the World Trade Organization. To the contrary, in the absence of the possibility of consideration of such issues by the dispute settlement system, there is a much greater possibility that the balance of WTO Members' rights and obligations will be unfairly and inappropriately tilted. Without the possibility of review in dispute settlement of the justification of balance-of-payments measures, the consensus decisionmaking practices of the WTO would mean that the Member applying those measures would have free rein to decide when and for how long to keep such measures in place, with no possibility of review.

Consider the case of India. It is not appropriate to equate what Roessler refers to as India's "procedural" right, a right to maintain balance-of-payments measures until it decides to remove them within a time period it sets, with the procedural right of the United States, a right to ask an independent three-person panel to consider the justification issue with the advice of the IMF and subject to appeal. Moreover, consideration of the justification of BOP measures is not done without any normative framework. The key issue under GATT Article XVIII:B is the adequacy of a Member's reserves. The IMF can, and did in the India case, opine on the adequacy of India's reserves by applying its normative standards.

Consideration of this issue in dispute settlement does not upset the political-judicial balance or the balance of Members' rights and obligations. Rather, it ensures that these balances are appropriately maintained in light of Members' procedural agreements (the Uruguay Round understandings) and substantive agreements on the justification issue.[6]

Generally, when considering the issue of balance within the WTO system, I think it is important that panels and the Appellate Body do not create rules that cause them to reject cases on *a priori* grounds. To do so risks upsetting the balance of rights and obligations. The fundamental purpose of the dispute settlement system is to provide security and predictability to the multilateral trading system. It cannot do that if certain obligations are viewed as too political to be reviewed in dispute settlement. It may well be that panels and the Appellate Body should defer to a Member's decision in a specific case (for example, where the justification issue is a close one), but that does not mean that the dispute settlement system should not consider the claims in the first instance.

Political Control of Judicial Action

Political control of judicial action in the WTO is a much broader issue than the precise role of panels in balance-of-payments and Article XXIV cases. Because of the wide array of WTO obligations, some of which are phrased in imprecise terms, some decisions of panels or the Appellate Body may be viewed as inappropriate by a significant number of WTO Members. In such a case, what can Members do to change the result?

Formally, Members can effectively change a judicial decision by amending the relevant treaty text on which it was based, adopting an interpretation of that text, or waiving in general or in specific cases the obligation resulting from the judicial decision.[7] As a practical matter, a substantive amendment would be nearly impossible, except perhaps in the context of the results of a global negotiation, since each WTO Member would have to accept formally the amendment before it would be bound. An interpretation could be adopted by a vote of 75 percent of the WTO membership, but the general WTO practice of consensus decisionmaking would probably mean that an interpretation could not be adopted unless the prevailing party in a dispute was willing to accept it. Although a waiver also requires a 75 percent vote, it might be easier to obtain for these reasons: (1) the waiver would not formally change the results of the dispute settlement system and (2) voting is possible in the case of a waiver since (a) waivers were the subject of voting in GATT and (b) the WTO General Council decision under which waivers are normally adopted does explicitly note the possibility of a Member asking for a vote (suggesting that such a request would not involve the opprobrium that such a request would normally entail).[8]

The foregoing possibilities may not be all that effective because of the consensus decisionmaking practice. To avoid that problem, it would be necessary to accept less than unanimity in certain cases by (1) changing WTO decisionmaking rules in general or (2) designing a procedure applicable only to proposals to modify dispute settlement decisions. The first option is unlikely. A procedure applicable only to proposals to modify dispute settlement decisions could be designed. But would it undermine the legitimacy of the dispute settlement system in general or lead to the politicizing of the system in specific cases? One possible way to reduce those risks would be to have a filtering body that would decide if the procedures would be applicable. While practicable, this would be equivalent to creating a super Appellate Body of sorts, and one may wonder if that is wise or necessary.

To date, it does not seem that WTO Members have had major problems with the substance of the decisions made by the Appellate Body. While the losing parties often complain, they are seldom joined by neutral Members. Indeed, given that panels and the Appellate Body are part of the WTO system (panels are typically composed of government officials, and the Appellate Body members are appointed for four-year terms by the WTO membership), they are unlikely to stray out of step with the general views prevailing in the system on the meaning of the substantive provisions. If they do, a waiver could correct the problem. The current means of political control over the judicial side are imperfect, but they may be sufficient.

Notes

1. Panel and Appellate Body Reports, *India—Quantitative Restrictions on Imports of Agricultural, Textile and Industrial Products*, WT/DS90/R and WT/DS90/AB/R, adopted September 22, 1999 by the DSB.

2. Understanding on Balance-of-Payments Provisions of GATT 1994, note 1; Understanding on the Interpretation of Article XXIV of GATT 1994, para. 12.

3. While it is true that a proposal to grant this authority in more explicit terms was not included in the understanding in the case of balance-of-payments measures, it is equally true that a proposal to limit this authority was not included in the case of Article XXIV. See MTN.TNC/W/125 (December 13, 1993), quoted in Theofanis Christoforou, "Multilateral Rules as a Constraint on Regional Rules: A Regional Perspective," in Paul Demaret,

Jean-François Bellis, and Gonzalo García Jiménez, eds., *Regionalism and Multilateralism after the Uruguay Round: Convergence, Divergence and Interaction* (Brussels: European Interuniversity Press, 1997), pp. 757, 764–65. However, given the clarity of the existing text, consideration of this ambiguous negotiating history is neither appropriate nor helpful under the standard rules for treaty interpretation.

4. Panel Report, *Republic of Korea—Restrictions on Imports of Beef,* adopted November 7, 1989, BISD 36/268, p. 304.

5. Ibid., pp. 302–03.

6. The same analysis applies to the Article XXIV issue with two caveats: (1) the issue of whether a regional trading agreement complies with Article XXIV is more complex than the question of reserve adequacy under the balance-of-payment rules and there is no international body to turn to for expert advice; and (2) the Appellate Body has suggested that panels should always first consider the compatibility of a regional trading agreement with the requirements of Article XXIV. Given the complexity of this issue, it would be preferable for panels to avoid it where possible. That was the approach taken by the *Turkey Textiles* panel, which did not rule that panels cannot consider the consistency of regional trading agreements with Article XXIV, only that they should leave that issue to the appropriate WTO committee to the extent possible.

7. WTO Agreement, Articles IX, X.

8. See WT/L/93 (November 25, 1995).

J. H. H. WEILER

14 | The Rule of Lawyers and the Ethos of Diplomats: Reflections on WTO Dispute Settlement

No other area of the World Trade Organization (WTO) has received more attention than its dispute settlement procedures, arguably the most important systemic outcome of the Uruguay Round. This is not surprising from the perspective of the WTO itself. The Dispute Settlement Understanding (DSU) was, it is argued, part of a Marrakech "historical deal" fundamental to the outcome of the Uruguay Round. Moreover, the provisions for multilateral dispute resolution are horizontal in nature, extending to all dimensions of the covered agreements. It is not surprising, too, from the perspective of the academic community of WTO watchers: everyone interested in the WTO supposedly is a specialist on dispute settlement. This includes the sprinkling of political scientists who have come to appreciate the profound importance of the WTO, the many economists and political economists who have appreciated it for years, and the rapidly growing number of trade lawyers. The five-year official review of the process, one of the many casualties of Seattle, brought all this attention into sharp focus.[1]

Much of the reflection on dispute settlement has focused on the "juridification" of the WTO.[2] It has been pointed out *ad nauseam* that third-party dispute resolution under the General Agreement on Tariffs and Trade (GATT) required the consent of the disputants to begin the process

My thanks to Sungjoon Cho for his research assistance.

and to accept its results. These two features compromised foundational principles of the rule of law and chilled the utility of dispute resolution, especially for the economically and politically unequal. Imagine a domestic legal dispute under municipal law in which the defending party must give its consent not only to "go to law" but also to accept the results of the legal process: heads I win, tails you lose.

Inevitably, the legal paradigm shift in the WTO occasioned by the acceptance of compulsory adjudication with binding outcomes has attracted the most comment—and with good empirical justification. Measured in quantitative terms, activity under the new DSU by panels and by the Appellate Body can be described as frenetic.[3] Equally inevitably, WTO dispute settlement in general and the Appellate Body and its jurisprudence in particular are taking their rightful place alongside other major transnational and international courts.[4]

The issue of legitimacy has become an essential part of the field. This chapter is meant as a footnote to the theme of legitimacy explored by Robert Hudec, Robert Howse, and others.[5] My interest is primarily in the *internal* organizational features of dispute settlement and their impact on the grander *external* contexts. By internal I refer to the world of the WTO and its principal institutional actors: the delegates and delegations, the Secretariat, the panels, and even the Appellate Body, among others. By external I refer to the universe outside the formal WTO: the real world of states and their constitutional organs (such as parliaments, governments, and courts) as well as the world of multinational corporations, nongovernmental organizations (NGOs), the media, and citizens.

My thesis has two intertwined threads and may be stated simply. First, I suggest the existence of an asynchronous development in the transition from the GATT to the WTO. Despite the undisputed and much vaunted shift in legal paradigm of WTO dispute settlement, a considerable lag has occurred in the internal appreciation and internalization of the new architecture, a lag reflected in the attitude of the delegates, the Secretariat, and other internal players as well as in many of the dispute settlement practices and procedures. The diplomatic ethos that developed in the context of the old GATT dispute settlement tenaciously persists despite the transformed and juridified WTO.

Second, one explanation for the lag, alongside personal and institutional inertia, is the need for internal legitimation of the new dispute settlement of the WTO. The persistent diplomatic ethos and the accompanying practices that support it are reassuring to the internal players and make the

legal revolution more palatable and easily digested. In some ways they cam-
ouflage the extent of the legal revolution. And yet this internal legitimation
is bought at a high price. It accounts for some dysfunctions of dispute settlement and undermines the external legitimation of the very same process.

Whether the shift in legal paradigm represents a victory for the rule
of law or merely a victory for the rule of lawyers is a serious matter on
which the jury is still out. Some thoughtful actors and observers wonder
whether the historical deal has truly advanced the deeper objectives of the
WTO, such as establishing stability and "peaceful economic relations."
But for now, and for the foreseeable future, the paradigm has shifted.
Therefore the persistence of diplomatic practices and habits in the context
of a juridical framework could undermine the very rule of law and some
of the benefits that the new Dispute Settlement Understanding was meant
to produce.

The Heritage and Ethos of Diplomacy

There is, of course, some measure of hyperbole in talking of a paradigm
shift in the WTO dispute resolution. Too quickly dismissed as "nonjuridi-
cal," the "old" dispute resolution process did result in more than a trickle of
panel decisions, all of which were written in "legalese." At least to some degree, they did what legal third-party dispute resolution is supposed to do:
ascertain facts, interpret a treaty (GATT), and apply the law as interpreted
to a dispute. This was done in very much the same manner as it is done
today under the new procedures.[6] Notwithstanding the need for positive
consensus of the losing party, most panel reports were adopted. And despite
the absence of an orderly regime of sanctions, most adopted reports were,
in fact, complied with.[7]

It is appropriate to think of the old dispute settlement process as
diplomacy through other means.[8] The following features justify such a characterization.

The Internal Nature of Disputes

A dominant feature of GATT was its self-referential and even communitarian ethos explicable in constructivist terms.[9] GATT successfully managed relative insulation from the "outside" world of international relations,
and it established among its practitioners a closely knit environment re-

volving around shared normative values (of free trade) and shared institutional ambitions. GATT operatives became a classical "network" of first-name contacts and friendly relationships. This phenomenon was a result of several factors: the relatively restricted and homogeneous membership of GATT, which eliminated much of the cold war tensions; the marginalization within national administrations of trade diplomats (considered a second-rate diplomatic career, often disdained by ministries of foreign affairs and left to the "lowlier" trade ministries); the supposedly technical and professional nature of the subject matter; and the consequent media indifference.[10] Within this ethos there was an institutional goal—preventing trade disputes from spilling into the wider circles of international relations. A trade dispute was an "internal" affair that needed to be resolved as quickly and smoothly as possible within the organization.[11]

The Discrete Nature of Disputes

Disputes might have raised broad systemic issues of relevance far beyond the immediate parties. The process, however, tended to treat disputes as discrete eruptions between members requiring "settlement." This would be attempted in the pre-panel stage, but even if the overt diplomacy failed, empanelment was a continuation of diplomacy by other means. A prime objective in selecting panelists was to find persons acceptable to the parties and most suitable to resolving the specific dispute. Very often they were diplomats or ex-diplomats belonging to the same internal WTO network. To be sure, some panels, like *Italian Tractors,* were potentially of huge systemic significance.[12] But, arguably, these were more the exception than the rule.

The Intergovernmental Nature of Disputes

Disputes were perceived as discrete problems between governments. The implications of GATT rules generally and the outcome of dispute resolution specifically to nongovernmental constituencies were only dimly perceived.

There are two principal explanations for this. The first is the classical "government is the state" fallacy. International law and international organizations condition a belief in equating the state with its government. It would be hard to conduct international relations and engage in international legal obligations without such an equation. Therefore, to regard

GATT disputes in this way would be almost natural. Second, until perhaps the tuna-dolphin disputes, GATT practitioners failed to understand the deep social and political domestic consequences of the regime of which they were custodians. They missed the implications for constituencies beyond governments in general and trade ministries in particular. They should, perhaps, be forgiven since these constituencies often lived in the same blissful ignorance.

The Confidential Nature of Disputes

This happy state of mutual ignorance was in part the result of the diplomatic ethos of confidentiality. Confidentiality is the hallmark of diplomacy. It often is a critical ingredient in "getting to yes" in delicate negotiations.[13] In GATT dispute resolution there was a double level of confidentiality. Once a panel was established, only a narrow range of actors, even within the GATT, were privy to the proceedings. At its conclusion, the outside world was treated to a perfunctory account. Panel reports for many years were hard to come by in a timely fashion except for a privileged few. The secrecy surrounding the dispute resolution process is one of the clearest indications of its perception as diplomacy through other means.

Jurisprudence and Jurists' Prudence

The compliance pull of the old GATT was impressive, given its voluntary nature. In talking to panelists of that era one gets the impression, difficult to prove empirically, of an ethos that favored 5:4 outcomes rather than 9:0 decisions. Crafting outcomes that would command the consent of both parties and thus be adopted was the principal task of the panelists. Custodianship over GATT law was far from the minds and the ability of many panelists. The drafting of reports was left in the hands of the Secretariat. The law played an important constraining role, but it was construed in a context that put a premium on settlement and acceptability. The tuned process often combined the diplomatic skill of the panel with the legal expertise of the Secretariat. Most panel reports are written in the reporting style of the third party: "the panel considered," or "the panel deliberated." The writer was typically the legal secretary to the panel, himself or herself a member of the Secretariat reporting to his or her supervisor. Often the legal deliberation had taken place between the legal secretary and other members of the Secretariat and not, in any meaningful sense, within the panel.[14]

The Paradigm Shift: The Rule of Lawyers and the Culture of Law

With all the attention given to the shift to compulsory adjudication, binding outcomes, and the creation of the Appellate Body, there is one dimension that is insufficiently articulated and understood.[15] Juridification is a package deal. It includes the rule of law and the rule of lawyers. It does not affect only the power relations between members, the compliance pull of the agreements, the ability to settle disputes definitively, and the prospect of authoritative interpretations of opaque provisions. It imports the norms, practices, and habits—some noble, some self-serving, some helpful, some disastrous, some with a concern for justice, some arcane and procedural— of legal culture. It would be nice if one could take the rule of law without the rule of lawyers. But with one, you get the other. The WTO moved to the rule of law without realizing that the accompanying legal culture is as integral as the compliance and enforcement dimensions of the DSU shift.

Juridification means that practicing lawyers will be involved early in all stages of dispute management. In many states lawyers will be responsible for dispute management—a trend that will grow with juridification. Ministries of trade worldwide are scurrying to beef up their legal departments. The WTO itself is in the business of providing legal services to poor members.[16] Much of legal culture is at odds with the ethos of diplomacy. Here is a partial inventory. First, disputes that go to adjudication are not settled; they are won and lost. The headlines talk of "victory" and "defeat" (a typical newspaper headline declares that the United States or the European Union "went down to defeat in a ruling by . . .").

Second, law is meant to be a dispassionate discipline of rigorous and objective analysis. It is at times, but not when two parties believe the law is on their side and decide to litigate. Then law becomes a profession of passion and rhetoric. Even the most reserved and self-controlled practitioners desire to win strong. There are less than a handful of cases in the history of the WTO where a compromise was found and a dispute settled once a panel started its work. At that point the parties, led by legal teams, go for the jugular.

Third, law is practiced by men and women who are like all other professionals: they are people with ambition, searching for job satisfaction. The international relations expert will explain that the new DSU makes legal resolution more attractive to members because it can, for example, equalize egregious disparities of power that exist at the negotiation table.[17] At the negotiating table, Venezuela is Venezuela and the United States is the United States. The name of the game is power. At the Bar of Law it is an altogether different paradigm, or at least is meant to be so. All are meant to be equal. A huge factor in the decision whether to go for legal resolution will have been the conscious and often subconscious input of lawyers driven by ambition and their particular professional deformations. "We can win in court" becomes in the hands of many lawyers an almost automatic trigger to "we should bring the case." Surgeons like to operate. Lawyers like to litigate and win cases.

Fourth, juridification involves an empowerment of lawyers both within the WTO itself and within the members. It is salutary for the rule of law when politicians, even of powerful states, are forced to ask their lawyers "is it legal?" before they embark on a course of action.[18] Empowering lawyers makes them much more central and consequently explains the infusion of legal culture into WTO discourse.

Fifth, the Appellate Body was put in place to give states an additional guarantee of review and revision; states had given up their veto power over adoption of panel reports. The very existence of the Appellate Body reflects a shift in organizational legal culture. The Appellate Body in style, content, and self-understanding is a high court. It reviews panel reports in precisely the same way that higher courts review first-instance decisions in a municipal legal system. That is how it should be. And there is an inevitable spillover into the style, content, and self-understanding of the panels. Underlying the pre-WTO ethos of panels was, consciously and subconsciously, the 5-4 ethos: crafting an opinion consistent with the legal advice given by the Secretariat but, at the same time, an opinion that would settle the dispute by being adopted by both parties. The gasoline decision of the Appellate Body, the first it rendered, sent a sharp notice to panels and the WTO Secretariat, a notice that has become a permanent feature of the Appellate Body's jurisprudence. Though the Appellate Body approved most aspects of the panel report (and this has been the case in most instances), it was sharply critical of the legal reasoning of the panel on many of the points. The message was clear: this is a legal process; here the law rules. The new ethos, conscious and subconscious, underlying the panel process is no longer the 5-4 mentality. It is "getting it (legally) right" or "making it appeal proof."[19]

Finally, I note the inevitable changes in the DSU process brought about by jurisprudence. For example, the ruling in *Banana III* allowed member states to employ private lawyers in their litigation, and the *Turtle-Shrimp* and *Asbestos* cases opened up the process to *amici* briefs.[20] Both decisions (on legal representation and *amici*) offended some of the diplomatic reflexes described earlier. They contradicted many delegations' perceptions of disputes as internal, discrete, and intergovernmental. Yet in both decisions the Appellate Body was doing no more than most conservative and prudent courts would do to ensure the integrity and fairness of legal process.

This last point, trivial as it may appear, encapsulates a crucial element of my thesis. The paradigm shift introduced by compulsory adjudication, binding outcomes, and the establishment of an Appellate Body does not only occasion an important shift in legal culture (an "is" statement) but must (an "ought" statement) be so accompanied. There are important normative elements associated with legal process on which its legitimacy depends. Some are rooted in legal principles such as the principles of natural justice—*nemo judex in propria causa* and *audi alteram partem*.[21] Fairness and openness are other legal principles. Sound legal reasoning, coherence, consistency, and communicativeness may not be strict legal principles, but they are indispensable to legitimate legal process.

Lawyers and Diplomats: The Dissonance

And yet, the transition from diplomacy to law has not been easy. In some of the features of the current system dissonance persists. The dissonance is almost inevitable, and its correction, where such correction is needed, will not be painless or without cost. In some cases a zero-sum game exists between internal and external legitimacy.

Nomenclature

Words, language, and rhetoric often signify cultural values, a certain mind-set, and aspirations. They can mask a discomforting reality and often a slide into self-deception. Here are two examples from the world of sport. Americans conduct each year a sporting event, the World Series. Teams of only two North American states participate. In this appellation we have everything: a culture and a mind-set that consider what lies between the Atlantic and the Pacific as "the world;" a mask over the discomforting reality that in this all-American sport, baseball, other nations, such as Cuba and Japan, have achieved an excellence that equals and perhaps surpasses the originators'. No commentary is needed for our continued use of the words "Olympic Games" to describe an event plagued by organizational corruption, by a willful conversion supported by its promoters to the ethos of profit, and by the addiction of its participants to celebrity and corporate sponsorship. The Olympics have lost any vestige of the innocence conveyed by the word "game," but it suits us to pretend otherwise.

Consider the nomenclature "dispute settlement" (rather than judicial process) and "Appellate Body" (rather than High Trade Court, or something similar). The WTO sticks tenaciously to these terms. As noted earlier, many delegations viewed the Appellate Body as a super panel that would give a losing party another bite at the cherry, given that the losing party could no longer block adoption of the panel. The delegations did not fully understand the judicial nature, let alone constitutional nature, of the Appellate Body.[22] And yet the Appellate Body is a court in all but name. It even has a constitutional dimension. De jure, the DSU leaves the final interpretation of the agreements in the hands of the General Council and the Ministerial Conference.[23] De facto, unless the WTO is to break the hallowed principle of consensus, that power has shifted to the Appellate Body. The circumstances would have to be utterly unique to envisage a consensus in the General Council or the Ministerial Conference to overturn an interpretation or decision of the Appellate Body. In interviews many delegations told me, with some incredulity, "We have created a court."

They are right. That is what the Appellate Body is. The nomenclature is convenient for some domestic constituencies, notably the U.S. Congress. There is a long tradition among some members of Congress to abhor all manner of "world courts." Yet the failure to call a court a court diminishes the external legitimacy of the WTO in general and the Appellate Body more specifically. It feeds the Gnomes-of-Geneva syndrome. The accusation that important issues of world and domestic sociopolitical and economic policy are being decided by "faceless" bureaucrats reflects this syndrome. "Appellate Body" is almost as bureaucratic (and internally comforting) a term as "panel." But the appellation robs the institution of the authority and respect that its decisions would have if its name matched its real function. My preference would be for an official name—the International Court of Economic Justice—and a diminutive—the World Trade Court.

The Panel System: Composition and Selection

Very little has changed at the panel level in the World Trade Organization's administration of justice. The Secretariat still has the key role in selecting panelists. In terms of the profile of panelists, the rosters have changed only slightly, and the profile of panels has changed only moderately to reflect the new culture of juridification. Panels are still ad hoc and transient, with no coordination among them. Keeping all the old features masks the importance of the change that has taken place, thus increasing internal legitimacy and making the transition smoother. Even if the context in which the panels now operate has changed radically, the same method, the same cast of characters, and the same modus operandi have been comfortingly kept intact.

The ad hoc, individualistic selection of panelists and the isolated manner in which they operated were consistent with an era when the prime task was to resolve discrete disputes. Today, however, panel decisions are part of a broad normative matrix involving delicate socioeconomic issues. Outcomes are relevant far beyond the specific parties to the dispute. The old system simply will not do.

There must be more continuity and continuous contact among panelists so an institutional identity can emerge and a common ethos can develop. This does not necessarily mean the creation of a permanent First Instance in Geneva. (In my view, however, this would be desirable.) But it could mean a more stable and limited roster, such as suggested by the European Union, greater automaticity of selection, and a reconsideration of the nationality exclusion rule that prevents the selection of the most qualified persons for many of the disputes involving the major players.

The profile of the ideal individual panelist, or the ideal panel, given the new reality of WTO dispute resolution, is not reflected in the current roster nor in the selection and composition of panels. The professional backgrounds of panelists should be commensurate with the gravity and profundity of the issues decided in a globalized world. This has conspicuously not been the case in some of the most important instances. "Who decides" is an important element in the paradigm of legitimacy. Instead, internal legitimacy is bought at the expense of external legitimacy.

Secrecy

The secrecy of the procedures is a throwback to the diplomatic phase of GATT development. There is still a place for secrecy in the consultation phases leading up to the establishment of the panels. There is no place for it once a panel is established. The disclosure of confidential commercial information or secret state documents is a problem that domestic courts also face, and there are many solutions to it. Secrecy is inconsistent with the principles of open government and the transparency of legal proceedings. It also is inconsistent with the significant issues now under dispute. The panels and the Appellate Body fulfill the same functions and cover the same issues that national courts and the European Court of Justice fulfill in the European Union. It is only because WTO discourse has been dominated by civil servants to whom confidentiality and secrecy are second nature that this practice has continued to prevail.

NGOs and Amici Briefs

The issue of nongovernmental organizations and *amici* briefs is a delicate one. It involves a clash of legal cultures: North America versus the rest of the world.[24] Wholesale opening of the WTO to nongovernmental organizations (most of which would be Western) could skew the system considerably. Of course, the system is already skewed in all kinds of directions, principally by unequal access of private actors (notably multinationals) to governments.[25]

But there is more to this debate than East and West, North and South. It also embodies the tension between diplomatic ethos and legal culture. For the diplomats, the WTO historically has been "their" organization and allowing in NGOs will inhibit it from achieving its goals and will compromise its integrity.[26] The diplomatic ethos views with horror any attempt by the WTO to question the legitimacy of formal governmental positions. But for lawyers, and particularly judges, the notion of excluding voices affected by one's decision and not hearing arguments by them runs counter not only to the ethic of open and public process but to the principles of natural justice.

The modus operandi established by the Appellate Body seems a perfect example of the interplay between external and internal legitimacy. Allowing *amici* briefs in principle (external legitimacy) will be counterbalanced, at least at first, by a prudence and conservatism in implementing the principle (internal legitimacy). Go too far in one direction, and the Appellate Body will find itself under severe internal challenge. Go too far in the other direction, and it will not only become a target of outside attacks but will open itself to attack for bowing to political pressure. One should allow a reasonable amount of time to pass before judgment is made as to the success of the "World Trade Court" in finding the appropriate balance.

Politicians' (typically short-lived) legitimacy often depends on outputs (results). Political institutions' legitimacy, of a more enduring nature, depends on inputs (process). The legitimacy of courts that is meant to transcend specific results depends on the integrity of process and on the quality of their reasoning. To reject, with no explanation, applications to submit *amici* briefs is a privilege of emperors, not of courts. The legitimacy of courts rests in part on their capacity to listen to the parties, to deliberate impartially, and to motivate and explain their decisions.

The Role of the Secretariat

Juridification has put the Secretariat in an impossible position. De jure, they are not players but facilitate the play of others. That, of course, is comforting nonsense. In dispute settlement, the Secretariat is the purveyor of objective legal advice and legal services to panels. De facto, they are the repository of institutional memory, of horizontal and temporal coherence, of long-term hermeneutic strategy—all the things that the panel system, as a first-instance judicial tier, should be, but is unable to be. The Secretariat has, and should have, a point of view on the best legal outcome of the dispute. Supposedly the notion of providing "objective legal advice" should protect them from partisanship and the appearance of partisanship. But only nonlawyers with a primitive understanding of hermeneutics and legal process can believe that.[27]

The result is schizophrenia in the Secretariat concerning its role in the settlement of disputes. The views of the Secretariat as to the proper outcome of a dispute are consciously and subconsciously pushed upon the panel. The ability of panels to be aware of this and to resist it varies considerably. Many panelists have told me that they feel they cannot meaningfully challenge the legal secretary on points of law. This reticence may not have been so critical in the GATT phase of dispute settlement. But when the law controls as much as it does today, this shifts even more power from the panel to the Secretariat. This is no secret, and the only novelty, if any, is putting it on paper so explicitly.[28] The Secretariat and the legal secretary to the panel have a point of view concerning the best outcome of the process. On the "micro" panel level, the relationship between panels and legal secretary is skewed in terms of command of the law; the relationship also is neither transparent nor healthy for a judicial system. The legal secretary reports to his or her supervisor. The primary loyalty of the legal secretary is not to the judges. The career of the legal secretary does not depend on the views of the panel. Indeed, panelists are never officially asked to report back on the legal secretary. The directors of the Secretariat will have no idea about the working relationship or the satisfaction or dissatisfaction of the panel with the legal secretary. Generally speaking, this schizophrenic situation is an invidious position to be put in, and many of the young, highly competent and skilled lawyers who fill this essential job do not know how to find the correct balance.

Organizationally, at the "macro" level, the process is equally unhealthy. The Secretariat gives legal advice that inevitably favors one of the parties. This advice has huge influence over panelists (in the selection of which the Secretariat plays a key role). Would it not be better to allow the Secretariat to present its legal opinion to the panel (and the Appellate Body) in each case, so that the opinion can be evaluated and given the weight it deserves by the panels and the Appellate Body and contested by the member disfavored by this advice? Would the panels and the Appellate Body not profit from having this advice by the Secretariat openly and transparently challenged? The relationship between the legal secretary and the panel could be simplified and redefined to become something less complicated and more akin to a clerk. The diplomatic ethos abhors the notion of the Secretariat "taking sides" in any dispute. But consider the following. The Commission of the European Union is meant to play a nonpartisan role in EU politics. And yet this principle of nonpartisanship is not considered compromised by its practice of submitting a brief with its position in every dispute that goes before the European Court of Justice. To be sure, the Secretariat of the WTO is not the Commission of the European Union and should not become one. But would its neutrality be compromised if its legal service would do openly what it now does surreptitiously? The Secretariat has an important role to play in the dispute settlement process. It is time to make that role open, transparent, and respectable.

The Appellate Body

On the whole, the legitimation strategy of the Appellate Body has been hermeneutic prudence and institutional modesty with a keen eye on balancing internal and external legitimacy.[29] On one issue, however, the Appellate Body has not fully understood the implications of the shift in legal paradigm. In its decisions (sometimes gratuitously scathing of panel decisions) and in the organization of its work, it has not grasped this: it is to be the custodian of the judicial element of dispute settlement, and it has an institutional responsibility toward the panels. The Appellate Body should socialize, institutionalize, and valorize the work of panels, pending a more profound overhaul by the members of the WTO. This can be done in the Appellate Body's reports and in many discrete actions within the WTO. Here, too, there is a lesson to be learned from the European Court of Justice. The ECJ understood early on how critical it was to develop a productive relationship with national courts. One way it did this was to embark on an ambitious program to meet as many national judges as it could and to instill in the national judges a partnership in ensuring the rule of law within the European Union. The task of the Appellate Body in this respect is to make the panelists feel that they are part of the judicial branch of the WTO and share the same ethos and set of values—the pursuit of justice within the oft-elusive rule of law.

Notes

1. See World Trade Organization, "Decision on the Application and Review of the Understanding on Rules and Procedures Governing the Settlement of Disputes, April 15, 1994, Ministerial Decisions and Declarations," in "Marrakech Agreement Establishing the World Trade Organization, 15 April 1994, Final Act Embodying the Results of the Uruguay Round of Multilateral Trade Negotitations," in *Legal Instruments—Results of the Uruguay Round,* vol. 33, *International Legal Materials* (1994), p. 1259.

2. See Arie Reich, "From Diplomacy to Law: The Juridicization of International Trade Relations," *Northwestern Journal of International Law and Business,* vol. 17 (1996–97), p. 776.

3. According to Hudec and others, 207 complaints were filed under the GATT 1947 framework from 1948 to 1989. Robert E. Hudec and others, "A Statistical Profile of GATT Dispute Settlement Cases: 1948–1989," *Minnesota Journal of Global Trade,* vol. 2 (1993), p. 4. Under the new WTO system, in the first five years alone (from January 1995 to November 2000) 210 complaints were notified to the WTO. See WTO, "Dispute Settlement: Overview of the State-of-Play of WTO Disputes" (www.wto.org/english/tratop_e/dispu_e/dispu_e.htm).

4. See, for example, Andrea Kupfer Schneider, "Getting Along: The Evolution of Dispute Resolution Regimes in International Trade Organizations," *Michigan Journal of International Law,* vol. 20 (1999), p. 697; Alec Stone Sweet, "Judicialization and the Construction of Governance," *Comparative Political Studies,* vol. 31 (1999).

5. See, for example, Robert E. Hudec, *Essays on the Nature of International Trade Law* (London: Cameron May, 1999), chap. 2; Robert Howse, "Adjudicative Legitimacy and Treaty Interpretation in International Trade Law: The Early Years of WTO Jurisprudence," in Joseph H. H. Weiler, ed., *The EU, the WTO, and the NAFTA: Towards a Common Law of International Trade* (Oxford University Press, 2000), p. 35; and Ernst-Ulrich Petersmann, "Constitutionalism and International Organizations," *Northwestern Journal of International Law and Business,* vol. 17 (1996–97), p. 398.

6. Indeed, during the mid-1950s, the GATT dispute settlement system underwent its first dramatic shift to juridification. No longer was a dispute referred to a "working party" composed of governmental representatives; it was referred instead to a "panel" of trade experts who acted on their own and not on behalf of certain governments. This development heralded a shift from a "negotiating" atmosphere to a more "judicial" procedure. See John H. Jackson, *The World Trading System,* 2d ed. (MIT Press, 1997), pp. 115–16.

7. See Hudec and others, "A Statistical Profile," pp. 7–8.

8. See Robert E. Hudec, "The GATT Legal System: A Diplomat's Jurisprudence," *Journal of World Trade Law,* vol. 4 (1970), pp. 615–16; Reich, "From Diplomacy to Law."

9. For a general understanding of constructivism and its application in different contexts, see Friedrich Kratochwil, *Rules, Norms, and Decisions: On the Conditions of Practical and Legal Reasoning in International Relations and Domestic Affairs* (Cambridge University Press, 1989); Alexander Wendt, "Collective Identity Formation and the International State," *American Political Science Review,* vol. 88 (1994), p. 384; Peter J. Katzenstein, ed., *The Culture of National Security: Norms and Identity in World Politics* (Columbia University Press, 1995); Martha Finnemore, *National Interest in International Society* (Cornell University Press, 1996).

10. A change in all of these factors contributed to the political problems now facing the WTO. Membership is far larger and more heterogeneous; there are much deeper divisions and tensions between North and South, East and West, Europe and the United States; maintaining the previous clubiness has become far more difficult.

11. There were exceptions to this, and some disputes became visible beyond the GATT horizon. Examples include the 1962 Uruguayan claim against all developed countries, the so-called Chicken War of the 1960s, and the U.S.-EC Domestic International Sales Corporation cases.

12. "Italian Discrimination against Imported Agricultural Machinery," panel report adopted on October 23, 1958, *GATT Basic Instruments and Selected Documents,* 7th supp. (1958), p. 60.

13. "Good faith negotiation does not require total disclosure. Perhaps the best answer to a question such as 'What is the most you would pay if you had to?' would be along the following lines: 'Let's not put ourselves under such a strong temptation to mislead. If you think no agreement is possible, and that we may be wasting our time, perhaps we could disclose our thinking to some trustworthy third party, who can then tell us whether there is a zone of potential agreement.' In this way it is possible to behave with full candor about information that is not being disclosed." Roger Fisher, William Ury, and Bruce Patton, eds., *Getting to Yes: Negotiating Agreement without Giving In* (Penguin, 1983), p. 134. See also A. Abba Eban, *Diplomacy for the Next Century* (Yale University Press, 1998), p. 78.

14. The title of this section comes from Ted L. Stein, "Jurisprudence and Jurists' Prudence: The Iranian-Forum Clause Decisions of the Iran-U.S. Claims Tribunal," *American Journal of International Law,* vol. 78 (1984), p. 1.

15. See John H. Jackson, *The World Trade Organization: Constitution and Jurisprudence* (London: Royal Institute of International Affairs, 1998), pp. 98–99. "[O]ne can detect a pretty strong rule-oriented approach," he writes. "The appeal case reports so far read much more like a judicial opinion of a national court than did some of the much earlier GATT cases. . . . Similarly, the participating governments are finding that the process requires

them to be much more 'legalistic' in their advocacy, to the extent of feeling the need to seek non-government expertise to assist them in cases."

16. See, for example, Trade and Development Center, "Establishing the Advisory Center on WTO Law" (www.itd.org/links/acwladvis.htm); WTO, "Dispute Settlement," art. 27, para. 2.

17. The threat of legal resolution, however, should have a similar effect. Recourse to legal resolution or adjudication eliminates, to a large degree, room for political maneuvering by big powerful states. Because a neutral third party hears and judges on a dispute, even big powerful states have the risk of losing the case in the tribunal. When relevant case law for a specific dispute favors a small state, the small state enjoys higher leverage at the negotiating table than the big one by using the threat of legal resolution. The existence of jurisprudence leads the big one to realize that it will eventually lose the case if the dispute ends up in the courtroom.

18. Or, at a minimum, politicians will ask their lawyers what the legal costs will be if their policy violates the WTO law. The legal costs include, *inter alia,* the monetary loss in terms of withdrawal of concessions. In the aftermath of *Banana III,* the arbitrators found that the level of nullification and impairment suffered by Ecuador amounted to U.S.$201.6 million a year. In the aftermath of *Hormones,* the arbitrators determined the level of nullification suffered by the United States to be equal to U.S.$116.8 million. See WTO, "Dispute Settlement."

19. One detects, too, a new approach in some panel reports. Given that there is a review instance, some panels, instead of adopting the "appeal-proof" approach, may be ready to "push the envelope" more than they might have dared without an appeal process. Once a good dialogue has been established between panels and the Appellate Body, this might not be a bad development: the panels—responsibly, judiciously, and within the province of legitimate hermeneutics—becoming the experimenters and the Appellate Body supervising uncalled for judicial innovation.

20. See *Banana III* case and "United States—Import Prohibition of Certain Shrimp and Shrimp Products," Appellate Body report adopted on November 6, 1998, WT/DS58/AB/R, pt. 5, "Panel Proceedings and Nonrequested Information."

21. No person can judge a case in which he or she is a party. All parties must be heard.

22. I use "constitutional" with a small *c* to connote a court interpreting the constituent document.

23. The definite or authoritative interpretation of a specific treaty provision, which involves rights and obligations of member states and is tantamount to amending the treaty, is in the hands of the General Council. See WTO, "Decision on the Application and Review of the Understanding on Rules and Procedures Governing the Settlement of Disputes, April 15, 1994," art. IX, para. 2: "The Ministerial Conference and the General Council shall have the exclusive authority to adopt interpretations of this Agreement and of the Multilateral Trade Agreements." See also WTO, "Understanding on Rules and Procedures Governing the Settlement of Disputes," art. 3, para. 2: "Recommendations and rulings of the DSB cannot add to or diminish the rights and obligations provided in the covered agreements." Para. 9 states: "The provisions of this Understanding are without prejudice to the rights of Members to seek authoritative interpretation of provisions of a covered agreement through decision-making under the WTO Agreement or a covered agreement which is a Plurilateral Trade Agreement."

24. Many scholars advocate openness and transparency in the WTO dispute settlement system. See, for example, Steve Charnovitz, "Participation of Nongovernmental Organizations in the World Trade Organization," *University of Pennsylvania Journal of International Economic Law*, vol. 17 (1996), p. 331; Daniel C. Esty, "Linkages and Governance: NGOs at the World Trade Organization," *University of Pennsylvania Journal of International Economic Law*, vol. 19 (1998), p. 709.

25. Philip M. Nichols, "Extension of Standing in World Trade Organization Disputes to Nongovernment Parties," *University of Pennsylvania Journal of International Economic Law*, vol. 17 (1996), p. 295.

26. See Philip M. Nichols, "Realism, Liberalism, Values, and the World Trade Organization," *University of Pennsylvania Journal of International Economic Law*, vol. 17 (1996), p. 851.

27. This is not meant to imply bad faith. Objectivity in areas of high legal indeterminacy and judicial discretion is a complicated matter. In legal disputes the lawyers on both sides claim to present objective legal arguments and yet they disagree.

28. The situation is different in most other judicial settings. Legal clerks to judges in international tribunals, even if on the "organigram" of the tribunal, are appointed by, work permanently with, and are answerable to "their" judge. In other panel situations, such as the North American Free Trade Agreement and other free trade agreements, professional support staff are appointed ad hoc to assist the panelists. In this respect the WTO practice is more the exception than the rule. I say this with no prejudice either to the integrity or the extraordinary competence of legal secretaries in the Secretariat and in the Appellate Body.

29. See Howse, "Adjudicative Legitimacy."

JOEL P. TRACHTMAN

Part Four Summary

L egitimacy, efficiency, and equity are related concepts. I begin with an analysis of the terms *constitu-*
tionalization, subsidiarity, and *legitimacy* and then seek to link ideas about
legitimacy, the focus of part four, to concerns regarding efficiency and
equity.

Analysis: Constitutionalization, Subsidiarity, and Legitimacy

Constitutionalization is sometimes used to refer to the development of
a constitution of a national state, like the United States. No one suggests
that the WTO will ever be constitutionalized in this sense. But all organizations have a constitution of some sort—a set of rules by which they are
constituted. Constitutionalization as it applies to governmental, intergovernmental, or international organizations has the following components:

—*Basic law, rule of recognition, or* grundnorm. This feature anticipates
the making of further rules, which will be recognized according to some
underlying rule.

—*Horizontal allocation of power.* Within any governmental organization there are usually various centers or branches delegated different com-

I thank Marc Busch and Bob Hudec for their thoughtful comments.

ponents of power. In national governments we often think of executive, legislative, and judicial branches. Frieder Roessler's chapter suggests an a priori concern for balance among branches. Sometimes these horizontal allocations of power represent particular constituencies. Thus the Council of the European Communities contains representatives of the member states, while its Parliament represents its people.[1]

—*Vertical allocation of power.* In any multilevel organization, like a federal government, there will be vertically allocated authority. When we speak of the legitimacy of the WTO, we focus on its power vis-à-vis its member states in comparative or relative terms.

—*Vertical supremacy.* This issue, a component of vertical allocation of power, raises the question of whether WTO law is supreme over the law of member states. The answer depends on the forum in which the conflicting norms are considered. An essential feature of all international law is that it is supreme over national law, at least in international courts. Within domestic courts, treatment as supreme may vary, and more subtle devices like the U.S. "Charming Betsy" rule (requiring that statutes be interpreted insofar as possible to comply with international law) may apply.

—*Horizontal supremacy.* This raises the question of whether WTO law is supreme over other international law.[2] Significantly, WTO dispute resolution is not intended to apply directly substantive non-WTO international law. From a practical perspective within the WTO legal system, WTO law is supreme over non-WTO international law. But it is more accurate to say that non-WTO international law simply is not applicable as a direct source of norms in WTO dispute resolution.

—*Direct effect.* Direct effect is the characteristic pursuant to which international law may be applicable within national courts. Direct effect, along with supremacy and judicial review, are the key components of constitutionalization by the European Court of Justice.

—*Judicial review.* Judicial review may be vertical or horizontal. That is, courts may review measures of lower level governments, or they may review measures of other branches at the same level. Roessler's chapter concerns the question of horizontal judicial review, and he criticizes the *India–Quantitative Restrictions* decision of the WTO Appellate Body, which establishes the principle of horizontal judicial review.

—*Substantive rules.* Constitutions may contain substantive rules of a more basic order, such as human rights or free trade norms.

These components of constitutionalization emphasize its heterogeneity. Furthermore, each component serves a different social purpose. For example, we often think of direct effect as making international law more enforceable (assuming that law applied as domestic law is more strongly enforceable). We would expect these features to have differential utility, depending on the particular social context.

There is no single scale or path of constitutionalization. Rather, constitutionalization is a continuum—a matter of degree. John Jackson is correct when he states that the WTO charter, even if it is a "mini charter," is constitutional in nature. This emperor has constitutional clothes; it makes little analytical sense to ignore them. Some feel that from a public relations standpoint it is useful to do so.

Constitutionalization is descriptive of societies that develop constitutional features over time; constitutionalism is normative, asserting that more constitutional features should be developed.[3] Adherents of constitutionalism presumably believe it will address a social need for these types of structures. Perhaps they see an imbalance between social cohesion and decisionmaking capacity—and are concerned that decisionmaking capacity exceeds underlying social cohesion. Alternatively, perhaps constitutionalism is intended to promote cohesion. The last is a "law and social change" issue: to what extent can new legal structures change behavior? Which comes first, the cohesion or the constitution? The chapters by Robert Howse and Kalypso Nicolaïdis and by Robert Keohane and Joseph Nye seem to assume that the cohesion must come first, but surely legal structures can play an interstitial role.

Subsidiarity, of course, is related to the vertical-allocation-of-power component of constitutionalization. To me, subsidiarity is a question and not an answer. It asks what vertical assignment of authority will maximize the preferences of the individual constituents. Where Howse and Nicolaïdis call for subsidiarity-based deference, they use a version of subsidiarity intended to connote a preference for governance at a lower level. My problem with this preference is that it does not tell us where to stop in our search for a lower level of governance. I also wonder, with Steve Charnovitz, what the basis for deference is. Why is it suggested to impose this extra-positive legal constraint?

The term *legitimacy*, like the terms *constitutionalization, subsidiarity*, and *equity*, is often used to express satisfaction or dissatisfaction with a particular outcome. From my contractarian perspective, legitimacy has two main meanings. First, it can refer to the ability of a particular governance structure to transmit the preferences of individuals. In this sense we seek governance structures that better reflect individual preferences.[4] This approach is consistent with methodological individualism. As Keo-hane and Nye argue, effectiveness in achieving goals is an element of le-gitimacy. This might be called the "accountability" element of legitimacy. If we think of governments as agents of individuals, the extent to which they act in accordance with their principals' aggregate preferences is the extent of their accountability. To the extent that the low-hanging fruit of trade liberalization has already been harvested, as Keohane and Nye point out, new trade agreements may provide diminishing returns. In this sense, legitimacy may be reduced. Second, legitimacy means the extent to which individuals perceive that their governance structure reflects their prefer-ences (or reflects their preferences to the maximum extent appropriate in a world where preferences are aggregated).[5] There is a marketing and pub-lic relations feature of legitimacy: to what extent does the government convince individuals that their preferences are being satisfied as much as possible?

The first meaning of legitimacy is the same as efficiency. Government is viewed as a preference-satisfying social structure that competes, through elections or through geographic mobility, for legitimacy. However, the sec-ond meaning suggests that the most successful government may not be the one that best satisfies citizens' preferences; it is the government that best convinces its constituents that it best satisfies their preferences.[6] Thus Coca-Cola is successful not just because it tastes good, but because it is marketed well. Of course, it is hard to market a bad product: if the gov-ernment is not somewhat successful at satisfying citizens' preferences, it is unlikely to be able to convince them that it is best.

What is the relationship between legitimacy and constitutionaliza-tion? These concepts are neither the same nor necessarily mutually sup-portive. Legitimacy refers to the "right" governance structure for a given social context. A certain level of constitutionalization may be legitimate in one context and illegitimate in another. Constitutionalization can enhance legitimacy, and legitimacy can support constitutionalization.

Recall the two components of legitimacy: legitimacy as efficiency and accountability may be enhanced by constitutional structures that improve the ability of individuals to agree on arrangements that are Pareto efficient, or perhaps potential Pareto efficient. This is the constitutional moment in the Buchanan sense.[7] However, unless people believe this is the case, they will not support constitutionalization that might be legitimate on effi-ciency grounds.

Synthesis: Legitimacy of Dispute Resolution and Treaty Making

I believe, with Dan Esty, that we cannot simply avoid centralized decisionmaking and thereby avoid crises of legitimacy. This is true for a simple reason: not to decide is to decide. The possibility of WTO central intervention has been identified; the public recognizes that the WTO could intervene or decline to intervene. For example, a decision by the WTO to decline to restrict U.S. extraterritorial regulation of foreign shrimp fishing—to protect U.S. "sovereignty"—is a decision to diminish the sovereignty of the flag states of the foreign shrimpers. The alternative decision diminishes U.S. sovereignty. From a Coase theorem perspective, one party always loses. The initial allocation of the "right" is important only because there are transaction costs, and for distributive reasons.

All vertical allocations of power are made to address issues of horizontal contention over power.[8] Trade law exists to regulate domestic laws about imports and exports of goods and services. Power is allocated to the WTO to regulate domestic laws. Thus the question is not whether to empower the WTO. The question is which state, on a horizontal plane, is to be the loser and which is to be the winner.

If I am correct that not to decide is to decide and that the WTO will sustain criticism from one side or another, Howse and Nicolaïdis, and Keohane and Nye, are misdirected. The WTO cannot avoid these issues. It can only decide them. These authors suggest that the WTO decide them in favor of states, but which states? There are states on both sides of the equation.

Sometimes the best place to handle cross-border issues is an international organization. In these cases, by declining to act, the WTO denies the international community a source of real benefits. If states have agreed that the WTO may intervene, legitimacy is surely not helped by reticence by the WTO, and none of the authors has suggested this.

A mechanism is needed to decide what issues the WTO should address. The leading mechanism is the political agreement of states, which will be influenced substantially by constituents' concerns about legitimacy. Sometimes these states will delegate the final decision about when to intervene to the dispute resolution process of the WTO. States prepare treaties that require interpretation. They implicitly delegate to the WTO dispute resolution system the authority to fill in the gaps. The Appellate Body has shown fierce allegiance to the language of the treaties themselves, but even so it cannot avoid interpolation, as in the *Shrimp-Turtle* case, for example. In fact, it has found in the words of the treaty a wide space for its own exercise of judgment.

Howse and Nicolaïdis, and Frieder Roessler, call for an interstitial approach to constitutional issues in dispute resolution. The Appellate Body, they say, should defer to member states' domestic policy on the one hand and the more political organs of the WTO on the other. There are two critiques of the deference strategy. The first is that it is too much, and the second is that it is not enough. Unfortunately, there can be no assurance that the authors, by staking out the territory in between, have gotten it just right.

Special preference or sensitivity to the domestic policy of member states is too much insofar as it departs from the intent of the states that are party to the relevant treaties.[9] If the states had wanted these preferences, they would have, and should have, provided for them either specifically or generally. Interpretations shading one way or another seem fundamentally illegitimate in this respect.

These preferences are too little insofar as they can only operate interstitially—where the relevant treaty leaves room for interpretation and that interpretation is not otherwise constrained. How can we be certain that this interstitial action will be sufficient to meet concerns regarding legitimacy? Normally, one would expect the customary rules of interpretation of public international law invoked by the Dispute Settlement Understanding to result in a unique interpretation. At least in theory, there should be little room for shading interpretations in favor of states or political branches. How can this strategy provide added legitimacy or avoid challenges?

Of course, sensitivity to political currents has been observed in both the U.S. Supreme Court and the European Court of Justice. There is no reason to expect less of the Appellate Body, although, as Keohane and Nye explain, the professional context in which these judges operate may affect their sensitivity. In turn, the professional context may be influenced by the perceived legitimacy of judicial activism in the WTO.

Given imperfect alternatives, what is the most legitimate or efficient mechanism for reflecting individual preferences? Weak legislative capacity is a problem: the WTO agreements can be amended only with great difficulty. For issues that alter the rights or obligations of members, some amendments require unanimity; others may be made upon acceptance by a two-thirds majority, but only bind states that accept them. Thus the legislative capacity of the WTO is quite limited. The adjudicative capacity of the WTO, however, was strengthened in 1994 (compared to GATT 1947).

This might be considered an imbalance similar to that experienced during the "Eurosclerosis" years of the European Community before the enhancement of legislative capacity in 1987 pursuant to the Single European Act.[10] A complex of political and economic circumstances led to the Single European Act of 1987, and we cannot expect the advent of majority voting in the WTO any time soon. However, it is worth noting the effects of weak legislative capacity on dispute resolution. First, to the extent there is strong social demand for new law, the major response will come from dispute resolution, if at all. If the Appellate Body remains fastidiously positivist in its approach, there will be little opportunity to satisfy this demand. Second, acts by the Appellate Body will be final; they will not be subject to legislative reversal. This may inspire the Appellate Body to *hubris* or caution. Much depends on the professional community within which the Appellate Body operates. Empirical research could be performed to understand how judges react in this context and in other contexts to nonreversibility.

Thus we have a conundrum: we cannot strengthen the WTO's legislative capacity without greater legitimacy, but the WTO's legitimacy is challenged by its reliance on dispute resolution to respond to the most important issues it faces.[11] We must look at the choices as they are in a context where not to decide is to decide: questions may be answered by dispute resolution, or we may allow more political bodies to answer them.

This conundrum has no easy solution: until the social reality of benefits from WTO activities justifies an assignment of greater legislative capacity, we should not enhance its legislative capacity. The social reality would come in the form of a constitutional moment as described by Buchanan.[12] States would recognize that by agreeing to majority voting; they could enter into agreements that would have beneficial effects that would exceed the costs (in terms of sovereignty).

But there is a gap that may be worth filling. Even if the social reality would justify majority voting, constituents must perceive this reality before it can be acted upon. This is a public relations or marketing problem, or perhaps a public education problem. It may be addressed by a number of activities, including the commitment of political leadership. National governments and the WTO should examine closely their options in this connection.[13] This activity would be supported by sound social choice–based research on the kinds of agreements that could be reached only through majority voting. Constituents need to be informed of the opportunities that are currently missed, in order to evaluate their worth, whether positive or negative, and the consequent value of modified constitutional arrangements.

Notes

1. Concern about a "democratic deficit" is concern about the distance between individuals and decisions made by their representatives. The term "deficit" suggests that there is a problem in the quantity of democracy; actually the substantive concern is with the quality of democracy.

2. See Joel P. Trachtman, "The Domain of WTO Dispute Resolution," *Harvard International Law Journal*, vol. 40 (1999), p. 333.

3. Thomas Cottier, "Limits to International Trade: The Constitutional Challenge," in *Proceedings of the 94th Annual Meeting of the American Society of International Law* (2000), p. 220.

4. See Neil Komesar, *Imperfect Alternatives: Choosing Institutions in Law, Economics and Public Policy* (University of Chicago Press, 1994).

5. No one in a society can expect that all his or her preferences will be perfectly reflected. For example, to the extent one has agreed to accept majority voting, one would expect to lose from time to time. However, one would accept that the system is legitimate if one exercised the amount of influence one had bargained for or deserved.

6. For example, some said Microsoft's DOS was not the best operating system for the original PCs but was the best-marketed operating system.

7. Geoffrey Brennan and James M. Buchanan, *The Reason of Rules: Constitutional Political Economy* (Cambridge University Press, 1985).

8. See Joel P. Trachtman, "Externalities and Extraterritoriality: The Law and Economics of Prescriptive Jurisdiction," in Jagdeep S. Bhandari and Alan O. Sykes, eds., *Economic Dimensions in International Law* (Cambridge University Press, 1997).

9. See Steven Charnovitz's comment in this volume.

10. See J. H. H. Weiler, "The Transformation of Europe," *Yale Law Journal*, vol. 100 (1991), p. 2403.

11. Trachtman, "The Domain of WTO Dispute Resolution."

12. Brennan and Buchanan, *The Reason of Rules*.

13. In his comments at the conference, Robert Hudec suggested that national governments have sometimes exaggerated the powers of the WTO.

PART FIVE

Governance

SYLVIA OSTRY

15 | World Trade Organization: Institutional Design for Better Governance

The term *trading system* is an anachronism today. The World Trade Organization (WTO) is increasingly centered on domestic regulation and legal systems instead of trade. But the shift in its focus is only one of the changes transforming the system. My first task is to summarize those changes, including the impact of the Uruguay Round (concluded in 1994), as well as changes in the policy ambience and the policy process. I then turn to the most urgent reforms needed to keep the system going and briefly note the long-term changes required in the international governance architecture.

Transformative Changes in the Trading System

The end of the cold war has profoundly affected the role of the United States in international economic policy not only because of a secular decline of congressional deference but also because the postwar spillover from "high" to "low" policy, which acted as a constraint on trade disputes, has greatly diminished. More pervasive albeit less obvious developments have altered the U.S. role as well.

Policy Ambience

The public showed little interest in the Uruguay Round negotiations. As Mike Moore, the WTO director-general, observed, "The Uruguay

Round was launched in the silence of public apathy."[1] The same could be said about the seven rounds of the General Agreement on Tariffs and Trade (GATT) launched between 1948 and 1973. The negotiations were handled by governments with lobbying by so-called distributional coalitions, chiefly business and trade unions. In the Uruguay Round the role of multinational corporations and farmers was unique because of the special character of the "new issues" (services, intellectual property, and investment) and the centrality of agriculture as a deal maker or breaker in the ultimate settlement. Although the United States led in launching and guiding all GATT negotiations, the negotiations ultimately depended on cooperation between the two big players, the United States and the European Community.

During the Seattle meeting of the WTO in 1999, many governments must have sorely missed the "silence of public apathy." The publicity in Seattle is attributable not only to the activity in the streets. It also reflects a more pervasive secular change in the industrialized countries—an alienation from the elite. V. O. Key Jr. wrote about the "permissive consensus" of the early postwar decades.[2] The general public had little detailed knowledge of international policy, and opinion polls demonstrated consistent support for the government's foreign policy, including trade policy. "When a permissive consensus exists," Key noted, "a government may be relatively free to work out a solution of the issue or it may be free to act or not to act."[3] The deference to government, and more broadly to the establishment, has dramatically declined since the 1960s in all countries in the Organization for Economic Cooperation and Development (OECD), as many recent polls have demonstrated.[4] Perhaps the Uruguay Round was the last gasp of the permissive consensus—and barely that.

Of course, there are many reasons for the decline in deference to government and to elites. One is the much wider access to information and the accelerating use of the Internet. Another is the ongoing debate in academia about the impact of trade on growth and equality and the growing emphasis on values and morals. According to opinion polls taken after the Seattle meeting, large majorities now want the environment and labor standards included in trade agreements.[5] These views, reflected in many OECD countries, are adamantly opposed by non-OECD countries, which represent two-thirds of the WTO membership.

The Political Economy

A second transformative change in the trading system involves the political economy of trade policymaking. Before the Uruguay Round the

GATT model of reciprocity worked well. Border barriers erected in the 1930s were reduced, and trade grew faster than output. The model was premised on the idea that protectionist lobbies could be offset by export interests. In these rounds developing countries negotiated mainly to secure unreciprocated market access to OECD countries. Most lacked the expertise and analytical resources for trade policymaking, but that did not matter much because of the nature of negotiations.

The Uruguay Round was dramatically different. The negotiation to launch the negotiation took almost as long as the Tokyo Round during the 1970s. After repeated U.S. efforts beginning in the early 1980s, the Uruguay Round was launched in September 1986 and formally concluded in April 1994, several years after the target date originally announced. The extraordinary difficulty in initiating and completing the round stemmed from two fundamental factors: the nearly insuperable problem of completing the unfinished business of past negotiations, most of all on agriculture matters, and the equally contentious issue of introducing new agenda items, notably trade in services, intellectual property, and, in a more limited way, investment. To avoid addressing the Common Agricultural Policy (CAP), the Europeans blocked the launch, and a number of developing countries led by Brazil and India were bitterly opposed to including the so-called new issues. The final trade-off involved a North-South deal across the old and new issues. In exchange for improved access for agricultural and labor-intensive products, the developing countries yielded on the new issues and accepted the restructuring of GATT.

The Uruguay Round launched the deepening integration of the global economy. The new issues did not involve the border barriers of the original GATT but domestic regulatory and legal systems embedded in the institutional infrastructure of the economy. The intrusiveness into domestic sovereignty bore little resemblance to the shallow integration of GATT. The barriers to access for service providers stemmed from laws, administrative actions, or regulations. Improved access required changes in domestic economic regulatory regimes and involved an inherent pressure for convergence. The telecommunications agreement set out a common framework for regulating competition in basic telecommunications. Including intellectual property rights radically transformed the trading system. The intellectual property negotiations covered comprehensive standards for domestic laws and, perhaps more important, detailed provisions for enforcing individual (corporate) property rights. The WTO shifted from the GATT model of negative regulation—what governments must not do—to positive regulation—what governments must do. This new agenda will require many developing countries to upgrade their institutional infrastructure with respect to governance, education, legal systems, and regulatory systems.

By the end of the 1980s, a major change in economic policy was under way. Economic reform—deregulation, privatization, liberalization—was seen as essential for higher growth. Even without the regulatory reform thrust from the Uruguay Round, the postwar economic regulatory state was no longer a dominant paradigm. Telecommunications and finance were regarded as essential building blocks in the soft infrastructure underpinning growth.

At the same time negotiations on social regulation—product standards, health, safety, and the environment—received less publicity and less attention from the ranks of senior policymakers. In OECD countries social regulation has accelerated since the 1960s. Economic regulation in advanced countries is withering, while social regulation is alive, well, and growing. Indeed, social regulation has grown by 300 to 400 percent in the industrialized countries since 1970.[6] This is not the case in developing countries, nor are they likely to embrace the social regulatory state unilaterally. Although the positive regulatory approach in social regulation is more procedural than substantive, the infrastructure implications are far-reaching. They involve sophisticated administrative procedures law as well as highly trained scientific human resources.

By 1999 the grand bargain of the Uruguay Round seemed to many developing countries to be a bad deal. They got less access than they had wanted, and the burden of the new agenda was far heavier than they had understood. During the preparatory meetings for Seattle, they argued for better access in agriculture and textiles, as well as an extension of time before implementation of the more difficult aspects of the new issues, and also enhanced technical assistance. So a North-South divide was expected in Seattle. The meeting ended, however, with a walkout by virtually all the developing countries—not over agriculture or textile tariffs, but because of the U.S. president's insistence on including labor standards that would be enforced by trade sanctions. While this proved to be the catalyst, the bitterest complaint of many of these countries was the undemocratic nature of the negotiation process.

Another major difference between GATT and the WTO is the greatly strengthened dispute settlement mechanism. Social regulatory issues have been particularly contentious. Inevitably, the dispute panels have been forced to interpret the relevant WTO rules. Because some WTO rules are deliberately imprecise or creatively ambiguous, they have been interpreted by internationally appointed judges. These judges make law: they define boundaries for domestic policy and reinforce the perception—and reality—of the intrusiveness of the new system.[7]

The Policymaking Process

While economists, businesspeople, and trade officials ponder how e-commerce will affect the market for goods and services, few seem to have given much though to how the Internet will affect the market for policy ideas and the policymaking process. The Internet is making the market for ideas contestable. Inexpensive, borderless, real-time networking provides nongovernmental organizations (NGOs) with economies of scale and scope by linking groups that are often widely disparate. Equally important, the Internet offers the opportunity to disseminate strategic knowledge formerly concentrated in governments and businesses.

There are three broad categories of NGO coalitions or networks: mobilization networks designed to rally support for specific activities; technical networks designed to provide specific information; and networks that I call a "virtual secretariat." The latter are dedicated to servicing developing countries.

MOBILIZATION NETWORKS.   Active at the Seattle meeting, the International Civil Society Opposing a Millennium Round (ICS) and People's Global Action (PGA) exemplify mobilization networks. The ICS claimed to represent more than 1,400 local, regional, and international nongovernmental organizations from more than eighty-seven countries (all of the OECD countries and a large number of developing countries).[8] The PGA, another broad coalition, described itself as "an instrument for coordination, not an organization."[9] Mobilization networks are coalitions of widely diverse NGOs that often have conflicting interests. With no center and no hierarchy, they pride themselves on their pure form of participatory democracy.

The carefully choreographed street operas and television sound bites in Seattle, however, carried a common theme—antiglobalization. The charge: the WTO is dominated by the interests of transnational corporations; its rules and procedures are undemocratic; it harms the environment; and it increases inequality within and among countries. One must distinguish between the loose networks of diverse NGOs and the organizations responsible for creating and marketing the message, such as Ralph Nader's Public Citizen and Global Trade Watch; the U.S.-based Preamble Centre; and Friends of the Earth in the United Kingdom. These "headquarters organizations" were aided in logistics planning by groups such as the Direct Action Network and the Ruckus Society, and in press relations and media management, by Turning Point. Some analysts have argued that these NGOs are part of a new industry—the protest business.[10]

The protest business seems to have combined three key ingredients: a salable message, a skillful media strategy, and money (from mass mailings and philanthropic institutions, mainly American).[11] The objective is to influence the policy process through public opinion. The new actors do not resemble the distributional coalitions sparring over the division of the pie.

TECHNICAL NETWORKS. Examples of technical networks are the Centre for International Environmental Law in Geneva and Washington; the International Institute for Sustainable Development in Winnipeg; the Institute for Agriculture and Trade Policy in Minneapolis; the International Centre for Trade and Sustainable Development in Geneva; WEED (World Economy, Ecology, and Development) in Bonn; and the Institute for Global Communications in Palo Alto. Their primary purpose is to facilitate greater NGO participation in the policy process by providing strategic and technical information, heavily weighted to environmental and legal issues. These technical groups mainly operate through institutional channels, both governmental and intergovernmental.

NETWORKS HELPING DEVELOPING COUNTRIES. Finally, a remarkable development is the proliferation of NGOs providing information and undertaking advocacy on behalf of developing countries. Examples are the Third World Network in Malaysia; the South Centre in Geneva; SEATINI (Southern and East African Trade and Information and Negotiations Initiative), with offices in African countries; Focus on the Global South in Thailand; and CUTS (Consumer Unity and Trust Society) in India. Northern nongovernmental organizations with a focus on southern issues in the WTO include Rongead (European NGO Network on Agriculture, Trade Environment and Development), based in France; Intrac (International NGO Research Centre), based in Oxford; and traditional development NGOs that now focus on trade and environmental issues, such as Oxfam, Christian Aid, and other religious organizations.

This South "virtual secretariat" provided a continual flow of information on negotiations in Geneva and helped formulate policy positions on major issues. They are not a homogeneous group, but, as Seattle demonstrated, their strategic assets of information and political know-how can provide a base for a significant increase in bargaining power in the WTO.

CONCLUSION.   The new prominence of NGOs in trade policymaking should be evaluated in a broad context. The American business community has maintained a low profile in WTO negotiations, unlike in the Uruguay Round. Apart from the service industries, the business community in Europe and the United States has demonstrated little generic or systemic interest. One can only speculate as to the reasons. Perhaps the Uruguay Round was a singular event because it radically transformed the GATT system and the stakes were very high. The global span of many corporations facilitates direct negotiation with governments. So, many of them ask, why bother with lengthy and tedious intergovernmental negotiations? Moreover, the restructuring of American corporations over the past decade has required a sharper focus on a limited number of governmental lobbying objectives with short-term impact on the bottom line. Thus Chinese accession to the WTO has been a top priority.

The most important lesson from the Seattle experience is the urgent need to reform the World Trade Organization, a necessary but not sufficient condition to ensure the survival of a global and rules-based trading system. In addition, change is needed in the existing architecture for international cooperation.

Governance of the WTO

In this section I examine three governance issues that are currently shaping the WTO: the need for a new policy forum, transparency, and the accession of China.

A Policy Forum

The Uruguay Round negotiators recognized that GATT would not provide an adequate foundation for the ambitious and comprehensive trading system embedded in the negotiating agenda. The Functioning of the GATT System (FOGS) negotiating group, promoted by a coalition of middle powers from developed and developing countries, recognized that the

368 SYLVIA OSTRY

alternative to a rules-based system would be a power-based system. Lacking power, these countries felt they had the most to lose.

The goals of the FOGS group were relatively modest: to make GATT more adaptable to change in the global economy through improved surveillance of country trade policy and regular Ministerial Conferences; to establish better linkages between GATT and the Bretton Woods institutions; and, most important, to strengthen the enforcement of the trading system's rules of the road by improving dispute settlement arrangements. Creating a new institution was not among these objectives.

In April 1990 Canada proposed a new institution, the WTO, a proposal quickly endorsed by the European Union. Although the EU had opposed stronger dispute settlement in the Tokyo Round, it became an active supporter of a new dispute settlement mechanism because of its growing concern about U.S. unilateralism. Unfortunately, an attempt to establish a successor to the Consultative Group of Eighteen (CG18)—GATT's policy forum for debate and discussion—failed. As a result, the WTO is a minimalist legalist institution.

In the light of the current debate on governance of the WTO, a brief history of the Consultative Group of Eighteen is useful.[12] It was established in July 1975 on a recommendation of the Committee of Twenty Finance Ministers after the breakdown of Bretton Woods. Its purpose was to provide a forum for senior officials to discuss policy issues—not to challenge the authority of the GATT Council. Membership was based on a combination of economic weight and regional representation, with provision for other countries to attend as alternates and observers or by invitation. Each meeting was followed by a comprehensive report to the GATT Council. In 1979 the GATT Council agreed to make CG18 permanent, but it was suspended in 1990 by the director-general for reasons that have never been made public.

As a forum for senior officials, the Consultative Group of Eighteen provided an opportunity to improve the coordination of policies. Papers were prepared by the secretariat on global economic issues such as balance of payments, related financial matters, and the nature and scope of cooperation with the International Monetary Fund. After the Tokyo Round, the CG18 was the only forum in GATT where agriculture was discussed, and (in the long lead-up to the Uruguay Round) trade in services. Indeed, the CG18 was the only forum for a full, wide-ranging, and often contentious debate on the basic issues of the round. There was an opportunity to analyze and explain issues without a commitment to specific negotiating positions.

The establishment of a policy forum (or executive committee) to foster comprehensive structural reform should be accorded highest priority. Since Seattle the mind-set in Geneva is pretty much that the WTO is not broken so why fix it? There has been a lot of discussion about *transparency*. Indeed, the opacity of that word has been significantly increased by distinguishing between *internal transparency* (adapting the traditional negotiating process to include more developing countries) and *external transparency* (improving access to documents and dealing with the demands of the NGOs for more participation). The internal transparency debate is gridlocked over how to design the main negotiating committee. In other words, what weights should be assigned to economic power, numbers, and geography? Even more conflicted is the external transparency debate about the role of NGOs.

A new policy forum could meet regularly at the official level and, as required, at the ministerial level to discuss these and other issues. The Trade Policy Review Mechanism (TPRM) is one possible model for the new forum. A committee of reasonable size and a rotating membership would ensure representation for all countries and regions within a given time frame. Alternately, the policy forum might be part of a new North-South package to include the so-called confidence-building measures of zero tariffs for the products of the poorest countries; extension of implementation periods for some measures such as TRIMs (Trade-Related Investment Measures), TRIPs (Trade-Related Aspects of Intellectual Property Rights), and customs valuation; and, most important, enhanced technical assistance and training.

The policy forum would be a great step forward, but it is unlikely to function effectively without an increase in the WTO's research capability. If member governments are unwilling to provide funding, private donors should be sought and other avenues explored. As the CG18 experience demonstrated, analytical papers on key issues are needed to launch serious discussions and to improve the diffusion of knowledge in national capitals. Today trade spans a growing range of international and domestic policies and is linked to other policy domains such as the environment and competition policy. The WTO could not possibly generate all its policy analysis in-house and remain reasonably small in size.

The WTO secretariat should consider establishing a research network linked to other institutions such as the OECD, the Bretton Woods institutions, private think tanks, and universities. Knowledge networks promote cooperation and coordination and foster consensus. Networking should include environmental, business, labor, and intergovernmental organizations such as the International Labor Organization (ILO) and the United Nations Environment Program (UNEP). Establishing a research or knowledge network could enhance the WTO director-general's ability to guide policy debate. The policy forum could become a broad meta-regime founded on mutually agreed basic principles and fostered by a combination of strategic assets: a knowledge infrastructure in the form of a research capability; a meeting infrastructure for knowledge diffusion, debate, and peer group pressure; and strategic planning and monitoring of policy performance. The new forum must not be a decisionmaking body and must report regularly to the General Council. Like the CG18, it should make recommendations to the Council and proffer suggestions for further analysis or action.

Transparency

The GATT decisionmaking system worked well because there were far fewer countries and the issues were less complex than they are today. The traditional Green Room process, inherited from GATT, has not been established by explicit rules but by a self-selection process. The number of Green Room participants is small and it varies. Those present include the large OECD countries, a group of middle powers, some of the most powerful developing countries, and a few of the transition economies. The demand for change came not only from the poor countries, which were largely excluded, but also from Pascal Lamy, commissioner for trade of the EU, whose term the "medieval process of decisionmaking" was widely quoted. Trade experts have made suggestions for structural reform.[13] Procedural changes also have been put forward in Geneva. None of these proposals, however, has been accepted. This is hardly surprising since any significant restructuring of the negotiating committee arrangements would involve "winners" and "losers."

Without an agreed target date for the launch of a new round, the countries now inside the Green Room have no incentive to agree to any change in its composition. The demands of the nongovernmental organizations are threefold: more access to WTO documents, the right to observer status and to present *amicus curiae* briefs before dispute settlement panels and the Appellate Body, and more participation in WTO activities such as committee meetings. In short, the NGOs want a seat at the table, though they usually stop short of a request to be included in negotiations. Through its website the WTO has already greatly improved access to documentation; the other two requests, however, will not be easily or quickly resolved.

The United States has been the strongest proponent of opening up the WTO dispute procedure, including the right of private parties to submit *amicus* briefs to panels and the Appellate Body. This proposal is supported not only by environmental, labor, and human rights groups but also by private lawyers who specialize in international trade and by their international business clients. Since *amicus* briefs often carry little weight in judicial decisions, it is likely that the next step will be a demand for the right to bring cases directly.

These demands are strongly rejected by the governments of the South and by the NGOs, which regard the present evidentiary-intensive and increasingly legalistic system as biased against them. A number of these countries have objected to the 1998 ruling in the *Turtle-Shrimp* case that opened the door to *amicus* briefs. This reaction underlines a broader complaint not confined to southern countries—namely that the Appellate Body is engaged in lawmaking. As Robert Hudec asserts, a demand for "a right to appear before an international tribunal is a partial repudiation of the role being performed by national governments in those proceedings."[14]

Suggestions to reduce the legalization of the WTO and even to go back to the GATT mode of diplomacy deserve to be considered. Governments, not judges, should determine the boundary line between international rules and domestic policy space.[15] The compact that underlay GATT involved liberalizing trade by reducing border barriers; creating rules to govern the liberalizing momentum; and safeguarding domestic policy space by rules to permit temporary blockage of imports under clearly specified terms. That compact is no longer relevant in the new global trading system. Sooner or later it must be renegotiated or the system will not survive.

The WTO is an intergovernmental organization, and most member governments want to keep it that way. They argue that NGOs should deal with their own governments. NGO advocates of participation respond that only they have a truly transnational vision, something lacking in national governments. For example, "a citizen who cares very deeply about ending whaling . . . will find his or her views better represented in international fora by the Worldwide Fund for Nature than by his or her own government, which has many goals it must simultaneously pursue."[16] But it is not clear what the word *citizen* means in this context. There are no world citizens, only citizens of nation states. Governments are accountable to their citizens, albeit some more so than others. How is accountability defined in the case of nongovernmental organizations? And what about transparency? Who and where are the members of the NGOs? What is their source of funding? Are they accountable to their membership or to their funders? These are some of the questions that would have to be settled before a meaningful proposal on participatory democracy in the WTO could be debated. Any such proposal would be fiercely opposed by most developing countries in the WTO—especially after their experience in Seattle.

Another complication is the enormous diversity among nongovernmental organizations. The main function of operational NGOs is service delivery in developing countries. Advocacy NGOs differ in focus and function: mobilization networks are in the protest business, and the technical groups lobby inside the system. There is no agreed taxonomy among the NGOs or the international institutions, especially the UN agencies with whom they have the closest contacts. And among these agencies and others, such as the World Bank or the Multilateral Environmental Agreements (MEAs), there is wide variation in the specific terms for accreditation and the nature of participation.[17]

As the influence of nongovernmental organizations has increased, their positions have come under more fire. Many NGO positions have been criticized as simplistic, ignorant, and driven by a need for media attention. The Brent Spar oil rig controversy is often cited as an example of a major policy shift catalyzed by Greenpeace's erroneous information. Other examples include the ongoing debate over genetically modified organisms (GMOs), as well as the attacks on the WTO, the IMF and the World Bank. If corporations seriously distort the truth and are exposed, they are accountable to shareholders. Democratic governments and unions in democratic countries are accountable as well. There is no comparable constraint on nongovernmental organizations—at least, no visible or obvious one.

In response to the criticism that they are unaccountable, some NGOs have undertaken new self-regulatory initiatives. There are now a number of codes of conduct drawn up by NGOs and monitored by them. These codes cover ethical practices, transparency, funding accountability, accuracy, and other issues. A comprehensive example of self-regulation at the global level is the NGO Steering Committee of the UN Commission on Sustainable Development, which includes NGOs, trade union representatives, and corporations.[18] This experiment is part of a broader trend toward "hybrid governance," a combination of "hard law" (implemented by governments or intergovernmental institutions) and "soft law" (codes of conduct that provide norms for guidance and emulation).

These developments will not place NGOs next to national governments at the WTO's global table. Certainly, such codes would assist the WTO in formulating more meaningful accreditation procedures for NGO participation in symposiums and other forums such as TPRM meetings on a voluntary basis.[19] Capacity building is needed in developing countries whose NGOs lack the personnel and expertise to implement the codes. The charge, by some southern countries, of neocolonialism is not without merit. Because the WTO administers global rules negotiated by nation states, it is argued that NGOs should be involved in the policy process through national mechanisms. But, of course, because of cultural, political, or legal differences, not all member countries are willing to permit this. As a recent survey by Freedom House demonstrates, 58 percent of the current WTO membership (calculated in terms of population) can be considered democracies. After China accedes, the percentage will fall to 43 percent.[20]

What is to be done? Certainly the WTO should monitor the new experiments in codes of conduct and perhaps convene a symposium to discuss these issues with NGOs, governments, unions, and business. Among the most important issues should be the national mechanisms required to involve accredited NGOs, parliamentarians, academics, and business groups in the formulation of policy. Through discussion and peer group pressure (and considerable patience), it may be possible to improve the transparency of policymaking in countries that at present may well regard the term *transparent governance* as an oxymoron.

Accession of China

A third WTO governance issue concerns the accession of China, a country that has not adopted the Western concept of law based on individual rights. Separation of powers is an alien idea; there is no independent judiciary. The Chinese concept of rule by law rather than rule of law is deeply embedded in thousands of years of history, in a tradition far older than Western legal tradition.

If China had joined GATT in the 1980s, the negotiations would have centered on traditional border barriers. That would have been difficult but not of overwhelming importance to the functioning of the institution. But the WTO is also about domestic regulatory reform, the independence of regulatory agencies governed by principles of competition, the rights of due process, and the protection of private property rights. The basic underpinning of the whole system is transparency, which includes the publication of

all laws and related regulations and judicial review of the rulemaking and
other actions of independent regulatory agencies.

The WTO concept of transparency is essentially an international system of administrative procedures law designed to control what government bureaucrats do and how they do it. The Chinese legal tradition did
not include the concept of control of the mandarins (except by the emperor)! One should expect that the transition to the Western legal system
may take decades.[21]

The accession protocol in Geneva allows transition periods of varying
length for different liberalization commitments. What is required is an
overall transition framework that would be time-certain and would include specified benchmarks for review by a WTO committee at designated
dates.[22] Full membership in the WTO would result at the end of the period when the Trade Policy Review Mechanism certified full adherence to
the transition protocol. To ensure the credibility of this mechanism, the
committee should have the right to apply sanctions for a specified period
if China failed to deliver the commitments at any of the designated benchmarks.

Finally, this approach to accession should be coordinated with World
Bank programs. Technical assistance should be jointly supplied by the Bank
and the World Trade Organization, although this would necessitate an increase in WTO training and legal resources. Since China's integration into
the WTO will require major restructuring of the state-owned enterprises
(SOEs), radical reform of the banking system, and extensive social reform,
including the creation of an effective social safety net, coordination with
World Bank programs is needed to ensure the sustainability of domestic reform and the liberalization process. The need for coordination between the
WTO and the World Bank is a broad issue that goes beyond institutional reform of the WTO. More coherent international policymaking is essential.

Coherence

One of the goals of the Functioning of the GATT System (FOGS)
group was to establish better linkages between GATT and the Bretton
Woods institutions. It was hoped that this would improve the coherence of
international policies. The only result of the group's seven years of negotiations was the (largely rhetorical) Ministerial Declaration on the Contribution of the World Trade Organization to Achieving Greater Coherence in

Global Economic Policymaking. The coherence objective of the Uruguay Round stemmed from the serious current account imbalances (the growing American deficit and the Japanese surplus), which had emerged in the first half of the 1980s and fanned the flames of protectionism in the U.S. Congress. The declaration concludes with an invitation to the director-general of the WTO "to review with the Managing Director of the International Monetary Fund and the President of the World Bank, the implications of the WTO's responsibilities for its cooperation with the Bretton Woods institutions, as well as the forms such cooperation might take, with a view to achieving greater coherence in global economic policymaking."[23] The review produced agreements with the International Monetary Fund at the end of 1996 and with the World Bank in the spring of 1997. These agreements detail who can attend certain meetings and what information can be exchanged. They also provide for consultation between secretariats on trade-policy-related issues. No mention is made of external imbalances and exchange rate misalignment.

Although the Uruguay Round objective of coherence in regard to exchange rate misalignment is pretty well dead, improved coordination among international institutions is more important today than the negotiators could have foreseen in 1986. So far as the Bretton Woods institutions are concerned, the main partner for cooperation must be the World Bank, as the China example suggests. This is because the Bank's approach to development policy changed markedly in the late 1990s.

The World Bank's development role now encompasses governance, economic regulation, competition policy, the legal system, education, social policies, competition policy, and the environment—the WTO's agenda. Trade policy and development policy are becoming more and more intertwined. What the WTO calls trade policy, the World Bank calls the second generation of reform.

As a result of an initiative by Renato Ruggiero, then the director-general, the WTO's Singapore Ministerial Meeting in December 1996 endorsed the Integrated Framework for Trade-Related Assistance to Least Developed Countries (IF). This was the first project involving the major international institutions in a coordinated approach to technical assistance for developing countries. Ruggiero called this important initiative, which focused on trade-related training programs for the poorest countries, "a new partnership against marginalization."

While it is not clear precisely what "trade-related" training means, the phrase carries echoes of GATT rather than the WTO. This is not to diminish the initiative—which will help the least developed countries improve their export capabilities, and therefore their growth potential—but to argue that it should be regarded as part of a much broader project that would include improved access for these countries' products and a comprehensive approach toward the upgrading of soft infrastructure. Granted, this will not be easy, as even the present integrated framework has hardly been a success. As reported in the World Bank's Development Committee report of March 2000, Uganda is the only country where new projects have been developed under the framework and an independent review has been established to assess the weaknesses of the IF process.[24]

There remain two other aspects of coherence relevant today: one concerns the environment and the other labor. Both are characterized by a strong North-South divide. Most developing countries firmly oppose linking environmental and labor issues with trade rules in the WTO. The two issues are, of course, very different. The environment is already a concern of the WTO, and trade and environment are linked in both positive and negative ways, as the most recent report by the WTO clearly demonstrated.[25] While a new WEO (World Environment Organization) with a clearly defined mission, policy influence, and analytic resources could launch the policy dialogue on the relationship between ecology and the economy, the likelihood of establishing a new international organization today is close to zero. A more practical approach would be to house all the existing multilateral environment agreements (MEAs) in UNEP (United Nations Environment Program), which would need more resources, with a mandate for review of the agreements and proposals to improve consistency among them. This would permit launching a joint project by the WTO and UNEP on the relationship between the MEAs and the WTO rules, which is one of the most important and contentious issues in this domain.

In addressing the North-South divide, I propose a new approach to the win-win policy of eliminating subsidies in selected sectors. Recent studies suggest that the subsidy reform benefits to developing countries in terms of increased growth are significant.[26] To stimulate an informed policy dialogue on this issue, the Committee on Trade and Environment, in cooperation with the OECD and the World Bank, should establish a Subsidies Policy Review Mechanism (SPRM) to discuss commissioned research on this issue in both the OECD and developing countries. The purpose of the SPRM would be to submit policy proposals to the Committee on Trade and Environment for consideration.

These suggestions are intended to promote more informed debate within the WTO on the linkage between trade and the environment. This highlights the difference with the other "trade and . . ." issue: labor. As was evident in Geneva and in Seattle, there is no agreement among members to bring that camel into the tent.

If the objective of the American and other OECD unions is to improve working arrangements in developing countries, the mandate rests with the International Labor Organization. (If it is not, then it is a matter for domestic policy designed to ameliorate the distributional consequences of adjustment to global forces.) But the ILO has no power of enforcement. Moreover, many of its developing-country members have resisted repeated attempts to improve enforcement capacity while at the same time opposing labor standards in the WTO. This dilemma must be resolved and the ILO monitoring and enforcement mechanisms strengthened. But development institutions will also have to play their role since labor standards are clearly linked to growth. What will be needed, in effect, is reform of the ILO and more effective coordination with the WTO, the World Bank, and UNCTAD.

While this macro approach to labor standards would rest on government policy, an innovative micro policy is now rapidly evolving independently of government and, indeed, generated by technical NGOs. The Washington-based Council on Economic Priorities (CEP) is a consumer organization established in 1969. In 1997 CEP established a separate accreditation agency (CEPAA), which developed a social accountability code that includes the ILO basic labor rights, in addition to rules on wages and hours. SA8000 was launched in 1998, on the fiftieth anniversary of the Universal Declaration of Human Rights. The codes are technically designed for auditors, and their development involved large corporations, unions, and nongovernmental organizations. They have been endorsed by international certification agencies. Monitoring of the developing-country subsidiaries of the transnational corporations that have adopted SA8000 will be carried out by a network of NGOs linked to CEPAA. While the information is designed for a consumer audience, the next step will be to involve investors, beginning with large pension funds. The core strategy of this micro policy is market-like: consumer and investor pressure will force an increasing number of firms to join the SA8000 crowd with a little help from global whistleblowers and the media. This policy innovation is new and a spin-off from the information technology revolution. As CEP has noted, "With instantaneous media connection and the internet . . . today's remote factory scandal can become tomorrow's global headline."[27]

SA8000 is just one example of an enormous proliferation in labor codes of conduct and labeling.[28] The codes and labels are voluntary and the product of self-regulation. A comprehensive survey of these developments and a project to evaluate their impact would be useful.

The European Union, like the United States, proposed that labor standards should not be discussed in a new WTO committee. A joint forum organized by the WTO and ILO, but outside both, was recommended. The purpose of the forum would be to analyze the relationship between trade policy, development, and core labor standards.[29] This forum would be the appropriate venue for the discussion of these innovations in "soft law." This would open the door for a discussion about the opportunities for hybrid governance rather than governmental or intergovernmental regulation.

Conclusion

I have explored ways of improving WTO governance—incremental initiatives rather than a new architecture. But even improved plumbing and interior decoration might not be feasible, because of the lacking ingredient: leadership. The hegemonic theory of Kindleberger would suggest that leadership is unlikely to be forthcoming. The end of the cold war, the decline of congressional deference in trade policy, and the increasing transatlantic friction hardly help.

Yet the global public goods of stability and predictability probably matter more today, when the threats to stability are far more diffuse and diverse, than they did in the twentieth century. These incremental improvements need not await a new round. Coalitions of middle powers have the greatest stake in a rules-based system. So, indeed, does the United States if there is a proliferation of bilateral and regional agreements that exclude the United States because of lack of fast-track authority. Coalitions allied with one or another of the global powers could begin the process and lay the groundwork for a new round at the next Ministerial Meeting, or least soon after. Indeed, without these changes it might be very unwise to wish for a new round, in case that wish were granted.

Notes

1. World Trade Organization, press release, Geneva, September 28, 1999.
2. V. O. Key Jr., *Public Opinion and American Democracy* (Knopf , 1963), pp. 27–53.
3. Key, *Public Opinion and American Democracy*, p. 35.

4. *The Economist,* July 17, 1999, pp. 49–50.

5. *The Economist,* April 15, 2000, p. 26; and Harris Poll, April 18, 2000 (wto-activist @jatp.org). See also *Business Week,* April 24, 2000, p. 202.

6. Organization for Economic Cooperation and Development, *Report on Regulatory Reform,* vol. 2: *Thematic Studies* (Paris, 1997), chap. 2, pp. 191–248.

7. See Marco C. E. J. Bronckers, "Better Rules for a New Millennium: A Warning against Undemocratic Developments in the WTO," *Journal of International Economic Law,* vol. 2, no. 4 (1999), pp. 547–66; and Gary P. Sampson, "Trade, Environment and the WTO: The Post-Seattle Policy Agenda," Overseas Development Council Policy Essay 27 (Johns Hopkins University Press, 2000).

8. (www.twnside.org.sg/souths/twn/title/wtomr-cx.htm).

9. (www.agp.org/agp/en/PGAenfos/about.htm).

10. See Grant Jordan and William A. Maloney, *The Protest Business? Mobilizing Campaign Groups* (Manchester University Press, 1997).

11. The *Chronicle of Philanthropy* (acwald@mindspring.ca) noted that after Seattle and Washington a conference of the National Network of Grantmakers drew some 350 participants to Boston to discuss why philanthropies should care about globalization and promote NGOs concerned with the issue.

12. "The Consultative Group of Eighteen," MTN.GNGIN14/W15, June 1987, secretariat document prepared for Negotiating Group on FOGS.

13. See, for example, Jeffrey J. Schott and Jayashree Watal, "Decision-Making in the WTO," International Economic Policy Brief (Washington: Institute for International Economics, March 2000); and Bhagiraith Lal Das, "Full Participation and Efficiency in Negotiations," *Third World Economics: Trends and Analysis* (Penang, Malaysia), January. 16–31, 2000, pp. 14–16.

14. Robert E. Hudec, "The New WTO Dispute Settlement Procedure: An Overview of the First Three Years," *Minnesota Journal of Global Trade,* vol. 8, no. 1 (1999), p. 470.

15. See, for example, Sampson, "Trade, Environment and the WTO"; Claude Barfield, *Free Trade, Sovereignty, Democracy: The Future of the World Trade Organization* (Washington: American Enterprise Institute Press, forthcoming).

16. Daniel C. Esty, "Non-Governmental Organizations at the World Trade Organization: Cooperation, Competition or Exclusion?" *Journal of International Economic Law,* vol. 1, no. 1 (1998), p. 133.

17. For a very useful review, see ICTSD, "Accreditation Schemes and Other Arrangements for Public Participation in International Fora," Geneva, November 1999.

18. This and other examples are discussed in Michael Edwards, "NGOs and Global Governance: Rights and Responsibilities" (London: Foreign Policy Centre, June 2000).

19. This is a proposal of the European Commission Trade Directorate that was submitted to a workshop on WTO institutional reform sponsored by the South Center and Oxfam, Geneva, February 2, 2000. It also recommends the establishment of a WTO Parliamentary Assembly.

20. David Jessup, executive director, *New Economy Information Service,* February 4, 2000 (www.newecon.org).

21. See Sylvia Ostry, "China and the WTO: The Transparency Issue," *UCLA Journal of International Law and Foreign Affairs,* vol. 3, no. 1 (1998), pp. 1–22.

22. See Mark A. Groom Bridge and Claude E. Barfield, *Tiger by the Tail: China and the World Trade Organization* (Washington: American Enterprise Institute Press, 1999), pp. 76–81.

23. "The Results of the Uruguay Round of Multilateral Negotiations: The Legal Texts, World Trade Organization" (Geneva, 1994), pp. 442–43.

24. Development Committee, "Trade, Development and Poverty Reduction" (Washington, March 31, 2000), pp. 31–140.

25. World Trade Organization, "Trade and Environment," Special Studies 4 (Geneva, 1999).

26. For analysis and a research review, see André de Moor and Peter Calamari, *Subsidizing Unsustainable Development* (Costa Rica and the Hague: Earth Council and Institute for Research on Public Expenditure, 1997).

27. Council on Economic Priorities, *SA8000: Setting the Standard for Corporate Social Accountability* (Washington, 1998) (cepaa.org).

28. For a useful review of this development, see Janelle Duller, "A Social Conscience in the Global Marketplace? Labour Dimensions of Codes of Conduct, Social Labeling and Investor Initiatives," *International Labour Review*, vol. 138, no. 2 (1999), pp. 22–129.

29. Pascal Lamy, "Inside U.S. Trade," speech by the EU commissioner for trade, November 30, 1999.

COMMENT BY

Rufus H. Yerxa

Sylvia Ostry's chapter combines well the practical and theoretical, and I agree with much of her analysis. My comment focuses on two aspects of how the World Trade Organization governs itself: decisionmaking within the WTO on matters related to new rules or negotiations and decision-making by panels and the Appellate Body within the new Disputes Settlement Understanding (DSU). I also explore how to deal with the concerns of those who fundamentally oppose the WTO system and who want to see it scrapped or changed.

Decisionmaking in the WTO

Many today persist in asking: "Is the WTO decisionmaking process now so flawed that it is in need of reform?" As an old General Agreement on Tariffs and Trade (GATT) and WTO negotiator, I am somewhat mystified and amused by this question and the proliferating number of reasons (or motives) for asking it. I continue to believe that there is very little wrong with the institutional structure for decisionmaking, only with our collective commitment to make it work.

The complaints about WTO governance arise from two different schools of thought: those who feel that the negotiating process is too undemocratic and those who believe you cannot manage a system with 130 countries all having an equal say in every decision. Ironically, proponents of these two polar extremes often act as if they agree about the nature of the problem and the need for reform. During the debate over congressional passage of the WTO agreement, Ralph Nader and Patrick Buchanan would often appear on television agreeing that Congress should reject the deal. Buchanan would say: "Do you really want Cuba to be deciding whether U.S. laws are legitimate?" Then Nader would chime in: "WTO decision-making is secretive, nontransparent and dominated by U.S. multinationals." From listening to them one could almost imagine that the WTO was a conspiracy between Cuba and American multinationals. Of course, those two gentlemen are not particularly interested in improving the WTO. Yet many who have a sincere interest in supporting open world trade echo the same views and ask what can help make the institution work better. The response to these concerns should begin by recognizing the difference between reality and perception.

One perception is that the WTO is somehow undemocratic in its treatment of member governments. There is very little foundation for this criticism. Any real differences in the relative power of countries come from their vastly differing sizes, populations, and trading interests. That is unavoidable. Given these realities, today's WTO is vastly more universal than the old GATT. Seattle itself is proof that significantly changing the rules requires a broad consensus of nations—large and small, developed and developing, trade dependent and trade poor.

Another perception is that the WTO is undemocratic with respect to the balance between interests—producers versus consumers, polluters versus environmentalists, capital versus labor. This is the real basis for Ralph Nader's opposition, and it deserves a good answer. Despite the intricacy and complexity of arguments against the WTO, the answer to those attacks is alarmingly simple: the WTO agreement reflects the sovereign decisions of virtually every democratically elected government in the world about the best way to regulate the global economy in the interests of all citizens. The United States can choose to walk away from this global consensus if it wants, but it cannot restructure the WTO unilaterally. A better course for Mr. Nader would be to try to convince governments to address his concerns about child labor (a concern I share wholeheartedly) in a constructive way by building up the rules. Achieving such objectives will not happen by tearing apart the WTO.

At the opposite extreme, it would be a mistake to fall prey to the thought that we could get better results in promoting free trade if we somehow changed the cumbersome and laborious task of achieving unanimity on all decisions. By better results I assume people mean faster results, rather than the kind of blockages that created the standoff in Seattle in 1999. Supporters of this view may have in mind some kind of UN-style Security Council for the WTO. But I believe this would be a major mistake, and to appreciate why we need to go back to Sylvia Ostry's history lesson.

Small and large countries' complaint about the old GATT rules was that they created a two-tiered regime. Only certain rules were universal, albeit important ones such as most favored nation (MFN) and national treatment. The rest were embodied in reciprocal codes with limited membership. Hence the vast majority of GATT members had very limited obligations. Not surprisingly, they were excluded from discussions about how to apply those rules. This two-tiered structure gave rise to complaints by all parties. Developing countries complained that it created a club of rich countries that made all the important decisions, and developed countries complained that most GATT members—mainly developing countries—were avoiding discipline altogether.

The single undertaking of the Uruguay Round was the grand bargain meant to solve all of those complaints. It created binding disciplines in all areas covered by the WTO agreements and imposed those disciplines on all members. In return for this strengthened trade regime it was assumed that all members would have to agree on any meaningful changes in the rules and that the negotiating structure to achieve changes would have to encompass all parties. The single undertaking was agreed to at the end of the Uruguay Round by complete and total consensus of more than 130 countries. When Peter Sutherland, the GATT director-general, brought down the gavel on that undertaking in Geneva, it was met with thunderous applause from every quarter.

But one should not underestimate the enormous difficulty experienced in getting all WTO members to buy into full disciplines in all areas—from agriculture and textiles to services and intellectual property. I do not see how we can even partly disenfranchise all of these countries without revisiting the question of their level of obligations. The real effect of trying to bring about fundamental changes in WTO decisionmaking would be nothing less than revisiting the agonizing decisions that gave rise to the single undertaking in the first place. Formal creation of a new mode of governance that is less universal and based upon something other than consensus would inevitably reopen the Uruguay Round Agreement and that would not be a good idea.

Moreover, it is not necessary. There is nothing wrong with the institution that leadership and a sense of common direction cannot fix, and any new structure will be utterly useless if those two factors are missing. The multilateral decisionmaking process worked in 1993 because everyone wanted the deal badly enough. A lot of informal consensus-building meetings and groupings successfully produced a truly multilateral agreement. We even had names for them: the Green Room, the Quad, the Cairns Group, the Dirty Dozen, the De La Paix Group, the Russin Group (named after the village where GATT Director-General Arthur Dunkel lived). We used small ministerials, large ministerials, and all kinds of gatherings of high officials to advance our work. More than thirty countries participated in the famous Green Room process, and those thirty represented all regions of the globe. None of this was formalized in the charter of the institution.

But it was a very effective accumulation of small groups and piecemeal negotiating structures designed to merge eventually into that most fragile and elusive of prey for trade negotiators—true consensus.

My cure for the problems of the WTO in the lead-up to Seattle and thereafter is quite simple: leave the formal decisionmaking structure alone and put in place people of talent and wisdom who know how to make it work. Then go to work on the slow, grueling, painful process of finding common ground. Seattle failed because there was no real consensus capable of withstanding the kind of criticism that is inevitable whenever you decide to resolve trade disputes and expand liberalization. I would have been far more troubled if Seattle had succeeded on the basis of some hastily engineered consensus that would have evaporated once the negotiators returned to Geneva.

The Dispute Settlement System

My second point concerns the dispute settlement system. This part of governance is critical, and the changes wrought by the Uruguay Round were considerable, although far less significant than the single undertaking. But the Disputes Settlement Understanding is the glue that holds the single undertaking together, and the tensions now apparent within the Dispute Settlement Body (DSB) are troublesome.

Once again historical perspective is needed. The old view of GATT was that a dispute system was intended to encourage and guide negotiations toward a solution. One of my best mentors, that great man Jules Katz, frequently reminded us that "all trade disputes are a prelude for negotiations." Some now raise the legitimate question: "Have we gotten away from the negotiation-based model by trying to put in place a more juridical system that is not working because key governments are incapable of implementing its decisions?"

I can understand this critique if one focuses only on the short term. Over time, however, I think the answer will be different. Fundamentally, this is a good system. It is true that some decisions are now being blocked at the implementation stage. But before the Uruguay Round they were all blocked at the adoption stage, so we are clearly making progress. At least now it is impossible to say that a panel or Appellate Body decision is irrelevant because it has not been adopted.

The fundamental objectives for having a dispute structure within an international organization are being realized. The rulings by panels and the Appellate Body are, for the most part, creating a solid and credible body of WTO law. They are given such prominence that they cannot be ignored even by the big powers, which may fight implementation of decisions for years. Where the rulings fail to totally resolve a dispute, the very existence of a panel decision can serve as a prelude for negotiations.

The real questions about what to do with the DSU are more mundane: Should there be a permanent body of panelists like the Appellate Body? How much greater access should private groups be given? How much more transparency should we mandate during panels? Beyond addressing those questions, we need to change the expectation that binding dispute settlement is somehow a miracle cure. In big cases it will still take negotiations to fully resolve disputes.

More troubling is the complaint of some small countries that the dispute settlement system is asymmetrical because big powers can ignore rulings and suffer retaliation, while small countries are forced to comply. This suggests that small countries would be better off with no binding dispute settlement. But any asymmetry would be even worse without the DSU because the large players would be even less constrained.

A central challenge is how we strengthen the DSU for all players—big and small—to move toward WTO-compatible laws. The real problem is that WTO disciplines go deeply into areas of domestic policy such as food safety. The only real solution is to let the world get used to this fact. Either we want to live in a world where we are increasing our commercial and economic interdependence, and thus inevitably our social and regulatory principles, or we do not. If we do, we will eventually become comfortable with an international juridical process. If we do not, we will find ourselves living with many of the imperfections and frustrations that have always characterized this system.

Addressing the Critics

What should we make of the challenge to the WTO's legitimacy brought on by the amazingly broad (and only fleetingly compatible) collection of interest groups and nongovernmental organizations that had their moment in Seattle? I assume that we can all agree they should have the opportunity to fully air their criticisms and their proposals for change. In time, and with true public debate, the valid criticisms will take root and the nutty ones will lose their virulence. Isn't that the essence of free speech in a democracy? If the critics succeed in changing the overwhelming judgment of governments and peoples across the globe that an open world economy based on sound rules is the best answer, then more power to them. I suspect they will never succeed. The WTO cannot have legitimacy unless these various ideas are fully aired in a democratic way and either accepted or rejected. I am not arguing that NGOs be allowed to capture the system, only that their concerns be addressed systematically.

At the heart of the legitimacy question is the dichotomy between turning the WTO into some supranational constitutionally based regime or, alternatively, stepping back from that paradigm to a loose system of free trade with regulatory diversity. My own view is that the Ralph Naders of the world are much too alarmed about the desire of people like me to go down the road of using the WTO as a vehicle for a forced integration of social and regulatory structures. Most people want to see nation states continue to have choices about how they regulate activity within their own borders, provided they do so in a manner that is nondiscriminatory and provided that the end justifies the means. We need to return to the traditional GATT concept that the rules are in the nature of a contract between governments. In the end you cannot force a partner to carry out a contract, but you can make him pay for the damage. Thus, even where the United States or some other party decides not to follow WTO rules—for example in the bananas or Foreign Investment Sales Corporation (FISC) disputes—the only final sanction is to allow the aggrieved party to redress the inequity by withdrawing equivalent concessions. This addresses many of the critics' concerns. If the WTO were to rule that one of our laws or regulations violates its rules, we must decide whether safeguarding that position outweighs our trade interests. If it does, so be it. But that is a democratic decision made by our government and not by activists in the street.

387

COMMENT BY
B. K. Zutshi

The institutional design of the World Trade Organization is basically sound. As an intergovernmental institution, it is as democratic as it can ever get. Furthermore, the causes of the failure at Seattle were complex and had little to do with the structure of the WTO. Seattle was essentially a leadership failure. This does not, however, mean that the institution cannot operate more efficiently.

The genesis of the debate on the architecture of the WTO is clearly the failed Seattle Ministerial meeting. Some assume that there is an inherent design fault in the WTO architecture necessitating changes that will lead to a more efficient discharge of three crucial functions: rulemaking, administration of the covered agreements, and dispute resolution. The debate has been formulated in terms of transparency and participation in the decisionmaking processes, both within the organization for its members and for the outside world, in particular for civil society as represented by nongovernmental organizations. Is there a design fault in the WTO? What are the issues in transparency and participation? How far can participation by outsiders be applied to an intergovernmental organization like the WTO?

The WTO is a sui generis organization. It is member driven and member administered; it is fully democratic inasmuch as the value of a member's vote is the same, irrespective of its trade share. Decisionmaking is by consensus, although voting is possible and provided for. There is open participation by all members in all organs of the WTO except the Balance of Payments Committee and the Committee on Budget and Finance. The WTO has a credible dispute resolution and enforcement system, perhaps the only one of its kind in any intergovernmental organization. It has a clearly defined competence, which is confined to trade relations among its members in covered agreements.

This architecture, drawn from the General Agreement on Tariffs and Trade (GATT), was adopted after examining various options, including the idea of having a decisionmaking body with limited membership, along the lines of the UN Security Council (with permanent and rotating membership), decisions by a weighted voting system based on trade shares, or greater delegation to the secretariat to administer the system. Developing countries expressed strong reservations about diluting the WTO's democratic character by providing for decisionmaking on a representational or on a trade-weighted basis. There was also little support for greater delegation to the secretariat; great value was attached to preserving the member-driven character of the organization (from personal knowledge as India's ambassador and permanent representative to GATT from June 1989 to October 1994).

Participation by WTO Members in Decisionmaking

There are two kinds of criticism about existing procedures and practices. First, the least developed countries' delegates are not present and do not participate in meetings where important decisions are made. Second, the so-called Green Room process is exclusive, or at least not inclusive enough. Small delegations are not always present in Geneva and are therefore unable to cover WTO meetings adequately. The essential problem is not a lack of transparency or a lack of opportunity to participate, but a lack of financial and human resources. A much greater effort is needed by the WTO and other international organizations to assist developing countries in capacity building. Small developing-country members will also need to pool their resources. The Caribbean Regional Negotiating Machinery (RNM) is an example of cooperation of this kind.

With the vastly increased scope of WTO agreements, the workload of daily meetings has risen appreciably. It is difficult, even for moderate-size delegations, to attend all meetings, and this is a particular problem for small delegations. The situation where delegations are unaware of meetings or not invited to them is serious and avoidable; this is a matter of leadership.

Small delegations have complained in the past about nontransparency and about being presented with faits accomplis, particularly during the process of setting an agenda and a negotiating mandate for rulemaking in a new round. The situation in Seattle no doubt was aggravated by the larger membership of the organization and greater interest by small developing-country delegations in the proceedings. But the basic nature of the problem has not changed with more members and more active participation by developing countries. The challenge is how to make the negotiating process both efficient and inclusive. This is essentially a leadership challenge, since the processes are run by representatives of the member countries themselves. Some experiences in the Uruguay Round negotiations are instructive.

Among the more difficult subjects negotiated in the Uruguay Round were services and Trade-Related Aspects of Intellectual Property Rights (TRIPs). As processes, these negotiations were conducted with skill and sensitivity toward all participants, particularly those from developing countries. This was largely because of the quality of leadership provided by the chairpersons of the negotiating groups. Small group meetings were convened, but the chairs took responsibility for keeping all interested delegations informed of developments. In services, negotiations were held in a small group first, then in a group of about twenty delegations, and finally in meetings open to all delegations. A similar arrangement was used in negotiating the Disputes Settlement Understanding.

There is no credible alternative to holding small group meetings to resolve difficult and contentious issues. If the practice is discontinued, it will drive the process of consultations outside the WTO building, with much greater harm to internal transparency. It is essential for those in charge of conducting negotiations to ensure that all delegations, which have an interest in a subject, are consulted and kept informed of developments if small group meetings are held.

Sylvia Ostry suggested that the WTO institute a forum where contentious issues could be debated in a nondecisionmaking context. She cited as a model the Consultative Group of Eighteen (CG-18), the GATT policy forum for debate. CG-18 was suspended in 1990 by the then director-general on the basis of informal consultations. The reason was that there were more aspirants for membership in the group than could be accommodated and still retain the character of the forum as small and representational. It seems unlikely that the nondecisionmaking character of such a forum will result in nonpartisan, objective consideration of subjects and issues for possible future negotiations. The experience of the working of CG-18 does not warrant any such conclusion.

Investing a forum with decisionmaking powers will not change the nature of members' participation, nor the character of the debate on a particular issue. It is not clear how an exclusive, restricted forum like CG-18 will promote participation and transparency. Any exclusive, restricted arrangement, even for the purpose of debate and discussion, will alter the basic democratic character of the organization. That the idea is a nonstarter has already become clear since Seattle. The related suggestion of off-loading research and analysis to academic institutions and think tanks looks equally unworkable. It would be difficult to choose among such institutions. A more fruitful avenue may be research cooperation between the WTO and other bodies of the United Nations, such as the UN Conference on Trade and Development (UNCTAD), the World Health Organization (WHO), and the World Intellectual Property Organization (WIPO).

External Transparency: Participation in WTO Deliberations

The clamor by nongovernmental organizations for a seat at the table has its origin in their perception that they can advance their specific agendas through the World Trade Organization and its dispute settlement mechanism, and through the use of trade sanctions. But making the WTO the sole arbiter of the international community's every little concern could lead to its breakdown.

The demand for participation in the deliberations of various WTO bodies by nongovernmental organizations is based on the notions of accountability and legitimacy prevalent in liberal democracies. But to what extent do these notions apply to the functioning of an intergovernmental organization? It is difficult to envisage an arrangement in which representatives accountable to their governments open their deliberations to NGOs accountable to none or to interest groups. The result is sure to be greater posturing. Open participation would encourage groups to play to the gallery, making deals much more difficult to achieve. At the least, it would take a heavy toll on the efficiency of the system.

Civil society and NGOs have a role to play in an intergovernmental organization, but the role must be played within national boundaries. When formulating their positions on issues under consideration in the World Trade Organization, NGOs must influence their own governments. Allowing NGOs to act as independent agents in the WTO, apart from being unworkable, would have serious implications for equity among members, giving rise to asymmetries of resources and influence between the North and the South. NGOs' claims of representing civil society are not sustainable on the basis of any objective criteria. Most of these organizations are opaque in their funding and functioning. Claims that they are more representative than the elected governments of democratic nations are, to put it mildly, a travesty. NGOs must work through their governments. There is, in my view, no workable alternative.

Access to the Dispute Settlement Process

Some have suggested opening the dispute settlement process to the public and giving NGOs the right to file *amicus* briefs. The question concerns the extent to which national practices can be introduced in the WTO dispute settlement process, how far is it feasible to do so, and what impact is it likely to have on equity among members and on the balance in their rights and obligations?

A shift in the orientation of the dispute settlement system from the political to the adjudicatory does not, in itself, imply application of all practices prevalent in national legal systems. These are not disputes between a state and an individual or between two individuals in a state; they are disputes between states that have entered into contractual obligations. The analogy with practices in national legal systems is not necessarily applicable. Unless open access to these processes is contemplated, selection for limited and controlled access will pose insurmountable problems. Although an Appellate Body judgment has held that *amicus* briefs can be accepted at their discretion, there is great uneasiness about this practice. If encouraged, it will result in great asymmetry in resources and influence between the North and South. The process will become even more expensive and burdensome for developing countries.

ROBERT D. HORMATS

16 | *Governance of the Global Trading System*

ven before the failure of the World Trade Organization's ministerial meeting in Seattle in 1999, a
move was under way to reexamine governance of that institution and of
the global trading system. Most experts recognize the need for reform.
Those who seek to change the WTO system face the difficult task of balancing the need for efficiency with the need for equity. They must find
ways to enable large countries to play a role consistent with their prominence in the international trading system. They also must ensure, however,
that developing countries play a role commensurate with their growing
power in the world economy. Moreover, developing nations' support will
be needed to reach agreement on key issues in future negotiations of the
World Trade Organization.

Equally complicated has been the task of forging agreement on how to
address newer issues such as the environment and workers' rights. And
there is the strategic question of whether the next step toward trade liberalization should be to tackle many issues in a single negotiation or relatively
few issues in separate sectoral negotiations. Should regional negotiations be
the primary vehicles for liberalization in the near future? Or is the WTO in
a position to take the next initiative, if only on the few items for which it al-

I am indebted to Oxford Analytica for its very useful updates and analysis of the running debate
over WTO reform.

ready has a clear mandate? Complicating the picture are domestic regulatory issues, such as antitrust. They have an increasingly significant impact on trade and investment, but so far have been addressed largely within the domain of domestic policy.

In addition to institutional and technical questions relating to reform, there are newer questions relating to what might be termed the "democratic gap." Some fear that globalization and the institutions that embody it are part of a process beyond the influence of the average citizen and even beyond the influence of governments to which citizens look to take care of their interests. The WTO is characterized by critics as representing forces that are disrupting the lives, values and communities of millions of people but forces over which most people have little control.

The WTO must find ways to identify with the concerns of average citizens of member countries as well as to expand commerce and improve global rules. It cannot just serve as a forum for officials, detached from the increased political attention trade is receiving. National trade officials will have to do a better job of demonstrating that their constituents' interests are being taken into account and that governments have policies to help people cope with the inevitable workplace disruption that comes from intensified domestic and international competition. In the final analysis good trade governance internationally depends on good economic governance domestically.

Organization

The World Trade Organization's decisionmaking process is awkward and cumbersome. Sheer size makes agreement difficult to reach. The General Agreement on Tariffs and Trade (GATT) started with twenty-three members in 1948. At the end of the Uruguay Round, in 1994, there were 110 members. The WTO now has 136 members. Roughly thirty more countries have applied to join. Virtually all of the new members are developing nations; many of them have become highly integrated into the global trading system in recent years and insist on greater participation in the WTO's decisionmaking process.

Developing nations were less insistent on a strong voice in GATT. They were, for the most part, willing to allow the United States and the European Union to run the show. This was because many developing countries were excused from full compliance with agreements reached in GATT negotiations. They enjoyed long phase-in periods before they had to implement most agreements. Large numbers of developing countries obtained generalized tariff preferences. And most received enormous benefits from most-favored-nation trade access to markets of industrialized nations. Many of them were, in effect, free riders in the system.

Following the Uruguay Round, most developing nations have had to implement all of the negotiated agreements as part of the "single undertaking principle." So, at a minimum, they have had to be better informed about what is happening in all the WTO negotiating sessions and how negotiations on all items will affect them. Many of these countries have had difficulty enforcing or implementing regulatory and other changes negotiated primarily by large countries—changes for which developing countries are held accountable even though many did not fully participate in the negotiations that produced them. As a result they now view with caution the negotiating process and insist on a far greater say in it.

Developing countries invoke the "consensus rule" more frequently than they did in the past. The consensus rule calls for decisions to be taken by vote. Each member has one vote, which it can use to block a consensus. In practice, however, decisions are taken on the basis of members forging a consensus before a vote. A consensus is interpreted to mean that no member states its direct opposition to a decision. The intent of this procedure is to give small nations a defense against pressure from large nations. But, of course, it allows each country a potential veto. The consensus rule enables individual nations to delay WTO decisions or to hold a potential agreement hostage in order to obtain concessions in other areas. Developing countries are not the only ones to use or threaten to use the veto, but they often see it as a useful tactic. The United States and the European Union frequently block initiatives before they get to this stage.

The WTO holds a ministerial conference every two years, far more frequently than did GATT (the next is in Doha, Qatar, in November 2001). These ministerials occupy an enormous amount of the time of members and WTO staff for several months in advance. The size of the meetings, and the need to address many issues in a very short period of time, have caused them to take on a frenetic air. The failure of the one in Seattle demonstrated the cost of poor preparation. It also highlighted the public embarrassment that can result from the chaos that surrounded such a high-profile event. Future meetings will likely be magnets for the kinds of demonstrations that made such a farce of the Seattle meeting—even though its failure was largely the result of what happened inside the hall rather than in the streets.

Compared with GATT, the WTO embraces a far wider range of issues. WTO rules cover many subjects that once were largely in the realm of domestic policy. The more complicated the issues, and the more profoundly they affect domestic constituencies, the harder it has been to achieve consensus. A large number of issues also require considerable technical expertise. Lacking a great deal of technical expertise, many developing nations find it difficult to fully participate in the WTO's work. Many of the poorest developing countries suffer an additional disadvantage: they cannot afford a full-time representative at the WTO or, if they can, they do not have the staff needed to prepare for highly complicated trade talks.

The main decisionmaking institution of the WTO, the General Council, includes all members. Its sheer size makes it unwieldy. This unwieldiness pushes most decisionmaking into small, informal meetings. These so-called Green Room meetings are normally attended only by countries with a direct interest in the subject under discussion. Members invited to attend are expected to represent the entire WTO membership on the issue under consideration, but the process often breeds suspicion among those not invited.

Suggested Changes in Governance

The above problems are well understood as governance defects of the WTO. But agreement on changes has proved difficult, for several reasons.

The European Union and the United States dominate the WTO. No progress can be made without their consent. And when they do agree, despite the consensus procedure, other nations or groups of nations cannot stand in their way without a major fight. They often anger smaller nations by agreeing on a given issue in advance of a major meeting and then informing others of that agreement. This creates resentment among nations excluded from the EU-U.S. negotiating process.

Green Room meetings meant to make decisionmaking more efficient often fail to achieve their intended results when participants cannot produce support among a broad enough group of nonattendees. Routinely, many developing nations are excluded from the Green Room meetings. In Seattle, many complained about this exclusion.

Another issue relates to nongovernmental organizations (NGOs). In an effort to broaden the base of domestic support for the WTO, U.S. officials have floated the idea of involving NGOs and other outside groups more actively in the WTO's work. Some developing countries have resisted this idea, arguing that participation in WTO deliberations should be limited to national governments that are WTO signatories. In the view of many developing countries, NGOs in developed countries often work directly against their trade interests. They do not want NGOs to file briefs or become more active observers in dispute settlement procedures or negotiations.

Nevertheless, nongovernmental organizations are likely to be more active in the coming years. Many are making particularly effective use of the Internet. Ways will need to be found for government officials to meet with them at the national and international levels to hear their views and demonstrate that their concerns are being addressed when they have merit —even if their policy formulas might not be accepted. In many cases the policy positions of individual NGOs differ radically from one another— especially the positions of NGOs in developed and developing countries: acceptance of one group's position often means rejection of another's. But individual governments must improve dialogue with NGOs to incorporate their views when and if they are valid and to argue against them when they are not valid.

Business and consumer groups will need to organize more effectively to ensure that their views are factored into WTO decisionmaking. They should do this proactively, rather than wait for a crisis or a major international meeting. They will need to address the human issues nongovernmental organizations raise in terms that average citizens can understand. And national governments will need to ensure that trade policy is not fragmented by responding to conflicting NGO pressures, a potential danger if national leaders lose sight of the broad national interests involved in expanded global trade.

National leaders must reinforce the political point that underlies the economic one. It will be very difficult to maintain international political harmony if international trade tensions increase or if some groups can take great advantage of open trade while others feel exploited by it. Politicians need to remind their citizens of the terrible condition of the world between World War I and World War II, a period when economic cooperation broke down. Claims that trade strengthens democracy or reduces chances of conflict are often exaggerated. Nonetheless, trade has a strong record of leading to improvements in domestic economies and in conditions for hundreds of millions of people, while empowering them vis-à-vis their governments. When disruptions do occur or environmental problem arise, they need to be addressed in ways that do not restrict trade or investment.

Specific proposals for reform of the WTO include creation of a council composed of the most significant participants in the world trading system. Opponents counter that this will further alienate the smaller nations. Another proposal is for an IMF-type executive board based on regional constituencies. But the WTO is a contractual organization in which countries are reluctant to give to a constituency representative the right to vote on matters of significant interest to them. The International Monetary Fund normally considers support for single-country programs, whereas the trade agreements of the WTO affect the lives and jobs of millions of people in many member countries. Ceding voting authority, as in the IMF or the World Bank, is an unlikely step for most members of the WTO.

Although these reform proposals have not attracted much support, most WTO members recognize that a situation in which all items are negotiated among all members, or even a great many of them, is unwieldy. Some type of representative group will be needed. But in the final analysis it will be hard to take the politics out of trade because it affects so many people in so many countries. A magic bullet that would produce efficient and fair trade governance quickly will remain elusive.

To bridge the gap, modest steps are under way to make the WTO more efficient while ensuring that developing countries do not feel disenfranchised. One constructive proposal is to hold negotiations among a small group of WTO members that are considered representative of the whole membership on the matter at hand; the substance of these discussions would quickly be conveyed to all members. Those nations not participating in the negotiations directly then could express their opinions on the matter, and their views would be considered when the small group met again.

Developing countries would need assistance in evaluating the impact on them of various proposals and possible negotiating outcomes—as well as in determining how they would implement specific proposals if accepted by the WTO membership. Steps would need to be taken to enable such countries to assess the progress of talks. The Internet could prove a useful and powerful tool in this respect, enabling dissemination of positions quickly to nonparticipants in a particular negotiation and allowing them to be in close touch with experts in their capitals. But no amount of automaticity will overcome the difficult negotiating barriers that exist substantively and organizationally. Hard bargaining will be needed to make progress on both.

More controversial are suggestions to introduce voting on some subjects that are noncontractual in nature, with a majority or supermajority being able to prevail. There also is little support for a recent initiative to institute a negotiating process among regional blocs. Few countries are willing to cede authority to others to negotiate for them. On numerous issues the interests of countries in the same region differ greatly.

Groups based on common interests, such as the Cairns Group of major agricultural exporters, will continue to form. For many subjects, however, this useful negotiating technique is hard to replicate because countries allied on one set of issues may differ on others. Agriculture is so singularly important to so many countries that the Cairns Group has had considerable influence and exhibited substantial cohesion.

Preparations for ministerial meetings could be improved. Before the Seattle conference WTO members made a vast number of proposals. Efforts to consolidate them in advance of the meeting and identify significant common ground proved fruitless. Failing to do this, officials sent a long draft declaration to the ministers. That declaration included many proposals on which there were deep divisions. It suggested few areas where political consensus was sufficient to reach agreement.

There seems to be broad agreement that better preparations are needed for future ministerial sessions of the WTO. Senior officials should meet well beforehand to develop issues for ministers in a coherent fashion. A lot more attention also must be paid in advance by political leaders. They must cultivate the domestic support needed for any new negotiation and to implement any deals reached. This attention was notably absent before Seattle.

Some countries want to establish the principle that a ministerial conference would be cancelled if preparations have not produced promising results. This idea to avoid huge fiascoes is refreshing, but it would deprive the world of the potential of using such conferences to galvanize consensus in advance as their opening date grows nigh.

The director-general of the WTO needs to establish the basis for an agreement on key issues before the ministerial conference. Major issues not resolved in advance are rarely resolved at high-level meetings. The role of the director-general can be a powerful one in selecting topics on which agreement is possible. This includes identifying potential trade-offs among issues. Compared with counterparts in the World Bank and IMF, the head of the WTO has been a less visible figure on the international economic landscape. The director-general now needs to push forward the international trade agenda at a high political level. Without this effort, the agenda is unlikely to advance very far.

Future Negotiations

The next question is when, how, and indeed whether to launch a new negotiating round. The Uruguay Round mandated negotiations on agriculture to "continue the reform process . . . of substantial progressive reductions in support and protection." This negotiation is expected to be completed by 2004. The General Agreement on Trade in Services (GATS) called for a new round to liberalize trade in services and improve rules on subsidies, safeguards, and government procurement. Finally, the Agreement on Trade-Related Aspects of Intellectual Property Rights (TRIPs) mandated new negotiations on a limited number of intellectual property issues.

In the next round, should a substantial number of items be on the agenda? Or is it preferable to conduct separate, or linked, negotiations on agriculture, services, and property rights and perhaps a few more issues? The European Union has supported a broad agenda for a new round. To make the concessions on agriculture that many exporters demand, the EU argues that it needs to obtain extensive concessions from other countries on items important to it, other than agriculture. But the European Union has appeared to be unwilling to offer much on agriculture to induce concessions by others in other areas. Its stance also has aroused suspicion in Washington and capitals of other big agricultural exporters; many suspect that the EU has ulterior motives in wanting a broader round with several controversial items on the agenda, such as antitrust. That formula, they charge, would allow the EU later to justify not giving concessions on agriculture on the grounds that other countries were not making sufficient concessions in these controversial areas.

The broader question is whether the political basis for a new multi-issue negotiating round can be established. For the time being the prospects are dim. Although President Bush and European leaders, meeting in Sweden in June 2001, committed to launching an "ambitious" track record later in the year, it will take much work to make that a success. Trade-offs are needed to ensure major EU concessions on agriculture, if sufficient trade-offs do in fact exist to change deep-seated political support for current EU policy. In many cases the goal should be sensible sectoral solutions that stand on their own. In some cases, solutions are not amenable to trade-offs. Taking a less rigorous approach to protection of intellectual property, for example, merely because another country opens its market for, say, meat is a position that is hard to defend.

In the United States the president is more likely to get congressional support for negotiations for the Free Trade Area of the Americas (FTAA) or for sectoral negotiations of finite scope with clear objectives than for a broader set of negotiations with a less clear outcome. As negotiations penetrate deeper into domestic policy, especially on regulatory matters, domestic constraints will increase. When negotiations were about trading increased access to the U.S. market for a foreign export in return for increased access for an American product to a foreign market, trade-offs were possible in many areas. But trade-offs become more difficult when dealing with antitrust, consumer protection, or environmental issues. The most promising near-term strategy would probably be to organize a series of sectoral negotiations under the umbrella of the WTO. These would include those issues already mandated and a few others (for example, an open and minimally regulated environment for the Internet and e-commerce). A broader, more "ambitious" road would be desirable, but a lot harder to pull off.

Internet and E-Commerce

Some of the thorny issues related to the Internet and e-commerce can be taken up in the GATS negotiations already scheduled. The Internet makes cross-border provision of services such as advertising, accounting, banking, communication, data processing, and software more immediate and more feasible than conventional modes of delivery. GATS negotiations provide a good opportunity to reinforce rules on national treatment and increased market access in such areas.

But governance issues are complicated. "All electronic transmissions consist of services," the EU asserts. It would like more items in this area to fall under GATS. But going that far could make treatment of some digitally transmitted e-commerce items (such as books, movies, music, and software) less liberal than if they were delivered in hard copy—where tariff bindings apply. Liberal market access under GATS covers only areas in which members have made specific commitments; in areas where members have not made commitments, less liberal treatment is allowed. Some items that face low or no tariffs when delivered in hard copy could be subject to high tariffs when delivered digitally. Already the EU has provoked controversy by announcing plans to impose a value-added tax on services transmitted electronically from abroad.

Other issues can be taken up by an e-commerce "work program." This was to have been initiated at the Seattle Ministerial, along with work on an agreement to extend the moratorium on duties on electronic transmissions over the Internet. A new WTO work program could address online delivery of less traditionally exported services, including education, legal services, and medical services. Among other things, it could find ways to ensure that domestic regulation and taxation of e-commerce and the Internet do not become nontariff barriers.

Every area of international business will be affected by the Internet. Without some consensus on the need to avoid heavy or discriminatory taxes and regulations, the global character of the Internet could be jeopardized or the Internet could become Balkanized by sharply different national or regional practices.

The highly technical nature of the Internet, and the newness of the many business and e-commerce models it has spawned, have led to very close collaboration between private sector representatives and governments around the world. In the Organization for Economic Cooperation and Development (OECD), for example, private sector representatives played a key role in work on electronic authentication, self-regulatory codes of conduct, and taxation. In talks on the Free Trade Area of the Americas, the private sector participated as a partner with governments in the Joint Committee of Experts on Electronic Commerce. These relationships should be continued and enhanced.

Broadening the Base for New Trade Talks

It is hard to imagine that a new round of WTO negotiations could embrace as wide a range of subjects as did past rounds. G8 leaders at the Okinawa Summit in July 2000 called for a new round with an "ambitious, balanced and inclusive agenda," yet no consensus to go forward could be reached by the end of that year. The goal expressed in Okinawa remains an enormous challenge.

The problem is deeper than the preparation of negotiating to determine the topics on which agreement might be possible. Globalization has increased dramatically with the expansion of trade, investment, and information flows. However, the ability of governments to forge a democratic consensus to support additional trade liberalization has lagged. National goals consistent with an improved global trading system have not been well articulated. Some argue that trade widens the income gap. They charge that even if economies gain as a whole, lower income groups will be injured by increased trade competition.

The current trade debate includes issues not only of economic trade-offs but also socioeconomic trade-offs. In a strictly economic trade-off, country A opens its markets further to country B's beef in return for country B opening its markets further to country A's computers. Now the debate combines economic values such as the desirability of expanded trade with socioeconomic values such as the desirability of improving the environment, labor standards, and human rights. So the argument frequently focuses on ways to use trade leverage to force improvements in these areas. That, in turn, raises the issue of whether or how to bring into the trade governance process those who advocate injecting these new issues into the trade debate.

The international leadership role of the United States is on the line. The success of the Clinton administration and leaders in the Congress in passing the China permanent normal trade relations (PNTR) bill and the African and Caribbean trade bills was a positive step. It reestablished momentum toward trade liberalization. But obtaining support for fast-track authority—now called trade promotion authority (TPA)—the next step in trade negotiations, will prove harder. Without such support, or without some acceptable alternative to TPA, the United States will be effectively out of the serious part of the negotiating process when it comes to a new WTO round, the Free Trade Area of the Americas, or an extension of the North American Free Trade Agreement (NAFTA) to Chile.

With no consensus on trade in the United States and no mandate for a new negotiation, regional negotiations, primarily involving other nations, are likely to drive the trade process. The United States may find itself on the sidelines and facing discrimination in a number of regional markets.

In working with nongovernmental organizations and engaging them to bring them into a new trade consensus in the United States, policymakers must ask several questions. Whom do these groups represent? And will their enhanced participation in the debate in the WTO weaken, or circumvent, representatives of national governments? After all, national representatives are supposed to represent all of their people, not just a vocal if well-motivated few. Many NGOs are asking legitimate questions, even if they often have the wrong answers. Their representations need to be sorted out between those that have merit and those that do not, with less emotion than of late.

Over time it will likely fall to national governments, rather than the WTO, to develop a more systematic dialogue with nongovernmental organizations. In the United States, NGOs are likely to become even more vocal on trade issues. Hence addressing their concerns in a rational way will become essential for progress toward a national consensus on trade policy. A dialogue hardly means agreement on all points. It cannot mean sacrificing the benefits of expansion of global trade and investment on which more and more jobs and countries, and enormous consumer benefits, depend. And many of their demands are non-negotiable from the start. But it does mean listening better and determining ways to respond to genuine concerns about labor rights, the environment, and human rights, where appropriate. Without improvements in domestic governance of trade policy, it will be hard to reestablish sufficient support for the next major steps in trade negotiations. There may now be a basis for a new dialogue between business, unions, environmentalists, and other groups on how to broaden the base of support for trade liberalization.

Many nongovernmental organizations want the WTO to play an increasingly interventionist or regulatory role. Such a role is inconsistent with the history of GATT and the WTO: their mission has been to reduce regulations and barriers to trade and investment. Environmentalists and supporters of better conditions for labor want to use trade sanctions to advance their objectives. They also want the WTO to monitor conditions in member countries to see that improved performance criteria are adhered to and to respond to complaints that violations have occurred.

At least for the moment, the WTO is not well positioned to assume these functions. Poor human rights policies, harmful environmental practices, and abusive working conditions reflect a country's state of development and domestic policies far more than their trade policies. In many cases these practices have little, if any, measurable impact on foreign trade or investment. A consensus on internationally acceptable procedures whereby the WTO would enforce good practices in these areas is highly unlikely. Modes of enforcement would be difficult to agree on even if a consensus was reached on ideal or acceptable domestic good practices.

On the other hand, there are bound to be areas in which market forces could be harnessed to strengthen labor and environmental practices. One positive step would be to develop higher levels of transparency, whereby consumers could have access to information on countries' human rights, environmental, and labor policies. These policies might then influence to a greater degree the purchasing decisions of consumers. That is already beginning to occur in some quarters. In addition, companies could develop voluntary codes of conduct and monitor compliance. Transparency also could be advanced through voluntary "social labeling"—certification that products were made under conditions that did not violate good environmental practices or basic labor protections. Other useful suggestions include strengthening the International Labor Organization and developing multilateral agreements to tackle environmental problems, rather than relying on trade sanctions, and giving weight to the environmental implications, as well as the anticompetitive implications, of subsidies.

Antitrust Issues

One of the most difficult governance issues in the coming decade will be competition, or antitrust, policy. As barriers at the border decline, restrictive business practices could become increasingly significant barriers to exporters and investors in a number of countries. Although a great deal of cooperation on this issue exists between the United States and the European Union, their approaches in the WTO differ considerably.

The EU has urged negotiation of a Competition Policy Agreement (CPA) that establishes a minimum set of binding standards governing competition policy and enforcement. It believes that this would establish a base for the subsequent progressive harmonization of such rules. The United States is reluctant to accede to a CPA of this type, in particular because of the binding nature of such an agreement. Instead it favors sustained expansion of cooperation among national and regional authorities based largely on bilateral agreements. It places greater emphasis than the EU on strengthening the commitment of regulatory authorities and governments to increased competition within their markets and among economies. It also is wary that a debate on this subject will be seized on by Japan and many developing countries to try to alter U.S. antidumping laws.

The challenge will be to craft an agreement that ensures that business practices within countries or regions that are signatories to an agreement do not restrict the access of foreign products or investors, or harm the interests of foreign consumers. Such an agreement is likely to be possible only if it does not require the complete harmonization of national policies but attempts to achieve broad conformity with agreed competition principles.

Implementation of such an agreement would pose special challenges. The initial signatories under the EU proposal would likely be the industrialized democracies plus the larger emerging economies. And a dispute settlement process relating to competition policy would probably need to differ from the normal WTO process. A dispute settlement panel should be composed of antitrust experts, practitioners, and judges as opposed to the normal generalist participants in traditional WTO panels. A complicated series of issues would have to be resolved as to how private parties would be able to obtain redress under any new WTO provisions.

In the final analysis, competition policy will pose one of the greatest challenges to WTO governance in this decade. Whether the process of increased cooperation involves primarily a higher degree of bilateral cooperation or a broader WTO agreement will be a major decision for the United States. There is already great resistance in the U.S. Congress to an enlarged role for the WTO—and extending the WTO's role to include antitrust issues is bound to encounter stiff opposition. In short, antitrust policy is an unlikely candidate for inclusion in the next round of negotiations.

Regional Trade Agreements

One of the more complicated challenges for trade governance will be to reconcile the growing number of regional and bilateral free trade agreements with the rules and principles of the WTO. During the 1990s the number of regional trade agreements more than doubled. Virtually all WTO members now participate in one or more of these agreements. Even Japan, which once resisted regional agreements, is seeking to negotiate bilateral deals. Once the bedrock of GATT and WTO, the most-favored-nation (MFN) principle (now referred to in the United States as normal trade relations) has become the exception rather than the rule.

GATT built in provisions for signatories to make exceptions to MFN—Article XXIV. This permitted groups of countries to eliminate trade barriers among themselves while maintaining their then-current barriers toward nonparticipating countries. It permitted the creation of customs unions and free trade areas that eliminate duties and other restrictions to "substantially all the trade" between members. It was justified on grounds that GATT did not want to prevent groups of countries, such as those in Western Europe, from expanding trade among themselves. In fact, such expansion was a major U.S. objective after World War II. The European Economic Community, now the EU, proved to be the largest of these regional trade groups and the prototype for many countries. NAFTA and Mercosur (the Southern Cone Common Market) are also established under this provision.

Working parties called for under GATT to consider the consistency of regional trade agreements with international rules have had difficulty in reaching conclusions. Nonmembers have often charged that these agreements failed to cover "substantially all the trade" and "other restrictions on commerce" required by Article XXIV. The United States and the European Union have frequently differed over this coverage issue. The United States has charged that EU expansion practices were inconsistent with the GATT principle that members of such groups engage in full internal free trade. Absence of free trade in farm products has been a particular irritant. Also there have been differences over rules-of-origin practices, which often are seen as unduly biased in favor of members of such groups and discriminatory against nonmembers.

Agreement was reached in the Uruguay Round on an Understanding on the Interpretation of Article XXIV. And the WTO has established a Committee on Regional Trade Agreements to examine regional deals. However, agreement on roughly sixty agreements remains deadlocked because of disagreement on various provisions.

The broader question for trade governance in the future will be whether regional trade groups continue to be the driving force in trade liberalization today. The major trading countries are finding it difficult to agree on an agenda for a new global round or even a mini round. If there is no multilateral round, a proliferation of new regional or bilateral free trade agreements could undermine the MFN concept and ultimately the role of the WTO. And with the United States at least temporarily paralyzed by lack of fast-track authority, U.S. products will be disadvantaged in the process.

Conclusion

The growth in the number and scope of regional free trade agreements is but one reason for restoring momentum to the multilateral negotiating process. Agreement on a major new round is possible at the WTO Ministerial Meeting in Qatar in November 2001. If this fails, another possible scenario is to negotiate in parallel on specific subjects, such as agriculture and services, as mandated by the Uruguay Round. But favorable prospects for any broader negotiating effort, or even for these more specific talks, will require considerably stronger domestic support.

America's next negotiation needs to be at home, to reestablish sufficient consensus in support of a new international trade initiative—such as the FTAA or a broader round. Other nations face a similar task. At Seattle no major country had much enthusiasm or much domestic political support for new negotiations on controversial issues. Those who seek to liberalize trade and investment will have to devote more attention to those in society who believe they are disadvantaged by globalization or believe governments are neglecting social and human concerns. That will be a joint task for the WTO and member governments.

President John F. Kennedy said of President Franklin D. Roosevelt that he could be a good neighbor abroad because he was a good neighbor at home. In the future it will be difficult if not impossible for governments to be good or effective global trading partners unless they attend to the domestic concerns of those who see themselves or others as adversely affected by liberalized trade and by globalization.

COMMENT BY
Pierre Jacquet

My comment attempts to place governance of the World Trade Organization (WTO), the theme of Robert Hormats's excellent chapter, in the
broader context of global governance. I begin with the word "governance,"
or "gouvernance" in French. Unlike "gouvernement," which connotes a
single centralized actor, "gouvernance" refers to the mechanisms likely to
produce collective action among independent sources of decisionmaking
power.

There are three such mechanisms of governance. The first is delegation of power, and the European Monetary Union is an example. Eleven
member states decided to delegate monetary sovereignty to a single European central bank. The second mechanism is rules (for example, WTO
commitments), and the third is policy coordination. The challenges to
world governance consist in finding the proper mix of these different approaches to produce consistent action by the largest number of independent countries.

Global Governance

Robert Hormats usefully addresses fundamental questions about the
future of the WTO and the strategy that should be adopted with respect to
multilateral trade negotiations. He also hints, without further developing
the argument, that the debate has changed from one about economic values and the desirability of expanded trade to one about social values and the
desirability of improving the environment, labor standards, and human
rights. In fact, the distinction is superfluous. Values—whether defined in
economic, social, or spiritual and moral terms—are part of the economic
analysis because they enter the "utility function," the economist's standard
approach to the measurement of welfare. Global governance must allow for
wide differences in individual countries' tastes and decide whether an argument that invokes such differences is genuine or a cover for protection. This
is a serious and contentious question exemplified by the transatlantic dispute on hormone-treated beef. Countries can legitimately have different
degrees of risk aversion.

This is a crucial issue for the WTO, the outcome of decades of negotiations based on trade liberalization with a view to reaping the benefits from trade. Focusing on the way the WTO works will not quiet the growing demand for better global governance. Like Daniel Esty, I believe that many people want their governments to address broader issues relating to globalization as well as trade.

Given the limited stock of political capital, time, and energy, and the relative efficiency of courses of action available for international action, should further trade liberalization be the top priority of the WTO, or other issues? This is the key question rather than "Is trade liberalization welfare improving?" The quasi-exclusive focus on trade in Seattle did not address the broader globalization concerns in the minds of many persons. Whether we like it, and whether the WTO is the right place to deal with these issues or not, the global environment, consumer safety, labor standards, and human rights are concerns that require international action. There was pressure in some quarters to "burden" the WTO with these concerns because the WTO is the only international institution with some implementation power, however imperfect. Whether we think of it as inviting compliance to international law or compensation, the WTO's dispute settlement mechanism is effective in assessing how countries respect their commitments. The International Labor Organization (ILO) or the many environmental agencies pale in comparison.

I do not have precise suggestions to offer on how global governance should proceed. This must come from intense international debate. There are two polar approaches. One is to think of the WTO as the depository for a constitution of globalization; this approach is much too demanding in terms of political commitment. The other is to envision multi-agency management of globalization, with each agency having its own dispute settlement procedure (DSP).[1] Coordination among all of these DSPs is an obvious problem. In between these two approaches is another way. The dispute settlement procedure could be taken out of the WTO and its mandate broadened to cover national commitments in all areas, not simply trade.

All international sanctions are imperfect and, more often than not, costly to those who impose them. This is also true for trade sanctions, which "punish" "innocent" exporters for the misbehavior of the exporting countries, and "innocent" importers in the country that imposes them. But trade sanctions are easy to implement, and it is probably hard to think of credible nontrade sanctions at this stage.

Discussion is needed on how trade liberalization efforts fit in with other legitimate concerns. That leads to discussion of the international architecture of global governance. This discussion has already started on financial issues. It needs to be extended. Progress is crucial to restore the momentum of trade liberalization and of the WTO.

WTO Governance

I now focus on the "narrower" subject of WTO governance. There is no place for GATT nostalgia. The option of going back to the nice old days is closed. Crucial challenges confront policymakers beyond simply making the decision process in Geneva more effective and efficient. I explore four of them.

The Return of the North-South Divide

How exactly can developing countries reap the benefits from globalization? Openness is a necessary condition for development, but there are so many other necessary conditions that the message about the benefits from globalization is too incomplete to be fully operational. Industrial countries seem to believe the message on a selective basis as far as they are concerned: it is good to open markets, except in sensitive sectors, such as agriculture, steel, and textiles. Jeffrey Sachs convincingly pointed out in chapter 5 that agriculture was not as crucial in world trade or in poor countries' development interests as the international debate suggests. But agriculture is crucial in another respect, namely the consistency and credibility of the developed countries' messages about the benefits from trade.

Another dimension to the North-South divide is noteworthy. Most demands for consideration of nontrade questions have emerged in rich countries and are supported by rich countries' nongovernmental organizations. Clearly, the extension of international negotiations to labor, safety, and environmental issues is going to be contentious in a North-South context. This argues for undertaking such efforts along largely independent negotiating lines. As Seattle demonstrated, linking trade issues with these newer issues can be counterproductive. The WTO should concentrate on the trade agenda, although "trade" should be defined broadly to encompass all issues dealing with market access—among others, direct investment and competition policy.

The Limits of "Enlightened Mercantilism"

There are two problems with the trade-off approach (based on reciprocity) that has been so successful so far. First, it is fundamentally misleading: benefits from trade come essentially from imports; exports are there to make imports affordable. The kind of misinterpretation that has been at the core of the trade-off approach of exchanging liberalizing "concessions" can indeed be enlightened, but probably not indefinitely. Good economics does not necessarily make good politics. Some elected officials who understand the benefits from trade actually hesitate to recognize them openly. Many governments have made a very poor job of selling openness in their own countries, a crucial aspect of the necessary interaction between world and domestic governance.

The second difficulty with the trade-off approach is that it exhibits decreasing returns. Because of the broadening of the trade agenda, negotiations often have to take a sector-specific route, along which reciprocity cannot help. The way forward is a sound analysis about the benefits from openness. Sectoral adjustment should not be undertaken on reciprocity grounds but because it is necessary and useful. For example, the debate in Europe on agricultural protection should not turn on how to dismantle protection under the pressure from our trade partners but on how to make European agriculture efficient—which indeed requires policy reform. Domestic politics requires finding a sound, consistent, indigenous solution, irrespective of any trade-off. Once the solution has been found, trade-offs become superfluous and will not necessarily bring that solution closer. The prospect of a trade-off may help shift the balance of domestic political forces toward undertaking the adjustment effort, but it does not produce the desirable adjustment solution. This is why the farm debate, in Europe, needs to focus on the future of farming and of farm policies, and on the change from a quantitative bias toward something else that needs to be defined.

Leadership

Regardless of the organization of the WTO's decisionmaking process, leadership is needed to get things done. As is well known, the United States has been the benevolent leader since the end of World War II. There is a widespread impression, however, that it is becoming less inclined to continue that role. The Seattle failure was also a failure of U.S. leadership. The difficulty is that the list of potential leadership candidates is very short. Europe could emerge, but it would first need to make a credible down payment in terms of market opening and to express political unity in a more systematic way. This will not happen overnight, but the posture taken by the European Union at Seattle had the merit of being consistent and forward-looking.

A Deficit in World Politics

Despite its benefits, trade liberalization is not produced naturally. The discipline implied by openness needs to be anchored in a political framework. The world had such a framework during the cold war, however partial and unsatisfactory. But the end of the cold war has left high politics loose and idle. Regional politics may work as a substitute in producing the kind of trade liberalization that can be seen as a building block for global liberalization. But for that to happen, the WTO must be effective at monitoring the extent of regional liberalization and at binding the results in a multilateral framework. This requires political commitment at the multilateral level, an ingredient that is currently in short supply.

The political motive was very strong at the beginning of European integration, but it was based on motivations that have lost their immediate raison-d'être (reconciliation, reconstruction, a bulwark against Soviet expansionism). The question of the finality of European integration has resurfaced and may prove quite contentious between member states. Both the quest for world governance and the process of European integration may ultimately hinge on how to produce supportive politics. Most European projects, including the monetary union, were driven by a political motive. Interestingly, economic integration has supported this political motivation, uniting those who believed in the benefits of integration and those whose primary purpose was political. Now, however, Europe recognizes that economic integration per se does not create political integration, and the debate has turned toward pursuing political integration on its own merits.

Conclusion

The World Trade Organization faces the double challenge of enlarging and deepening. It needs to enlarge because there are new trade issues and more countries want to join, China being the next very meaningful addition. At the same time the discussion process that supports the negotiations needs to find ways to involve the civil society. The WTO must deepen because its decisionmaking process is cumbersome, and the larger the number of members, the more cumbersome it becomes. As Hormats argues, this calls for urgent reform.

Notes

1. For a discussion, see Pierre Jacquet, Jean Pisani-Ferry, and Dominique Strauss-Kahn, "Trade Rules and Governance: A Long-Term Agenda," CEPII Working Paper 2000–22 (December 2000).

COMMENT BY

Geoff Raby

A serving ambassador is in a difficult position when asked to discuss the question of leadership of the World Trade Organization (WTO). In what is known among delegates in Geneva as a member-driven organization, a comment on leadership is invariably a comment on the members themselves. In diplomacy we only say nice things about each other—at least, in public. Nevertheless, it is important to try to comment on such a vital issue, for it is important that the voices of practitioners are also heard in this discussion.

The question of leadership is inescapably one for the membership. Leadership responsibility rests squarely with member governments. If there is a problem with leadership, the director-general cannot solve it. To be sure, the director-general's position is an important one. If the position is used judiciously, the director-general can play a key role behind the scenes bridging differences between delegations and building consensus. Practically, however, the director-general is the head of the secretariat and, as such, is just as constrained as the secretariat.

One of the most important misconceptions about the WTO is that the secretariat is an independent agent or actor in international affairs. This misconception about the WTO as an institution frequently leads to misplaced demands by the public that the WTO can do this thing or that thing.

In fact, the WTO as an institution can do little in its own right. If the public wants something done on the environment or labor standards or debt relief, it is up to the members to achieve action through the difficult process of consensus building among the entire membership. The WTO secretariat can assist through research papers, advice, and administrative support. In this sense, the WTO is best thought of as a "passive" institution.

If there is a leadership deficit, it is a failure of member governments to provide the necessary leadership. A comparative question also merits consideration. Was the WTO better led at some other time, say in the 1980s when the Uruguay Round was launched, than it is now, and if so, in what ways? As these questions illustrate, a discussion on the leadership of the WTO will be heavily subjective and inescapably impressionistic.

It is probably because of these concerns that Robert Hormats, in his admirable chapter, does not tackle directly the question of whether there is a leadership deficit. Instead he provides a valuable and balanced survey of current public debate on the WTO from a North American perspective. There is, however, enough to suggest that Hormats accepts the position that there is a leadership deficit in the WTO. Less obvious are the nature and source of that deficit and what might be done about it.

Hormats addresses several important topical issues concerning governance, broadly defined: NGO participation, nontrade concerns (labor and the environment), and internal decisionmaking. He also identifies a number of areas around which support for a new round might be built. A third important area is regionalism and, by implication, the systemic harm that the proliferation of regional arrangements could do to the multilateral trading system. It is in the lack of considered answers from governments to these challenges that Hormats seems to imply there is a leadership deficit.

Governance

The assertion that there is a "democratic deficit" is a popular criticism of the World Trade Organization. It is often made by NGOs that would like to be able to involve themselves directly in the WTO, rather than having their views and interests mediated through national processes of democratic decisionmaking.

Hormats rightly lays responsibility for the uneasiness about a possible democratic deficit at the feet of national governments. If there is a democratic deficit, or merely the perception of one, it is up to national governments to strengthen their domestic consultative and policymaking processes. Expanded information flows directly between the WTO and interested publics may well be in everyone's interest, but the question "How representative is the work of the WTO?" is one for member governments to decide. "In the final analysis," Hormats argues, "good trade governance internationally depends on good trade governance domestically."

He cautions that while better trade governance will require a better dialogue with domestic interests over trade issues, governments will need to be careful that trade policy does not become fragmented or paralyzed. He warns of the danger that governments may lose sight of the overall national interest as sectional groups organize and oppose each other. Again he places responsibility on national political leaders to remind their citizens of the immense benefits they receive from a stable and predictable framework of multilateral trade rules and disciplines.

Turning to the WTO itself, Hormats raises several pertinent points about internal decisionmaking or, in the jargon of the post-Seattle WTO, "internal transparency." Curiously, this topic is discussed far less inside the WTO than outside it. It is true, as Hormats notes, that the WTO has grown massively since its early days as GATT, but the consultative and decisionmaking processes are largely unchanged. The "consensus rule," central to the strength of the WTO, presents a major difficulty. It slows the pace of work and often leads to minimalist outcomes. Hormats's message is clear: governments must behave responsibly. The ever-growing range and complexity of issues, together with a big and expanding membership, greatly complicate decisionmaking.

Sensibly, he rejects calls for major institutional reforms, such as establishing a constituency system like those that operate in the International Monetary Fund (IMF) or World Bank. He draws the pragmatic conclusion that trade policy and the negotiation of binding trade disciplines are simply too political for delegating authority to others. While he makes many suggestions, the drawbacks of each are such that we are left with the conclusion that, though very imperfect, what we have is about the best we are likely to get in the foreseeable future. One is reminded of Sir Winston Churchill's famous dictum: "Democracy is the worst form of government except all those other forms that have been tried from time to time."

Turning to the future challenges for governance, Hormats is rightly concerned about the North Atlantic shift in focus from securing and advancing commercial interests to pursuing social values through trade measures. The chapter asks some urgent questions. Whom do NGOs represent? What is the legitimacy of their representatives? What authority can they claim compared with the representatives of elected governments? Such groups, as we saw on the streets of Seattle, often want more intervention by governments, more regulation, and more control—demands that sit oddly with their libertarian critique of governments. As Hormats observes, such positions are "inconsistent with the history of GATT and the WTO." Their mission has been "to reduce regulations and the barriers to trade and investment." Put another way, the GATT and WTO system has sought to take governments out of trade.

Hormats does not regard the WTO as the place to deal with these issues despite the tremendous temptation for governments to shift these issues to it. The onus is placed squarely on national governments to strengthen trade governance at home and to build support for a new round of multilateral trade negotiations.

Addressing the Leadership Deficit

Returning to the question posed at the outset, is leadership lacking, and if so, from whom? Hormats offers important observations for practitioners and policymakers. By highlighting the responsibilities of national governments for leading and managing the multilateral trading system, he helps to shift the focus of discussion to where it properly belongs.

Trade governance may begin at home, but greater collective leadership of the WTO by national governments is also required. Members of the WTO have the responsibility to be actively engaged in explaining the need for and benefits from a rules-based multilateral trading system. Moreover, members need to explain more clearly the case for trade liberalization. It is difficult to understand how some governments can continue to remain in the WTO but not argue the case for liberalization.

Governments also need to be precise about what the WTO is and is not. It is not an emerging arm of world governance. It is not the IMF or the World Bank. Rather, it is a passive body run by and for its members. Similarly, the WTO is not an agent of globalization. It provides members a forum in which they can negotiate the reduction of barriers and enforce compliance with their freely negotiated individual contracts.

Governments should also say more clearly what the WTO does. They should be vigorous in their defense of a multilateral rules-based trading system that protects the weak and constrains the strong from acting unilaterally. Governments need to explain better how an international system of stable rules, and a mechanism to discipline governments not to accommodate sectional interests but to play by the rules, have made and will continue to make a substantial contribution to international security and world peace.

Governments, however, must be supported in these efforts. Business must also argue the case in favor of the rules-based trading system administered by the WTO. Business too often enjoys the public good of the organization without being willing to defend it in the face of hostile criticism from well-organized and vocal groups expressing minority views.

The "social agenda" enumerated in the chapter provides the biggest challenge to leadership in the future. While acknowledging the legitimacy of the concerns behind the social agenda, governments must take responsibility for ensuring that these issues are not allowed to distract from the WTO's core business. For domestic reasons many governments find it convenient to push on the WTO's door with these issues even though there is no consensus that the door should be opened and is unlikely ever to be opened. Meanwhile, the constant hammering distracts attention from the urgent business of building a more open and fair international economy.

Far-sighted leadership from governments is required if the WTO is to get on with its core business while finding ways to address the legitimate concerns of citizens in rich and poor countries alike in a balanced way that does not amount to back-door protectionism. New forums and bodies may or may not be required. The members of the WTO should not shy away from such a discussion. Indeed, such a discussion should begin sooner rather than later.

GARY HUFBAUER

Part Five Summary

The new millennium! A time to shake things up! What needs more shaking than the International Monetary Fund, the World Bank, and the World Trade Organization? These warhorses have served long and well since Bretton Woods, but hasn't the time come to rejuvenate their DNA? So goes popular thinking in the wake of the Asian crisis, the Russian mess, failures in Africa, Seattle street theater, and the trashing of McDonald's in France. I resist the temptation to comment on the International Monetary Fund and the World Bank except to observe that these Washington institutions are far more needful of reform than the World Trade Organization.

What about WTO governance? No one says it is perfect. What needs changing? In part 5 of this volume, five ambassadors (Sylvia Ostry, Rufus Yerxa, B. K. Zutshi, Robert Hormats, and Geoff Raby) and two academics (Pierre Jacquet and myself) stoutly defend a core proposition: GATT in its long life and the WTO in its short one have been tremendous successes. Accordingly, when it comes to governance reform, the authors are raging moderates. World trade has flourished over the past fifty years, thanks in good measure to policy liberalization orchestrated in Geneva. Lower trade barriers negotiated in the European Union, the North American Free Trade Agreement, and other regional forums have certainly contributed. Plummeting transportation and communication costs since 1950 have likewise accelerated global trade and investment—two sides of the same coin as

Raymond Vernon first perceived in the 1960s.[1] But on my scorecard, GATT/WTO receives the most credit for the dramatic postwar growth in world commerce, growth that has regularly exceeded world GDP expansion by 2 percent to 4 percent a year and indeed has paced the most prosperous half-century in human history. Flourishing commerce, joined at the hip with international investment, has spread new technology around the globe, harvesting absolute and comparative advantage, enabling specialized production of both intermediate and final goods, with great economies of scope and scale. Unlike the financial system, the trading system did not fall apart during the debt crisis of the 1980s or the Asian crisis of the 1990s largely because of the dense network of mutual commitments negotiated under GATT and WTO auspices.

Bert Lance, one of President Jimmy Carter's cronies from Georgia, was renowned for his aphorism "If it ain't broke, don't fix it." Lance was overly disposed toward the status quo, as much as anything to slow Carter's endless tinkering. The aphorism that emerged from part 5 might be stated (in undiplomatic language), "If it ain't working right, just fix what ain't working." Five things need fixing. Leadership, not organizational shuffling, is the main challenge.

Leadership and the New Issues

Governance questions become most insistent when leadership is most hesitant. Robert Hormats stressed that the outlook for U.S. trade leadership is not bright. The battle over congressional approval of China permanent normal trade relations (PNTR) stands as a caution. Despite the minimum concessions required of the United States, the maximum concessions required of China, and the logic of Chinese membership in the WTO, the Clinton administration and the business community had to lobby hard to secure approval of PNTR.[2] We will be lucky if President George W. Bush puts trade legislation near the top of his agenda.

The European Union faces similar difficulties. Enlargement to Central Europe will challenge the EU with difficult adjustments in agriculture and old economy industries. Western Europe's slow but sure embrace of the new economy brings its own challenges—mergers and acquisitions, restructuring, and layoffs. Since the departure of Sir Leon Brittan, no one in Brussels seems eager to add an ambitious WTO Round to the demanding internal agenda. Rather than pleading negotiating incapacity (the U.S. excuse), the EU seeks delay by overloading the agenda.

Integration of world markets is a threatening process, even to winners, as Hormats emphasized. Liberalization coupled with new technology enables the value-added chain to be sliced ever more finely, making production more footloose and requiring far greater flexibility in the workplace. Absolute advantage, the economic rule when inputs can move from place to place, occupies more economic space, while comparative advantage, the economic rule when inputs are geographically confined, occupies less. In the process the public sector is constrained, lest high taxes and regulatory burdens drive slices of the value-added chain to other states or other countries. Households must assume greater responsibility for educating their children, financing their health care, and saving for their old age. These changes are disquieting and even disruptive, especially to middle-age and elderly workers. The consequent backlash against the most visible agents of globalization—multinational corporations and the WTO—was perceptively foretold in 1998 by Raymond Vernon in *In the Hurricane's Eye*.[3]

The skeptical attitude toward further liberalization in the United States and Europe, even in the midst of record prosperity, is compounded, as Pierre Jacquet observed, by the declining utility of "enlightened mercantilism." Practitioners of enlightened mercantilism basically say to one another, "I'll trade my bad tariff for your bad tariff; we'll both benefit from import liberalization; and we'll both sell the deal at home by trumpeting better market access abroad." Enlightened mercantilism is losing its punch because average protection in the Organization for Economic Cooperation and Development (OECD) is already low, and peak protection is concentrated in politically powerful industries. OECD countries find it devilishly difficult to shave the peaks off their textile, clothing, steel, or agricultural protection. At the same time many emerging countries, with high average tariffs and insulation from foreign investors, still need the cover of enlightened mercantilism to sell liberalization at home.

Another troubling question faces the big trading powers. Pierre Jacquet summarized their dilemma. Do the big powers want the WTO to continue its aggressive push on liberalization, or do they want to open environment and labor agendas? The panelists unanimously condemned an expansion of the WTO mandate to encompass the new issues. Geoff Raby warned that inserting the new issues in the WTO agenda would be following the sentiments of the North Atlantic seaboard (the East Coast of the United States, the eastern provinces of Canada, and Western Europe) rather than the demands of the world at large. B. K. Zutshi flatly stated that adding environment and labor to the WTO agenda would simply be a device for postponing the legitimate demands of developing countries—better market access for specialty agriculture, textiles and clothing, and processed goods.

Stronger environmental and labor standards are commendable. But the standards and their implementation need not be negotiated in the WTO. The International Labor Organization has new vitality, while like-minded countries are negotiating ad hoc environmental agreements right and left.[4] Implementation of standards does not require trade sanctions. Carrots can work as well as sticks (for example, World Bank grants), and sticks can take the form of labels, public "sunshine," and civil fines rather than trade sanctions.

Reconciling these differences and meeting these challenges call for new leaders to fire up the WTO engine. Leaders can come from small industrial powers and emerging markets as well as from the quad (the United States, the European Union, Japan, and Canada). Australia, Brazil, Chile, China, Mexico, and even India can help carry the banner. To do their work, leaders must be inspired by vision—the vision of spreading the "new economy" throughout the OECD countries and emerging markets and bringing the flavor of prosperity to 3 billion people living far from affluence. Vision needs to be accompanied by a negotiating plan. Here the authors had two concrete suggestions. Geoff Raby recommended an early focus on eliminating industrial tariffs as a way of jump-starting the WTO for more difficult tasks, such as liberalizing agriculture and reforming the antidumping system. Rufus Yerxa suggested that more contentious issues (competition and investment policy, financial liberalization, government procurement) be pursued in a code framework, rather than the single undertaking formula that dominated the Uruguay Round.

The "Protest Industry" and Other NGOs

Sylvia Ostry dissected the movement of nongovernmental organizations, sharply distinguishing the "protest industry" (populated by groups like Greenpeace, Public Citizen, or the Sierra Club) from expert associations that may exist only in cyberspace ("virtual NGOs"). The hard-core protest industry thrives on media attention; the attention in turn draws revenue from dues-paying members and foundations. Media attention comes from disrupting WTO meetings and misstating WTO rulings.[5] By contrast, expert associations operate outside the public limelight. They do not need much money since they operate on a volunteer basis with few paid staff members. Expert associations are dedicated to particular issues, such as the breadth of biotechnology patents, antidumping procedures, or the privacy and taxation of e-commerce.

Other than disbanding, or inviting NGO leaders into the Council, the World Trade Organization can no sooner reach a modus vivendi with the hard-core protest industry than India can reach a settlement with Pakistan over Kashmir. Expert NGOs are another matter. They are worth listening to. As a general proposition, however, the authors argued that the right vehicle for NGOs—whatever their coloration—is through national governments, rather than direct access to the WTO. If there is a "democratic deficit" in the WTO, it is because the nongovernmental organizations are not getting a proper hearing in their capitals, as Geoff Raby noted. It is a national problem, not an international problem. B. K. Zutshi insisted that if NGOs somehow grab a place at the WTO table, developing countries will be pushed to the back row just when larger trading volumes are edging the emerging nations closer to the Green Room.

The Green Room Process

Carrying on the tradition of the GATT, the WTO largely operates by consensus. But, as Pascal Lamy has warned, 135 members cannot all sit at the same table and negotiate anything. This obvious point has led to the much-criticized Green Room process—small gatherings at crucial junctures to reach key decisions. The Green Room is unevenly representative, and that is part of the problem. The critical members include the European Union, the United States, Japan, and Canada. China will soon join this club. But the novel development in the Green Room process is the rise of issue coalitions—a role pioneered by the Cairns group on agriculture during the Uruguay Round.

Suggestions have been offered for formalizing the Green Room.[6] The ambassadors on the governance panel, led by Sylvia Ostry, argued that precious time would be wasted if the design of a more formal structure becomes a precondition for the next WTO round. As part of the wrap-up bargain, after trade concessions have been exchanged, a new governance structure might be created, loosely modeled after the IMF and World Bank models (country groups represented by a single spokesperson and organized around geography or issues).

Dispute Settlement

A major achievement at the birth of the WTO was its dispute settlement system, designed to produce conclusive findings within a relatively short time period.[7] The WTO dispute settlement mechanism (DSM) has gotten a good workout, both at the panel level and the appellate level. Between 1995 and 2000, more than 180 consultation requests between members were filed. More than 60 cases led to the establishment of panels; in about 30 cases (after going through the full panel and appellate process), reports were adopted; in another 30 cases the parties are still working through the system. B. K. Zutshi argues that this record shows the WTO is becoming too legalistic. Like other ambassadors, they urged that members practice self-restraint in bringing cases.

In my opinion this is a well-intentioned but naïve recommendation. Aside from the DSM, small trading powers have little hope of getting the major powers to pay attention to their legitimate grievances. Moreover, the European Union is staring at an avalanche of cases against agricultural subsidies in 2003, when the "peace clause" negotiated in the Uruguay Round expires. The new cases will come on top of EU losses in the beef hormones and banana cases. The EU's response, evidenced in the Foreign Sales Corporation case, is to accumulate bargaining chips by bringing cases against objectionable foreign practices. Practices of the United States, Canada, and Australia are especially inviting targets.

Rufus Yerxa quoted the late ambassador Jules Katz: "All trade disputes are a prelude to negotiations." Taking this view, the current crop of trade disputes—especially disputes where the losing party refuses to implement the Appellate Body report—are simply a warm-up for the next WTO round. Perhaps the negotiators will conclude that the panels and Appellate Body have been too aggressive. They may rewrite the rules so that a substantial minority of WTO members (representing, for example, at least one-quarter of members *and* one-quarter of world trade) could block adoption of an Appellate Body report. Negotiators may also rewrite the rules to encourage redress other than prohibitive barriers against a handful of products; for example, compensation might be paid to injured parties and financed by low rate tariffs on *all* the offending country's exports.

While these basic questions are being thrashed out, some NGOs and corporations are seeking direct access to the WTO's dispute settlement system. Governance panelists think direct access would badly strain the system. National governments act as gatekeepers, balancing the interests of conflicting domestic groups and the possible costs of retaliation, before bringing cases to the WTO. Direct access would dispense with the gatekeeper, allowing more cases to reach the DSM and putting a stronger spotlight on the WTO as "usurper" of national sovereignty.

An intriguing alternative to direct access is to create an auxiliary arbitration system where corporations, nongovernmental organizations, and provincial, state, and even federal governments could voluntarily submit to dispute settlement under the substantive rules of the WTO and the decisions of the Appellate Body. No party could bring a case before the auxiliary arbitration system unless it had previously deposited its own undertaking to be bound by adverse rulings.

Short of direct access, many NGOs want more "hallway hospitality" in the corridors of the World Trade Organization. Robert Hormats points out that large corporations have informally worked their way into the GATT/WTO system, and the nongovernmental organizations are simply seeking parity. They long for the sort of welcome they enjoyed in the Kyoto Protocol on greenhouse gases in 1997 and the Cartegena Protocol on biosafety concluded in Montreal in 2000. WTO dispute panels could invite *amicus* briefs in appropriate cases—from NGOs, corporations, and state and local governments—limited to be sure in number and length. Sylvia Ostry thinks that *amicus* briefs, however restricted, are a bad idea. I disagree.

Resources

The WTO is incredibly understaffed relative to the legitimate demands placed on it. It should not get in the business of providing technical assistance to members who may have trouble coping with the complex requirements of WTO commitments. Providing technical assistance is a worthy task but one far beyond the prospective resources of the WTO. Africa, South Asia, and China all need technical assistance that will easily cost hundreds of millions of dollars. Geoff Raby forcefully insisted that multilateral development banks can best provide the required assistance. The assistance, however, should be tailored to help correct administrative shortcomings revealed by the WTO's periodic Trade Policy Review Mechanism (TPRM) reports.

Instead of forging into the technical assistance business, the WTO can use more resources in two areas. First, with additional staff and an independent stance, the WTO could carry out hard-hitting studies of key policy areas. Possible subjects would include the workings of intellectual property protection in developing countries (who benefits? who pays?), the spread and costs of antidumping systems, the use of subsidies by federal and subfederal governments, and how to adapt customs and tax procedures to e-commerce. The list of timely—and controversial—subjects is large. Cooperative staffing between the United Nations Conference on Trade and Development (UNCTAD) and the WTO might carry out some of these studies.[8]

Second, the World Trade Organization needs more resources to carry out its dispute settlement tasks, even if (as several authors urge), the system is reformed to restrain its litigious tendencies. Panelists and Appellate Body jurists are seriously overworked, and even with reforms their workload will become heavier. The WTO operates on a slender budget of about $100 million a year. An additional $30 million would do wonders.

Notes

1. Raymond Vernon's seminal writings on direct investment and trade and product cycle were synthesized in *Sovereignty at Bay: The Multinational Spread of U.S. Enterprises* (Basic Books, 1971).

2. See Gary Clyde Hufbauer and Daniel H. Rosen, "American Access to China's Market: The Congressional Vote on PNTR," International Economics Policy Brief 00-3 (Washington: Institute for International Economics, April 2000).

3. Raymond Vernon, *In the Hurricane's Eye: The Troubled Prospects of Multinational Enterprises* (Harvard University Press, 1998). This book, his last, was published well before the OECD's Multilateral Agreement on Investment collapsed and the WTO's Ministerial at Seattle was tear-gassed.

4. Several environmental agreements have been negotiated or are under deliberation among like-minded countries (not necessarily organized along North-South lines). Examples are the Convention on International Trade in Endangered Species, the Panama Agreement on Dolphins, the Montreal Protocol on Ozone, the Kyoto Protocol on Greenhouse Gases, the Cartegena Protocol on Biosafety, the Treaty on Persistent Organic Pollutants, the Conference on Parties to Climate Change, and a U.S./East Asian agreement on shrimp/turtles. For an excellent survey of the "new" ILO, see Kimberly Ann Elliott, "The ILO and Enforcement of Core Labor Standards," International Economics Policy Brief 00-6 (Washington: Institute for International Economics, 2000).

5. The textbook of misstatement is Lori Wallach and Michelle Sforza, *Whose Trade Organization? Corporate Globalization and the Erosion of Democracy* (Washington: Public Citizen, 1999). For a corrective analysis, see U.S. Alliance for Trade Expansion, *A Guide to Whose Trade Organization?* Washington, December 16, 1999.

6. See, for example, Jeffrey J. Schott and Jayshree Watal, "Decision-Making in the WTO," International Economics Policy Brief 00-2 (Washington: Institute for International Economics, March 2000).

7. For a quick overview, see William J. Davey, "The WTO Dispute Settlement System," *Journal of International Economic Law*, vol. 3, no. 1 (March 2000). For a longer exposition, see the special issue of *Journal of International Economic Law*, vol. 2, no. 2 (June 1999). In progress is a thoughtful monograph by Claude Barfield, *More Than You Can Chew: The New WTO Dispute Settlement System* (American Enterprise Institute, forthcoming).

8. Under the able guidance of Rubens Ricupero, UNCTAD has practically reinvented itself since the heyday of the G-77. It has a highly professional staff capable of carrying out first-rate studies.

JONATHAN T. FRIED

General Summary

The contributors to this volume have examined the international framework for trade—in particular the linkages between its efficiency, equity, and legitimacy. As a practitioner and trade negotiator who "survived" Seattle, I add three observations.

First, today's trade agenda is more about strengthening markets than about opening markets. As tariffs and other border barriers to trade fall, international rulemaking on trade has moved inland, with an increasing focus on nontariff measures such as technical standards, licenses and approvals, and inspection procedures. Areas once considered within "domestic jurisdiction"—transparency and objectivity in setting rules domestically, due process principles of prepublication of laws and regulations, civic participation in the rulemaking process, and independent administrative and judicial review of economic regulation—are now the subject of international negotiations. The trade agenda of today promotes principles of inclusiveness and democratic participation, as a matter of equity and legitimacy, along with efficiency and good economic governance.

Second, this focus in trade matters has parallels in other aspects of international economic policy. In the wake of the financial crisis that spread through emerging markets in 1997, finance ministers concluded that, contrary to some popular media, the root of the problem did not lie in the free flow of capital. Rather, difficulties arose in large measure because accurate information was lacking on risk as well as on the liquidity and reserves of banks and other institutions. Regulatory and supervisory regimes for oversight of the financial sector were inadequate to steer investment to productive opportunities and away from speculative ventures (or "crony capitalism"). The finance ministers began to recognize that opening financial services to competition from abroad would increase demand for accurate information and promote a more sober assessment of lending risk.

The finance ministers also learned that the consequences of the crisis were exacerbated by the absence of social safety nets and adequate investment in workers. With no savings to draw on, consumers reduced their spending precipitously in many affected economies. Had governments invested in appropriate forms of unemployment insurance or welfare, more money would have remained available in the economy, more consumer spending would have been maintained, and the social impact of the crisis would have been lessened significantly.

Having learned these lessons of the late 1990s, finance ministers have now taken the lead on a similar agenda of regulatory reform and economic good governance. Their agenda underscores the importance of inclusiveness of stakeholders (a concrete reflection of democratic principles of rulemaking and administration). It also takes into account the social dimension, or "equity."

My third observation concerns the interests of developing countries, interests that are remarkably similar. Seattle highlighted developing countries' difficulties implementing WTO disciplines. Despite a grace period under the Uruguay Round agreements, developing countries still lack the capacity, they argue, to administer an increasingly complex set of rules and regulations as the WTO agreements now require.

Taking these three observations together, I suggest that today's trade agenda cannot be considered in isolation from other aspects of good economic governance. And this "good government" agenda encompasses political and social, as well as economic, dimensions. The logic is irrefutable: the well-being of developed countries in a globalized economy will increasingly depend on the health and vitality of markets abroad. Making the pie bigger requires the sustainable development of emerging economies.

For such development to be sustainable in the long to medium term, it is the market, and private business, that will generate the economic activity that will create growth. And business will go where there is a regulatory environment conducive to doing business: one characterized by transparency and predictability; where governments invest in "human capital" (social safety nets and education that enables workers to keep pace with structural adjustment); and where participants in the economy, those who are governed, have a say in how they are governed.

If this diagnosis is correct and trade is but one contributor, and by no means the most central, to sustainable development and growth, the consequent questions of international governance must be asked. Political inclusiveness and democratic institution building, social programs and improved education, and investment in skills upgrading, lifelong learning, and "human capital" must accompany the evolution of good economic governance. Are international institutions up to the task? Should we do more to bring together the work and expertise of the Bretton Woods institutions with the WTO and with the resources and expertise of the United Nations—and by so doing, to bring together, in the name of governance, questions of efficiency, equity, and legitimacy?

Contributors

Americo Beviglia Zampetti is administrator, Directorate-General for Trade, European Commission.

Jagdish Bhagwati is the Arthur Lehman Professor of Economics and professor of political science, Columbia University.

Steven Charnovitz practices law at Wilmer, Cutler & Pickering, Washington, D.C.

Richard N. Cooper is the Maurits C. Boas Professor of International Economics, Harvard University.

William Davey is the Edwin M. Adams Professor of Law, University of Illinois School of Law.

Alan Deardorff is the John W. Sweetland Professor of International Economics, University of Michigan School of Public Policy.

David Dollar is research manager at the Development Research Group of the World Bank.

Daniel C. Esty is director of the Center for Environmental Law and Policy, School of Forestry and Environmental Studies, Yale University.

Jonathan T. Fried is senior assistant deputy minister and G-7 finance deputy for Canada, Department of Finance.

Jeffrey Frankel is the James W. Harpel Professor of Capital Formation and Economic Growth, John F. Kennedy School of Government, Harvard University.

Gary Horlick is a partner at O'Melveny & Myers, Washington, D.C.

Robert Hormats is vice chairman of Goldman, Sachs (International).

Robert Howse is professor of law, University of Michigan Law School.

Robert E. Hudec is professor emeritus and formerly the Melvin C. Steen and Corporate Donors Professor, University of Minnesota Law School.

Gary C. Hufbauer is the Reginald Jones Senior Fellow, the Institute for International Economics.

Motoshige Itoh is professor of studies of contemporary economy at the Graduate School, Division of Economics, University of Tokyo.

Pierre Jacquet is deputy director of the Institut Français des Relations Internationales (IFRI).

Robert O. Keohane is the James B. Duke Professor of Political Science, Duke University.

David W. Leebron is dean and Lucy G. Moses Professor of Law, Columbia University School of Law.

Kalypso Nicolaïdis is lecturer in international relations, St. Antony's College, Oxford University.

Joseph S. Nye Jr. is dean and the Don K. Price Professor of Public Policy, John F. Kennedy School of Government, Harvard University.

Sylvia Ostry is distinguished research fellow, Munk Centre for International Studies, University of Toronto.

Roger B. Porter is the IBM Professor of Business and Government, John F. Kennedy School of Government, Harvard University.

Geoff Raby is ambassador, Australian Permanent Mission to the World Trade Organization.

Dani Rodrik is the Rafiq Hariri Professor of International Political Economy, John F. Kennedy School of Government, Harvard University.

Frieder Roessler was director of the GATT Legal Affairs Division.

Jeffrey Sachs is the Galen L. Stone Professor of International Trade, John F. Kennedy School of Government, Harvard University.

André Sapir is professor of economics at the Free University of Brussels and adviser to the Directorate-General for Economic and Financial Affairs, European Commission.

Pierre Sauvé is head of the Trade Policy Linkages Division, Trade Directorate, Organization for Economic Cooperation and Development.

F. M. Scherer is the Aetna Professor of Public Policy and Corporate Management, emeritus, John F. Kennedy School of Government, Harvard University.

Debora Spar is professor of business administration, Graduate School of Business, Harvard University.

Arvind Subramanian is division chief, African Department, International Monetary Fund.

Alan O. Sykes is the Frank and Bernice Greenberg Professor of Law, University of Chicago School of Law.

Joel P. Trachtman is academic dean and professor of international law, Fletcher School of Law and Diplomacy, Tufts University.

Craig VanGrasstek is president of Washington Trade Reports and professional lecturer, School of International Service, American University.

J. H. H. Weiler is the Jean Monnet Chair and Manley Hudson Professor of Law, Harvard Law School.

Alan Winters is professor of economics, School of Social Sciences, University of Sussex.

Rufus Yerxa is associate general counsel, Monsanto.

B. K. Zutshi is former ambassador of India to the World Trade Organization.

Index